PENGUIN BOOKS

THE ANNOTATED
GILBERT AND SULLIVAN: 1

Ian Bradley was born in 1950 in Berkhamsted, Hertford-shire, and educated at Tonbridge School and New College, Oxford, where he obtained a First Class Honours degree in modern history. He stayed on at Oxford to complete a doctoral thesis on early nineteenth-century politics. After a brief period with the B.B.C., he joined the staff of *The Times* where he spent five years writing on political, historical and educational topics. Since 1982 he has combined free-lance writing and school teaching.

He is the author of six books, ranging in their subject matter from Victorian Evangelicalism to the birth of the Social Democratic Party. He is now working on a philosophical study of the British Liberal tradition and its relevance to the emerging post-industrial society.

Ian Bradley has been a Gilbert and Sullivan addict ever since he was taken by his parents to the Savoy Theatre as a small boy to see a performance of *Iolanthe*. Among his other loves are spa towns, remote railway stations, fishing ports, Scotland and the American Mid-West. Penguin also publish a companion volume of annotated Gilbert and Sullivan containing *Trial by Jury, The Sorcerer, Patience, Princess Ida, Ruddigore* and *The Yeomen of the Guard*.

THE ANNOTATED
GILBERT
AND
SULLIVAN: 1

Introduced and edited by Ian Bradley

PENGUIN BOOKS

PENGUIN BOOKS

Published by the Penguin Group
27 Wrights Lane, London W8 5TZ, England
Viking Penguin Inc., 40 West 23rd Street, New York, New York 10010, USA
Penguin Books Australia Ltd, Ringwood, Victoria, Australia
Penguin Books Canada Ltd, 2801 John Street, Markham, Ontario, Canada L3R 1B4
Penguin Books (NZ) Ltd, 182–190 Wairau Road, Auckland 10, New Zealand

Penguin Books Ltd, Registered Offices: Harmondsworth, Middlesex, England

This edition first published 1982
Reprinted with revisions 1985 (twice), 1988

Introduction and notes copyright © Ian Bradley, 1982
All rights reserved

Made and printed in Great Britain by
Hazell Watson & Viney Limited
Member of BPCC plc
Aylesbury Bucks
Set in Palatino

CONTENTS

PREFACE

Gilbert and Sullivan's operas exist to be sung, hummed, whistled, performed, watched, listened to, read and enjoyed, not to be annotated. The notes on the left-hand pages in this book are intended first and foremost to enhance the enjoyment of the lines opposite. They are not designed to provide an exhaustive record of every single textual change that has occurred in the last hundred or so years. This book is offered to its readers as a source of innocent merriment, and, I hope, of some interesting information, not as an academic treatise.

A word on the text is needed. There is, alas, no such thing as a definitive version of the Savoy Operas. In the case of every work, what was performed on the first night varied from what was printed in the original libretto sent to the Lord Chamberlain for licensing, and further, often substantial, alterations were made subsequently. Vocal scores differ in wording from libretti, both in manuscript and printed editions, and there are occasional discrepancies between British and American versions of the same work. 'Gags', both authorized and unauthorized, introduced by members of the D'Oyly Carte Opera Company during performances, creep in and out of successive editions of the libretto. Mrs Helen D'Oyly Carte, who ran the company from 1901 to 1913, often asked Gilbert to authorize a correct version of the operas, but he never did so.

The texts which are printed in this volume are as accurate as I can make them. They broadly follow the versions contained in the current set of libretti published by Chappells, which are used by most amateur and professional companies performing the operas, and the two-volume edition of the Savoy Operas which was prepared by Dame Bridget D'Oyly Carte and Mr Colin Prestige and published by the Oxford University Press in 1962–3. Some slight differences will be found, however, where I have tried to bring the text into line with current practices in performance. Essentially, the version of the operas printed in this book is that in which they were most recently performed by the D'Oyly Carte Opera Company before its sad demise in February 1982 and in which they are now generally performed by other amateur and professional societies. In that, it differs from the version contained in the paperback edition of the Savoy Operas published by Macmillans, which is, generally speaking, that performed fifty or so years ago.

I have received much help in the preparation of this book. First and foremost I would like to thank Dame Bridget D'Oyly Carte, who placed her fascinating collection of letters and marked libretti at my disposal and allowed me to quote from copyright material. I would also like to thank her secretary, Mr Albert Truelove, and Mr Peter Riley, the last general manager of the D'Oyly Carte Company, for all their help and for sharing their knowledge of G & S.

My grateful thanks are also extended to the Royal General Theatrical Fund Association, 11 Garrick Street, London WC2, as owner of the subsisting copyright in Sir William S. Gilbert's unpublished writings, for allowing me to publish various lines which are in copyright to be found in the Lord Chamberlain's licence copies of the operas, and to publish extracts from various letters written by Sir William Gilbert which are still subject to copyright. I would also like to thank Mr Colin Prestige, the Association's solicitor and himself a leading authority on Gilbert and Sullivan.

Various people have helped me with specific queries. Dr Nicholas Ostler supplied me with translations and comments on Japanese phrases in *The Mikado*, and the staff of the historical section of the National Maritime Museum answered my questions about certain nautical expressions in *H.M.S. Pinafore*. The staffs of the Pierpont Morgan Library, New York, where Reginald Allen's splendid collection of Gilbert and Sullivan material is lodged, the music library of the Berkeley campus of the University of California, and the students' room of the manuscript department of the British Library have all been very helpful. Chappells were also kind enough to send me a reference copy of Reginald Allen's *The First Night Gilbert and Sullivan*, which is now, sadly, out of print.

I would also like to thank John Denny and Peter Carson of Penguin Books for their help and encouragement and Judith Wardman for her splendid copy-editing, which has prevented at least one or two howlers from getting into print. For those that remain, needless to say, I alone am responsible. My parents made many useful suggestions on the first draft of my typescript, and I owe a special debt of gratitude to my brother, whose early passion for Gilbert and Sullivan began to grip me just, I fear, as it was beginning to wane in him.

My final thanks must go to all the members of the D'Oyly Carte Opera Company, off-stage as well as on it, who have been chiefly responsible for my love of the works of Gilbert and Sullivan, just as they must have been for countless thousands around the world. I dedicate this book to them, in gratitude for all the pleasure they have given me, and in the hope that before long they will be back again to perform the Savoy Operas – all of them – as only they know how.

Rather than give a lengthy bibliography at the end of this book, I list here the books (many of them, alas, now out of print) from which I have derived the greatest benefit, and the greatest amusement, in the task of preparing this volume:

Reginald Allen, *The Life and Work of Sir Arthur Sullivan* (The Pierpont Morgan Library, New York, 1975).

Reginald Allen, *The First Night Gilbert and Sullivan* (Chappell & Co., London, 1958).

Leslie Ayre, *The Gilbert and Sullivan Companion* (Pan Books, London, 1974).

Leslie Baily, *The Gilbert and Sullivan Book* (Cassell, London, 1952).

Leslie Baily, *Gilbert and Sullivan and their World* (Thames & Hudson, London, 1973).

Harry Benford, *The Gilbert and Sullivan Lexicon* (Richards Rosen Press, New York, 1978).

Sidney Dark and Rowland Grey, *W. S. Gilbert: His Life and Letters* (Methuen, London, 1923).

W. A. Darlington, *The World of Gilbert and Sullivan* (Thomas Crowell, New York, 1950).

G. E. Dunn, *A Gilbert and Sullivan Dictionary* (Allen & Unwin, London, 1936, and Da Capo Press, New York, 1971).

James Ellis (editor), *The Bab Ballads by W. S. Gilbert* (The Belknap Press of Harvard University Press, Cambridge, Massachusetts, 1970).

Isaac Goldberg, *The Story of Gilbert and Sullivan* (New York, 1928).

Martyn Green's Treasury of Gilbert and Sullivan (Simon & Schuster, New York, 1961).

Michael Hardwick, *The Osprey Guide to Gilbert and Sullivan* (Osprey, London, 1972).

Hesketh Pearson, *Gilbert and Sullivan* (Penguin Books, Harmondsworth, 1950).

J. W. Steadman (editor), *Gilbert Before Sullivan* (Chicago University Press, Chicago, 1967).

I have taken advantage of a reprinting of this book to correct some mistakes which appeared in the first edition. For pointing out errors to me, I am extremely grateful to the Revd D. G. Bell of Blackpool, the Revd Arthur King of Harrogate, Keith Peterson of New York, Colin Prestige, George Low, Arthur Jacobs and, above all, Michael Walters, who found a distressingly large number of howlers in my notes. He also declared himself to be somewhat sceptical about the oft-repeated story of the sword falling from the wall in Gilbert's study (see page 257), but I have chosen to keep it in my notes until it is definitely proved apocryphal. It is too good to leave out. I hope he will forgive me.

I.C.B.

H.M.S. PINAFORE

OR

THE LASS THAT LOVED A SAILOR

DRAMATIS PERSONÆ

THE RT. HON. SIR JOSEPH PORTER, K.C.B. (*First Lord of the Admiralty*)
CAPTAIN CORCORAN (*Commanding H.M.S. Pinafore*)
TOM TUCKER (*Midshipmite*)
RALPH RACKSTRAW (*Able Seaman*)
DICK DEADEYE (*Able Seaman*)
BILL BOBSTAY (*Boatswain*)
BOB BECKET (*Boatswain's Mate – Carpenter*)
JOSEPHINE (*the Captain's Daughter*)
HEBE (*Sir Joseph's First Cousin*)
MRS CRIPPS (LITTLE BUTTERCUP) (*a Portsmouth Bumboat Woman*)
First Lord's Sisters, his Cousins, his Aunts, Sailors, Marines, etc.

SCENE. – Quarter-deck of H.M.S. *Pinafore*, off Portsmouth.
ACT I. – Noon.   ACT II. – Night.

H.M.S. PINAFORE

H.M.S. Pinafore was the fourth work on which Gilbert and Sullivan collaborated and their first big success. First performed at the Opéra Comique theatre just off the Strand on 25 May 1878, it ran for a total of 571 performances. This equalled the record for an initial West End run, which was held by a farce called *Our Boys*.

The talents of William Schwenck Gilbert, the failed barrister who prefered writing plays, and Arthur Sullivan, the serious composer who always felt comic operas to be rather beneath him, had first been brought together in 1871 by John Hollingshead, owner and manager of the Gaiety Theatre. The opera which they wrote for him, *Thespis, or the Gods Grown Old*, was staged at the theatre at the end of that year without success. The dramatist and composer continued to work separately until they were brought together again in 1875 by Richard D'Oyly Carte, an enterprising young theatrical manager and entrepreneur. The first result of this new collaboration, *Trial by Jury*, opened at Carte's Royalty Theatre in Soho on 25 March 1875 and ran for 175 performances.

The relative success of *Trial by Jury* encouraged Richard D'Oyly Carte to commission further works from Gilbert and Sullivan and to establish his own permanent opera company to perform them. The Opéra Comique was leased as the base for the Comedy Opera Company. The first fruit of this new, more permanent arrangement between the three men was *The Sorcerer*, which opened on 17 November 1877 and ran for 175 performances. The next was *H.M.S. Pinafore*.

With *H.M.S. Pinafore* Gilbert and Sullivan found the magic touch which they were to apply to another eight operas over the next decade. The establishment of a permanent company enabled them to write parts which suited the particular talents of individual singers. The nautical theme of the opera appealed strongly to Gilbert, who had seafaring blood in his veins. His father had been a naval surgeon, and Gilbert liked to claim that a more distant ancestor was Sir Humphrey Gilbert, the Elizabethan navigator who landed at Newfoundland in 1583 and established the first English colony in North America. Jokes about the Navy had figured prominently in the *Bab*

Ballads which Gilbert had written for the humorous magazine *Fun* (a rival to the better-known *Punch*) in the 1860s. Indeed, the ballads supplied several of the ideas and characters on which the opera was based.

H.M.S. Pinafore also provided the perfect vehicle for Sullivan to display his gifts for melody and for evocative mood music. Amazingly, he struggled to compose the opera while wracked with pain as the result of a stone in his kidneys. He wrote later: 'It is, perhaps, rather a strange fact that the music of *Pinafore*, which was thought to be so merry and spontaneous, was written while I was suffering agonies from a cruel illness. I would compose a few bars, and then be almost insensible from pain. When the paroxysm was passed, I would write a little more, until the pain overwhelmed me again.'

Early on, it looked as though *H.M.S. Pinafore* might prove to be a flop. Partly because of a fierce June heatwave, the Opéra Comique was far from full, and by July nightly takings were down to less than £40. The cast took a voluntary cut of a third in their salaries, and there were constant threats that the show would have to close. However, Sullivan gave it a boost by conducting a selection of music from the opera at the summer promenade concerts at the Royal Opera House, Covent Garden. By the end of August the weather was cooler and the theatre was full. The music had caught on, and shops in London were inundated with requests for the piano score.

H.M.S. Pinafore had no such difficulties in establishing itself on the other side of the Atlantic. In the absence of international copyright agreements, the opera was first performed in the United States by a 'pirate' company in Boston on 25 November 1878. Within a few months *Pinafore* mania was sweeping the States and more than fifty unauthorized companies were playing the piece across the country. In New York alone the opera was at one stage being performed simultaneously in eight separate theatres within five blocks of each other. There were all-negro and all-Catholic productions and performances on canal boats and Mississippi paddle steamers. One enterprising pilot in Newport, Rhode Island, learning that *H.M.S. Pinafore* was shortly to arrive there, even rowed several miles out to sea so as to be sure of getting the job of piloting her into the harbour.

Clearly, Gilbert, Sullivan and D'Oyly Carte could not let the pirates have a monopoly of performing, and reaping the profits from their own work. In the autumn of 1879 the three men sailed across the Atlantic with a cast drawn from the Comedy Opera Company. The first authorized performance of *H.M.S. Pinafore* in the United States opened at the Fifth Avenue Theater, New York, on 1 December 1879.

H.M.S. Pinafore has had a particularly illustrious set of fans. Crown Prince William of Prussia, later Kaiser William II, greeted Sullivan on a visit to Kiel in 1881 with a rendering of 'He polished up the handle of the big front door'. Like many leading figures in the Navy, Admiral Lord Fisher, First Sea Lord at the beginning of the 1914–18 war, loved the opera and was frequently in the audience of D'Oyly Carte Company performances. Sir Harold Wilson,

British Prime Minister from 1964 to 1970 and 1974 to 1976, first developed his life-long love of Gilbert and Sullivan when he played the part of a midshipman when a boy. On 16 June 1977 the D'Oyly Carte Opera Company performed *H.M.S. Pinafore* before the Queen, the Duke of Edinburgh and other members of the Royal Family at Windsor Castle. It was the first Royal Command performance of a Gilbert and Sullivan opera there since *The Gondoliers* had been performed for Queen Victoria in 1891.

Pinafore has also long been a special favourite of schools and amateur operatic societies. Appropriately, it was the first Gilbert and Sullivan opera to be performed by amateurs when the Harmonists' Choral Society staged it at the Kingston upon Thames Drill Hall on 30 April 1879. Since then there can have been few evenings when the 'airs from that infernal nonsense *Pinafore*' could not have been heard wafting from some school hall or church room.

1–2 *Scene*: The stage set for *H.M.S. Pinafore* was based on the quarter-deck of Lord Nelson's famous flagship H.M.S. *Victory*, which is still preserved in dry dock at Portsmouth. Gilbert visited Portsmouth with Sullivan six weeks before *Pinafore* was due to open and made a careful inspection of the *Victory* and other ships there. From the many sketches he made he designed the set for the opera.

In the copy of the libretto sent to the Lord Chamberlain for licensing purposes in May 1878, Gilbert specified that the set should show 'an old-fashioned three decker' with a raised poop, the deck on stage right and the mainmast on stage left. He also dated the action of the opera as 1840.

Gilbert took great care to ensure that every detail of the set was correct. It was a source of great pride to him when he was complimented by senior naval officers who came to see *Pinafore* on the accuracy of the ship's furnishings. He even had the sailors' costumes made by official Navy tailors in Portsmouth to ensure their authenticity.

3–12 *We sail the ocean blue*
This rollicking opening chorus establishes the location of H.M.S. *Pinafore*, riding at anchor outside Portsmouth. In his original note on the set for Act I, Gilbert had written 'View of Portsmouth in distance'. This town in Hampshire on the south coast of England was the site of the first ever naval dockyard in Britain, built by King Henry VIII in 1540, and has been one of the country's major naval bases ever since.

12 *plenty of time for play*: The phrase appears in this form in the original manuscript score of the opera and in the first published edition of the libretto. It appears in some editions of the libretto as 'plenty of time to play', but this seems to have been a printing error which got perpetuated.

18–33 *I'm called Little Buttercup*
The famous waltz song in which Little Buttercup (real name, as we learn from the list of *Dramatis personæ*, Mrs Cripps) introduces herself to the crew of H.M.S. *Pinafore* originally began 'For I'm called Little Buttercup' and is used again in the entr'acte played as the curtain rises on Act II. Sullivan had a pet parrot, Polly, to whom he taught the tune. 'It might not be quite a perfect rendering of the music', the composer remarked, 'but it was certainly quite as good as Gilbert's attempts.'

Little Buttercup herself was an importation from one of the *Bab Ballads* which Gilbert wrote during the 1860s. Under a different name, she is the central character in a ballad entitled 'The Bumboat Woman's Story', which anticipates one of the sub-plots in *H.M.S. Pinafore* in telling of the love between Poll Pineapple and a naval officer, Lieutenant Belaye.

ACT I

SCENE. – *Quarter-deck of H.M.S. Pinafore. Sailors, led by* BOATSWAIN, *discovered cleaning brasswork, splicing rope, etc.*

CHORUS.

We sail the ocean blue,
And our saucy ship's a beauty;
We're sober men and true,   5
And attentive to our duty.
When the balls whistle free
O'er the bright blue sea,
We stand to our guns all day;
When at anchor we ride   10
On the Portsmouth tide,
We've plenty of time for play.

(*Enter* LITTLE BUTTERCUP, *with large basket on her arm.*)

RECITATIVE.

Hail, men-o'-war's men – safeguards of your nation,
Here is an end, at last, of all privation;   15
You've got your pay – spare all you can afford
To welcome Little Buttercup on board.

ARIA.

I'm called Little Buttercup – dear Little Buttercup,
  Though I could never tell why,
But still I'm called Buttercup – poor little Buttercup,   20
  Sweet Little Buttercup I!

22 *jacky*: Twists of tobacco soaked in rum and sold to sailors for chewing. In another of Gilbert's *Bab Ballads*, the King of Canoodle-Dum orders that 'every lady and every lady's lord should masticate jacky (a kind of tobaccy) and scatter its juice abroad'.

26 *I've tea and I've coffee*: In the original libretto this was 'and excellent coffee'.
27 *Soft tommy*: Soft bread, usually in the form of fresh rolls.
28 *conies*: Wild rabbits.
   polonies: Cold smoked pork sausages named after the town of Bologna, in Italy, where they were first made.

33 *Come, of your Buttercup buy*: At the end of her song Buttercup distributes the wares from her basket to the sailors, traditionally saving until last a large stick of peppermint rock which she gives to the midshipman to whom she says 'And that's for you, my little man.' Although this line is not printed in any libretto, it has regularly occurred in D'Oyly Carte productions.
34 *Boatswain*: The crew member who first greets Buttercup, and who has been supervising the work of the sailors on deck, is the boatswain (pronounced 'bosun'). He is the warrant officer in charge of sails, rigging, anchors and cables and with direct responsibility for all work carried out on deck. It is, in fact, slightly unclear whether Bill Bobstay of H.M.S. *Pinafore* is a full-fledged boatswain or merely a boatswain's mate. He appears in both guises in different editions of the libretto and even in different places in the same edition. We may as well give him the benefit of the doubt, particularly as Gilbert refers to him as boatswain both in his letters about producing the opera and in the early libretto sent to the Lord Chamberlain to be licensed.
35 *Spithead*: The stretch of water lying off Portsmouth in the east Solent. A traditional assembly point for British war fleets, it was the scene of a famous naval mutiny in 1797 when the British Channel fleet refused to go to sea during the war against Revolutionary France.
41 *Dick Deadeye*: The odious and mis-shapen Deadeye is perhaps the nearest that Gilbert comes in the Savoy Operas to creating the archetypal stage villain of Victorian melodrama, whom the audience would be expected to hiss whenever he came on stage. Sir Despard Murgatroyd in *Ruddigore* is a more self-conscious example of the species.
   For Dick's name, Gilbert deliberately chose a nautical term. A deadeye is a wooden block with three holes, used for tightening or extending the shrouds of a sailing ship. Two other members of the *Pinafore* crew were also given names with nautical connotations, although they appear only in the list of *Dramatis personæ* and are never heard on stage. Bill Bobstay, the boatswain, takes his name from the rope used to draw down the bowsprit of a ship and keep it steady, counteracting the upward force of the foremast stays. Bob Becket, the boatswain's mate, is called after the ring or loop of rope used for holding spars.

I've snuff and tobaccy, and excellent jacky,
  I've scissors, and watches, and knives;
I've ribbons and laces to set off the faces
  Of pretty young sweethearts and wives.   25

I've treacle and toffee, I've tea and I've coffee,
  Soft tommy and succulent chops;
I've chickens and conies, and pretty polonies,
  And excellent peppermint drops.

Then buy of your Buttercup – dear Little Buttercup,   30
  Sailors should never be shy;
So, buy of your Buttercup – poor Little Buttercup;
  Come, of your Buttercup buy!

BOAT. Aye, Little Buttercup – and well called – for you're the rosiest, the roundest, and the reddest beauty in all Spithead.   35

BUT. Red, am I? and round – and rosy! May be, for I have dissembled well! But hark ye, my merry friend – hast ever thought that beneath a gay and frivolous exterior there may lurk a canker-worm which is slowly but surely eating its way into one's very heart?

BOAT. No, my lass, I can't say I've ever thought that.   40

(*Enter* DICK DEADEYE. *He pushes through sailors, and comes down.*)

DICK. *I* have thought it often. (*All recoil from him.*)

BUT. Yes, you look like it! What's the matter with the man? Isn't he well?

BOAT. Don't take no heed of *him*; that's only poor Dick Deadeye.

DICK. I say – it's a beast of a name, ain't it – Dick Deadeye?   45

BUT. It's not a nice name.

DICK. I'm ugly too, ain't I?

BUT. You are certainly plain.

DICK. And I'm three-cornered too, ain't I?

BUT. You are rather triangular.   50

DICK. Ha! ha! That's it. I'm ugly, and they hate me for it; for you all hate me, don't you?

ALL. We do!

DICK. There!

BOAT. Well, Dick, we wouldn't go for to hurt any fellow-creature's   55 feelings, but you can't expect a chap with such a name as Dick Deadeye to be a popular character – now can you?

DICK. No.

BOAT. It's asking too much, ain't it?

DICK. It is. From such a face and form as mine the noblest sentiments   60

66 *Ralph Rackstraw*: It has been suggested that this name was also drawn from a seafaring term. A rack is sailors' slang for a berth on board ship, so the *Pinafore* hero's name could be interpreted as bedding straw. This seems to me a far-fetched suggestion. What is beyond doubt, however, is that his first name should be pronounced 'Rafe'. It has to rhyme with 'waif' in Little Buttercup's song 'A many years ago' (Act II, lines 461 and 463).

69–80 *The Nightingale/Sighed for the moon's bright ray*
The original version of this haunting song, as printed in the first edition libretto, began 'The nightingale/Loved the pale moon's bright ray' but was otherwise identical to the present version.

    Several American audiences had the dubious pleasure of hearing this and Ralph's other songs sung by a soprano. Early productions of *Pinafore* in the United States followed the burlesque tradition of casting females in the romantic male leads. Thus the first Ralph Rackstraw in Boston was one Rose Temple, and the first on the west coast was Alice Oates.

81 *I know the value of a kindly chorus*: An appropriate line for a Gilbert and Sullivan principal to sing, since the Savoy Operas broke new ground in musical theatre in using the chorus to represent real people with a meaningful role in the action rather than just as a passive vehicle for setting a scene or telling a story. This elevation of the role of the chorus is something for which countless members of amateur operatic societies have cause to thank Gilbert, even if they may occasionally feel inclined to agree with Mad Margaret's definition of madness in *Ruddigore* as the singing of choruses in public.

83 *pain and sorrow*: In early libretti, though not in the first vocal score, this phrase appears as 'pain and trouble'.

85 *loves a lass*: The first of three rather excruciating puns which Gilbert inflicts on the *Pinafore* audience. The others are the play on 'birth' and 'berth' (lines 429–30) and Captain Corcoran's remark to Josephine that a photograph of Sir Joseph Porter may put her in a better frame of mind (line 237).

sound like the black utterances of a depraved imagination. It is human nature – I am resigned.

RECITATIVE.

BUT.   But, tell me – who's the youth whose faltering feet
      With difficulty bear him on his course?
BOAT. That is the smartest lad in all the fleet –   65
      Ralph Rackstraw!
BUT.   Ralph! That name! Remorse! Remorse!

(*Enter* RALPH.)

MADRIGAL – RALPH.

    The Nightingale
    Sighed for the moon's bright ray,   70
      And told his tale
    In his own melodious way!
      He sang 'Ah, well-a-day!'

ALL.   He sang 'Ah, well-a-day!'

    The lowly vale   75
    For the mountain vainly sighed,
      To his humble wail
    The echoing hills replied.
      They sang 'Ah, well-a-day!'

ALL.   They sang 'Ah, well-a-day!'   80

RECITATIVE.

    I know the value of a kindly chorus,
      But choruses yield little consolation
    When we have pain and sorrow too before us!
      I love – and love, alas, above my station!

BUT. (*aside*). He loves – and loves a lass above his station!   85
ALL (*aside*). Yes, yes, the lass is much above his station!

(*Exit* LITTLE BUTTERCUP.)

88–108 *A maiden fair to see*
As originally written by Gilbert, the second verse of this song had slightly different words:

> A suitor, lowly born,
> With hopeless passion torn,
>   And poor beyond concealing,
> Has dared for her to pine,
> At whose exalted shrine
>   A world of wealth is kneeling!

The plight of Ralph Rackstraw is foreshadowed in Gilbert's Bab Ballad 'Joe Golightly', which tells of a poor sailor, born in a workhouse, who is in love with the First Lord of the Admiralty's daughter, Lady Jane:

> Whene'er he sailed afar
> Upon a Channel cruise, he
> Unpacked his light guitar
> And sang this ballad (Boosey):

> The moon is on the sea, willow!
> The wind blows towards the lee, willow!
> But though I sigh and sob and cry,
> No Lady Jane for me, willow!

> She says, ''Twere folly quite, willow!
> For me to wed a wight, willow!
> Whose lot is cast before the mast',
> And possibly she's right, willow!

112 *foremast hands*: Gilbert originally wrote 'foremast jacks', later substituted 'blue jackets' and finally produced 'foremast hands' for the 1908 revival of *Pinafore*. The term refers to those members of a ship's company who serve 'before the mast', i.e. all below the rank of officer.

117 *quarter-deck*: The stretch of deck to the aft of the mainmast where the officers and midshipmen had their quarters. Only commissioned officers could linger on the quarter-deck.

117–18 *fore-yard arm*: The ends of the large wooden spar which crossed the mast and from which sails were set. Flag signals were generally hoisted on the yard arms, and in the days when the code of punishments aboard included death by hanging they were also used for that purpose.

118–19 *main-truck*: A circular wooden cap fitted on the highest point of the mainmast.

119 *slacks*: A traditional nautical term for trousers.

BALLAD – RALPH.

A maiden fair to see,
The pearl of minstrelsy,
  A bud of blushing beauty;   90
For whom proud nobles sigh,
And with each other vie
  To do her menial's duty.

ALL.   To do her menial's duty.

A suitor, lowly born,   95
With hopeless passion torn,
  And poor beyond denying,
Has dared for her to pine
At whose exalted shrine
  A world of wealth is sighing.   100

ALL.   A world of wealth is sighing!

Unlearned he in aught
Save that which love has taught
  (For love had been his tutor);
Oh, pity, pity me –   105
Our captain's daughter she,
  And I that lowly suitor!

ALL.   And he that lowly suitor!

BOAT. Ah, my poor lad, you've climbed too high; our worthy captain's
child won't have nothin' to say to a poor chap like you. Will she, lads?   110
ALL. No, no!
DICK. No, no, captains' daughters don't marry foremast hands.
ALL (*recoiling from him*). Shame! Shame!
BOAT. Dick Deadeye, them sentiments o' yourn are a disgrace to our
common natur'.   115
RALPH. But it's a strange anomaly, that the daughter of a man who
hails from the quarter-deck may not love another who lays out on the fore-
yard arm. For a man is but a man, whether he hoists his flag at the main-
truck or his slacks on the main-deck.
DICK. Ah, it's a queer world!   120
RALPH. Dick Deadeye, I have no desire to press hardly on you, but
such a revolutionary sentiment is enough to make an honest sailor
shudder.

126 *Captain Corcoran*: Once again, Gilbert borrowed from his earlier works to create the character of Captain Corcoran. He bears a close resemblance, for example, to the hero of the Bab Ballad 'Captain Reece':

> Of all the ships upon the blue
> No ship contained a better crew
> Than that of worthy CAPTAIN REECE,
> Commanding of *The Mantelpiece.*

> He was adored by all his men,
> For worthy CAPTAIN REECE, R.N.,
> Did all that lay within him to
> Promote the comfort of his crew.

There is more than a hint of Corcoran too in Captain Bang, a pirate chief in *Our Island Home*, a musical entertainment for which Gilbert wrote the words in 1870, who boasts:

> I'm a hardy sailor, too;
> I've a vessel and a crew,
> When it doesn't blow a gale
> I can reef a little sail.
> I never go below
> And I generally know
> The weather from the 'lee',
> And I'm never sick at sea.

143 *I can hand, reef, and steer*: This same line is given to Lieutenant Belaye in the Bab Ballad 'The Bumboat Woman's Story'. He also makes the additional boast, not made by Captain Corcoran, that he can 'fire my big gun too'. To hand is to take in and furl a sail; to reef is to reduce the area of a sail exposed to the wind by partially furling it.

144 *ship a selvagee*: A selvagee is a strop of spun yarn either plaited into a stout rope or tied together into parallel lengths. It was used as a strap to fasten round a shroud or stay or for making a sling to lift heavy weights. One of the *Bab Ballads*, 'The Mystic Selvagee', tells of Sir Blennerhasset Portico, a Captain in the Royal Navy, who believes in removing selvagees from the maintop-stays of ships.

150–51 *What, never?/Well, hardly ever*: This became a popular catch-phrase in Britain and even more in the United States as *Pinafore* mania swept both sides of the Atlantic in the winter of 1878–9. One American newspaper editor is said to have called all his reporters into his office and complained that the phrase had occurred twenty times in the previous day's paper. 'Never let me see it again,' he ordered. 'What, never?' came the inevitable reply. 'Well, hardly ever,' he found himself responding.

Boat. My lads, our gallant captain has come on deck; let us greet him
as so brave an officer and so gallant a seaman deserves.   125

(*Enter* Captain Corcoran.)

RECITATIVE.

Capt. My gallant crew, good morning.
All (*saluting*). Sir, good morning!
Capt. I hope you're all quite well.
All (*as before*). Quite well; and you, sir?   130
Capt. I am in reasonable health, and happy
      To meet you all once more.
All (*as before*). You do us proud, sir!

SONG – Captain.

Capt.   I am the Captain of the *Pinafore*;
All.   And a right good captain, too!   135
Capt.   You're very, very good,
            And be it understood,
        I command a right good crew.
All.   We're very, very good,
            And be it understood,   140
        He commands a right good crew.
Capt.   Though related to a peer,
        I can hand, reef, and steer,
            And ship a selvagee;
        I am never known to quail   145
        At the fury of a gale,
            And I'm never, never sick at sea!
All.   What, never?
Capt.   No, never!
All.   What, *never*?   150
Capt.   Well, hardly ever!
All.   He's hardly ever sick at sea!
        Then give three cheers, and one cheer more,
        For the hardy Captain of the *Pinafore*!

Capt.   I do my best to satisfy you all –   155
All.   And with you we're quite content.
Capt.   You're exceedingly polite,
            And I think it only right
         To return the compliment.

168 *I never use a big, big D*: The idea of a sailor who didn't swear was evidently something which Gilbert found particularly amusing. In 'The Bumboat Woman's Story' he alluded to the 'gentle, well-bred crew' of the gunboat *Hot Cross Bun*:

> When Jack Tars growl, I believe they growl with a big, big D—
> But the strongest oath of *The Hot Cross Buns* was a mild 'Dear me!'

The same subject also features in another Bab Ballad, 'The Bishop of Rum-ti-Foo':

> Some sailors whom he did not know
> Had landed there not long ago,
> And taught them 'Bother', also 'Blow',
> (Of wickedness the germs).
> No need to use a casuist's pen
> To prove that they were merchantmen;
> No sailor of the Royal N.
> Would use such awful terms.

175 *Captain of the Pinafore*: In an interview in *The World* in 1880 Gilbert admitted that the name *Pinafore* 'was suggested entirely by rhyme . . . something had to rhyme with "three cheers more"'. He had originally christened his operatic vessel H.M.S. *Semaphore*, but it was changed to *Pinafore* at Sullivan's suggestion.

184 *ancestral timber*: A suitably nautical if rather highfalutin expression for the family tree.

ALL.	We're exceedingly polite,	160
	And he thinks it's only right	
	To return the compliment.	
CAPT.	Bad language or abuse,	
	I never, never use,	
	Whatever the emergency;	165
	Though 'Bother it' I may	
	Occasionally say,	
	I never use a big, big D –	
ALL.	What, never?	
CAPT.	No, never!	170
ALL.	What, *never*?	
CAPT.	Well, hardly ever!	
ALL.	Hardly ever swears a big, big D –	
	Then give three cheers, and one cheer more,	
	For the well-bred Captain of the *Pinafore*!	175

(*After song exeunt all but* CAPTAIN.)

(*Enter* LITTLE BUTTERCUP.)

RECITATIVE.

BUT. Sir, you are sad! The silent eloquence
      Of yonder tear that trembles on your eyelash
      Proclaims a sorrow far more deep than common; 180
      Confide in me – fear not – I am a mother!

CAPT. Yes, Little Buttercup, I'm sad and sorry –
       My daughter, Josephine, the fairest flower
       That ever blossomed on ancestral timber,
       Is sought in marriage by Sir Joseph Porter, 185
       Our Admiralty's First Lord, but for some reason
       She does not seem to tackle kindly to it.

BUT. (*with emotion*). Ah, poor Sir Joseph! Ah, I know too well
       The anguish of a heart that loves but vainly!
       But see, here comes your most attractive daughter. 190
       I go – Farewell!   (*Exit.*)

CAPT. (*looking after her*). A plump and pleasing person! (*Exit.*)

(*Enter* JOSEPHINE *, twining some flowers which she carries in a small basket.*)

194–205 *Sorry her lot who loves too well*
The ballad which introduces Josephine may sound familiar to those who have never
heard *H.M.S. Pinafore* but have seen the Joseph Papp production of *The Pirates of
Penzance*. For some reason, Papp gave Mabel Josephine's ballad to croon immediately
after her long duet with Frederic in Act II.

208 *Sir Joseph Porter, K.C.B.*: Snob that he is, Captain Corcoran cannot resist making the
most of Sir Joseph Porter's knighthood. K.C.B. stands for Knight Commander of the
Bath. This is the second class of the Order of the Bath, the first being Grand Cross of
the Bath (G.C.B.) and the third Companion of the Bath (C.B.). There are two other
K.C.B.s in the Savoy Operas: Sir Marmaduke Pointdextre in *The Sorcerer* and our old
friend Captain Corcoran, who reappears as Captain Sir Edward Corcoran in *Utopia
Limited* (see the note to Act II, line 538).

227–8 *solecisms that society would never pardon*: After this line, Gilbert originally intended
Captain Corcoran to have a ballad highlighting the English obsession with the
outward marks of class and status rather than the inner qualities of character and
creativity. The song occurs in the copy of the intended libretto sent to the Lord
Chamberlain but was jettisoned before the first performance. Here it is:

BALLAD – CAPTAIN.
Reflect my child, he may be brave
As any in the Royal navy
And daily fill a watery grave
The locker of poor Davy.
But ah! What gallant act
Could counteract
The fearful social ban
That falls on man
Who with his knife's sharp blade devours his prey!

ENSEMBLE.
In truth I fear
The sneer
That would disgrace
Each face
When he with blade of knife devoured his prey.

He may a second Shakespeare be,
Endowed with faulty* creative
But what avail such gifts, if he
Confounds accusative with dative,
In what far nook of earth
Would mortal worth,
Or strength of lung or limb,
Atone for him
Whose verbs don't tally with the nominative.

ENSEMBLE.
Oh, I can tell
Too well
How people frown
Him down
Whose verbs don't tally with the nominative.

*This should surely be 'faculty' and must be a misprint in the licence copy.

BALLAD – JOSEPHINE.

Sorry her lot who loves too well,
   Heavy the heart that hopes but vainly,   195
Sad are the sighs that own the spell,
   Uttered by eyes that speak too plainly;
      Heavy the sorrow that bows the head
      When love is alive and hope is dead!

Sad is the hour when sets the sun –   200
   Dark is the night to earth's poor daughters,
When to the ark the wearied one
   Flies from the empty waste of waters!
      Heavy the sorrow that bows the head
      When love is alive and hope is dead!   205

(*Enter* CAPTAIN.)

CAPT. My child, I grieve to see that you are a prey to melancholy. You should look your best to-day, for Sir Joseph Porter, K.C.B., will be here this afternoon to claim your promised hand.

JOS. Ah, father, your words cut me to the quick. I can esteem –   210 reverence – venerate Sir Joseph, for he is a great and good man; but oh, I cannot love him! My heart is already given.

CAPT. (*aside*). It is then as I feared. (*Aloud.*) Given? And to whom? Not to some gilded lordling?

JOS. No, father – the object of my love is no lordling. Oh, pity me, for   215 he is but a humble sailor on board your own ship!

CAPT. Impossible!

JOS. Yes, it is true – too true.

CAPT. A common sailor? Oh fie!

JOS. I blush for the weakness that allows me to cherish such a passion.   220 I hate myself when I think of the depth to which I have stooped in permitting myself to think tenderly of one so ignobly born, but I love him! I love him! I love him! (*Weeps.*)

CAPT. Come, my child, let us talk this over. In a matter of the heart I would not coerce my daughter – I attach but little value to rank or wealth, but   225 the line must be drawn somewhere. A man in that station may be brave and worthy, but at every step he would commit solecisms that society would never pardon.

JOS. Oh, I have thought of this night and day. But fear not, father, I have a heart, and therefore I love; but I am your daughter, and therefore I am   230 proud. Though I carry my love with me to the tomb, he shall never, never know it.

243 *the loud nine-pounders*: These were the smallest long cannons carried on Royal Navy ships in the first half of the nineteenth century. Large warships like the *Pinafore* would have them mounted on the fo'c'sle and quarter-decks, with bigger eighteen- and thirty-two-pounders providing the main armament on lower decks.

247–58 *Sir Joseph's barge is seen*
In early editions of the libretto, the first four lines of this chorus take the form of a repeat of the first four lines of the sailors' opening chorus.

Although the last words of the second and fourth lines are printed as 'beauties' and 'duties' in some modern editions of the libretto, they appear as 'beauty' and 'duty' in the vocal score and are often sung in that form.

The rhyming of 'beauty' and 'duty' occurs in fifteen separate songs in the Savoy Operas. Four of them are in *H.M.S. Pinafore* (the opening chorus and its reprise here, Ralph's ballad 'A maiden fair to see', Josephine and Ralph's duet 'Refrain, audacious tar', and Josephine's song 'A simple sailor, lowly born').

261–70 *Gaily tripping*
Like so much else in *Pinafore*, the chorus of female relatives who make their entrance to this infectiously gay tune have their origins in the *Bab Ballads*. The worthy Captain Reece, whom we have already come across as the prototype of Captain Corcoran, has ten female cousins, a niece, six sisters, an aunt or two and a widowed mother whom he philanthropically unites to unmarried members of his crew. For *Pinafore* Gilbert transfers the relatives to the First Lord of the Admiralty, just as he changes Joe Golightly's love for the First Lord's daughter into Ralph Rackstraw's passion for his captain's daughter.

CAPT. You *are* my daughter after all. But see, Sir Joseph's barge approaches, manned by twelve trusty oarsmen and accompanied by the admiring crowd of sisters, cousins, and aunts that attend him wherever he 235 goes. Retire, my daughter, to your cabin – take this, his photograph, with you – it may help to bring you to a more reasonable frame of mind.

JOS. My own thoughtful father!

> (*Exit* JOSEPHINE. CAPTAIN *remains and ascends the poop-deck.*)

BARCAROLLE (*invisible*).

> Over the bright blue sea 240
> Comes Sir Joseph Porter, K.C.B.,
> > Wherever he may go
> Bang-bang the loud nine-pounders go!
> > Shout o'er the bright blue sea
> For Sir Joseph Porter, K.C.B. 245

(*During this the Crew have entered on tiptoe, listening attentively to the song.*)

CHORUS OF SAILORS.

> Sir Joseph's barge is seen,
> > And its crowd of blushing beauties,
> We hope he'll find us clean,
> > And attentive to our duties. 250
> We sail, we sail the ocean blue,
> > And our saucy ship's a beauty.
> We're sober, sober men and true
> > And attentive to our duty.
> We're smart and sober men, 255
> > And quite devoid of fe-ar,
> In all the Royal N.
> > None are so smart as we are.

(*Enter* SIR JOSEPH'S FEMALE RELATIVES.

> *They dance round stage.*) 260

REL.	Gaily tripping,
	Lightly skipping,
	Flock the maidens to the shipping.
SAILORS.	Flags and guns and pennants dipping!
	All the ladies love the shipping. 265
REL.	Sailors sprightly

275–92 *I am the monarch of the sea*
Sir Joseph Porter's entrance is normally accompanied by a Royal Marine guard, consisting of a sergeant and two privates who present arms as the First Lord of the Admiralty steps on to the quarter-deck of the *Pinafore*.

When George Grossmith, the principal comic baritone with D'Oyly Carte's Comedy Opera Company, who created so many of what might be termed the 'patter song roles', first made his entrance on the opening night of *H.M.S. Pinafore*, he was made up to look like Lord Nelson. However, as the opera progressed there was little doubt in the audience's mind about the identity of the real model for Sir Joseph Porter. In background, character and attitudes he was strikingly similar to William Henry Smith, founder of the newsagent's business which still bears his name, who had been appointed First Lord of the Admiralty the previous year.

Until the post was abolished in 1964 with the incorporation of the Admiralty into the Ministry of Defence, the First Lord of the Admiralty was the Government minister in charge of the Navy. Although the office was a political one, carrying a seat in the Cabinet, it was often held in the nineteenth century by someone with personal experience in the Navy and nearly always by someone of aristocratic, or at the very least upper-middle-class, background. Smith had never been to sea and had risen from the humble origins of selling newspapers at railway-station bookstalls. Sir Joseph Porter was in a very similar position, as his next song was to make clear.

293–340 *When I was a lad I served a term*
It was this song which firmly established W. H. Smith as the model for Sir Joseph Porter in the eyes of the British public. Gilbert himself had rather mischievously denied the suggestion in a letter he wrote to Sullivan late in 1877 when he was still working out the songs of the proposed new opera:

> Among other things there is a song for the First Lord – tracing his career as office boy in cotton broker's office, clerk, traveller, junior partner, and First Lord of Britain's Navy. I think a splendid song can be made of this. Of course there will be no personality in this – the fact that the First Lord in the opera is a Radical of the most pronounced type will do away with any suspicion that W. H. Smith is intended.

Of course, Gilbert knew perfectly well that everyone would think of W. H. Smith when they heard Sir Joseph Porter chronicling his rise from office boy to ruler of the Navy and urging those who would emulate him to stick close to their desks and never go to sea. Following the success of the opera, Smith, who remained as First Lord until the fall of Disraeli's Government in 1880, became universally known as 'Pinafore Smith'. 'When I was a lad' was even played by a Royal Marine band when he went down to launch a ship at Devonport, although strict orders had gone out from the Port Admiral that music from *Pinafore* should on no account be performed.

In fact, as he indicated, Gilbert's satire was directed much more against the system which put in charge of Government departments those who were wholly ignorant of their affairs than against W. H. Smith as an individual. In a summary of *H.M.S. Pinafore* which he later wrote for children, Gilbert explained his creation of Sir Joseph Porter: 'You would naturally think that a person who commanded the entire British Navy would be the most accomplished sailor who could be found, but that is not the way in which such things are managed in England'.

294 *an Attorney's firm*: Until 1873 those lawyers (other than barristers) who practised in the courts of equity were called solicitors and those in common law courts attorneys. The Judicature Act of that year brought the two groups together under the common title of solicitors of the Supreme Court.

296 *I polished up the handle of the big front door*: In the winter of 1881 Sullivan accompanied the Duke of Edinburgh on a Baltic cruise on board H.M.S. *Hercules*. At Kiel they were

	Always rightly Welcome ladies so politely.	
SAILORS.	Ladies who can smile so brightly, Sailors welcome most politely.	270
CAPT. (*from poop*).	Now give three cheers, I'll lead the way. Hurrah! hurrah!	
ALL.	Hurray! hurray! hurray!	

(*Enter* SIR JOSEPH *with* COUSIN HEBE.)

SONG – SIR JOSEPH.

	I am the monarch of the sea,	275
	The ruler of the Queen's Navee,	
	Whose praise Great Britain loudly chants.	
COUSIN HEBE.	And we are his sisters, and his cousins, and his aunts!	
REL.	And we are his sisters, and his cousins, and his aunts!	
SIR JOSEPH.	When at anchor here I ride,	280
	My bosom swells with pride,	
	And I snap my fingers at a foeman's taunts;	
COUSIN HEBE.	And so do his sisters, and his cousins, and his aunts!	
ALL.	And so do his sisters, and his cousins, and his aunts!	
SIR JOSEPH.	But when the breezes blow,	285
	I generally go below,	
	And seek the seclusion that a cabin grants!	
COUSIN HEBE.	And so do his sisters, and his cousins, and his aunts!	
ALL.	And so do his sisters, and his cousins, and his aunts!	
	His sisters and his cousins,	290
	Whom he reckons up by dozens,	
	And his aunts!	

SONG – SIR JOSEPH.

When I was a lad I served a term
As office boy to an Attorney's firm.
I cleaned the windows and I swept the floor,   295
And I polished up the handle of the big front door.
  CHORUS. – He polished, etc.
 I polished up that handle so carefullee
That now I am the Ruler of the Queen's Navee!
  CHORUS. – He polished, etc.   300

As office boy I made such a mark
That they gave me the post of a junior clerk.
I served the writs with a smile so bland,

greeted by Prince William of Prussia, who bowed to the composer and sang 'He polished up the handle of the big front door'. Sullivan noted 'I burst out laughing and so did everyone. It was too funny'. Seven years later William was the Kaiser.

303 *I served the writs*: To serve a writ is to deliver a legal document, often summoning a person to appear in court.

310 *an articled clerk*: One undergoing a form of apprenticeship before becoming a fully qualified solicitor.

312 *the Institute*: The Law Society, the governing body for solicitors, which organizes qualifying examinations for entry into the profession, was also known as the Law Institute.

326 *a pocket borough*: A parliamentary seat in the gift of a single individual, normally a wealthy landowner. Pocket boroughs, which contained at the most only a handful of electors and in some cases had none at all, were effectively abolished in the Great Reform Act of 1832. The Fairy Queen in *Iolanthe* has 'a borough or two' at her disposal and puts Strephon into the House of Commons by this means.

And I copied all the letters in a big round hand –
      CHORUS. – He copied, etc.   305
    I copied all the letters in a hand so free,
    That now I am the Ruler of the Queen's Navee!
      CHORUS. – He copied, etc.

In serving writs I made such a name
That an articled clerk I soon became;   310
I wore clean collars and a brand-new suit
For the pass examination at the Institute.
      CHORUS. – For the pass examination, etc.
    That pass examination did so well for me,
    That now I am the Ruler of the Queen's Navee!   315
      CHORUS. – That pass examination, etc.

Of legal knowledge I acquired such a grip
That they took me into the partnership.
And that junior partnership, I ween,
Was the only ship that I ever had seen.   320
      CHORUS. – Was the only ship that he, etc.
    But that kind of ship so suited me,
    That now I am the Ruler of the Queen's Navee!
      CHORUS. – But that kind, etc.

I grew so rich that I was sent   325
By a pocket borough into Parliament.
I always voted at my party's call,
And I never thought of thinking for myself at all.
      CHORUS. – He never thought, etc.
    I thought so little, they rewarded me   330
    By making me the Ruler of the Queen's Navee!
      CHORUS. – He thought so little, etc.

Now, landsmen all, whoever you may be,
If you want to rise to the top of the tree,
If your soul isn't fettered to an office stool,   335
Be careful to be guided by this golden rule –
      CHORUS. – Be careful, etc.
    Stick close to your desks and never go to sea,
    And you all may be Rulers of the Queen's Navee!
      CHORUS. – Stick close, etc.   340

SIR JOSEPH. You've a remarkably fine crew, Captain Corcoran.
CAPT. It *is* a fine crew, Sir Joseph.

343 *a very small midshipman*: Midshipman is a non-commissioned rank in the Royal Navy just below the officer level. Traditionally young men destined to become officers serve first for a three-year period as midshipmen before becoming sub-lieutenants.

In some editions of the *Pinafore* libretto the midshipman (or midshipmite, as he is sometimes called) appears in the list of *Dramatis personæ* and is given the name Tom Tucker. It is, however, a very minor part, with no lines to say and no notes to sing, and it is traditionally played by a small boy. The former British Prime Minister Sir Harold Wilson began his life-long love affair with Gilbert and Sullivan when he played the part in a production of *Pinafore* by the Milnsbridge Baptist Amateur Operatic Society near his home town of Huddersfield, Yorkshire, in 1926.

364 *Dick comes forward*: Dick Deadeye's step forward in response to Sir Joseph's request did not feature in the earliest productions of *H.M.S. Pinafore*. Like several of Dick's lines, this particular bit of stage business was added, quite possibly on the suggestion of Richard Temple, the singer who created the role of Deadeye. It was approved by Gilbert in the libretto prepared for the 1908 revival of the opera at the Savoy Theatre.

366 *Ralph Rackstraw, three paces to the front – march*: This order was also added with Gilbert's approval for the 1908 revival, the original line being simply 'Ralph Rackstraw, come here'. It is the cue for a typical piece of D'Oyly Carte business, described by Martyn Green in his *Treasury of Gilbert and Sullivan*. As Ralph steps forward, he salutes Sir Joseph and stamps his right foot. Sir Joseph, a little taken aback by this, inspects him and indicates that he wants him to turn round. Ralph does so and again stamps his foot. His response to Sir Joseph's first comment, 'You're a remarkably fine fellow', is to stamp his foot yet again. Not to be outdone, Sir Joseph stamps his right foot too, only to bring it down hard on his left toes.

374 *topman*: A seaman stationed at the top of a mast, either to attend to the sails, or as a marksman during an engagement.

379 *all sailors should dance hornpipes*: The hornpipe was originally a wind instrument, which gave its name to the vigorous solo dance associated particularly with sailors from the eighteenth century onwards. It is said that the hornpipe was danced at sea in order to keep the blood circulating and to ward off scurvy. Sullivan wrote a hornpipe to be danced by the *Pinafore* crew after their first singing of 'A British tar is a soaring soul', but it was cut out after the first night. The one danced by Richard Dauntless in Act I of *Ruddigore* has, however, been allowed to remain and is a splendid example of the genre.

SIR JOSEPH (*examining a very small midshipman*). A British sailor is a splendid fellow, Captain Corcoran.

CAPT. A splendid fellow indeed, Sir Joseph.   345

SIR JOSEPH. I hope you treat your crew kindly, Captain Corcoran.

CAPT. Indeed I hope so, Sir Joseph.

SIR JOSEPH. Never forget that they are the bulwarks of England's greatness, Captain Corcoran.

CAPT. So I have always considered them, Sir Joseph.   350

SIR JOSEPH. No bullying, I trust – no strong language of any kind, eh?

CAPT. Oh, never, Sir Joseph.

SIR JOSEPH. What, *never*?

CAPT. Well, hardly ever, Sir Joseph. They are an excellent crew, and do their work thoroughly without it.   355

SIR JOSEPH. Don't patronize them, sir – pray, don't patronize them.

CAPT. Certainly not, Sir Joseph.

SIR JOSEPH. That you are their captain is an accident of birth. I cannot permit these noble fellows to be patronized because an accident of birth has placed you above them and them below you.   360

CAPT. I am the last person to insult a British sailor, Sir Joseph.

SIR JOSEPH. You are the last person who did, Captain Corcoran. Desire that splendid seaman to step forward.

(DICK *comes forward.*)

SIR JOSEPH. No, no, the other splendid seaman.   365

CAPT. Ralph Rackstraw, three paces to the front – march!

SIR JOSEPH (*sternly*). If what?

CAPT. I beg your pardon – I don't think I understand you.

SIR JOSEPH. If you *please*.

CAPT. Oh, yes, of course. If you please. (RALPH *steps forward.*)   370

SIR JOSEPH. You're a remarkably fine fellow.

RALPH. Yes, your honour.

SIR JOSEPH. And a first-rate seaman, I'll be bound.

RALPH. There's not a smarter topman in the Navy, your honour, though I say it who shouldn't.   375

SIR JOSEPH. Not at all. Proper self-respect, nothing more. Can you dance a hornpipe?

RALPH. No, your honour.

SIR JOSEPH. That's a pity: all sailors should dance hornpipes. I will teach you one this evening, after dinner. Now tell me – don't be afraid – how   380
does your captain treat you, eh?

RALPH. A better captain don't walk the deck, your honour.

ALL. Aye! Aye!

SIR JOSEPH. Good. I like to hear you speak well of your commanding

387 *I can hum a little, your honour*: Traditionally Ralph, in keeping with his common origins, drops the 'h' in 'hum', and Sir Joseph, temporarily forgetting his rapid rise from a similarly lowly station, does the same in the next line before he quickly corrects himself.

395 *grog*: In 1740 Admiral Vernon introduced a daily issue of rum diluted with water to all men serving in the Royal Navy. His intention was to mitigate the evil effects of the raw spirit which most sailors had previously taken in copious quantities. The name given to the diluted rum derived from the Admiral's nickname, 'Old Grog', a reference to the grogram trousers he habitually wore. The Navy abolished the daily issue of grog in 1970.

396 *seven bells*: The twenty-four-hour day on board ship is divided into six watches, each four hours long. The ship's bell is rung every half hour, so there are eight bells in each watch. Seven bells therefore marks the last half hour of the watch.

404 *The expression, 'if you please'*: In making Sir Joseph Porter such a stickler for good manners and good language, Gilbert may have been having another little dig at W. H. Smith, who was known to have strong views on both matters. Brought up by strict Methodist parents, and himself an evangelical Anglican, Smith deplored coarseness and lewdness of any kind.

423 *Messmates*: In Army and Navy parlance, the mess is the place where meals are served and eaten. The word mess originally meant a small portion of food and so came to be used for a group of people who sat together for meals and were served from the same dishes.

officer; I daresay he don't deserve it, but still it does you credit. Can you 385
sing?

RALPH. I can hum a little, your honour.

SIR JOSEPH. Then hum this at your leisure. (*Giving him MS. music.*) It
is a song that I have composed for the use of the Royal Navy. It is designed
to encourage independence of thought and action in the lower branches of 390
the service, and to teach the principle that a British sailor is any man's equal,
excepting mine. Now, Captain Corcoran, a word with you in your cabin, on
a tender and sentimental subject.

CAPT. Aye, aye, Sir Joseph. (*Crossing.*) Boatswain, in commemoration of
this joyous occasion, see that extra grog is served out to the ship's company 395
at seven bells.

BOAT. Beg pardon. If what, your honour?

CAPT. If what? I don't think I understand you.

BOAT. If you *please*, your honour.

CAPT. What! 400

SIR JOSEPH. The gentleman is quite right. If you *please*.

CAPT. (*stamping his foot impatiently*). If you *please*! (*Exit.*)

SIR JOSEPH.	For I hold that on the seas
	The expression, 'if you please',
	A particularly gentlemanly tone implants.
COUSIN HEBE.	And so do his sisters, and his cousins, and his aunts!
ALL.	And so do his sisters, and his cousins, and his aunts!

405

(*Exeunt* SIR JOSEPH *and* RELATIVES.)

BOAT. Ah! Sir Joseph's a true gentleman; courteous and considerate to
the very humblest. 410

RALPH. True, Boatswain, but we are not the very humblest. Sir Joseph
has explained our true position to us. As he says, a British seaman is any
man's equal excepting his, and if Sir Joseph says that, is it not our duty to
believe him?

ALL. Well spoke! well spoke! 415

DICK. You're on a wrong tack, and so is he. He means well, but he
don't know. When people have to obey other people's orders, equality's out
of the question.

ALL (*recoiling*). Horrible! horrible!

BOAT. Dick Deadeye, if you go for to infuriate this here ship's company 420
too far, I won't answer for being able to hold 'em in. I'm shocked! that's what
I am – shocked!

RALPH. Messmates, my mind's made up. I'll speak to the captain's
daughter, and tell her, like an honest man, of the honest love I have for her.

ALL. Aye, aye! 425

RALPH. Is not my love as good as another's? Is not my heart as true as
another's? Have I not hands and eyes and ears and limbs like another?

435 *What is to be done with this here hopeless chap*: In answer to this question, in D'Oyly Carte productions the crew have traditionally indicated by making a splashing sound that Dick should be thrown overboard.

438–55 *A British tar is a soaring soul*
This stirring three-part glee, in its tune slightly reminiscent of the popular sea shanty 'Tom Bowling', is the first of Gilbert's two great patriotic songs in *H.M.S. Pinafore*. The second is, of course, 'He is an Englishman'. In producing such flag-waving stuff Gilbert was reflecting the general mood of the country at the time *Pinafore* was written. Disraeli's decision to send the British fleet to Constantinople in February 1878 to defend it from possible Russian attack produced a wave of patriotism and military adventurism throughout Britain, which lasted for more than two months and was only just beginning to subside as *Pinafore* took to the stage. It was during this period, indeed, that the word jingoism was added to the English language as a result of the popular music-hall song written by G. W. Hunt at the same time that Gilbert was writing *Pinafore*:

> We don't want to fight, but by Jingo if we do,
> We've got the ships, we've got the men, and got the money too.
> We've fought the Bear before, and while we're Britons true,
> The Russians shall not have Constantinople.

447 *His eyes should flash*: Some of the striking anatomical postures demanded in this song were anticipated in the *Bab Ballads*. In 'Peter the Wag', a London policeman finds that the citizens of the capital are less than helpful when he asks them directions:

> Their eyes would flash – their teeth would grind –
> Their lips would tightly curl –
> They'd say, 'Thy way thyself must find,
> Thou misdirecting churl!'

The curling lip also finds its way into another Bab Ballad, 'The Scornful Colonel':

> At sight of snobs his lip would curl –
> His lips would quiver, twist, and twirl
> In an astonishing degree –
> He often curled his lip at me.

ALL. Aye, aye!
RALPH. True, I lack birth —
BOAT. You've a berth on board this very ship.   430
RALPH. Well said – I had forgotten that. Messmates – what do you say?
Do you approve my determination?
ALL. We do.
DICK. *I* don't.
BOAT. What is to be done with this here hopeless chap? Let us sing   435
him the song that Sir Joseph has kindly composed for us. Perhaps it will
bring this here miserable creetur to a proper state of mind.   (*Exit* DICK.)

GLEE – RALPH, BOATSWAIN, BOATSWAIN'S MATE, *and* CHORUS.

A British tar is a soaring soul,
  As free as a mountain bird,
His energetic fist should be ready to resist   440
  A dictatorial word.
His nose should pant and his lip should curl,
His cheeks should flame and his brow should furl,
His bosom should heave and his heart should glow,
And his fist be ever ready for a knock-down blow.   445
    CHORUS. – His nose should pant, etc.

His eyes should flash with an inborn fire,
  His brow with scorn be wrung;
He never should bow down to a domineering frown,
  Or the tang of a tyrant tongue.   450
His foot should stamp and his throat should growl,
His hair should twirl and his face should scowl;
His eyes should flash and his breast protrude,
And this should be his customary attitude – (*pose*).
    CHORUS. – His foot should stamp, etc.   455

(*All dance off excepting* RALPH, *who remains, leaning
pensively against bulwark.*)

(*Enter* JOSEPHINE *from cabin.*)

JOS. It is useless – Sir Joseph's attentions nauseate me. I know that he is
a truly great and good man, for he told me so himself, but to me he seems   460
tedious, fretful, and dictatorial. Yet his must be a mind of no common order,
or he would not dare to teach my dear father to dance a hornpipe on the
cabin table. (*Sees* RALPH.) Ralph Rackstraw! (*Overcome by emotion.*)
RALPH. Aye, lady – no other than poor Ralph Rackstraw!

465 *How my heart beats*: In early editions of the libretto this line read 'How my head beats!' This was almost certainly a misprint.

470–71 *the Cimmerian darkness*: In the *Odyssey*, Homer says that the Cimmerians dwell in a land beyond the ocean where the sun never shines.

471 *a living ganglion*: The *Oxford English Dictionary* variously defines a ganglion as a tumour or swelling of a tendon, enlargement or knot of a nerve, collection of grey matter in the central nervous system, and (as here) a centre of force, activity or interest, a point from which many lines diverge.

478 *Jove's armoury*: The armour of Jove, alias Jupiter, alias Zeus, the king of the gods in classical mythology, was thunder and lightning. He takes a prominent role in two of the operettas of Gilbert and Sullivan's French contemporary Jaques Offenbach (*Orpheus in the Underworld* and *La Belle Helène*), and appears in *Thespis*.

Ralph's anything but simple eloquence is, of course, designed to show Josephine that he is not lacking in the accomplishments which come with gentlemanly birth and breeding. Inevitably it has precisely the opposite effect.

484 *Oh, my heart, my beating heart*: The word 'beating' was added by Gilbert for the 1908 revival, as was the subsequent phrase, 'Common! oh, the irony of the word!'

496–515 *Refrain, audacious tar*

In early editions of the libretto, instead of being obliged to repeat the first four lines of this song as she is now, Josephine had another four:

> Proud lords to seek my hand
> In throngs assemble,
> The loftiest in the land,
> Bow down and tremble!

Those lines make Josephine sound even more like Lady Jane, the First Lord of the Admiralty's daughter whom, it may be remembered, Joe Golightly unsuccessfully wooed in the Bab Ballad:

> The First Lord's daughter, proud,
> Snubbed Earls and Viscounts nightly,
> She sneered at Barts, aloud,
> And spurned poor Joe Golightly.

Jos. (*aside*). How my heart beats! (*Aloud.*) And why poor, Ralph? 465
Ralph. I am poor in the essence of happiness, lady – rich only in never-ending unrest. In me there meet a combination of antithetical elements which are at eternal war with one another. Driven hither by objective influences – thither by subjective emotions – wafted one moment into blazing day, by mocking hope – plunged the next into the Cimmerian 470 darkness of tangible despair, I am but a living ganglion of irreconcilable antagonisms. I hope I make myself clear, lady?
Jos. Perfectly. (*Aside.*) His simple eloquence goes to my heart. Oh, if I dared – but no, the thought is madness! (*Aloud.*) Dismiss these foolish fancies, they torture you but needlessly. Come, make one effort. 475
Ralph (*aside*). I will – one. (*Aloud.*) Josephine!
Jos. (*indignantly*). Sir!
Ralph. Aye, even though Jove's armoury were launched at the head of the audacious mortal whose lips, unhallowed by relationship, dared to breathe that precious word, yet would I breathe it once, and then perchance 480 be silent evermore. Josephine, in one brief breath I will concentrate the hopes, the doubts, the anxious fears of six weary months. Josephine, I am a British sailor, and I love you!
Jos. Sir, this audacity! (*Aside.*) Oh, my heart, my beating heart! (*Aloud.*) This unwarrantable presumption on the part of a common sailor! (*Aside.*) 485 Common! oh, the irony of the word! (*Crossing, aloud.*) Oh, sir, you forget the disparity in our ranks.
Ralph. I forget nothing, haughty lady. I love you desperately, my life is in your hand – I lay it at your feet! Give me hope, and what I lack in education and polite accomplishments, that I will endeavour to acquire. 490 Drive me to despair, and in death alone I shall look for consolation. I am proud and cannot stoop to implore. I have spoken and I wait your word.
Jos. You shall not wait long. Your proffered love I haughtily reject. Go, sir, and learn to cast your eyes on some village maiden in your own poor rank – they should be lowered before your captain's daughter! 495

DUET – Josephine *and* Ralph.

Jos.   Refrain, audacious tar,
                          Your suit from pressing,
                      Remember what you are,
                          And whom addressing!
(*Aside.*)   I'd laugh my rank to scorn   500
                          In union holy,
                      Were he more highly born
                          Or I more lowly!
Ralph.   Proud lady, have your way,
                          Unfeeling beauty!   505

509 *That sails the water*: In early editions of the vocal score the word 'ploughs' occurs instead of 'sails', as it still does in Josephine's line in 'Never mind the why and wherefore'. The libretto, however, has always had 'sails' in this song.

532 *Rejects my humble gift, my lady*: Until 1908 the *Pinafore* libretto had the word 'love' where the vocal score had 'gift'. The latter is much more appropriate, as it rhymes with 'adrift' two lines down.

It is interesting that Ralph here addresses his remarks to Cousin Hebe, a figure who so far has not assumed any great importance in the opera. In fact, Gilbert originally conceived Hebe's to be a more substantial speaking part and wrote several dialogue exchanges between her and Sir Joseph, with whom she was supposed to be infatuated. However, the actress who was due to play Hebe, Mrs Howard Paul, left the company shortly before the first night of *Pinafore*. The untried girl brought in hastily to replace her, Jessie Bond (who was destined to become one of the first great stars of the D'Oyly Carte Opera Company), protested that she was a singer rather than an actress, and so Gilbert cut out most of the lines he had given to Hebe.

537 *I told you so*: After Dick's verse, the copy of *H.M.S. Pinafore* sent to the Lord Chamberlain for licensing purposes has the following exchange between the First Relative (a figure who appears only in the licence copy, where she has the singing lines later given to Hebe) and Ralph:

> FIRST RELATIVE.   Reject a British tar! The cream
> Of all the virtues highly rated.
>
> RALPH.   Impossible as it may seem,
> The fact's precisely as I've stated.

You speak and I obey,
　It is my duty!
I am the lowliest tar
　That sails the water,
And you, proud maiden, are　　　　　　　　510
　My captain's daughter!
(*Aside.*)　　My heart with anguish torn
　Bows down before her,
She laughs my love to scorn,
　Yet I adore her!　　　　　　　　　　　515

(*Repeat refrain, ensemble, then exit* JOSEPHINE *into cabin.*)

RALPH (*Recitative*).　Can I survive this overbearing
　Or live a life of mad despairing,
　My proffered love despised, rejected?
　No, no, it's not to be expected!　　　　520
　　　　(*Calling off.*)
　　Messmates, ahoy!
　　　Come here! Come here!

(*Enter* SAILORS, HEBE, RELATIVES, *and* BUTTERCUP.)

ALL.　　　　Aye, aye, my boy,　　　　　525
　　　　What cheer, what cheer?
　　　　　Now tell us, pray,
　　　　　Without delay,
　　　　　What does she say –
　　　　What cheer, what cheer?　　　　530

RALPH (*to* COUSIN HEBE).
　　　　The maiden treats my suit with scorn,
　　　　　Rejects my humble gift, my lady;
　　　　She says I am ignobly born,
　　　　　And cuts my hopes adrift, my lady.
ALL.　　　　　Oh, cruel one.　　　　　535
DICK.　　　She spurns your suit? Oho! Oho!
　　　　I told you so, I told you so.
SAILORS *and* RELATIVES.

Shall { we / they } submit? Are { we / they } but slaves?
　　Love comes alike to high and low –
　　Britannia's sailors rule the waves,　　　540
　　　And shall they stoop to insult? No! No!

558 *For Josephine I fall*: Threats to commit suicide occur in two of the Savoy Operas, and there is an actual suicide in another: the unfortunate John Wellington Wells takes his own life at the end of *The Sorcerer* as it is the only way of removing the magic spell which has wrought such havoc to the happily married folks of Ploverleigh.

Of those who threaten to take their own lives because of unrequited love, Ralph comes nearest to executing the deed. Nanki-Poo, discovered by Ko-Ko in the act of preparing a rope with which to hang himself in Act II of *The Mikado*, must be counted a pretty close runner-up. Ko-Ko's own threat to Katisha later in the same opera that he will kill himself unless she immediately consents to marry him must surely be taken rather less seriously.

561 *Ah! stay your hand! I love you*: Gilbert loves the dramatic device of the last-minute intervention by the leading lady just as the hero is resigning himself to utter despair. It occurs again in *The Pirates of Penzance* when Mabel rushes on to assure Frederic that there is one maiden who loves him.

DICK.	You must submit, you are but slaves;
	A lady she! Oho! Oho!
	You lowly toilers of the waves,
	She spurns you all – I told you so!
RALPH.	My friends, my leave of life I'm taking,
	For oh, my heart, my heart is breaking.
	When I am gone, oh, prithee tell
	The maid that, as I died, I loved her well!
ALL (*turning away, weeping*).	
	Of life, alas! his leave he's taking,
	For ah! his faithful heart is breaking;
	When he is gone we'll surely tell
	The maid that, as he died, he loved her well.

545

550

(*During Chorus* BOATSWAIN *has loaded pistol, which
he hands to* RALPH.)

555

RALPH.	Be warned, my messmates all
	Who love in rank above you –
	For Josephine I fall!

(*Puts pistol to his head. All the sailors stop their ears.*)

(*Enter* JOSEPHINE.)

560

JOS.	Ah! stay your hand! I love you!
ALL.	Ah! stay your hand – she loves you!
RALPH (*incredulously*). Loves me?	
JOS.	Loves you!
ALL.	Yes, yes – ah, yes, – she loves you!

565

ENSEMBLE.

JOSEPHINE, HEBE *and* RALPH.

Oh joy, oh rapture unforeseen,
For now the sky is all serene;
The god of day – the orb of love –
Has hung his ensign high above,
The sky is all ablaze.

570

With wooing words and loving song,
We'll chase the lagging hours along,

589–601 *This very night*

This complicated number with its numerous quick parts constitutes a modern producer's (and conductor's) nightmare. Gilbert, however, tackled it with meticulous planning and painstaking drilling of his cast, as he did every single song in the Savoy Operas. He planned all the staging and movements initially on a model set, with coloured wooden blocks representing each principal and member of the chorus. Once he had got his ideas straight he translated them to his prompt-book and to the company, who were taken through every movement and piece of business as though they were part of a military operation.

And if $\left\{\begin{array}{l} \text{I find} \\ \text{we find} \end{array}\right\}$ the maiden coy,

$\left.\begin{array}{l} \text{I'll} \\ \text{We'll} \end{array}\right\}$ murmur forth decorous joy

In dreamy roundelays!   575

DICK DEADEYE.

He thinks he's won his Josephine,
But though the sky is now serene,
A frowning thunderbolt above
May end their ill-assorted love
    Which now is all ablaze.   580

Our captain, ere the day is gone,
Will be extremely down upon
The wicked men who art employ
To make his Josephine less coy
    In many various ways.   585

JOSEPHINE, HEBE *and* RALPH.

Oh joy, oh rapture unforeseen, etc.

DICK. Our captain soon, unless I'm wrong,
Will be extremely down upon, etc.   (*Exit* DICK.)

JOS.	This very night,
HEBE.	With bated breath
RALPH.	And muffled oar –
JOS.	Without a light,
HEBE.	As still as death,
RALPH.	We'll steal ashore.
JOS.	A clergyman
RALPH.	Shall make us one
BOAT.	At half-past ten,
JOS.	And then we can
RALPH.	Return, for none
BOAT.	Can part them then!
ALL.	This very night, etc.

590
595
600

(DICK *enters.*)

DICK. Forbear, nor carry out the scheme you've planned;
She is a lady – you a foremast hand!
Remember, she's your gallant captain's daughter,   605
And you the meanest slave that crawls the water!

612–15 *Let's give three cheers for the sailor's bride*
This happy, foot-tapping tune starts off the overture to *H.M.S. Pinafore*, the broad themes of which were sketched out by Sullivan, with the details filled in probably by Alfred Cellier, a fellow composer who conducted the Savoy Operas for five years. The other numbers which feature in the overture are the section beginning 'I'd laugh my rank to scorn' from 'Refrain, audacious tar', 'Never mind the why and wherefore', and 'A British tar is a soaring soul', which, as here in Act I, provides a rousing finale.

  615 *For the honest love of a sailor true*: In the libretto sent to the Lord Chamberlain these lines, sung by the entire company, follow at this point and precede 'For a British tar':

> Though a lad in the fore
> He's the pride of the fleet;
> He can pull at an oar,
> He can tug at a sheet.
> When danger is near
> He's the pick of the crew –
> Then give him a cheer
> And his true love too.

ALL.   Back, vermin, back,
                            Nor mock us!
                        Back, vermin, back,
                            You shock us!   610

                                            (*Exit* DICK.)

        Let's give three cheers for the sailor's bride
        Who casts all thought of rank aside –
        Who gives up home and fortune too
        For the honest love of a sailor true!   615

            JOSEPHINE, HEBE *and* RELATIVES.

    For a British tar is a soaring soul
    As free as a mountain bird!
    His energetic fist should be ready to resist
    A dictatorial word!
    His eyes should flash with an inborn fire,   620
    His brow with scorn be wrung;
    He never should bow down to a domineering frown,
    Or the tang of a tyrant tongue.

                        SAILORS.

    His nose should pant and his lips should curl,
    His cheeks should flame and his brow should furl,   625
    His bosom should heave and his heart should glow,
    And his fist be ever ready for a knock-down blow.

                        ENSEMBLE.

    His foot should stamp and his throat should growl,
    His hair should twirl and his face should scowl,
    His eyes should flash and his breast protrude,   630
    And this should be his customary attitude – (*pose*).

                    GENERAL DANCE.

                    END OF ACT I

1 *Captain discovered singing*: For Act II of *Pinafore* Captain Corcoran is traditionally kitted out in full naval mess dress, i.e. tails, black tie, white waistcoat and gold striped trousers. Some versions of the libretto have him accompanying himself on the guitar, others, as here, on the mandolin.

There is a celebrated D'Oyly Carte Company story attached to this scene. At an early rehearsal of the first ever production of *Pinafore*, Gilbert told Rutland Barrington, the company's principal bass baritone, who was playing the part of Corcoran, to 'walk slowly toward the left stage, then sit on the skylight pensively.' When Barrington, who weighed over thirteen stone, followed the latter part of the direction, both the skylight and the surrounding woodwork collapsed under him. 'No,' said Gilbert, 'that's expensively.'

4–19 *Fair moon, to thee I sing*
This song has echoes of the Bab Ballad 'Joe Golightly'. Joe, it may be recalled, was infatuated with the First Lord of the Admiralty's daughter, and was constantly singing ballads to the moon to the accompaniment of his light guitar. This so annoyed his captain that he was given the terrible punishment of twelve years' solitary confinement with 500,000 lashes twice a day.

The day after the first night of *H.M.S. Pinafore*, after reading the reviews together, Gilbert and Sullivan decided to cut 'Fair moon'. They presumably felt that it gave a slow start to Act II and held up the action. Rutland Barrington himself was none too happy with the song and would have preferred a topical patter song. Despite all these reservations, however, 'Fair moon' was retained.

ACT II

Same Scene. Night. Awning removed. Moonlight. CAPTAIN *discovered singing on poop-deck, and accompanying himself on a mandolin.* LITTLE BUTTERCUP *seated on quarter-deck, gazing sentimentally at him.*

SONG – CAPTAIN.

Fair moon, to thee I sing,
   Bright regent of the heavens,   5
Say, why is everything
   Either at sixes or at sevens?
I have lived hitherto
   Free from the breath of slander,
Beloved by all my crew –   10
   A really popular commander.
But now my kindly crew rebel,
   My daughter to a tar is partial,
Sir Joseph storms, and, sad to tell,
   He threatens a court martial!   15
    Fair moon, to thee I sing,
       Bright regent of the heavens,
    Say, why is everything
       Either at sixes or at sevens?

BUT. How sweetly he carols forth his melody to the unconscious moon! 20
Of whom is he thinking? Of some high-born beauty? It may be! Who is poor
Little Buttercup that she should expect his glance to fall on one so lowly! And
yet if he knew – if he only knew!

CAPT. (*coming down*). Ah! Little Buttercup, still on board? That is not
quite right, little one. It would have been more respectable to have gone on 25
shore at dusk.

BUT. True, dear Captain – but the recollection of your sad pale face
seemed to chain me to the ship. I would fain see you smile before I go.

35 *such a one as this*: Printed as 'such an one as this' in some editions of the libretto, this phrase recurs in *The Pirates of Penzance* in Frederic's song 'Oh, is there not one maiden breast', with its lines 'To rescue such an one as I' and 'To such an one, if such there be'.

40 *The poor bumboat woman*: Bumboats were vessels used for conveying provisions to ships lying off ports.

46–94 *Things are seldom what they seem*
  This is one of two songs in the Savoy Operas (the other being the 'If you go in' trio in *Iolanthe*) which are made up almost entirely of adaptations of traditional proverbs and sayings. I have tried to unravel the originals and explain their meanings in the following notes.
48 *Highlows*: Laced ankle boots of the kind typically worn by Victorian women and very different from patent leather shoes.
49 *Jackdaws strut in peacock's feathers*: This is taken from Aesop's fable about the jackdaw which decked itself out in peacock's feathers to impress other birds and in fact only became a general laughing-stock.
52 *Black sheep dwell in every fold*: A familiar English saying, meaning that there are bad individuals in every group, which is first found, according to the *Oxford Dictionary of English Proverbs*, in Sir Walter Scott's *Old Mortality* (1816).
53 *All that glitters is not gold*: Adapted from the line 'All that glisters is not gold' in Shakespeare's *The Merchant of Venice*, Act II, Scene 7.
54 *Storks turn out to be but logs*: This is taken from another of Aesop's fables, 'King Log and King Stork', which tells of a group of frogs who appealed to Jupiter for a king, and, being dissatisfied with the log given to them, found him replaced by a stork. The normal saying is 'Neither a log nor a stork'.
55 *Bulls are but inflated frogs*: In Aesop's fable 'The Frog and the Ox', the mother frog wanted to impress her children by making herself as big as an ox which was grazing nearby. She puffed herself up and burst.
58 *Drops the wind and stops the mill*: The nearest proverb I can find to this is 'No weather ill, if wind be still'.
59 *Turbot is ambitious brill*: Both turbot and brill are large flat fish, often weighing up to forty pounds, but whereas the former is regarded as a considerable delicacy, the latter is not.
60 *Gild the farthing if you will*: I can find no original for this phrase, but its meaning is clear enough. Until its withdrawal from circulation in 1961, the farthing, worth a quarter of a penny, was the coin of lowest value in Britain.

CAPT. Ah! Little Buttercup, I fear it will be long before I recover my
accustomed cheerfulness, for misfortunes crowd upon me, and all my old   30
friends seem to have turned against me!

BUT. Oh no – do not say 'all', dear Captain. That were unjust to one, at
least.

CAPT. True, for you are staunch to me. (*Aside.*) If ever I gave my heart
again, methinks it would be to such a one as this! (*Aloud.*) I am touched to   35
the heart by your innocent regard for me, and were we differently situated,
I think I could have returned it. But as it is, I fear I can never be more to you
than a friend.

BUT. I understand! You hold aloof from me because you are rich and
lofty – and I poor and lowly. But take care! The poor bumboat woman has   40
gipsy blood in her veins, and she can read destinies.

CAPT. Destinies?

BUT. There is a change in store for you!

CAPT. A change?

BUT. Aye – be prepared!   45

DUET – LITTLE BUTTERCUP *and* CAPTAIN.

BUT.   Things are seldom what they seem,
                Skim milk masquerades as cream;
                Highlows pass as patent leathers;
                Jackdaws strut in peacock's feathers.

CAPT. (*puzzled*).   Very true,   50
                So they do.

BUT.   Black sheep dwell in every fold;
                All that glitters is not gold;
                Storks turn out to be but logs;
                Bulls are but inflated frogs.   55

CAPT. (*puzzled*).   So they be,
                Frequentlee.

BUT.   Drops the wind and stops the mill;
                Turbot is ambitious brill;
                Gild the farthing if you will,   60
                Yet it is a farthing still.

CAPT. (*puzzled*).   Yes, I know,
                That is so.
                Though to catch your drift I'm striving,
                It is shady – it is shady;   65
                I don't see at what you're driving,
                Mystic lady – mystic lady.

BOTH.   Stern conviction's o'er $\left\{ \begin{array}{c} me \\ him \end{array} \right\}$ stealing,

75 *Once a cat was killed by care*: The saying 'Care killed the cat', which dates at least from the sixteenth century, means that you can worry yourself to death.

76 *Only brave deserve the fair*: The phrase 'None but the brave deserve the fair' occurs in John Dryden's ode for St Cecilia's Day, *Alexander's Feast* (1697). It is also used, in that latter form, in the 'If you go in' trio in *Iolanthe*.

79 *Wink is often good as nod*: The traditional saying is the other way round: 'A nod is as good as a wink' (first recorded use in Dorothy Wordsworth's journal in 1802).

80 *Spoils the child who spares the rod*: The phrase 'Spare the rod and spoil the child' derives from a biblical saying (Proverbs 23.13).

81 *Thirsty lambs run foxy dangers*: This comes from another of Aesop's fables, which tells how a lamb was devoured by a wolf while it was off-guard drinking from a stream.

82 *Dogs are found in many mangers*: A 'dog in a manger' is a mean-spirited individual who will not allow another to use something even though he does not want it himself. The phrase derives from yet another of Aesop's fables, in this case about a dog that fixed his place in a manger and would not allow an ox to come near the hay, even though he did not want it himself.

85 *Paw of cat the chestnut snatches*: The expression 'Take the chestnuts out of the fire with the cat's paw' means to use somebody else to do your dirty work. It is said to derive from a monkey belonging to Pope Julius II (1443–1513) which made a cat pull its chestnuts out of the fire.

86 *Worn-out garments show new patches*: A paraphrase of another biblical quotation, 'No man seweth a piece of cloth into an old garment' (Mark 2.21).

87 *Only count the chick that hatches*: 'Don't count your chickens before they are hatched' is a favourite English saying which is first recorded back in 1575.

88 *Men are grown-up catchy-catchies*: I cannot offer an entirely satisfactory explanation for this phrase. The most likely one seems to be that 'catchy-catchy' was either a term of endearment given to babies when throwing them up in the air and catching them, or a phrase used in children's games like 'he' and 'touch'.

103 *Time alone can tell*: For the 1908 revival of *H.M.S. Pinafore* at the Savoy Theatre, Gilbert agreed to an additional few lines for Captain Corcoran at this point. The lines, which had been introduced by Rutland Barrington into his performance, went: 'Ah! Here comes the First Lord of the Admiralty. I will talk with him on the subject! Happily we are still on speaking terms.' They were cut in 1914.

	That the mystic lady's dealing	
	In oracular revealing.	70
Capt.	Yes, I know –	
But.	That is so!	
Capt.	Though I'm anything but clever,	
	I could talk like that for ever:	
	Once a cat was killed by care;	75
	Only brave deserve the fair.	
But.	Very true,	
	So they do.	
Capt.	Wink is often good as nod;	
	Spoils the child who spares the rod;	80
	Thirsty lambs run foxy dangers;	
	Dogs are found in many mangers.	
But.	Frequentlee,	
	I agree.	
Capt.	Paw of cat the chestnut snatches;	85
	Worn-out garments show new patches;	
	Only count the chick that hatches;	
	Men are grown-up catchy-catchies.	
But.	Yes, I know,	
	That is so.	90
(*Aside.*)	Though to catch my drift he's striving,	
	I'll dissemble – I'll dissemble;	
	When he sees at what I'm driving,	
	Let him tremble – let him tremble!	

ENSEMBLE.

Though a mystic tone $\left\{ \begin{array}{c} I \\ you \end{array} \right\}$ borrow, 95

$\left. \begin{array}{l} \text{You will} \\ \text{I shall} \end{array} \right\}$ learn the truth with sorrow,

Here to-day and gone to-morrow;

Yes, I know –

That is so!

    (*At the end exit* Little Buttercup *melodramatically.*) 100

Capt. Incomprehensible as her utterances are, I nevertheless feel that they are dictated by a sincere regard for me. But to what new misery is she referring? Time alone can tell!

105–6 *Captain Corcoran, I am much disappointed with your daughter*: In the licence copy of the libretto sent to the Lord Chamberlain, when it was still planned that Cousin Hebe's would be a bigger speaking part, she accompanies Sir Joseph in this entrance and repeats most of his remarks to the Captain, greatly to the First Lord's annoyance. This version was, of course, never performed.

127–44 *The hours creep on apace*
In this long passage of dramatic and heavily orchestrated recitative, Sullivan consciously imitates the florid style and exaggerated intensity of Italian opera.

136 *Rare 'blue and white'*: Blue-and-white oriental ceramics were much in vogue in the late 1870s and early 1880s, particularly among followers of the aesthetic movement. In *Patience*, Reginald Bunthorne, the fleshly poet, proclaims himself 'Such a judge of blue-and-white and other kinds of pottery' in Act I and 'A blue-and-white young man' in Act II.

138 *Gillow's*: A famous firm of house furnishers in London's Oxford Street which later amalgamated to become Waring and Gillow, now situated in the Brompton Road.

(*Enter* SIR JOSEPH.)

SIR JOSEPH. Captain Corcoran, I am much disappointed with your   105
daughter. In fact, I don't think she will do.
CAPT. She won't do, Sir Joseph!
SIR JOSEPH. I'm afraid not. The fact is, that although I have urged my
suit with as much eloquence as is consistent with an official utterance, I have
done so hitherto without success. How do you account for this?   110
CAPT. Really, Sir Joseph, I hardly know. Josephine is of course sensible
of your condescension.
SIR JOSEPH. She naturally would be.
CAPT. But perhaps your exalted rank dazzles her.
SIR JOSEPH. You think it does?   115
CAPT. I can hardly say; but she is a modest girl, and her social position
is far below your own. It may be that she feels she is not worthy of you.
SIR JOSEPH. That is really a very sensible suggestion, and displays
more knowledge of human nature than I had given you credit for.
CAPT. See, she comes. If your lordship would kindly reason with her   120
and assure her officially that it is a standing rule at the Admiralty that love
levels all ranks, her respect for an official utterance might induce her to look
upon your offer in its proper light.
SIR JOSEPH. It is not unlikely. I will adopt your suggestion. But soft,
she is here. Let us withdraw, and watch our opportunity.   125

(*Enter* JOSEPHINE *from cabin.* SIR JOSEPH *and* CAPTAIN *retire.*)

SCENA – JOSEPHINE.

The hours creep on apace,
    My guilty heart is quaking!
Oh, that I might retrace
    The step that I am taking!   130
    Its folly it were easy to be showing,
    What I am giving up and whither going.
On the one hand, papa's luxurious home,
    Hung with ancestral armour and old brasses,
Carved oak and tapestry from distant Rome,   135
    Rare 'blue and white', Venetian finger-glasses,
Rich oriental rugs, luxurious sofa pillows,
And everything that isn't old, from Gillow's.
And on the other, a dark and dingy room,
    In some back street with stuffy children crying,   140
Where organs yell, and clacking housewives fume,
    And clothes are hanging out all day a-drying.

145 *A simple sailor, lowly born*: The licence copy of *Pinafore* sent to the Lord Chamberlain omits lines 145 to 156 (from 'A simple sailor' to 'solemn duty') and has instead the following extension of Josephine's recitative:

> And then his relations,
> Their mean and sordid lives,
> Their vulgar explanations and their oaths,
> His father's a mechanic, I dare say,
> His soapy mother washing all the day,
> I do not mean herself, but dirty clothes.
> His sisters, what a theme for lover's sonnets!
> I think I see them in their Sunday bonnets,
> Oh dear, those bonnets,
> Oh dear, *dear*, dear, those bonnets.
> Oh no, no, no,
> I could not stand those bonnets.
> And yet he is so fair – so gentle, too,
> So young – so tender-hearted and so true,
> And so judicious in his observation,
> And then
> 'Tis he whom I would wed – not his relations!
> Yes, yes,
> 'Tis he, 'tis he – not his relations.

164 *your lordship*: Josephine's mode of addressing Sir Joseph is, in fact, wrong. 'Your lordship' would only be correct if he were a peer of the realm; the fact of being First Lord of the Admiralty is not sufficient to justify the title. Captain Corcoran makes the same mistake in line 120, and all three repeat it in the trio 'Never mind the why and wherefore'. Perhaps Gilbert deliberately caused the Captain and his daughter, arch-snobs that they are, to commit precisely the kind of social solecism that they would have found unpardonable in others. More likely, however, he needed something to rhyme with 'on board-ship'.

173–228 *Never mind the why and wherefore*
Always the most encored song in *Pinafore*, and one of the most popular in all the Savoy Operas, 'Never mind the why and wherefore' was described in the *Standard* review of the first night as 'a movement in E so vivacious and tuneful that even the First Lord has to retire at intervals behind the wardroom skylight and relieve his feelings by a dance, in which his dignified playfulness is delightful to behold'.

177 *Though your tastes are mean and flighty*: One of several instances where the words in the vocal score are different from those in the libretto. The former has 'her tastes' and in line 178 'her fortune', the latter, as here, 'your tastes' and 'your fortune'.

With one cracked looking-glass to see your face in,
And dinner served up in a pudding basin!

    A simple sailor, lowly born,   145
       Unlettered and unknown,
    Who toils for bread from early morn
       Till half the night has flown!
    No golden rank can he impart –
       No wealth of house or land –   150
    No fortune save his trusty heart
       And honest brown right hand!
    And yet he is so wondrous fair
    That love for one so passing rare,
    So peerless in his manly beauty,   155
    Were little else than solemn duty!
Oh, god of love, and god of reason, say,
Which of you twain shall my poor heart obey!

        (SIR JOSEPH *and* CAPTAIN *enter.*)

SIR JOSEPH. Madam, it has been represented to me that you are 160
appalled by my exalted rank. I desire to convey to you officially my
assurance, that if your hesitation is attributable to that circumstance, it is
uncalled for.

JOS. Oh! then your lordship is of opinion that married happiness is *not*
inconsistent with discrepancy in rank?   165

SIR JOSEPH. I am officially of that opinion.

JOS. That the high and the lowly may be truly happy together, provided
that they truly love one another?

SIR JOSEPH. Madam, I desire to convey to you officially my opinion
that love is a platform upon which all ranks meet.   170

JOS. I thank you, Sir Joseph. I *did* hesitate, but I will hesitate no longer.
(*Aside.*) He little thinks how eloquently he has pleaded his rival's cause!

          TRIO.

    SIR JOSEPH, CAPTAIN, *and* JOSEPHINE.

CAPT.   Never mind the why and wherefore,
               Love can level ranks, and therefore,
               Though his lordship's station's mighty,   175
                  Though stupendous be his brain,
               Though your tastes are mean and flighty
                  And your fortune poor and plain,
CAPT. *and*   Ring the merry bells on board-ship,
SIR JOSEPH.   Rend the air with warbling wild,   180

196 *In the lower middle class*: It hardly behoves Sir Joseph Porter, who started life as an office boy polishing the handle of the big front door, to speak so disdainfully of the lower middle class. But, of course, he has risen so far and he is such a snob, for all his egalitarian pronouncements, that he feels he can. The chorus of peers in *Iolanthe* have even more contempt for this particular segment of society, whom they bracket with tradesmen and the masses in the general command to bow down before them.

206 *Rend with songs the air above*: In early editions of the libretto this line was printed as 'Fill with songs the air above'. This was almost certainly a misprint.

215 *Ring the merry bells on board-ship*: This line has traditionally been the cue for some typical D'Oyly Carte business, particularly in encores. Among the imaginary bells that the First Lord has pretended to play have been a front-door bell, carillon, hurdy-gurdy, triangle, hand bells, telephone and a church bell, the 'rope' of which he inevitably loses control of so that he is carried up into the air.

There are other standard bits of business which D'Oyly Carte First Lords have practised during encores of this song. John Reed, who joined the company in 1951, took over the principal comic roles in 1959 and retired, to everyone's great sadness, in 1979, leaned on the ship's wheel and sent it spinning round, signalled in semaphore for help and finally jumped overboard.

For the union of $\left\{ \begin{array}{c} \text{his} \\ \text{my} \end{array} \right\}$ lordship

    With a humble captain's child!

CAPT.   For a humble captain's daughter –

JOS.   For a gallant captain's daughter –

SIR JOSEPH.   And a lord who rules the water –   185

JOS. (*aside*).   And a *tar* who ploughs the water!

ALL.   Let the air with joy be laden,

    Rend with songs the air above,

For the union of a maiden

    With the man who owns her love!   190

SIR JOSEPH.   Never mind the why and wherefore,

    Love can level ranks, and therefore,

Though your nautical relation (*alluding to* CAPT.)

    In my set could scarcely pass –

Though you occupy a station   195

    In the lower middle class –

CAPT. *and*   Ring the merry bells on board-ship,

SIR JOSEPH.   Rend the air with warbling wild,

For the union of $\left\{ \begin{array}{c} \text{my} \\ \text{his} \end{array} \right\}$ lordship

    With a humble captain's child!   200

CAPT.   For a humble captain's daughter –

JOS.   For a gallant captain's daughter –

SIR JOSEPH.   And a lord who rules the water –

JOS. (*aside*).   And a *tar* who ploughs the water!

ALL.   Let the air with joy be laden,   205

    Rend with songs the air above,

For the union of a maiden

    With the man who owns her love!

JOS.   Never mind the why and wherefore,

    Love can level ranks, and therefore   210

I admit the jurisdiction;

    Ably have you played your part;

You have carried firm conviction

    To my hesitating heart.

CAPT. *and*   Ring the merry bells on board-ship,   215

SIR JOSEPH.   Rend the air with warbling wild,

For the union of $\left\{ \begin{array}{c} \text{my} \\ \text{his} \end{array} \right\}$ lordship

    With a humble captain's child!

CAPT.   For a humble captain's daughter –

JOS.   For a gallant captain's daughter –   220

SIR JOSEPH.   And a lord who rules the water –

233 *this glorious country*: Originally the phrase was 'this happy country of ours'. It was altered to its present version, with Gilbert's authorization, for the 1908 revival of *Pinafore* at the Savoy Theatre.

236 *Elysian*: The Elysian fields were the abode of the blessed in Greek mythology.

247 *the kind commander that you are*: In the original vocal score this is 'the gallant captain that you are'.

252 *the mystic sailor that you are*: The original vocal score has this as 'the silly sailor that you are'.

257 *the simple captain that you are*: Once again, the original vocal score has 'the gallant captain that you are'.

Jos. (*aside*).   And a *tar* who ploughs the water!
(*Aloud.*)   Let the air with joy be laden.
CAPT. *and* SIR JOSEPH.   Ring the merry bells on board-ship –
Jos.   For the union of a maiden –   225
CAPT. *and* SIR JOSEPH.   For her union with his lordship.
ALL.   Rend with songs the air above
                       For the man who owns her love!

                                (*Exit* JOSEPHINE.)

     CAPT. Sir Joseph, I cannot express to you my delight at the happy   230
result of your eloquence. Your argument was unanswerable.

     SIR JOSEPH. Captain Corcoran, it is one of the happiest characteristics
of this glorious country that official utterances are invariably regarded as
unanswerable.   (*Exit* SIR JOSEPH.)

     CAPT. At last my fond hopes are to be crowned. My only daughter is to   235
be the bride of a Cabinet Minister. The prospect is Elysian. (*During this speech*
DICK DEADEYE *has entered.*)

     DICK. Captain.

     CAPT. Deadeye! You here? Don't! (*Recoiling from him.*)

     DICK. Ah, don't shrink from me, Captain. I'm unpleasant to look at,   240
and my name's agin me, but I ain't as bad as I seem.

     CAPT. What would you with me?

     DICK (*mysteriously*). I'm come to give you warning.

     CAPT. Indeed! do you propose to leave the Navy then?

     DICK. No, no, you misunderstand me; listen!   245

DUET.

CAPTAIN *and* DICK DEADEYE.

DICK.   Kind Captain, I've important information,
             Sing hey, the kind commander that you are,
         About a certain intimate relation,
             Sing hey, the merry maiden and the tar.
BOTH.   The merry maiden and the tar.   250

CAPT.   Good fellow, in conundrums you are speaking,
             Sing hey, the mystic sailor that you are;
         The answer to them vainly I am seeking;
             Sing hey, the merry maiden and the tar.
BOTH.   The merry maiden and the tar.   255

DICK.   Kind Captain, your young lady is a-sighing,
             Sing hey, the simple captain that you are,
         This very night with Rackstraw to be flying;
             Sing hey, the merry maiden and the tar.

260 *The merry maiden and the tar*: In this particular refrain the Captain sings 'The much too merry maiden', while Deadeye sings the usual 'The merry, merry maiden'.

264 *the cat-o'-nine-tails*: A whip with nine lashes, used in both the Army and the Navy for punishing offenders. Its use in the Army was formally abolished in 1881. In the Navy an Act of 1866 limited any punishment to a maximum of forty-eight lashes. Use of the cat, which was traditionally administered by the boatswain's mate, was subsequently suspended, first in peace-time and then in wartime, but it has never formally been abolished in the senior service. The difficulty of wielding the cat-o'-nine-tails in the cramped confines of a ship gave rise to the expression 'There's not even room to swing a cat.'

286 *Hymen*: The Greek god of marriage, who crops up again in the version of *The Pirates of Penzance* sung at the first night in New York, and printed in the licence copy sent to the Lord Chamberlain, when in the finale of Act II Mabel sings:

> Tomorrow morning early we will quickly be parsonified –
> Hymeneally coupled, conjugally matrimonified.

Hymen also gets a mention in Gilbert and Sullivan's first collaboration, *Thespis*, when Mercury laments in a song about the muddled state of the gods: 'But alas that determined young bachelor Hymen refuses to wed anybody at all'.

BOTH.   The merry maiden and the tar.   260

CAPT.   Good fellow, you have given timely warning,
               Sing hey, the thoughtful sailor that you are,
               I'll talk to Master Rackstraw in the morning:
               Sing hey, the cat-o'-nine-tails and the tar.
                                          (*Producing a 'cat'.*)   265
BOTH.   The merry cat-o'-nine-tails and the tar!

CAPT. Dick Deadeye – I thank you for your timely warning – I will at
once take means to arrest their flight. This boat cloak will afford me ample
disguise – So! (*Envelops himself in a mysterious cloak, holding it before his face.*)
DICK. Ha, ha! They are foiled – foiled – foiled!   270

(*Enter Crew on tiptoe, with* RALPH *and* BOATSWAIN *meeting* JOSEPHINE,
*who enters from cabin on tiptoe, with bundle of necessaries, and accompanied
by* LITTLE BUTTERCUP.)

ENSEMBLE.

               Carefully on tiptoe stealing,
                    Breathing gently as we may,   275
               Every step with caution feeling,
                    We will softly steal away.
                    (CAPTAIN *stamps. – Chord.*)
ALL (*much alarmed*).   Goodness me –
                                 Why, what was that?   280
DICK.   Silent be,
                                 It was the cat!
ALL (*reassured*).   It was – it was the cat!
CAPT. (*producing cat-o'-nine-tails*).   They're right, it was the cat!
ALL.   Pull ashore, in fashion steady,   285
                              Hymen will defray the fare,
                         For a clergyman is ready
                              To unite the happy pair!
                              (*Stamp as before, and Chord.*)
ALL.   Goodness me,   290
                              Why, what was that?
DICK.   Silent be,
                              Again the cat!
ALL.   It was again that cat!
CAPT. (*aside*).   They're right, it was the cat!   295
CAPT. (*throwing off cloak*).   Hold! (*All start.*)

315 *the port division*: The crews of men-o'-war were traditionally divided into port and starboard watches, one of which was always on duty while the other rested. The practice is still continued on submarines. Ralph here proclaims himself one of the most junior members of the port watch.

316 *epauletted scorn*: A splendidly Gilbertian term for naval snobbery. Epaulettes, heavy and ornate shoulder badges fringed with cord, were worn by both Navy and Army officers until 1855, when the Army gave them up, leaving this particular piece of decorative adornment to the senior service.

323–35 *He is an Englishman*

The second great patriotic number in *H.M.S. Pinafore*, 'He is an Englishman' belongs to a clutch of fervently nationalistic songs in the Savoy Operas which also includes 'A British tar is a soaring soul', 'When Britain really ruled the waves' from *Iolanthe*, 'The Darned Mounseer' from *Ruddigore*, and the stirring finale from *Utopia Limited*, 'There's a little group of isles beyond the wave'. Apart from 'The Darned Mounseer', which offended several Frenchmen with its anti-Gallic sentiments, 'He is an Englishman' is the only one to contain somewhat disparaging references to other countries. In that respect it has distinct similarities with Michael Flanders and Donald Swann's famous 'Song of Patriotic Prejudice' from *At the Drop of a Hat*, 'The English, the English, the English are best'.

A correspondent to *The Times* in 1955 suggested that 'He is an Englishman' was based on a patriotic song popular in the 1870s which ran:

> 'Tis a glorious charter – deny it who can –
> That lives in the words 'I'm an Englishman'.

However, I doubt whether Gilbert needed any such direct inspiration in the generally patriotic atmosphere which prevailed in Britain during the period in which *Pinafore* was written.

When Gilbert and Sullivan went to the United States in the winter of 1879 to present the authorized version of *H.M.S. Pinafore*, one impresario suggested that they should americanize the opera, changing its name to *U.S.S. Pinafore*, hoisting the Stars and Stripes instead of the White Ensign, and anchoring the ship off Jersey Beach. Gilbert, who was appalled by the idea, humoured the man (and himself) by suggesting a new version of the boatswain's song:

> He is American!
> Though he himself has said it,
> 'Tis not much to his credit,
> That he is American.
> For he might have been a Dutchman,
> An Irish, Scotch or such man,
> Or perhaps an Englishman!
> But in spite of hanky-panky,
> He remains a true-born Yankee,
> A cute American.

Needless to say, that version was never performed.

Pretty daughter of mine,
  I insist upon knowing
  Where you may be going
With these sons of the brine,   300
  For my excellent crew,
Though foes they could thump any,
Are scarcely fit company,
  My daughter, for you.

CREW.   Now, hark at that, do!   305
Though foes we could thump any,
We are scarcely fit company
  For a lady like you!

RALPH.   Proud officer, that haughty lip uncurl!
  Vain man, suppress that supercilious sneer,   310
For I have dared to love your matchless girl,
  A fact well known to all my messmates here!

CAPT.   Oh, horror!

RALPH *and* JOS. $\left\{\begin{array}{l} \text{I,} \\ \text{He,} \end{array}\right\}$ humble, poor, and lowly born,

  The meanest in the port division –   315
    The butt of epauletted scorn –
    The mark of quarter-deck derision –

$\left.\begin{array}{l} \text{Have} \\ \text{Has} \end{array}\right\}$ dared to raise $\left\{\begin{array}{l} \text{my} \\ \text{his} \end{array}\right\}$ wormy eyes

Above the dust to which you'd mould $\left\{\begin{array}{l} \text{me} \\ \text{him} \end{array}\right.$

  In manhood's glorious pride to rise,   320

$\left.\begin{array}{l} \text{I am} \\ \text{He is} \end{array}\right\}$ an Englishman – behold $\left\{\begin{array}{l} \text{me!} \\ \text{him!} \end{array}\right.$

ALL.   He is an Englishman!

BOAT.   He is an Englishman!
  For he himself has said it,
  And it's greatly to his credit,   325
That he is an Englishman!

ALL.   That he is an Englishman!

BOAT.   For he might have been a Roosian,
A French, or Turk, or Proosian,
Or perhaps Itali-an!   330

ALL.   Or perhaps Itali-an!

BOAT.   But in spite of all temptations
To belong to other nations,
  He remains an Englishman!

ALL.   For in spite of all temptations, etc.   335

343 *damme*: This is the only swear word to occur in full in the text of the Savoy Operas. Major-General Stanley's 'But *damme*, you don't go' said in exasperation to the policemen in Act II of *The Pirates*, although found in nearly every production, is not actually printed in the libretto. In *Utopia Limited*, King Paramount is twice given the aside 'Da—!' but the word is never finished.

The utterance of 'damme' by the young actor playing Captain Corcoran in the special series of matinées of *Pinafore* which Richard D'Oyly Carte put on at the Opéra Comique in the winter of 1879–80, with a cast composed entirely of children, caused great distress to Lewis Carroll, the author of *Alice in Wonderland*. Carroll, who had some years earlier written to Sullivan suggesting that he might compose the music for a dramatic version of *Alice*, commented after seeing the children's version of *Pinafore*:

> One passage was to me sad beyond words. It occurs when the captain utters the oath 'Damn me!' I cannot find words to convey to the reader the pain I felt in seeing dear children taught to utter such words to amuse ears grown callous to their ghastly meaning. Put the two ideas side by side: Hell (no matter whether you believe in it or not; millions do), and those pure young lips thus sporting with its horrors – and then find what fun in it you can! How Mr Gilbert could have stooped to write, and Sir Arthur Sullivan could have prostituted his noble art to set to music, such vile trash, it passes my skill to understand.

357 *My amazement – my surprise*: George Grossmith, playing the part of Sir Joseph in the opening run of *Pinafore*, found himself moved to utter these words towards the end of a performance on the evening of 31 July 1879 when the stage of the Opéra Comique was suddenly invaded by a gang of roughs. They had been hired by three former co-directors of the Comedy Opera Company who, having been bought out by Richard D'Oyly Carte, and seeing the great popularity of *Pinafore*, decided to claim the scenery and costumes as theirs and to mount a rival production of the opera in a nearby theatre.

The invaders raised the cry of 'Fire!' to divert the audience's attention while they tried to grab what they could off the stage. However, led by Buttercup, the crew of the *Pinafore* successfully repelled the boarders and they were forced off the stage at bayonet point by the marines who were about to escort Ralph off to his dungeon cell. Carte's former co-directors were later made to pay damages in court, and in August 1879 he rechristened his own company Mr D'Oyly Carte's Opera Company, so that there could be no possible confusion about its identity or its boss.

368 *To your cabin with celerity*: In his *Treasury of Gilbert and Sullivan*, Martyn Green, principal comic singer with the D'Oyly Carte Opera Company from 1934 to 1939 and from 1946 to 1951, says that a traditional joke in the company when *Pinafore* was being performed was 'Who's playing Celerity tonight?'

375 *To refrain from language strong*: Sir Joseph Porter's strong reaction to Captain Corcoran's bad language may well have been intended as a further dig at the puritanical W. H. Smith.

CAPT. (*trying to repress his anger*).
>> In uttering a reprobation
>> To any British tar,
>> I try to speak with moderation,
>> But you have gone too far.
>> I'm very sorry to disparage   340
>> A humble foremast lad,
>> But to seek your captain's child in marriage,
>> Why, damme, it's too bad!

    (*During this,* COUSIN HEBE *and* FEMALE RELATIVES *have entered.*)

ALL (*shocked*).   Oh!   345
CAPT.   Yes, damme, it's too bad!
ALL.   Oh!
CAPT. *and* DICK DEADEYE.   Yes, damme, it's too bad.

    (*During this,* SIR JOSEPH *has appeared on poop-deck. He is*
>> *horrified at the bad language.*)   350

HEBE.   Did you hear him – did you hear him?
>> Oh, the monster overbearing!
>> Don't go near him – don't go near him –
>> He is swearing – he is swearing!
SIR JOSEPH.   My pain and my distress,   355
>> I find it is not easy to express;
>> My amazement – my surprise –
>> You may learn from the expression of my eyes!
CAPT.   My lord – one word – the facts are not before you;
>> The word was injudicious, I allow –   360
>> But hear my explanation, I implore you,
>> And you will be indignant too, I vow!
SIR JOSEPH.   I will hear of no defence,
>> Attempt none if you're sensible.
>> That word of evil sense   365
>> Is wholly indefensible.
>> Go, ribald, get you hence
>> To your cabin with celerity.
>> This is the consequence
>> Of ill-advised asperity!   370
>> (*Exit* CAPTAIN, *disgraced, followed by* JOSEPHINE.)
ALL.   This is the consequence
>> Of ill-advised asperity!
SIR JOSEPH.   For I'll teach you all, ere long,
>> To refrain from language strong,   375

388 *the fo'c'sle*: The forecastle, or forward part of the ship, was so called because it was raised and protected like a castle so that it could command the enemy's deck during an engagement. Decked over, the fo'c'sle normally housed the ship's bell, galley chimney and ladder to the bowsprit. It was customary for the crew's quarters to be in the fo'c'sle and those of the officers aft on the quarter-deck: hence the significance of Ralph's remarks.

392 *Darling*: This line was added for the revival of *Pinafore* in 1908. Gilbert sanctioned it, no doubt reflecting that the Edwardian audience could take what might have seemed a little too strong for the sensibilities of the Victorians. Traditionally, Sir Joseph faints into the ever-ready arms of Cousin Hebe on hearing the girl whom he had presumed was soon to become his thus addressing a common sailor.

400 *Pray, don't*: This phrase was substituted for the original 'Away with him' in the 1908 revival. Dick Deadeye's line 'They have!' was also added at the same time.

405–26 *Farewell, my own*
This is the only octet in the Savoy Operas. There is one sestet ('I hear the soft note of the echoing voice' in *Patience*) and another song ('When Britain sounds the trump of war' from *Utopia Limited*) where there are six solo singers, but for the most part individual songs are for five or fewer voices.

For I haven't any sympathy for ill-bred taunts!
HEBE. No more have his sisters, nor his cousins, nor his aunts.
ALL. For he is an Englishman, etc.

(*Enter* JOSEPHINE.)

SIR JOSEPH. Now, tell me, my fine fellow – for you *are* a fine fellow — 380
RALPH. Yes, your honour.
SIR JOSEPH. How came your captain so far to forget himself? I am
quite sure you had given him no cause for annoyance.
RALPH. Please your honour, it was thus-wise. You see I'm only a
topman – a mere foremast hand — 385
SIR JOSEPH. Don't be ashamed of that. Your position as a topman is a
very exalted one.
RALPH. Well, your honour, love burns as brightly in the fo'c'sle as it
does on the quarter-deck, and Josephine is the fairest bud that ever
blossomed upon the tree of a poor fellow's wildest hopes. 390

(JOSEPHINE *rushes to* RALPH'S *arms.*)

JOS. Darling! (SIR JOSEPH *horrified.*)
RALPH. She is the figurehead of my ship of life – the bright beacon that
guides me into my port of happiness – the rarest, the purest gem that ever
sparkled on a poor but worthy fellow's trusting brow! 395
ALL. Very pretty, very pretty!
SIR JOSEPH. Insolent sailor, you shall repent this outrage. Seize him!
(*Two Marines seize him and handcuff him.*)
JOS. Oh, Sir Joseph, spare him, for I love him tenderly.
SIR JOSEPH. Pray, don't. I will teach this presumptuous mariner to 400
discipline his affections. Have you such a thing as a dungeon on board?
ALL. We have!
DICK. They have!
SIR JOSEPH. Then load him with chains and take him there at once!

OCTET.

RALPH.   Farewell, my own, 405
                   Light of my life, farewell!
               For crime unknown
                   I go to a dungeon cell.

JOS.   I will atone.
                   In the meantime farewell! 410
               And all alone
                   Rejoice in your dungeon cell!

419 *No telephone*: This was a very up-to-date reference in 1878. Alexander Graham Bell had been granted a patent for his new invention only two years earlier. The world's first clearly audible telephone message had been transmitted by Bell to a friend on another floor of his house in Boston on 10 March 1876, and the first telephone exchange was opened at New Haven, Connecticut, in January 1878. London had its first telephone company in June 1878, the month after *Pinafore* opened, and its first exchange a year later.

Gilbert had a telephone installed in his home in 1882, and he also ordered one for the prompt desk at the Savoy Theatre so that he could monitor performances and rehearsals in his study. He also persuaded Sullivan to install a telephone at his home, and it was there, on 13 May 1883, at a party to mark the composer's forty-first birthday, that a distinguished group of guests, headed by the Prince of Wales (later Edward VII), heard a direct relay of parts of *Iolanthe* from the Savoy stage. This was probably the first ever live 'broadcast' of an opera.

428 *My pain and my distress*: Sir Joseph's next four lines, and Buttercup's four-line recitative which follows them, were not in the original *Pinafore* libretto. The licence copy sent to the Lord Chamberlain has this passage of dialogue instead:

> SIR JOSEPH. Josephine, I cannot tell you the distress I feel at this most painful revelation. I desire to express to you, officially, that I am hurt.
>
> HEBE. If you have five and twenty minutes to spare I will explain how it has effected [*sic*] me.
>
> SIR JOSEPH. Do *not* interfere.
>
> HEBE. Crushed.
>
> SIR JOSEPH. You, whom I honoured by seeking in marriage, you but the daughter of a captain in the Royal Navy.
>
> BUTTERCUP. Hold! I have something to say to that.
>
> HEBE. You had better be quiet.
>
> SIR JOSEPH. On the contrary, she had better proceed.
>
> HEBE. Of course, anybody but me. Go on, vulgar old woman.

Although Hebe's part was written out before the first performance, Sir Joseph's dialogue, without her interruptions, was kept in early productions. So was Buttercup's 'Hold! I have something to say to that', after which Sir Joseph said 'You?' Buttercup replied 'Yes, I!' before launching into her song 'A many years ago'.

SIR JOSEPH.　A bone, a bone
　　　　　　　　I'll pick with this sailor fell;
　　　　　　　　Let him be shown　　　　　　　　　　　415
　　　　　　　　At once to his dungeon cell.

BOATSWAIN, BOATSWAIN'S MATE, DICK DEADEYE, *and* COUSIN HEBE.
　　　　　　　　He'll hear no tone
　　　　　　　　Of the maiden he loves so well!
　　　　　　　　No telephone
　　　　　　　　Communicates with his cell!　.　　　　420

BUT. (*mysteriously*).　But when is known
　　　　　　　　The secret I have to tell,
　　　　　　　　Wide will be thrown
　　　　　　　　The door of his dungeon cell.

ALL.　　　　　　For crime unknown　　　　　　　　425
　　　　　　　　He goes to a dungeon cell!
　　　　　　　　　　　(RALPH *is led off in custody.*)

SIR JOSEPH.　My pain and my distress
　　　　　　　　Again it is not easy to express.
　　　　　　　　My amazement, my surprise,　　　　430
　　　　　　　　Again you may discover from my eyes.
ALL.　　　　　　How terrible the aspect of his eyes!
BUT.　　　　　　Hold! Ere upon your loss
　　　　　　　　You lay much stress,
　　　　　　　　A long-concealèd crime　　　　　　435
　　　　　　　　I would confess.

SONG – BUTTERCUP.

　　　　　　　　A many years ago,
　　　　　　　　When I was young and charming,
　　　　　　　　As some of you may know,
　　　　　　　　I practised baby-farming.　　　　　　440
ALL.　　　　　　Now this is most alarming!
　　　　　　　　When she was young and charming,
　　　　　　　　She practised baby-farming,
　　　　　　　　A many years ago.
BUT.　　　　　　Two tender babes I nussed:　　　　445
　　　　　　　　One was of low condition,
　　　　　　　　The other, upper crust,
　　　　　　　　A regular patrician.

455 *I mixed those children up*: Gilbert made much of the dramatic possibilities of people being mixed up when they were babies. It is the central feature of the plot of *The Gondoliers*, where there is first confusion about whether it was Marco or Giuseppe Palmieri who was the heir to the throne of Barataria taken away as a baby to be reared by a gondolier, and then there is the added twist provided at the end by the prince's foster-mother, Inez, when she reveals that in fact it was neither of them, but rather Luiz.

The swapping of identities at birth also forms the basis of two of the *Bab Ballads*. 'The Baby's Vengeance' tells the story of how Paley Vollaire had crept into the cradle of his foster-brother and so inherited an enormous fortune, leaving the rightful heir, Frederick West, poor and forced to earn a living as a dustman. 'General John' describes a situation even closer to that in *Pinafore*. Private James of the Sixty-seventy-first Regiment gets the idea that he and his commanding officer, General John, 'were cruelly changed at birth'. The general generously accepts his story and swops places with the private.

472 *That is the idea I intended to convey, officially*: This, and Sir Joseph's next line, were both formally incorporated in the *Pinafore* libretto with Gilbert's approval for the 1908 revival. They were probably originally introduced, like many of the added lines, as 'ad-libs' by the D'Oyly Carte principals. Buttercup's line 'Aye! aye! yer 'onour' was added in 1914.

476–7 *Ralph enters as Captain; Captain as a common sailor*: This rapid transformation, calling for a speedy change of costume by the two principals involved, directly recalls the last verse of the Bab Ballad 'General John':

> So GENERAL JOHN as PRIVATE JAMES
> Fell in, parade upon;
> And PRIVATE JAMES, by change of names,
> Was MAJOR-GENERAL JOHN.

Traditionally the former Captain Corcoran shows his fall in station by adopting a common Cockney accent from now on and dropping his 'h's. Archibald Grosvenor undergoes a similar transformation of accent when he appears at the end of *Patience* having shed his aestheticism and become an ordinary, matter-of-fact young man.

ALL (*explaining to each other*).
          Now, this is the position:
          One was of low condition,   450
          The other a patrician,
          A many years ago.
BUT.   Oh, bitter is my cup!
          However could I do it?
          I mixed those children up,   455
          And not a creature knew it!
ALL.   However could you do it?
          Some day, no doubt, you'll rue it,
          Although no creature knew it,
          So many years ago.   460
BUT.   In time each little waif
          Forsook his foster-mother,
          The well-born babe was Ralph –
          Your captain was the other!!!
ALL.   They left their foster-mother,   465
          The one was Ralph, our brother,
          Our captain was the other,
          A many years ago.

SIR JOSEPH. Then I am to understand that Captain Corcoran and Ralph were exchanged in childhood's happy hour – that Ralph is really the   470 Captain, and the Captain is Ralph?

BUT. That is the idea I intended to convey, officially!

SIR JOSEPH. And very well you have conveyed it, Miss Buttercup.

BUT. Aye! aye! yer 'onour.

SIR JOSEPH. Dear me! Let them appear before me, at once!   475

(RALPH *enters as* CAPTAIN; CAPTAIN *as a common
sailor.* JOSEPHINE *rushes to his arms.*)

JOS. My father – a common sailor!

CAPT. It is hard, is it not, my dear?

SIR JOSEPH. This is a very singular occurrence; I congratulate you   480 both. (*To* RALPH.) Captain Rackstraw, desire that remarkably fine seaman to step forward.

RALPH. Corcoran. Three paces to the front – march!

CAPT. If what?

RALPH. If what? I don't think I understand you.   485

CAPT. If you please.

SIR JOSEPH. The gentleman is quite right. If you *please*.

RALPH. Oh! If you *please*. (CAPTAIN *steps forward*.)

501 *Sad my lot and sorry*: In early productions the lines from 'Sad my lot and sorry' to the beginning of the quartet were sung as recitative, with the chorus repeating Sir Joseph's line 'What shall I do? I cannot live alone!' They were subsequently changed to spoken dialogue.

519 *In dreamy roundelay*: The licence copy sent to the Lord Chamberlain has the following additional lines after the end of the quartet for Josephine, Hebe, Ralph and Deadeye:

ALL.

Tomorrow night,
With loving spouse,
He'll go ashore,
And then he'll plight
His marriage vows
For evermore.
A clergyman, etc.

The song presumably continued as a reprise of the chorus towards the end of Act I.

SIR JOSEPH (*to* CAPTAIN). You are an extremely fine fellow.
CAPT. Yes, your honour. 490
SIR JOSEPH. So it seems that you were Ralph, and Ralph was you.
CAPT. So it seems, your honour.
SIR JOSEPH. Well, I need not tell you that after this change in your
condition, a marriage with your daughter will be out of the question.
CAPT. Don't say that, your honour – love levels all ranks. 495
SIR JOSEPH. It does to a considerable extent, but it does not level them
as much as that. (*Handing* JOSEPHINE *to* RALPH.) Here – take her, sir,
and mind you treat her kindly.
RALPH *and* JOS.   Oh bliss, oh rapture!
CAPT. *and* BUT.   Oh rapture, oh bliss! 500
SIR JOSEPH.   Sad my lot and sorry,
          What shall I do? I cannot live alone!
HEBE.   Fear nothing – while I live I'll not desert you.
          I'll soothe and comfort your declining days.
SIR JOSEPH. No, don't do that. 505
HEBE.   Yes, but indeed I'd rather –
SIR JOSEPH (*resigned*). Oh, very well then.
          To-morrow morn our vows shall all be plighted,
          Three loving pairs on the same day united!

QUARTET.

JOSEPHINE, HEBE, RALPH, *and* DEADEYE.

Oh joy, oh rapture unforeseen, 510
The clouded sky is now serene,
The god of day – the orb of love,
Has hung his ensign high above,
   The sky is all ablaze.

With wooing words and loving song, 515
We'll chase the lagging hours along,
And if $\left\{\begin{array}{l}\text{he finds}\\ \text{I find}\end{array}\right\}$ the maiden coy,
We'll murmur forth decorous joy,
   In dreamy roundelay.

CAPT.   For he's the Captain of the *Pinafore*. 520
ALL.   And a right good captain too!
CAPT.   And though before my fall
          I was captain of you all,
          I'm a member of the crew.
ALL.   Although before his fall, etc. 525

538 *For the former Captain of the Pinafore*: In early productions this line was sung as: 'For the faithful seamen of the *Pinafore*'. That was, in fact, a more appropriate refrain, because in *Utopia Limited* (1893) Captain Corcoran reappears, surprisingly but impressively transformed into Captain Sir Edward Corcoran, K.C.B., and sings the following song:

> I'm Captain Corcoran, K.C.B.,
> I'll teach you how we rule the sea,
> And terrify the simple Gauls;
> And how the Saxon and the Celt
> Their Europe-shaking blows have dealt
> With Maxim gun and Nordenfeldt
> (Or will, when the occasion calls).
> If sailor-like you'd play your cards,
> Unbend your sails and lower your yards,
> Unstep your masts – you'll never want 'em more.
> Though we're no longer hearts of oak,
> Yet we can steer and we can stoke,
> And, thanks to coal, and thanks to coke,
> We never run a ship ashore!

Well, hardly ever run a ship ashore, he is forced to admit under familiar questioning from the chorus. So Corcoran evidently manages to rise again through the ranks to his former position. Of Captain Rackstraw, however, we hear no more.

540 *Though I could never tell why*: In early productions Buttercup sang 'I'm sure I shall never know why' here.

545 *And when I've married thee*: It is just as well that Hebe is Sir Joseph's cousin, and not a sister or an aunt, since marriage with either of those relations would be prohibited according to the rules of kindred and affinity in the Prayer Book.

555 *That he is an Englishman*: For several years during the ultra-patriotic and jingoistic Edwardian period, performances of *H.M.S. Pinafore* did not end with this line but with a rendering of 'Rule, Britannia'. It can be heard on the 1908 D'Oyly Carte recording. A master copy of the *Pinafore* libretto dating from 1923 and now in the D'Oyly Carte archives has 'Rule, Britannia' printed after the end of 'He is an Englishman' and before the curtain. Against it there is a handwritten note by Rupert D'Oyly Carte which reads: 'Rule Britannia was not originally sung and is not sung by my company now (1924).' It is not in the 1923 D'Oyly Carte recording.

CAPT. I shall marry with a wife,
In my humble rank of life! (*turning to* BUT.)
   And you, my own, are she –
I must wander to and fro,
But wherever I may go,   530
   I shall never be untrue to thee!

ALL.   What, never?
CAPT.   No, never!
ALL.   What, *never*?
CAPT.   Well, hardly ever!   535
ALL.   Hardly ever be untrue to thee.
Then give three cheers, and one cheer more
For the former Captain of the *Pinafore*.

BUT. For he loves Little Buttercup, dear Little Buttercup,
   Though I could never tell why;   540
But still he loves Buttercup, poor Little Buttercup,
   Sweet Little Buttercup, aye!
ALL.   For he loves, etc.

SIR JOSEPH. I'm the monarch of the sea,
   And when I've married thee (*to* HEBE),   545
I'll be true to the devotion that my love implants.
HEBE. Then good-bye to your sisters, and your cousins, and your
    aunts,
Especially your cousins,
Whom you reckon up by dozens,
Your sisters, and your cousins, and your aunts!   550

ALL. Then good-bye, etc.
For he is an Englishman,
   And he himself hath said it,
   And it's greatly to his credit
That he is an Englishman!   555

CURTAIN

THE
PIRATES
OF
PENZANCE

OR
THE SLAVE OF DUTY

DRAMATIS PERSONÆ

MAJOR-GENERAL STANLEY
THE PIRATE KING
SAMUEL (*his Lieutenant*)
FREDERIC (*the Pirate Apprentice*)
SERGEANT OF POLICE
MABEL
EDITH
KATE } (*General Stanley's Daughters*)
ISABEL
RUTH (*a Pirate Maid of all Work*)
Chorus of Pirates, Police, and General Stanley's Daughters.

ACT I. – A Rocky Sea-shore on the Coast of Cornwall.
ACT II. – A Ruined Chapel by Moonlight.

THE PIRATES OF PENZANCE

The Pirates of Penzance has the unique distinction among Gilbert and Sullivan's operas of having received its première in the United States of America. It opened at the Fifth Avenue Theater, New York, on 31 December 1879, with the composer himself conducting.

Gilbert and Sullivan were in America with Richard D'Oyly Carte and his company to present the authorized version of *H.M.S. Pinafore*. When they set out from Britain in October 1879 they had already made substantial progress on the next opera for the company to perform, which they intended should be premiered in the States.

To his horror Sullivan discovered when he unpacked his bags on arrival at New York that he had left behind in Britain all the music he had written for Act I of the new work. So, working partly from memory and partly from scratch in the periods when he was not either rehearsing or conducting *Pinafore*, he feverishly set about reconstructing the lost songs as well as working on the numbers in the Second Act. To this day, a plaque set in the wall of No. 45, East 20th Street, where his hotel stood, records that 'On this site Sir Arthur Sullivan composed *The Pirates of Penzance* during 1879'.

Sullivan worked furiously to complete the opera in time for the scheduled first performance on the last day of the year. He slaved away right through Christmas Day and finally finished the full score at 7 a.m. on 28 December, the day before the dress rehearsal and two days before the opening night. In these last forty-eight hours he also had to face the added headache of a threatened strike by the members of the orchestra, who claimed that the new work was an opera rather than an operetta and they should therefore be paid on a higher scale.

Sullivan countered the threat by announcing that he would bring over the orchestra of the Royal Opera House, Covent Garden, which, he said, had nothing much to do until the start of the opera season in the spring and would gladly come to New York for not much more than expenses. In the meantime, the piece would be played with accompaniment from himself on the piano and his friend and associate Alfred Cellier on the harmonium. In the face of this display of British *sang-froid* the American musicians backed down, much to the relief of Sullivan, who later admitted: 'the idea of getting the Covent Garden band over was hardly less absurd than the ludicrous idea of using the pianoforte and harmonium in a big theatre'.

The day of the opening performance was an ordeal for the composer. He finally finished the overture at 5 a.m. and spent the morning rehearsing the orchestra at the theatre. After breakfasting at his hotel at 1.45 he went to bed but was unable to sleep. In the evening he had twelve oysters and a glass of champagne at the New York Club before taking his position in the orchestra pit. 'Went into the orchestra more dead than alive,' his diary records, 'but got better when I took the stick in my hand. Fine reception. Piece went marvellously well. Grand success.' After the triumphant première, there was a grand party to see in the New Year and Sullivan did not finally get to his bed until 3.30 the following morning.

In order to protect the British copyright, a performance of *The Pirates of Penzance* had, in fact, already been given in the Bijou Theatre, Paignton, Devon, the day before the New York opening. The reason for this remote venue was not its proximity to the location of the opera but rather the fact that the members of the D'Oyly Carte touring company were in nearby Torquay performing *H.M.S. Pinafore*. For their single performance of the new opera, the cast read from handwritten sheets of music newly arrived from America, and wore their *Pinafore* costumes with only minimal changes, like scarves round the heads of those playing pirates. The music for a number of the songs had still not reached Paignton when the performance took place, and the modern major-general was one of several characters who had to introduce himself in verse rather than song.

The London première of *The Pirates* took place on 3 April 1880 at the Opéra Comique. The opera ran for almost exactly a year, closing on 2 April 1881 after 363 performances. Meanwhile, it was by now so successful in the United States that it was being performed by four separate companies established by D'Oyly Carte. The original Fifth Avenue company went on to Boston; a second company played in Philadelphia; a third opened at Newark, New Jersey, and went on to tour Pennsylvania, Ohio, Indiana, Michigan, Missouri, Kansas, Nebraska, Iowa, Minnesota and Wisconsin; and a fourth, launched in Buffalo, went from Chicago and St Louis to New Orleans, Memphis, Nashville and Louisville.

Both the plot and the music of *The Pirates of Penzance* have continued to delight audiences on both sides of the Atlantic ever since. Surprisingly, Gilbert had not originally intended the opera to be about pirates at all. Its first provisional title was *The Robbers* and it was to be about the relations between a group of burglars and a group of policemen. While in the United States he decided to recast the burglars as pirates, who had already figured in one of his previous plays, *Our Island Home* (1870). The policemen, luckily, remained as an object for Gilbert's gentle satire along with the Army, the

House of Lords and, of course, the overpowering sense of duty which is the opera's main theme and which provides its sub-title.

Sullivan found that the songs, and particularly the duets, with which he was provided by Gilbert in *The Pirates* gave him full scope to show his potential as an operatic composer. Indeed one has some sympathy with the striking musicians of the Fifth Avenue Theater. *The Pirates* comes closer to grand opera than any other of the works of Gilbert and Sullivan, with the possible exception of *The Yeomen of the Guard*. The composer himself wrote to his mother: 'The music is infinitely superior in every way to the *Pinafore* – tunier, and more developed – of a higher class altogether'. Nor, at a less lofty level, did he neglect the comic possibilities of a chorus of British bobbies, for whom he provided two of the most popular tunes in the entire Savoy Operas.

The Pirates of Penzance was the first production of the new D'Oyly Carte Opera Company, in which Gilbert, Sullivan and D'Oyly Carte each took one third of the profits. It firmly established the trio on a successful partnership which was to continue, with some ups and downs, for the next twenty years.

Recently *The Pirates of Penzance* has been given a new lease of life by Joseph Papp in his production which opened in New York's Central Park on 15 July 1980 and which has since played to packed houses both on Broadway and in the West End of London. Whatever purists may think of casting rock singers to play Frederic and Mabel and putting electric guitars and synthesizers in the orchestra pit, there can be no denying the verve and excitement of the production, which must have introduced many newcomers to the genius of Gilbert and Sullivan. It is also particularly appropriate that the city in which the opera first opened should be the scene of its renaissance almost exactly a century later.

1–5 *Scene: The Pirates of Penzance* is not the only Savoy Opera to be set in Cornwall. The action of *Ruddigore* takes place in the fictitious fishing village of Rederring in the same county. There is, of course, nothing fictitious about Penzance, which is an important fishing, market and tourist centre on the south coast of Cornwall, the terminus of the main West Country railway line from London and the most westerly town in England.

Gilbert originally conceived a very different opening to the opera from the present one. The description of the scene in the copy sent to the Lord Chamberlain for licensing reads 'A cavern by the sea-shore. Pirates discovered carousing. Thomas, the Pirate King, waiting on them, busying himself with wiping glasses etc. and generally acting as a servant while the others are enjoying themselves.'

6 *Pour, oh, pour the pirate sherry*: In the licence copy, and in early vocal scores, in keeping with Gilbert's original intention to portray the Pirate King as the servant of his band, this chorus begins:

> Pour, oh King, the pirate sherry;
> Fill, oh King, the pirate glass, etc.

9 *bumper*: A well-filled glass or mug.

10 *For to-day our pirate 'prentice*: In the licence copy, and presumably in the original Paignton performance of the opera, while this first verse was given to Samuel, the next (beginning 'Two-and-twenty now he's rising') was given to another pirate, James. ''Prentice' is, of course, short for 'apprentice'. Indentures are sealed agreements binding an apprentice to his master for a particular period of time.

ACT I

SCENE. – *A rocky sea-shore on the coast of Cornwall. In the distance is a calm sea, on which a schooner is lying at anchor. As the curtain rises groups of pirates are discovered – some drinking, some playing cards.* SAMUEL, *the Pirate Lieutenant, is going from one group to another, filling the cups from a flask.* FREDERIC *is seated in a despondent attitude at the back of the scene.*   5

OPENING CHORUS.

Pour, oh, pour the pirate sherry;
   Fill, oh, fill the pirate glass;
And, to make us more than merry,
   Let the pirate bumper pass.

SAM.   For to-day our pirate 'prentice   10
                Rises from indenture freed;
            Strong his arm and keen his scent is,
                He's a pirate now indeed!

ALL.   Here's good luck to Frederic's ventures!
            Frederic's out of his indentures.   15

SAM.   Two-and-twenty now he's rising,
                And alone he's fit to fly,
            Which we're bent on signalizing
                With unusual revelry.

ALL.   Here's good luck to Frederic's ventures!   20
            Frederic's out of his indentures.
            Pour, oh, pour the pirate sherry, etc.

(FREDERIC *rises and comes forward with* PIRATE KING, *who enters.*)

32–3 *scuttling a Cunarder*: To scuttle is to sink. The Cunard line was founded by Samuel
Cunard (1787–1865), who in 1839 established the British and North American Royal
Mail Steam Packet Company to run regular mail and passenger services between
Liverpool and the East Coast of North America. In 1878 it was re-formed as a public
company with the title The Cunard Steam-Ship Company. It was a Cunard liner, the
Aurania, which took Richard D'Oyly Carte and his company secretly to the United
States in the summer of 1885 to perform *The Mikado* (see p. 259). Cunard still runs
passenger services across the Atlantic in its flag-ship, the *QE2*.

33 *cutting out a P. & O.*: To cut out is to capture or destroy one ship in a fleet by separating
it from the rest. The Peninsular and Oriental Steam Navigation Company, better
known as the P. & O., began in 1835 as the Peninsular Steam Navigation Company,
with a regular steamer service to the Iberian peninsula, including the carrying of mail
to Gibraltar. It acquired its present name in 1840, having started a service on the
Gibraltar–Alexandria route, and later extended its operations through the Suez Canal
to India, Ceylon and the Far East.

In early productions of *The Pirates* in the United States, including the première, the
Pirate King did not refer to the P. & O. but to the White Star Line, which was
presumably better-known across the Atlantic. Founded as the Oceanic Steam
Navigation Company in 1869 by Thomas Henry Ismay, the line operated services on
both the North Atlantic and the Australian routes. Its liner *Oceanic*, launched in 1870
for the Liverpool to New York run, was the world's first express luxury liner. In 1934
the line was merged with Cunard to form Cunard White Star Ltd.

never shipped a handspike: A handspike is a lever, generally made of wood, fitted into a
windlass or capstan to heave up an anchor or heavy chain.

43–60 *When Frederic was a little lad*
Gilbert's original intention, as revealed in the licence copy of *The Pirates* sent to the
Lord Chamberlain, was to have no dialogue at all until the end of this number, which
was conceived as a duet for Frederic and Ruth rather than a solo as now. The opening
chorus was to be followed immediately by a song for the Pirate King, after which there
was to be a recitative for Frederic covering much the same points as those now
contained in the dialogue in lines 24 to 42. Then came the duet for Frederic and Ruth.
I reproduce the entire sequence below, as it appears in the licence copy (i.e. with a
serious lack of punctuation; unlike all the other Savoy Opera libretti sent to the Lord
Chamberlain before their first performance, that for *The Pirates* is not printed but
written out in an evidently hurried long-hand, a further sign of the pressures under
which the opera was completed).

This sequence is interesting both in its own right, in showing, for example, a very
different character for the Pirate King from the one later adopted, and also because it
seems to have been the version which was performed at Paignton on 30 December
1879. It follows straight on from the opening chorus:

KING.	Yes I am a Pirate King!
ALL.	You are!
	Hurrah for our Pirate King!
KING.	And it is, it is a glorious thing
	To be a Pirate King!
ALL.	Hurrah,
	Hurrah for our Pirate King.
KING.	It's true I have to work all day
	Like a genial help in a humble way
ALL (*significantly*).	You should!
	You should if you'd be our king!

KING. Yes, Frederic, from to-day you rank as a full-blown member of
our band.   25
ALL. Hurrah!
FRED. My friends, I thank you all, from my heart, for your kindly
wishes. Would that I could repay them as they deserve!
KING. What do you mean?
FRED. To-day I am out of my indentures, and to-day I leave you for   30
ever.
KING. But this is quite unaccountable; a keener hand at scuttling a
Cunarder or cutting out a P. & O. never shipped a handspike.
FRED. Yes, I have done my best for you. And why? It was my duty
under my indentures, and I am the slave of duty. As a child I was regularly   35
apprenticed to your band. It was through an error – no matter, the mistake
was ours, not yours, and I was in honour bound by it.
SAM. An error? What error?
FRED. I may not tell you; it would reflect upon my well-loved Ruth.

(RUTH *rises and comes forward.*)   40

RUTH. Nay, dear master, my mind has long been gnawed by the
cankering tooth of mystery. Better have it out at once.

SONG – RUTH.

When Frederic was a little lad he proved so brave and daring,
His father thought he'd 'prentice him to some career sea-faring.
I was, alas! his nurserymaid, and so it fell to *my* lot   45
To take and bind the promising boy apprentice to a *pilot* –
A life not bad for a hardy lad, though surely not a high lot,
Though I'm a nurse, you might do worse than make your boy a pilot.

I was a stupid nurserymaid, on breakers always steering,
And I did not catch the word aright, through being hard of hearing;   50
Mistaking my instructions, which within my brain did gyrate,
I took and bound this promising boy apprentice to a *pirate*.
A sad mistake it was to make and doom him to a vile lot.
I bound him to a pirate – you – instead of to a pilot.

I soon found out, beyond all doubt, the scope of this disaster,   55
But I hadn't the face to return to my place, and break it to my master.
A nurserymaid is not afraid of what you people *call* work,
So I made up my mind to go as a kind of piratical maid-of-all-work.
And that is how you find me now, a member of your shy lot,
Which you wouldn't have found, had he been bound apprentice to a pilot.   60

KING.   But to cook your meals I don't refuse
         And I black piratical boots and shoes
         I clean your knives, I bake your bread
         I light your fires – I make your beds
         I answer all the bells that ring
         Cling! cling! cling! cling! cling! cling!
         For if I said I'd rather not
         (I know you! I know you!)
         You would depose me like a shot!
ALL.   We would!
         Hurrah for our Pirate King!
KING.   Well many a king on a first class throne
         If he wants to call his crown his own
         Must manage somehow to get through
         More dirty work than ever I do
         Though I wash and boil
         And scrub and toil
         And answer bells that ring cling! cling!
ALL.   Cling! cling! cling! cling! cling! cling!
KING.   But menial duties carry no sting
         When one reflects what a glorious thing
         It is to be a king
ALL.   Hurrah!
         Hurrah for our Pirate King!
         So pour, oh King, the pirate sherry etc.

                    RECITATIVE.
FRED.   My generous friends, with all my heart I thank you
         Although as brethren I no longer rank you!
ALL.   Oh, oh?
         How so?
         Although with all his heart he thanks us
         As brethren he no longer ranks us!
         Oh, oh!
         How so? How so? How so? How so?
FRED.   Bear with me pray
         Although I bring you tidings that will grieve you
         This very day
         I'm out of my indentures and I leave you.
ALL.   You leave us?
FRED.   I leave you!
         Don't estimate me at too high appraisement
ALL.   Wonder, surprise, confusion and amazement.
FRED.   I've always loathed your pillaging and branding
         But for a most absurd misunderstanding
         Upon the part of one who little knew you
         I never should have been apprenticed to you.
         Once more – don't estimate me at too high appraisement
ALL.   Once more surprise, confusion and amazement.
                    DUET AND CHORUS.
FRED.   When I was but a child of three
         I proved so brave and daring
         My father thought he'd prentice me
         To some career seafaring

RUTH. Oh, pardon! Frederic, pardon! (*Kneels.*)

FRED. Rise, sweet one, I have long pardoned you.

RUTH (*rises*). The two words were so much alike!

FRED. They were. They still are, though years have rolled over their heads. But this afternoon my obligation ceases. Individually, I love you all   65
with affection unspeakable, but, collectively, I look upon you with a disgust that amounts to absolute detestation. Oh! pity me, my beloved friends, for such is my sense of duty that, once out of my indentures, I shall feel myself bound to devote myself heart and soul to your extermination!

ALL. Poor lad – poor lad! (*All weep.*)   70

KING. Well, Frederic, if you conscientiously feel that it is your duty to destroy us, we cannot blame you for acting on that conviction. Always act in accordance with the dictates of your conscience, my boy, and chance the consequences.

SAM. Besides, we can offer you but little temptation to remain with us.   75
We don't seem to make piracy pay. I'm sure I don't know why, but we don't.

FRED. *I* know why, but, alas! I mustn't tell you; it wouldn't be right.

KING. Why not, my boy? It's only half-past eleven, and you are one of us until the clock strikes twelve.

SAM. True, and until then you are bound to protect our interests.   80

ALL. Hear, hear!

FRED. Well, then, it is my duty, as a pirate, to tell you that you are too tender-hearted. For instance, you make a point of never attacking a weaker party than yourselves, and when you attack a stronger party you invariably get thrashed.   85

KING. There is some truth in that.

FRED. Then, again, you make a point of never molesting an orphan!

SAM. Of course: we are orphans ourselves, and know what it is.

FRED. Yes, but it has got about, and what is the consequence? Every one we capture says he's an orphan. The last three ships we took proved to   90
be manned entirely by orphans, and so we had to let them go. One would think that Great Britain's mercantile navy was recruited solely from her orphan asylums – which we know is not the case.

SAM. But, hang it all! you wouldn't have us absolutely merciless?

FRED. There's my difficulty; until twelve o'clock I would, after twelve I   95
wouldn't. Was ever a man placed in so delicate a situation?

RUTH. And Ruth, your own Ruth, whom you love so well, and who has won her middle-aged way into your boyish heart, what is to become of *her*?

KING. Oh, he will take you with him.

(*Hands* RUTH *to* FREDERIC.)   100

FRED. Well, Ruth, I feel some little difficulty about you. It is true that I admire you very much, but I have been constantly at sea since I was eight

A servant girl in his employ
He sent in charge of my lot
Instructing her to bind his boy
Apprentice to a pilot –

KING, SAMUEL & JAMES: A pilot?

FRED.   A pilot.
A very respectable line of life, though certainly not a high lot.

KING, SAMUEL & JAMES.   An odd mistake
You surely make
You mean of course a Pirate

FRED.   No, no, no, no.
A *pi*lot, *pi*lot, a *pi*lot, a *pi*lot.
A highly respectable line of life though certainly not a high lot –
I hope I'm clear

KING.   Yes, yes, we hear
Now pray do not get irate
You said 'a respectable line of life' we thought you meant a pirate

ALL.   He said 'a respectable line of life' we thought he meant a pirate

RUTH (*coming forward*).
Ah me, I was that nurserymaid
Forgive my interfering
My strict commands I disobeyed
Through being hard of hearing
His father's words were spoken that wild
That in my brain did gyrate
And I understood he wished his son
Apprenticed to a pirate

KING, JAMES & SAMUEL.   A pirate?

RUTH.   A pirate.
A very contemptible line of life, with a premium at a high rate.

KING, SAMUEL & JAMES.   An odd mistake
You surely make
You mean of course a pilot.

RUTH (*irritated*).   No, no, no, no
A pirate, a pirate, a pirate, a pirate.
A very contemptible line of life, you stupid triumvirate,
I hope I'm clear?

KING.   Yes, yes, we hear
Though ours is not a vile lot
You said 'a contemptible line of life', we thought you meant a pilot.

ALL.   She said 'a contemptible line of life', we thought she meant a pilot.

The licence copy then continues with this dialogue line:

> FRED. Yes my friends, my being apprenticed to you was entirely due to my excellent nurse's mistake.
> RUTH. Oh pardon, pardon, pardon.

126 *Well, it's the top of the tide*: The original version, found in the licence copy and performed at Paignton, contained another piece of recitative at this point instead of the dialogue which begins 'Well, it's the top of the tide':

> SAMUEL.   Your Majesty, we must get underway
> To lose the tide we should be worse than crazy

years old, and yours is the only woman's face I have seen during that time. I think it is a sweet face.

RUTH. It is – oh, it is! 105

FRED. I say I *think* it is; that is my impression. But as I have never had an opportunity of comparing you with other women, it is just possible I may be mistaken.

KING. True.

FRED. What a terrible thing it would be if I were to marry this innocent 110 person, and then find out that she is, on the whole, plain!

KING. Oh, Ruth is very well, very well indeed.

SAM. Yes, there are the remains of a fine woman about Ruth.

FRED. Do you really think so?

SAM. I do. 115

FRED. Then I will not be so selfish as to take her from you. In justice to her, and in consideration for you, I will leave her behind. (*Hands* RUTH *to* KING.)

KING. No, Frederic, this must not be. We are rough men who lead a rough life, but we are not so utterly heartless as to deprive thee of thy love. I think I am right in saying that there is not one here who would 120 rob thee of this inestimable treasure for all the world holds dear.

ALL (*loudly*). Not one!

KING. No, I thought there wasn't. Keep thy love, Frederic, keep thy love. (*Hands her back to* FREDERIC.)

FRED. You're very good, I'm sure. 125

(*Exit* RUTH.)

KING. Well, it's the top of the tide, and we must be off. Farewell, Frederic. When your process of extermination begins, let our deaths be as swift and painless as you can conveniently make them.

FRED. I will! By the love I have for you, I swear it! Would that you 130 could render this extermination unnecessary by accompanying me back to civilization!

KING. No, Frederic, it cannot be. I don't think much of our profession, but, contrasted with respectability, it is comparatively honest. No, Frederic, I shall live and die a Pirate King. 135

SONG – PIRATE KING.

> Oh, better far to live and die
> Under the brave black flag I fly,
> Than play a sanctimonious part,
> With a pirate head and a pirate heart.
> Away to the cheating world go you, 140
> Where pirates all are well-to-do;
> But I'll be true to the song I sing,
> And live and die a Pirate King.

KING.   Is it essential we put out today?
To tell the truth I feel a little lazy –
How would it be if I remained behind?
On this hot day the cavern is delicious

JAMES.   We rather think your majesty would find
That course of action highly injudicious

ALL (*drawing knives*). We rather think, etc.

SAMUEL.   Who would there be to knot and reef and splice
Or take in canvas when the storm is lowering

KING (*sighing*). True, true – I thank you for your very good advice.
(*loading himself with kegs etc.*)
The cares of government are overpowering.
For I am a Pirate King etc.

After repeating the final refrain of the Pirate King's song, the pirates depart, leaving Ruth and Frederic alone, and the dialogue continues as now (line 168).

144 *For I am a Pirate King*: The Pirate King, played by Prince Charles when he was a boy at Gordonstoun School in 1967 and turned into an Errol-Flynn-type swashbuckling matinée idol by Joseph Papp, is one of the most likeable villains in the Savoy Operas. In an earlier musical play, *Our Island Home*, written in 1870 in collaboration with the composer Thomas German Reed, Gilbert had created a character who is in many ways the prototype of the Pirate King in *The Pirates of Penzance*. Captain Bang introduces himself in a similar if rather more threatening way:

> Oh tremble! I'm a Pirate Chief;
> Who comes upon me comes to grief,
> For I'm a murderer and a thief;
> A Pirate Captain, I.
> I spare nor age nor sex nor rank.
> For every one my fetters clank,
> Until they're made to walk the plank,
> A Pirate Captain, I.

The story of Captain Bang in *Our Island Home* also anticipates the plight of Frederic in *The Pirates*. He is the only son of an indulgent father and mother who had asked him, when he was seven, what he wanted to be. He replied that he had a hankering for a seafaring life, but didn't want to be away from home for long, so he told them that he wanted to be a pilot. 'My kind papa consented and sent me with my nurse to the nearest sea-front, telling her to apprentice me to a pilot. The girl – a very good girl, but stupid, – mistaking her instructions, apprenticed me to a pirate of her acquaintance and bound me over to serve him diligently and faithfully until I reached the age of 21'.

172 *You will find me a wife of a thousand*: This same joke occurs in the Bab Ballad 'Haunted', in which a man reflects on the social ghosts which haunt him:

> I pass to critical seventeen:
> The ghost of that terrible wedding scene,
> When an elderly colonel stole my queen,
> And woke my dream of heaven:
> No school-girl decked in her nursery curls
> Was my gushing innocent queen of pearls;
> If she wasn't a girl of a thousand girls,
> She was one of forty-seven!

Gilbert, who was himself forty-six when he wrote *The Pirates*, seems to have found

	For I am a Pirate King.	
ALL.	You are!	145
	Hurrah for the Pirate King!	
KING.	And it is, it is a glorious thing	
	To be a Pirate King.	
ALL.	It is!	
	Hurrah for our Pirate King!	150
KING.	When I sally forth to seek my prey	
	I help myself in a royal way:	
	I sink a few more ships, it's true,	
	Than a well-bred monarch ought to do;	
	But many a king on a first-class throne,	155
	If he wants to call his crown his own,	
	Must manage somehow to get through	
	More dirty work than ever *I* do,	
	For I am a Pirate King.	
ALL.	You are!	160
	Hurrah for the Pirate King!	
KING.	And it is, it is a glorious thing	
	To be a Pirate King!	
ALL.	It is!	
	Hurrah for our Pirate King!	165

(Exeunt all except FREDERIC.)

(Enter RUTH.)

RUTH. Oh, take me with you! I cannot live if I am left behind.

FRED. Ruth, I will be quite candid with you. You are very dear to me, as you know, but I must be circumspect. You see, you are considerably older than I. A lad of twenty-one usually looks for a wife of seventeen. 170

RUTH. A wife of seventeen! You will find me a wife of a thousand!

FRED. No, but I shall find you a wife of forty-seven, and that is quite enough. Ruth, tell me candidly, and without reserve: compared with other women – how are *you*? 175

RUTH. I will answer you truthfully, master – I have a slight cold, but otherwise I am quite well.

FRED. I am sorry for your cold, but I was referring rather to your personal appearance. Compared with other women, are you beautiful?

RUTH (*bashfully*). I have been told so, dear master. 180

FRED. Ah, but lately?

RUTH. Oh, no, years and years ago.

FRED. What do you think of yourself?

RUTH. It is a delicate question to answer, but I think I am a fine woman.

FRED. That is your candid opinion? 185

RUTH. Yes, I should be deceiving you if I told you otherwise.

women in their forties a source of particular amusement. In the judge's song in *Trial by Jury* we are told that the rich attorney says of the daughter whom he is hoping to marry off:

> She may very well pass for forty-three
> In the dusk, with a light behind her!

191 *Can it be Custom House*: For the most part, the Joseph Papp production of *The Pirates* sticks faithfully to Gilbert's original dialogue. At this point, however, Papp makes a small concession to his American audience by substituting 'the Coastguard' for 'Custom House' in Frederic's speech. 'Custom House' anyway seems a strange phrase to use to describe the officers of Her Majesty's Department of Customs and Excise. 'The revenuemen' would be more usual.

203–20 *You told me you were fair as gold*
This duet is the first of several songs in *The Pirates* in which Sullivan's music comes nearer to being in the category of grand opera than operetta. He was, of course, a serious composer, with several operas, oratorios, a symphony and numerous hymn tunes and songs to his credit, and it was in those areas that he believed his true talents lay and that he was happiest working. Yet, although his serious music was played and recognized, it never brought him the same fame and popularity as the Savoy Operas.

Several critics shared Sullivan's view that the comic opera collaborations with Gilbert were really beneath his talents. One wrote of *The Pirates*: 'Certain passages in the first duet between Frederic and Ruth and elsewhere, where the composer becomes serious in spite of himself, make one regret what might have been, or, perhaps, might still be if Mr Sullivan would attempt a genuine dramatic effort'.

In fact, Sullivan went on to write at least one major dramatic grand opera. *Ivanhoe*, based on the story by Sir Walter Scott, opened in January 1891 at the new Royal English Opera House (now the Palace Theatre), which Richard D'Oyly Carte had built to be the home of English grand opera. Although it ran for 155 consecutive performances, a record for grand opera, it has hardly ever been heard since, and Carte was forced to abandon his plans to do for English grand opera what he had so successfully done for English comic opera.

FRED. Thank you, Ruth, I believe you, for I am sure you would not practise on my inexperience; I wish to do the right thing, and if – I say *if* – you are really a fine woman, your age shall be no obstacle to our union! (*Chorus of Girls heard in the distance.*) Hark! Surely I hear voices! Who has 190
ventured to approach our all but inaccessible lair? Can it be Custom House? No, it does not sound like Custom House.

RUTH (*aside*). Confusion! it is the voices of young girls! If he should see them I am lost.

FRED. (*looking off*). By all that's marvellous, a bevy of beautiful maidens! 195
RUTH (*aside*). Lost! lost! lost!

FRED. How lovely! how surpassingly lovely is the plainest of them! What grace – what delicacy – what refinement! And Ruth – Ruth told me she was beautiful!

RECITATIVE.

FRED.	Oh, false one, you have deceived me!	200
RUTH.	I have deceived you?	
FRED.	Yes, deceived me! (*Denouncing her.*)	

DUET – FREDERIC *and* RUTH.

FRED.   You told me you were fair as gold!
RUTH (*wildly*). And, master, am I not so?
FRED.   And now I see you're plain and old.   205
RUTH.   I am sure I am not a jot so.
FRED.   Upon my innocence you play.
RUTH.   I'm not the one to plot so.
FRED.   Your face is lined, your hair is grey.
RUTH.   It's gradually got so.   210
FRED.   Faithless woman, to deceive me,
              I who trusted so!
RUTH.   Master, master, do not leave me!
              Hear me, ere you go!
              My love without reflecting,   215
              Oh, do not be rejecting.
        Take a maiden tender – her affection raw and green,
              At very highest rating,
              Has been accumulating
        Summers seventeen – summers seventeen.   220

230 *in this alarming costume*: This phrase originally went 'in this detested costume'. The word 'detested' was almost certainly dropped because it proved difficult to sing. The same reason probably explains the substitution of 'innocence' for the original 'ignorance' in line 207. 'Detested costume' appears in all editions of the vocal score, so it was probably before the first performance.

234–62 *Climbing over rocky mountain*
This song was substantially 'lifted' from Gilbert and Sullivan's first joint work, *Thespis*. There it was sung by a troupe of actors who had come to Mount Olympus for a picnic. In adapting it for the new opera, Gilbert made only one change, substituting the line 'Till the bright sea-shore they gain!' for the original 'Till the mountain top they gain' and altering the original 'hardy lads and lasses' to the 'hardy little lasses' of line 242. Even with those alterations, the song still seems a trifle incongruous in its setting. Gaining access to a Cornish beach hardly requires 'Climbing over rocky mountain' or 'Scaling rough and rugged passes' in the way that ascending Mount Olympus no doubt would.

The verses sung by Edith and Kate are also taken from the same song in *Thespis*, although here Gilbert was careful to make more alterations to suit the different circumstances of *The Pirates*. The lines now given to Kate, for example, were rather different when sung by the Thespians climbing Mount Olympus:

> Far away from grief and care,
> High up in the mountain air,
> Let us live and reign alone
> In a world that's all our own.
> Here enthroned in the sky,
> Far away from mortal eye,
> We'll be gods and make decrees,
> Those may honour them who please.

'Climbing over rocky mountain' is, in fact, one of only two songs in *Thespis* of which the music still survives. The other is the ballad 'Little Maid of Arcadee'.

The licence copy of *The Pirates* has an eight-line introductory chorus for General Stanley's daughters before they embark on 'Climbing over rocky mountain'. This was presumably sung at the Paignton performance:

ENSEMBLE.

RUTH.	FREDERIC.	
Don't, beloved master,	Yes, your former master	
Crush me with disaster.	Saves you from disaster.	
What is such a dower to the dower	Your love would be uncomfortably	
I have here?	fervid, it is clear,	
My love unabating	If, as you are stating,	225
Has been accumulating	It's been accumulating	
Forty-seven year – forty-seven year!	Forty-seven year – forty-seven year!	

(*At the end he renounces her, and she goes off in despair.*)

RECITATIVE – FREDERIC.

What shall I do? Before these gentle maidens
I dare not show in this alarming costume.   230
No, no, I must remain in close concealment
Until I can appear in decent clothing!

(*Hides in cave as they enter climbing over the rocks.*)

GIRLS.   Climbing over rocky mountain,
Skipping rivulet and fountain,   235
Passing where the willows quiver
By the ever-rolling river,
    Swollen with the summer rain;
Threading long and leafy mazes
Dotted with unnumbered daisies;   240
Scaling rough and rugged passes,
Climb the hardy little lasses,
    Till the bright sea-shore they gain!

EDITH.   Let us gaily tread the measure,
Make the most of fleeting leisure;   245
Hail it as a true ally,
Though it perish by and by.

ALL.   Hail it as a true ally,
    Though it perish by and by.

EDITH.   Every moment brings a treasure   250
Of its own especial pleasure,

With timid step and watchful eye
And pleasing palpitation
We will continue bye and bye
Our work of explanation
This cavern will afford us rest
Within its shade romantic
While we inhale, with grateful zest,
The breath of the Atlantic

'Explanation' at the end of the fourth line should surely be 'exploration' and must have been a mistake made by the hasty transcriber of the licence copy.

271 *Who are only human beings down to the waist*: This idea is employed again in *Iolanthe*, where Strephon is a fairy down to the waist and a mortal below it.

291 *Ladies, do not shun me*: The line originally written by Gilbert was 'Ladies, do not shudder!' Once again, it was probably changed because it proved difficult to sing. 'Shun me' is in all editions of the vocal score. In the following line, 'wild profession' was substituted for the original 'vile profession', which still appears in some editions of the libretto and is often sung.

Though the moments quickly die,
Greet them gaily as they fly.

KATE.   Far away from toil and care,
Revelling in fresh sea air,   255
Here we live and reign alone
In a world that's all our own.
Here in this our rocky den,
Far away from mortal men,
We'll be queens, and make decrees –   260
They may honour them who please.

ALL.   Let us gaily tread the measure, etc.

KATE. What a picturesque spot! I wonder where we are!
EDITH. And I wonder where papa is. We have left him ever so far behind.
ISABEL. Oh, he will be here presently! Remember poor papa is not as   265
young as we are, and we have come over a rather difficult country.
KATE. But how thoroughly delightful it is to be so entirely alone! Why,
in all probability we are the first human beings who ever set foot on this
enchanting spot.
ISABEL. Except the mermaids – it's the very place for mermaids.   270
KATE. Who are only human beings down to the waist!
EDITH. And who can't be said strictly to set *foot* anywhere. Tails they
may, but feet they *cannot*.
KATE. But what shall we do until papa and the servants arrive with the
luncheon?   275
EDITH. We are quite alone, and the sea is as smooth as glass. Suppose
we take off our shoes and stockings and paddle?
ALL. Yes, yes! The very thing! (*They prepare to carry out the suggestion.
They have all taken off one shoe, when* FREDERIC *comes forward from cave.*)

FRED. (*recitative*). Stop, ladies, pray!   280
ALL (*hopping on one foot*).   A man!
FRED.   I had intended
Not to intrude myself upon your notice
In this effective but alarming costume,
But under these peculiar circumstances   285
It is my bounden duty to inform you
That your proceedings will not be unwitnessed!
EDITH.   But who are you, sir? Speak!   (*All hopping.*)
FRED.   I am a pirate!
ALL (*recoiling, hopping*).   A pirate! Horror!   290
FRED.   Ladies, do not shun me!

299–322 *Oh, is there not one maiden breast*
The rhyming of 'beauty' and 'duty', which we noted in four songs in *H.M.S. Pinafore*, occurs in only three in *The Pirates*, despite the opera's sub-title and theme. In addition to this song, they are the girls' recitative 'The question is, had he not been/A thing of beauty' and Mabel's solo 'Did ever maiden wake/From dream of homely duty'.

This song shows very clearly how far Sullivan's music can, at times, transcend Gilbert's words to give a wholly different effect from that achieved by reading the lyrics in print. The beginning of the second verse, and particularly the line 'Whose homely face and bad complexion', reads like a comic dig from the *Bab Ballads*. Yet when sung to Sullivan's powerful, swelling melody it strikes a note of extreme pathos.

Gilbert's original version of this song would have been even less suitable for setting to Sullivan's soul-stirring tune:

FREDERIC. Oh do not spurn the pirate's tear,
Nor deem his grief unreal and frothy,
He longs to doff his pirate gear
And turn tall-hatty and broad-clothy.
He hates his life upon the wave,
And longs 'on change' to try his luck, oh –
He loathes his rude and draughty cave,
And sighs for brick relieved with stucco.

ALL. We do not spurn the pirate's tear,
Nor deem his grief unreal and frothy.
He's right to drop his pirate gear
And turn tall-hatty and broad-clothy.

This evening I renounce my wild profession;
And to that end, oh, pure and peerless maidens!
Oh, blushing buds of ever-blooming beauty!
I, sore at heart, implore your kind assistance.   295

EDITH.   How pitiful his tale!
KATE.   How rare his beauty!
ALL.   How pitiful his tale!   How rare his beauty!

SONG – FREDERIC.

Oh, is there not one maiden breast
   Which does not feel the moral beauty   300
Of making worldly interest
   Subordinate to sense of duty?
Who would not give up willingly
   All matrimonial ambition,
To rescue such an one as I   305
   From his unfortunate position?

ALL.   Alas! there's not one maiden breast
   Which seems to feel the moral beauty
Of making worldly interest
   Subordinate to sense of duty!   310

FRED.   Oh, is there not one maiden here
   Whose homely face and bad complexion
Have caused all hopes to disappear
   Of ever winning man's affection?
To such an one, if such there be,   315
   I swear by Heaven's arch above you,
If you will cast your eyes on me –
   However plain you be – I'll love you!

ALL.   Alas! there's not one maiden here
   Whose homely face and bad complexion   320
Have caused all hope to disappear
   Of ever winning man's affection!

FRED. (*in despair*). Not one?
ALL.   No, no – not one!
FRED. Not one?   325
ALL.   No, no!

(MABEL *enters.*)

330 *Yes, 'tis Mabel*: In the licence copy, and likewise in the original Paignton performance, there was no recitative or solo song for Mabel after she had so dramatically responded to Frederic's plea. Instead, there was the following ensemble, sung, it would seem, to the same tune as Frederic's earlier solo:

FREDERIC.	Oh joy, of all the maidens here The fairest with the best complexion So sweet a face and eyes so clear Might chain an anchorite's affection!
MABEL.	Although indifferent I fear My face and form and my complexion These blemishes will disappear Before the ardour of affection!
EDITH.	Yes, yes, it is extremely clear Her homely face and bad complexion Have caused all hope to disappear Of ever winning man's affection
ALL.	Yes, yes, it is extremely clear etc.

343–56 *Poor wandering one*

This seductive waltz song, with its dazzling coloratura trills and cadences – the 'farmyard effects', as Sullivan called them – was at least in part a deliberate skit on the 'operacrobatics' which Gounod and other French and Italian opera composers had made fashionable. Whether parody or not, however, it stands as a perfect and delightful example of the genre.

As already noted above, 'Poor wandering one' was composed at the last minute for the American production of *The Pirates* and did not figure in the licence copy or the Paignton performance. The last line of the first section, following 'Thy steps retrace', was originally 'Be not afraid'. It was probably altered to 'Poor wandering one!' by Sullivan as being easier to set in that form.

MABEL.	Yes, one!	
ALL.	'Tis Mabel!	
MABEL.	Yes, 'tis Mabel!	330

RECITATIVE – MABEL.

Oh, sisters, deaf to pity's name,
> For shame!
It's true that he has gone astray,
> But pray
Is that a reason good and true   335
> Why you
Should all be deaf to pity's name?

ALL (*aside*).   The question is, had he not been
> A thing of beauty,
Would she be swayed by quite as keen   340
> A sense of duty?

MABEL.   For shame, for shame, for shame!

SONG – MABEL.

Poor wandering one!
Though thou hast surely strayed,
> Take heart of grace,   345
> Thy steps retrace,
Poor wandering one!
Poor wandering one!
If such poor love as mine
> Can help thee find   350
> True peace of mind –
Why, take it, it is thine!
> Take heart, fair days will shine;
> Take any heart – take mine!

ALL.   Take heart; no danger lowers;   355
Take any heart – but ours!

(*Exeunt* MABEL *and* FREDERIC.)

(EDITH *beckons her sisters, who form in a semicircle
around her.*)

360–75 *What ought we to do*: In the licence copy Edith and Kate's verses are replaced by a passage for Edith and the chorus:

EDITH.	Now stern propriety we know Bids us remain in solemn tether
ALL.	Yes, yes. Yes, yes.
EDITH.	While delicacy bids us go And leave the plighted pair together
ALL.	Yes, yes, yes, yes.
EDITH.	Suppose we make a compromise For oh, our hearts are not of leather.
ALL.	Yes, yes, yes, yes.
EDITH.	Suppose we stop and shut our eyes And talk discreetly of the weather?
ALL.	Yes, yes, yes, yes, We'll talk discreetly of the weather.

377–84 *How beautifully blue the sky*

The simultaneous singing of two tunes with completely different speeds and moods, which occurs here with dramatic effect, is a trick which Sullivan used several times in the Savoy Operas. It happens again in Act II of *The Pirates*, when Mabel and Edith's 'Go, ye heroes, go to glory' is sung over the policemen's 'When the foeman bears his steel'. Perhaps the most sophisticated example is the lead-in to the trio 'To sit in solemn silence' in *The Mikado*, where Nanki-Poo, Pooh-Bah and Pish-Tush each have their own tune to express their particular mood.

EDITH.

What ought we to do,   360
  Gentle sisters, say?
Propriety, we know,
  Says we ought to stay;
While sympathy exclaims,
  'Free them from your tether –   365
Play at other games –
  Leave them here together.'

KATE.

Her case may, any day,
  Be yours, my dear, or mine.
Let her make her hay   370
  While the sun doth shine.
Let us compromise,
  (Our hearts are not of leather.)
Let us shut our eyes,
  And talk about the weather.   375

GIRLS.   Yes, yes, let's talk about the weather.

CHATTERING CHORUS.

How beautifully blue the sky,
The glass is rising very high,
Continue fine I hope it may,
And yet it rained but yesterday.   380
To-morrow it may pour again
(I hear the country wants some rain),
Yet people say, I know not why,
That we shall have a warm July.

(*Enter* MABEL *and* FREDERIC.)   385

(*During* MABEL'S *solo the Girls continue chatter pianissimo,
but listening eagerly all the time.*)

SOLO – MABEL.

Did ever maiden wake
  From dream of homely duty,
To find her daylight break   390
  With such exceeding beauty?
Did ever maiden close

399–402 *Did ever pirate roll*
  In editions of the libretto up to 1914, Frederic's solo balanced Mabel's and had these extra lines, together with a final response from Mabel, which followed 'With peace and virtue beaming?':

> Did ever pirate loathed
> Forsake his hideous mission,
> To find himself betrothed
> To a lady of position?

MABEL.   Ah yes, ah, yes, I am a lady of position.

In fact the lines beginning 'Did ever pirate loathed' are now generally sung by Frederic in the ensemble which follows his solo.

415 *Nice companions for young ladies*: The original libretto had 'nice associates for young ladies'. The word was almost certainly changed before the opening night, no doubt because it was difficult to sing. 'Companions' appears in the earliest vocal score.
416 *Let us disappear*: This line should really read: 'Let us disap– *(shriek)*' for so it is always sung: the pirates appear before the ladies can finish the word.
  In the licence copy and the first Paignton performance the entrance of the pirates was slightly postponed, allowing the ladies to finish their chorus and giving Edith a chance to change her mind and ask Frederic whether there might not be another pirate for her to help along the path of virtue:

EDITH.   Stay, before we terminate this most romantic of adventures
Tell me, are there any others nearly out of their indentures
And prentice who desirous to give up his dreadful trade is
If so we will gladly help him

FRED.   No there isn't one, young ladies
All confirmed desperadoes they would certainly be termed.

EDITH *(disappointed)*. I'm sorry they are desperadoes but I'm glad they've been confirmed.

ALL.   We're sorry that they are desperadoes, but we're glad they've been confirmed.

Come, we must not lose our senses, etc.

Her eyes on waking sadness,
To dream of such exceeding gladness?

FRED.   Oh, yes! ah, yes! this is exceeding gladness.   395

GIRLS.   How beautifully blue the sky, etc.

SOLO – FREDERIC.

(During this, Girls continue their chatter pianissimo as before, but listening intently all the time.)

Did ever pirate roll
His soul in guilty dreaming,   400
And wake to find that soul
With peace and virtue beaming?

ENSEMBLE.

MABEL.	FREDERIC.	GIRLS.
Did ever maiden wake, etc.	Did ever pirate loathed, etc.	How beautifully blue the sky, etc.

RECITATIVE – FREDERIC.

Stay, we must not lose our senses;
Men who stick at no offences   405
Will anon be here.
Piracy their dreadful trade is;
Pray you, get you hence, young ladies,
While the coast is clear.

(FREDERIC *and* MABEL *retire.*)   410

GIRLS.   No, we must not lose our senses,
If they stick at no offences
We should not be here.
Piracy their dreadful trade is –
Nice companions for young ladies!   415
Let us disappear.

(During this chorus the Pirates have entered stealthily, and formed in a semicircle behind the Girls. As the Girls move to go off each Pirate seizes a girl. KING *seizes* EDITH *and* ISABEL, SAMUEL *seizes* KATE.*)*

438 *your pirate caravanserai*: 'Caravanserai' is a curious word to use in connection with Cornish pirates, being more usually associated with travellers in the Middle East. The word, which is of Persian origin, actually means a building for sheltering caravans with a large inner court for camels and mules, surrounded by rooms for the travellers to rest and store their goods. But I suppose some licence is permissible when you are trying to find something to rhyme with 'Wards in Chancery'.

440 *we are Wards in Chancery*: Even granted Gilbert's special fondness for Wards in Chancery (he makes Phyllis one in *Iolanthe*) it is a little difficult to see why Major-General Stanley's daughters should have been put into this category. Minors are normally put under the care and guardianship of the Court of Chancery if they are orphans or to protect them from their parents. Neither of those reasons would seem applicable here. The most likely explanation is that, faced with so many daughters to clothe and educate, Stanley himself had them made wards so that he could release money which they were due to inherit. Those due to inherit property when they come of age become wards of court if any legal question arises about the property.

441 *Major-General*: The most junior rank of general in the British Army; a major-general commands a division or district or holds a senior staff appointment. Above him comes a lieutenant-general, who commands a corps, and a full general, who commands an army in the field or holds a staff appointment of great importance.

ALL.	Too late!	420
PIRATES.	Ha! Ha!	
ALL.	Too late!	
PIRATES.	Ho! Ho!	

Ha! ha! ha! ha! Ho! ho! ho! ho!

ENSEMBLE.

(*Pirates pass in front of Girls.*)	(*Girls pass in front of Pirates.*)	425
PIRATES.	GIRLS.	

Here's a first-rate opportunity	We have missed our opportunity	
To get married with impunity,	Of escaping with impunity;	
And indulge in the felicity	So farewell to the felicity	
Of unbounded domesticity.	Of our maiden domesticity!	
You shall quickly be parsonified,	We shall quickly be parsonified,	430
Conjugally matrimonified,	Conjugally matrimonified,	
By a doctor of divinity,	By a doctor of divinity,	
Who resides in this vicinity.	Who resides in this vicinity.	

ALL.

By a doctor of divinity,
Who resides in this vicinity,   435
By a doctor, a doctor, a doctor,
Of divinity, of divinity.

MABEL (*coming forward*).

RECITATIVE.

Hold, monsters! Ere your pirate caravanserai
Proceed, against our will, to wed us all,
Just bear in mind that we are Wards in Chancery,   440
And father is a Major-General!

SAM. (*cowed*). We'd better pause, or danger may befall,
Their father is a Major-General.

GIRLS. Yes, yes; he is a Major-General!

(*The* MAJOR-GENERAL *has entered unnoticed, on rock.*)   445

GEN.	Yes, I am a Major-General!	
SAM.	For he is a Major-General!	
ALL.	He is! Hurrah for the Major-General!	
GEN.	And it is – it is a glorious thing	
	To be a Major-General!	450
ALL.	It is! Hurrah for the Major-General!	

452–96 *I am the very model of a modern Major-General*
Major-General Stanley introduces himself in one of the fastest and most famous of all the Gilbert and Sullivan patter songs. It must also be one of the most parodied. The American comedian Tom Lehrer set the entire table of chemical elements to the tune, beginning 'There's antimony, arsenic, aluminum, selenium'.

In its original version the song began 'I am the very pattern of a modern Major-General'. Its distinctive rhythm, with sixteen syllables to the line, is found in the Grand Duke Rudolph's song 'A pattern to professors of monarchical autonomy' in *The Grand Duke*, which contains the major-general-like line 'I weigh out tea and sugar with precision mathematical'.

455 *From Marathon to Waterloo*: The battle of Marathon was fought between the Greeks and the Persians in 490 B.C. A messenger ran the twenty-two miles from the battle site to Athens to convey the news of the Greek victory and dropped down dead on arrival. Marathon races take their name from this incident. The battle of Waterloo was fought between the English and the French in 1815 ten miles south of Brussels but won, according to the Duke of Wellington, on the playing fields of Eton.

458 *binomial theorem*: The law of the formation of any power of a binomial, i.e. an expression of two terms connected by the signs plus or minus, which was first expounded by Sir Isaac Newton. And if you can understand that, you are a cleverer man than I. There is an echo of the Major-General's mathematical ability in Gilbert's Bab Ballad 'My Dream', where the writer dreams that he is living in a land of highly numerate babies:

> For, as their nurses dandle them,
> They crow binomial theorem,
> With views (it seems absurd to us)
> On differential calculus.

461 *integral and differential calculus*: Differential calculus is the branch of mathematics dealing with the calculation of the rate of change of variable quantities. Integral calculus deals with the calculation of variable quantities from their rate of change and also with the calculation of areas and volumes. Together, these two branches are sometimes known as 'infinitesimal calculus', so the Major-General was doubtless very good at that too.

462 *beings animalculous*: An animalcule is a microscopic animal.

467 *King Arthur's and Sir Caradoc's*: The historical evidence for King Arthur, who is said to have been a British king who led the natives' fight against the advancing Saxons in the sixth century A.D., is scanty but there is an abundance of myth and legend about him and his knights of the Round Table. Sir Caradoc was one of those knights. An old ballad tells how the chastity of the ladies at King Arthur's court was tested by a boy using his mantle, a boar's head and a golden horn. Sir Caradoc's wife alone underwent the ordeal and proved her fidelity.

468 *hard acrostics*: Acrostics was a popular Victorian parlour game, rather like charades, in which players had to guess at one-word answers to a series of clues. The first letters of these answers spelt out the overall answer.

469 *elegiacs*: The classical verse form of alternating hexameters and pentameters in which elegies were written.
Heliogabalus: Perhaps the most dissolute of all Roman emperors. He ruled from A.D. 218 to 222 under the name Marcus Aurelius Antonius and was murdered by the pretorian guards. He is also mentioned in *Utopia Limited* when Tarara, the Public Exploder, says that the King of Utopia is 'one of the most Heliogabalian profligates that ever disgraced an autocratic throne'.

470 *conics*: The geometric properties of a cone when cut by imaginary planes.

SONG – MAJOR-GENERAL.

I am the very model of a modern Major-General,
I've information vegetable, animal, and mineral,
I know the kings of England, and I quote the fights historical,
From Marathon to Waterloo, in order categorical;   455
I'm very well acquainted too with matters mathematical,
I understand equations, both the simple and quadratical,
About binomial theorem I'm teeming with a lot o' news –
With many cheerful facts about the square of the hypotenuse.

ALL. With many cheerful facts, etc.   460

GEN. I'm very good at integral and differential calculus,
I know the scientific names of beings animalculous;
In short, in matters vegetable, animal, and mineral,
I am the very model of a modern Major-General.

ALL. In short, in matters vegetable, animal, and mineral,   465
He is the very model of a modern Major-General.

GEN. I know our mythic history, King Arthur's and Sir Caradoc's,
I answer hard acrostics, I've a pretty taste for paradox,
I quote in elegiacs all the crimes of Heliogabalus,
In conics I can floor peculiarities parabolous.   470
I can tell undoubted Raphaels from Gerard Dows and Zoffanies,
I know the croaking chorus from the *Frogs* of Aristophanes,
Then I can hum a fugue of which I've heard the music's din afore,
And whistle all the airs from that infernal nonsense *Pinafore*.

ALL. And whistle all the airs, etc.   475

GEN. Then I can write a washing bill in Babylonic cuneiform,
And tell you every detail of Caractacus's uniform;
In short, in matters vegetable, animal, and mineral,
I am the very model of a modern Major-General.

ALL. In short, in matters vegetable, animal, and mineral,   480
He is the very model of a modern Major-General.

GEN. In fact, when I know what is meant by 'mamelon' and 'ravelin,'
When I can tell at sight a Mauser rifle from a javelin,
When such affairs as sorties and surprises I'm more wary at,
And when I know precisely what is meant by 'commissariat',   485
When I have learnt what progress has been made in modern
     gunnery,
When I know more of tactics than a novice in a nunnery;

470 *parabolous*: Pertaining to parabolas. The usual adjective is 'parabolic', but try rhyming that with 'Heliogabalus'.

471 *undoubted Raphaels*: The Italian artist Raffaello Sanzio (1483-1520), better-known as Raphael, was one of the creators of the movement in art known as the Renaissance. In the mid-nineteenth century a group of artists calling themselves the Pre-Raphaelites sought to re-create the pre-Renaissance style of painting. It was the affectations of this latter group, and the aesthetic movement which they helped to create, which Gilbert satirized in *Patience*.

Gerard Dows: Gerard Dou (1613-75), a Dutch portrait painter and pupil of Rembrandt.

Zoffanies: Johann Zoffany (1725-1810), a portrait painter who was born in Germany but settled in England, becoming a founder member of the Royal Academy.

472 *the Frogs of Aristophanes*: *The Frogs*, with its croaking chorus 'Berkekekex, koax, koax', is perhaps the best-known of the plays of the Greek dramatist Aristophanes (*c.* 445–385 B.C.).

473 *fugue*: A musical composition based on a short theme which is contrapuntally harmonized and reintroduced from time to time. Among the Mikado's punishments designed to fit the crime is compulsory attendance by the music-hall singer at 'a series of masses and fugues and "ops" by Bach'.

474 *that infernal nonsense Pinafore*: This is one of two occasions when one Savoy Opera is mentioned in another. The Mikado of Japan is mentioned in *Utopia Limited*. Captain Corcoran of *H.M.S. Pinafore* makes a re-appearance in the same opera, but the name of his ship is not mentioned.

476 *Babylonic cuneiform*: A system of writing used extensively in the Near East from around the end of the fourth millennium B.C. to the end of the first century B.C. The characters were pressed into soft clay tablets with the slanted edge of a stylus and thus had a wedge-shaped appearance. The Latin word *cuneus* means wedge.

477 *Caractacus's uniform*: Caractacus was the Roman name for the British chief Caradoc (not to be confused with the much later Sir Caradoc), who maintained a fierce resistance to the Romans after they landed in Britain in A.D. 43. He usually went into battle clad only in body paint, so his uniform was not as difficult to describe as Major-General Stanley's boast suggests.

482 *'mamelon' and 'ravelin'*: Major-General Stanley need make no apology for being ignorant of these words, which are both archaic terms relating to earthworks and hardly necessary to the vocabulary of a modern major-general. A mamelon was a rounded hillock or mound suitable for use in an ambush or sniping attack; a ravelin was a detached outwork outside the main ditch of a fort.

483 *Mauser rifle*: Gilbert originally wrote 'Chassepôt rifle' here, and the line still appears in that form in certain editions of the libretto, including the Macmillan paperback. A Chassepôt rifle, named after its inventor, was used by the French in the Franco-Prussian War of 1870. Towards the end of his life, certainly after the 1907 revival of *The Pirates*, when 'Chassepôt' was still sung, Gilbert changed the phrase to 'Mauser rifle'. The Mauser rifle, better-known than the Chassepôt, was developed for the Prussian army in the early 1870s.

485 *commissariat*: The food and stores department of an army.

489 *sat a gee*: Sat on a horse ('gee-gee'). At this point in many productions of *The Pirates* the Major-General gallops around the stage on an imaginary horse. In the D'Oyly Carte encores of this verse, the Major-General surprised and confused the chorus by coming out with the line 'You'll say a better Major-General has never rode a horse'.

493 *But still in matters vegetable*: In early versions, the word 'learning' occurs instead of 'matters' in the Major-General's last verse and in the final chorus. The order of the phrase is, of course, normally 'animal, vegetable and mineral', as it was in the popular quiz series which ran through the 1950s and 1960s on BBC radio.

497 *now that I've introduced myself*: Like Sir Joseph Porter in *H.M.S. Pinafore*, Major-General Stanley was at least partly modelled by Gilbert on a well-known contemporary figure.

In short, when I've a smattering of elemental strategy,
You'll say a better Major-General has never *sat* a gee –

ALL. You'll say a better, etc.   490

GEN. For my military knowledge, though I'm plucky and adventury,
Has only been brought down to the beginning of the century;
But still in matters vegetable, animal, and mineral,
I am the very model of a modern Major-General.

ALL. But still in matters vegetable, animal, and mineral,   495
He is the very model of a modern Major-General.

GEN. And now that I've introduced myself I should like to have some
idea of what's going on.
KATE. Oh, papa – we —
SAM. Permit me, I'll explain in two words: we propose to marry your   500
daughters.
GEN. Dear me!
GIRLS. Against our wills, papa – against our wills!
GEN. Oh, but you mustn't do that! May I ask – this is a picturesque
uniform, but I'm not familiar with it – What are you?   505
KING. We are all single gentlemen.
GEN. Yes, I gathered that – anything else?
KING. No, nothing else.
EDITH. Papa, don't believe them; they are pirates – the famous Pirates
of Penzance!   510
GEN. The Pirates of Penzance! I have often heard of them.
MABEL. All except this gentleman – (*indicating* FREDERIC) – who was
a pirate once, but who is out of his indentures to-day, and who means to
lead a blameless life evermore.
GEN. But wait a bit. I object to pirates as sons-in-law.   515
KING. We object to Major-Generals as fathers-in-law. But we waive
that point. We do not press it. We look over it.
GEN. (*aside.*) Hah! an idea! (*Aloud.*) And do you mean to say that you
would deliberately rob me of these, the sole remaining props of my old age,
and leave me to go through the remainder of my life unfriended,   520
unprotected, and alone?
KING. Well, yes, that's the idea.
GEN. Tell me, have you ever known what it is to be an orphan?
PIRATES (*disgusted*). Oh, dash it all!
KING. Here we are again!   525
GEN. I ask you, have you ever known what it is to be an orphan?
KING. Often!

497 George Grossmith, who created the role in London, was given the elegantly twirled moustache and the slightly imperious manner of Sir Garnet Wolseley, one of the most dashing commanders in the British Army, who had led the British forces in the Ashanti Wars of 1873 and who was to be·sent out to Khartoum in 1885 to relieve General Gordon.

At the time when *The Pirates of Penzance* was being written, Lieutenant-General Wolseley (he had been promoted from Major-General the previous year) was leading a successful expedition to capture the rebellious Zulu king, Cetewayo. He returned to the War Office as quartermaster-general with specific responsibility for reforming the structure of the Army.

Unlike Major-General Stanley, Sir Garnet Wolseley was the very model of a modern military commander. In 1869 he had published *The Soldier's Pocket Book*, a manual of military organization and tactics which was the forerunner of the modern field service regulations. His considerable skills of organization and management gave rise to the saying 'All Sir Garnet', meaning all's well, while his military adventuring was commended in another of the Savoy Operas when Colonel Calverley in *Patience* sang of the 'Skill of Sir Garnet in thrashing a cannibal'.

Wolseley, who revelled in publicity, was delighted to be taken as the model for the modern Major-General and enjoyed singing the patter song to his friends and family at home.

Wolseley may not have been the only contemporary figure that Gilbert had in mind when he created the character of Major-General Stanley. Trevor Hearl, a historian of Victorian military education, believes that Sir Edward Hamley, commandant of the Staff College at Camberley from 1870 to 1877, may also have been a model for the modern Major-General. Hamley believed that military history was more valuable to soldiers than military science – a sentiment which would certainly have found favour with Major-General Stanley.

531 *I don't think we quite understand one another*: Feeling that the 'orphan'/'often' joke went on for too long and became rather laboured, the D'Oyly Carte Opera Company generally cut all the dialogue from this point until the Major-General's remark: 'When you said "orphan", did you mean "orphan" – a person who has lost his parents, or "often" – frequently?' Joseph Papp, however, retained the full exchange between the Major-General and the King.

It is interesting to note that Sir Garnet Wolseley was himself orphaned, or at least half-orphaned, at the age of seven, when his father died, leaving his mother to bring up four sons and three daughters, although it seems unlikely that this was the source of Gilbert's idea.

553 *How sad – an orphan boy*: At this point, and before the Major-General's solo, the licence copy, and presumably also the Paignton performance, had an ensemble which anticipates the later 'I'm telling a terrible story':

ENSEMBLE

GENERAL (aside)	GIRLS (aside)
Oh what a story I am telling	Oh what a fib papa is telling
My parents close to us are dwelling	His parents close to us are dwelling
These simple pirates I am selling	These simple privates* he is selling
Oh what a story I am telling	Oh what a fib papa is telling

PIRATES (in tears)
Oh sad indeed the tale he's telling
And pity from our bosoms welling
All ferocity is quelling
Sad indeed the tale he's telling

*This should presumably be 'pirates'.

GEN. Yes, orphan. Have you ever known what it is to be one?

KING. I say, often.

ALL (*disgusted*). Often, often, often. (*Turning away.*) 530

GEN. I don't think we quite understand one another. I ask you, have you ever known what it is to be an orphan, and you say 'orphan'. As I understand you, you are merely repeating the word 'orphan' to show that you understand me.

KING. I didn't repeat the word often. 535

GEN. Pardon me, you did indeed.

KING. I only repeated it once.

GEN. True, but you repeated it.

KING. But not often.

GEN. Stop: I think I see where we are getting confused. When you said 540 'orphan', did you mean 'orphan' – a person who has lost his parents, or 'often' – frequently?

KING. Ah! I beg pardon – I see what you mean – frequently.

GEN. Ah! you said often – frequently.

KING. No, only once. 545

GEN. (*irritated*). Exactly – you said often, frequently, only once.

RECITATIVE – GENERAL.

Oh, men of dark and dismal fate,
   Forgo your cruel employ,
Have pity on my lonely state,
   I am an orphan boy! 550

KING *and* SAM.   An orphan boy?

GEN.   An orphan boy!

PIRATES.   How sad – an orphan boy.

SOLO – GENERAL.

These children whom you see
   Are all that I can call my own! 555

PIRATES.   Poor fellow!

GEN.   Take them away from me
   And I shall be indeed alone.

PIRATES.   Poor fellow!

GEN.   If pity you can feel, 560
   Leave me my sole remaining joy –
See, at your feet they kneel;
Your hearts you cannot steel
  Against the sad, sad tale of the lonely orphan boy!

PIRATES (*sobbing*).   Poor fellow! 565

588–91 *Hail, Poetry, thou heaven-born maid*

Listening to this remarkable hymn to poetry, which is sung unaccompanied, it is not difficult to see why Sullivan was regarded as one of the leading composers of sacred music in Victorian Britain. He produced numerous anthems and sacred part-songs as well as forty-one hymn tunes. Among the hymns which are still sung to his tunes are 'Onward, Christian soldiers', 'Lead, kindly Light', 'Love Divine, all loves excelling', 'God moves in a mysterious way' and 'Rock of ages'.

Possibly because of Sullivan's difficulty in setting this hymn, Gilbert's original manuscript shows that the line 'Thou gildest e'en the pirate's trade' was rewritten four times, twice being changed to 'That gild'st the Pirates' trade' before it was finally restored to the original version.

> See at our feet they kneel;
> Our hearts we cannot steel
> Against the sad, sad tale of the lonely orphan boy!

SAM.　　　　The orphan boy!

SAM *and* KING.　　　　　　　　The orphan boy!　　　　570
> See at our feet they kneel, etc.

ENSEMBLE.

GENERAL (*aside*).	GIRLS (*aside*).	PIRATES (*aside*).
I'm telling a terrible story,	He's telling a terrible story,	If he's telling a terrible story,
But it doesn't diminish my glory;	Which will tend to diminish his glory;	He shall die by a death that is gory,
For they would have taken my daughters	Though they would have taken his daughters	One of the cruellest slaughters
Over the billowy waters,	Over the billowy waters.	That ever were known in these waters;
If I hadn't, in elegant diction,	It's easy, in elegant diction,	And we'll finish his moral affliction
Indulged in an innocent fiction;	To call it an innocent fiction,	By a very complete male-diction,
Which is not the same category	But it comes in the same category	As a compliment valedict*ory*,
As a regular terrible story.	As a regular terrible story.	If he's telling a terrible story.

(line 575 aligns at "these waters;" row)

KING.　　　Although our dark career　　　　　　　580
> 　　Sometimes involves the crime of stealing,
> We rather think that we're
> 　　Not altogether void of feeling.
> Although we live by strife,
> 　　We're always sorry to begin it,　　　　585
> For what, we ask, is life
> 　　Without a touch of Poetry in it?

ALL　　　　Hail, Poetry, thou heaven-born maid!
(*kneeling*).　Thou gildest e'en the pirate's trade:
> 　　　　　Hail, flowing fount of sentiment!　　590
> 　　　　　All hail, Divine Emollient! (*All rise.*)

KING.　You may go, for you're at liberty, our pirate rules protect you,
> And honorary members of our band we do elect you!

SAM.　　　　For he is an orphan boy.
CHORUS.　He is! Hurrah for the orphan boy.　　　　595

GEN.　　　And it sometimes is a useful thing
> 　　To be an orphan boy.
CHORUS.　It is! Hurrah for the orphan boy!

616–23 *Pray observe the magnanimity*

The licence copy and the original Paignton production had a different finale to Act I from that performed at the New York première and ever since. Instead of the final ensemble it has the following song for the Pirate King and chorus:

KING.	Comrades, let us join in plighting These, our honorary members May the fire of friendship's lightning Never sink to dust and embers
CHORUS.	May the fire, etc.
KING.	Oh remember – Major-General And remember – Wards in Chancery You are welcome – nine or ten – or all To our Pirate Caravanserai
ALL.	We ⎱ They ⎰ are welcome nine or ten in all. To { their / our } pirate caravanserai
KING.	For we all are orphan boys
ALL.	We are! Hurrah for the orphan boys
KING.	And it is, it is a Kindly Thing To spare all orphan boys
ALL.	It is! Hurrah for the orphan boys.

617 *dimity*: Cotton cloth with raised thread patterns, traditionally used for bedroom hangings.

ENSEMBLE.

Oh, happy day, with joyous glee
We ⎫
They ⎭ will away and married be;   600
Should it befall auspiciously,
My ⎫
Her ⎭ sisters all will bridesmaids be!

(RUTH *enters and comes down to* FREDERIC.)

RUTH.	Oh, master, hear one word, I do implore you!
	Remember Ruth, your Ruth, who kneels before you! 605
PIRATES.	Yes, yes, remember Ruth, who kneels before you!
FRED.	Away, you did deceive me! (*Pirates threaten* RUTH.)
PIRATES.	Away, you did deceive him!

RUTH.	Oh, do not leave me!
PIRATES.	Oh, do not leave her! 610

FRED.	Away, you grieve me!
PIRATES.	Away, you grieve him!

FRED.	I wish you'd leave me!
	(FREDERIC *casts* RUTH *from him. Exit* RUTH.)
PIRATES.	We wish you'd leave him! 615

ENSEMBLE.

Pray observe the magnanimity
We ⎫
They ⎭ display to lace and dimity!
Never was such opportunity
To get married with impunity,
But ⎰ we ⎱ give up the felicity   620
    ⎱ they ⎰
Of unbounded domesticity,
Though a doctor of divinity
Resides in this vicinity.

(*Girls and* GENERAL *go up rocks, while Pirates indulge in a wild dance of delight on stage. The* GENERAL *produces a British flag, and the* PIRATE KING 625 *produces a black flag with skull and cross-bones. Enter* RUTH, *who makes a final appeal to* FREDERIC, *who casts her from him.*)

END OF ACT I

4 *That dews that martial cheek*: The same imagery occurs towards the end of Act I of *Patience* in the Duke of Dunstable's line 'A tear-drop dews each martial eye'.

16 *heaven has lit her lamp*: This phrase is reminiscent of the first line of the much-loved Victorian parlour ballad 'The moon has raised· her lamp above' from Benedict's operetta *The Lily of Killarney*.

17 *The twilight hour is past*: Gilbert wrote this line as 'The midnight hour is past', and so it still appears in the Macmillan edition. Yet a little later on, at lines 49-51, he has Frederic announcing that 'At eleven, and before midnight I hope to have atoned for my involuntary association with the pestilent scourges by sweeping them from the face of the earth'. A note by Rupert D'Oyly Carte in his copy of the libretto reads: 'This seems to be Gilbert nodding or Frederic's watch is wrong'. Since 1930 the D'Oyly Carte Company has substituted 'twilight' for 'midnight' in Mabel's song to make chronological sense of this apparent paradox.

ACT II

Scene. – A ruined chapel by moonlight. Ruined Gothic windows at back.
General Stanley discovered seated pensively, surrounded by his daughters.

CHORUS.

Oh, dry the glistening tear
    That dews that martial cheek;
Thy loving children hear,   5
    In them thy comfort seek.
With sympathetic care
    Their arms around thee creep,
For oh, they cannot bear
    To see their father weep!   10

(Enter Mabel.)

SOLO – Mabel.

Dear father, why leave your bed
    At this untimely hour,
When happy daylight is dead,
    And darksome dangers lower?   15
See, heaven has lit her lamp,
    The twilight hour is past,
The chilly night air is damp,
    And the dews are falling fast!
Dear father, why leave your bed   20
When happy daylight is dead?

Chorus.   Oh, dry the glistening tear, etc.

*(*Frederic *enters.)*

Mabel. Oh, Frederic, cannot you, in the calm excellence of your wisdom,

34 *the stucco in your baronial hall*: This was originally 'the stucco on your baronial castle'. 'Stucco' is a word of Italian origin for a smooth plaster made of lime and sand, used to face walls. The original phrase is still found in American editions of the libretto and was used in Joseph Papp's production on both sides of the Atlantic.

35-6 *With the estate, I bought the chapel and its contents*: Gilbert's sharp social comment on the attitudes of the *nouveaux riches* in this and the next few lines is sometimes taken as a further dig at Sir Garnet Wolseley, who bought land as a way of establishing himself as a man of position and escaping from his relatively humble origins. I am doubtful, however, if Gilbert had this in mind when writing these lines. It was not a conspicuous part of Wolseley's make-up and he certainly never boasted about his newly acquired ancestors as Stanley does. He didn't need to: his own family were a junior branch of the well-established Staffordshire Wolseleys and had held land in County Carlow, Ireland, under William III.

43 *I assure you, Frederic*: The passage beginning 'I assure you' and ending 'most disastrous to myself' was added for the 1908 revival of *The Pirates* with Gilbert's apparent approval. It is also found in an expanded form, in the licence copy.

59–119 *When the foeman bares his steel*
The entrance of the Sergeant of Police (in the original New York production of *The Pirates* given the name Edward) and his trusty if rather nervous constables is one of the funniest moments in all the Savoy Operas. It almost invariably involves some business on stage. In D'Oyly Carte productions the sergeant trips up on some imaginary object on stage, which he ever afterwards steps gingerly over although no one else is troubled by it.

reconcile it with your conscience to say something that will relieve my   25
father's sorrow?

FRED. I will try, dear Mabel. But why does he sit, night after night, in
this draughty old ruin?

GEN. Why do I sit here? To escape from the pirates' clutches, I
described myself as an orphan, and, heaven help me, I am no orphan! I come   30
here to humble myself before the tombs of my ancestors, and to implore their
pardon for having brought dishonour on the family escutcheon.

FRED. But you forget, sir, you only bought the property a year ago, and
the stucco in your baronial hall is scarcely dry.

GEN. Frederic, in this chapel are ancestors: you cannot deny that. With   35
the estate, I bought the chapel and its contents. I don't know whose ancestors
they *were*, but I know whose ancestors they *are*, and I shudder to think that
their descendant by purchase (if I may so describe myself) should have
brought disgrace upon what, I have no doubt, was an unstained escutcheon.

FRED. Be comforted. Had you not acted as you did, these reckless men   40
would assuredly have called in the nearest clergyman, and have married
your large family on the spot.

GEN. I thank you for your proffered solace, but it is unavailing. I assure
you, Frederic, that such is the anguish and remorse I feel at the abominable
falsehood by which I escaped these easily deluded pirates, that I would go   45
to their simple-minded chief this very night and confess all, did I not fear
that the consequences would be most disastrous to myself. At what time
does your expedition march against these scoundrels?

FRED. At eleven, and before midnight I hope to have atoned for my
involuntary association with the pestilent scourges by sweeping them from   50
the face of the earth – and then, dear Mabel, you will be mine!

GEN. Are your devoted followers at hand?

FRED. They are, they only wait my orders.

RECITATIVE – GENERAL.

Then, Frederic, let your escort lion-hearted
Be summoned to receive a General's blessing,   55
Ere they depart upon their dread adventure.

FRED. Dear sir, they come.

(*Enter Police, marching in single file. They form in line facing audience.*)

SONG – SERGEANT, *with* POLICE.

When the foeman bares his steel,
          Tarantara! tarantara!   60

Sullivan had a particular reason for responding to Gilbert's idea of a chorus of singing policemen. As organist at St Michael's, Chester Square, a fashionable West End church, in the late 1860s, he had made its choir one of the best in London. 'We were well off for soprani and contralti', he wrote later, 'but at first I was at my wit's end for tenors and basses. However, close by St Michael's Church was Cottage Row Police Station, and here I completed my choir. The Chief Superintendant threw himself heartily into my scheme, and from the police I gathered six tenors and six basses, with a small reserve. And capital fellows they were. However tired they might be when they came off duty, they never missed a practice. I used to think of them sometimes when I was composing the music for *The Pirates of Penzance*.'

67 *emeutes*: A French word for brawls. One can see why Gilbert could not use the English word – the obvious rhyme in the next line would have severely shocked a Victorian audience. To rhyme with 'emeutes' the word 'boots' has to be pronounced in a rather strange way. The late Owen Brannigan, who played the Sergeant in many concert and stage versions of *The Pirates*, and whose performance is preserved on the HMV recording under Sir Malcolm Sargent, developed a particularly resonant rendition which can only (but poorly) be reproduced in print as 'bewts'.

The 'tarantara' refrain which figures so prominently in this song was originally conceived as having something of the same function and significance as a Wagnerian leitmotif. In a letter to Sullivan in August 1879, when he was still thinking in terms of robbers rather than pirates, Gilbert wrote:

> By the way, I've made great use of the 'Tarantara' business in Act II. The police always sing 'Tarantara' when they desire to work their courage to sticking-point. They are naturally timid, but through the agency of this talisman they are enabled to acquit themselves well when concealed. In Act II, when the robbers approach, their courage begins to fail them, but recourse to 'Tarantara' (pianissimo) has the desired effect. I mention this that you may bear it in mind in setting the General's 'Tarantara' song.

The phrase 'Tarantara, tarantara' was used as the title of a play about Gilbert and Sullivan by Ian Taylor, which was first performed at the Bristol Old Vic in May 1975.

We uncomfortable feel,
> Tarantara!
And we find the wisest thing,
> Tarantara! tarantara!
Is to slap our chests and sing   65
> Tarantara!
For when threatened with emeutes,
> Tarantara! tarantara!
And your heart is in your boots,
> Tarantara!   70
There is nothing brings it round,
> Tarantara! tarantara!
Like the trumpet's martial sound,
> Tarantara! tarantara!
Tarantara-ra-ra-ra-ra!   75

ALL.   Tarantara-ra-ra-ra-ra!

MABEL.   Go, ye heroes, go to glory,
Though you die in combat gory,
Ye shall live in song and story.
> Go to immortality!   80
Go to death, and go to slaughter;
Die, and every Cornish daughter
With her tears your grave shall water.
> Go, ye heroes, go and die!

ALL.   > Go, ye heroes, go and die!   85

SERGEANT *with* POLICE.

Though to us it's evident,
> Tarantara! tarantara!
These attentions are well meant,
> Tarantara!
Such expressions don't appear,   90
> Tarantara! tarantara!
Calculated men to cheer,
> Tarantara!
Who are going to meet their fate
In a highly nervous state,   95
> Tarantara! tarantara! tarantara!
Still to us it's evident
These attentions are well meant.
> Tarantara! tarantara! tarantara!

129 *Yes, but you don't go*: Although it is not in any of the printed editions of the libretto, the Major-General in exasperation finally utters the words 'But *damme*, you don't go' to the reluctant policemen. I have not been able to discover when this swear word was first introduced. It is not used on early recordings. But whenever it came in, it does not seem to have provoked the same outcry as Captain Corcoran's use of 'damme' in *H.M.S. Pinafore*. This whole passage is, of course, a skit on those scenes in grand opera where people spend a lot of time singing about something that they are just going to do but never seem to get round to doing it.

EDITH.	Go and do your best endeavour,	100
	And before all links we sever,	
	We will say farewell for ever.	
	Go to glory and the grave!	

GIRLS.	Go to glory and the grave!	
	For your foes are fierce and ruthless,	105
	False, unmerciful, and truthless.	
	Young and tender, old and toothless,	
	All in vain their mercy crave.	

SERG.	We observe too great a stress,	
	On the risks that on us press,	110
	And of reference a lack	
	To our chance of coming back.	
	Still, perhaps it would be wise	
	Not to carp or criticize,	
	For it's very evident	115
	These attentions are well meant.	

POLICE.	Yes, it's very evident
	These attentions are well meant, etc.

ENSEMBLE.

Chorus of all but Police.	*Chorus of Police.*
Go, ye heroes, etc.	When the foeman, etc.

GEN.	Away, away!	120
POLICE (*without moving*).	Yes, yes, we go.	
GEN.	These pirates slay.	
POLICE.	Tarantara!	
GEN.	Then do not stay.	
POLICE.	Tarantara!	125
GEN.	Then why this delay?	
POLICE.	All right – we go.	
	Yes, forward on the foe!	
GEN.	Yes, but you *don't* go!	
POLICE.	We go, we go!	130
	Yes, forward on the foe!	
GEN.	Yes, but you *don't* go!	
ALL.	At last they really go.	

(*Exeunt Police.* MABEL *tears herself from* FREDERIC *and exit, followed by her sisters, consoling her. The* GENERAL *and others follow.* FREDERIC *remains.*)   135

156–84 *When you had left our pirate fold*

As first performed, the second line of the paradox trio (as this song is generally called) had the word 'cheer' instead of 'raise'.

The licence copy has the following additional verses for Ruth and Frederic after the King's verse (which ends, in this version, with the line 'To tell it to our Prentice Boy'):

RUTH.

This is the jest and when unfurled
The truth of what we say 'twill show
You came into this wicked world
Just one and twenty years ago
But though since you by me were nursed
Years twenty one have passed away
You have not seen the twenty first
Recurrence of your natal day

FRED.

'Twill be our death that paradox.

(Puzzled)

Now let me see how can that be
I'm twenty one that's very clear
Moreover it is plain to me
Man has birthday once a year
To solve the quip I see no way
All common sense the statement mocks
I beg of you without delay
Explain this startling paradox.

At this point the King begins his chant, as in the present version.

RECITATIVE – Frederic.

Now for the pirates' lair! Oh, joy unbounded!
Oh, sweet relief! Oh, rapture unexampled!
At last I may atone, in some slight measure,
For the repeated acts of theft and pillage   140
Which, at a sense of duty's stern dictation,
I, circumstance's victim, have been guilty.

(King *and* Ruth *appear armed.*)

King.	Young Frederic! (*Covering him with pistol.*)
Fred.	Who calls? 145
King.	Your late commander!
Ruth.	And I, your little Ruth! (*Covering him with pistol.*)
Fred.	Oh, mad intruders,

How dare ye face me? Know ye not, oh rash ones,
That I have doomed you to extermination?   150

(King *and* Ruth *hold a pistol to each ear.*)

King.	Have mercy on us, hear us, ere you slaughter.
Fred.	I do not think I ought to listen to you.

Yet, mercy should alloy our stern resentment,
And so I will be merciful – say on!   155

TRIO – Ruth, King, *and* Frederic.

Ruth.   When you had left our pirate fold
     We tried to raise our spirits faint,
According to our custom old,
     With quip and quibble quaint.
But all in vain the quips we heard,   160
     We lay and sobbed upon the rocks,
Until to somebody occurred
     A startling paradox.

Fred.   A paradox?
Ruth.   A paradox!   165
A most ingenious paradox!
We've quips and quibbles heard in flocks,
But none to beat this paradox!

All.   A paradox, a paradox, etc.
Ha, ha, ha, this paradox!   170

King.   We knew your taste for curious quips,
     For cranks and contradictions queer,

186 *the Astronomer Royal*: A title used between 1675 and 1972 for the director of the Observatory at Greenwich. As the name implies, it was a royal appointment. The Astronomer Royal is now an honorary title bestowed on an outstanding British astronomer.

190 *leap-year*: The time taken for the earth to complete its orbit round the sun is 365.2421988 days (or 365 days, 5 hours, 48 minutes and 46 seconds). To make up the odd quarter day which is 'lost' every year by having only 365 days, an extra calendar day is added every four years at the end of February. A year is a leap year if its last two digits can be divided by four.

having been born in . . . February: Gilbert takes a certain amount of dramatic licence here. From this passage it is clear that *The Pirates of Penzance* is set at the end of February with Frederic about to celebrate his twenty-first, or more accurately his fifth and a quarter, birthday. Yet the atmosphere of the First Act, which we know to be set only a few hours before the Second, suggests the middle of summer. Surely the Major-General's daughters would not be taking off their shoes to paddle and singing 'How beautifully blue the sky' in what is traditionally one of the coldest months of the English winter. A paradox indeed!

And with the laughter on our lips,
  We wished you there to hear.
We said, 'If we could tell it him,   175
  How Frederic would the joke enjoy!'
And so we've risked both life and limb
  To tell it to our boy.

FRED. (*interested*).   That paradox?
KING (*laughing*).   That paradox. That most ingenious paradox!   180
         We've quips and quibbles heard in flocks
         But none to beat that paradox!
ALL.   A paradox, a paradox, etc.
         Ha, ha, ha, that paradox!

CHANT – KING.

For some ridiculous reason, to which, however, I've no desire to be disloyal,   185
Some person in authority, I don't know who, very likely the Astronomer
    Royal,
Has decided that, although for such a beastly month as February, twenty-
    eight days as a rule are plenty,
One year in every four his days shall be reckoned as nine-and-twenty.
Through some singular coincidence – I shouldn't be surprised if it were
    owing to the agency of an ill-natured fairy –
You are the victim of this clumsy arrangement, having been born in leap-
    year, on the twenty-ninth of February,   190
And so, by a simple arithmetical process, you'll easily discover,
That though you've lived twenty-one years, yet, if we go by birthdays,
    you're only five and a little bit over!
RUTH *and*   Ha! ha! ha! ha!
KING.   Ho! ho! ho! ho!
FRED.   Dear me!   195
         Let's see! (*counting on fingers*).
         Yes, yes; with yours my fingers do agree!
ALL.   Ha! ha! ha! ha! Ha! ha! ha! ha!
          (FREDERIC *more amused than any.*)
FRED.   How quaint the ways of Paradox!   200
         At common sense she gaily mocks!
         Though counting in the usual way,
           Years twenty-one I've been alive,
         Yet, reckoning by my natal day,
           I am a little boy of five!   205
KING *and* RUTH.   He is a little boy of five! Ha! ha! ha!
ALL.   A paradox, a paradox,

217-18 *I'm afraid you don't appreciate the delicacy of your position*: The position in which Frederic now finds himself is somewhat similar to the predicament of Captain Bang, the Pirate Chief in Gilbert's earlier musical play *Our Island Home*. Like Frederic (or, rather, like Frederic thinks he is), Bang is on the verge of celebrating his twenty-first birthday and so ending his association with the pirate band to which he was apprenticed by his stupid nurse. However, just before the time when his articles are due to expire he has the misfortune to capture his own parents, whom, by pirate law, he is obliged to slaughter instantly. Resourcefully, he manages to avoid this gruesome duty by working out that as he was born at Greenwich, and is now at a longitude fifty degrees east of Greenwich, allowing for the time difference he technically came of age twenty minutes before capturing his parents. So he is able to spare them and start his post-piratical existence untroubled.

243 *General Stanley*: This is the first mention of the Major-General's name in the course of the opera. It would have had two strong contemporary associations for British audiences at early performances. The Secretary of State for War from April 1878 to April 1880 was Sir Frederick Stanley, later the 16th Earl of Derby. In the Cabinet, Stanley was, of course, closely associated with W. H. Smith, the First Lord of the Admiralty and the model for Sir Joseph Porter in *H.M.S. Pinafore*. However, there is nothing to suggest that the War Secretary was in any way a model for the modern Major-General. The other well-known Stanley whose name might well have been rather more on Gilbert's mind when he cast around for a surname for his military adventurer was Henry Morton Stanley, the explorer and journalist, well-known in both the United States and Britain as the man who had 'discovered' David Livingstone in darkest Africa in 1871. At the time *The Pirates* was being written Stanley had just gone out to the Congo, where he was to spend five years colonizing and administering that territory.

A most ingenious paradox!

    Ha! ha! ha! ha! Ha! ha! ha! ha! (RUTH *and* KING *throw*
      themselves back on seats, exhausted with laughter.) 210

FRED. Upon my word, this is most curious – most absurdly whimsical.
Five-and-a-quarter! No one would think it to look at me!

RUTH. You are glad now, I'll be bound, that you spared us. You would
never have forgiven yourself when you discovered that you had killed *two of*
your comrades. 215

FRED. My comrades?

KING (*rises*). I'm afraid you don't appreciate the delicacy of your
position. You were apprenticed to us —

FRED. Until I reached my twenty-first year.

KING. No, until you reached your twenty-first *birthday* (*producing* 220
document), and, going by birthdays, you are as yet only five-and-a-quarter.

FRED. You don't mean to say you are going to hold me to that?

KING. No, we merely remind you of the fact, and leave the rest to your
sense of duty.

RUTH. Your sense of duty! 225

FRED. (*wildly*). Don't put it on that footing! As I was merciful to you
just now, be merciful to me! I implore you not to insist on the letter of your
bond just as the cup of happiness is at my lips!

RUTH. We insist on nothing; we content ourselves with pointing out to
you *your duty.* 230

KING. Your duty!

FRED. (*after a pause*). Well, you have appealed to my sense of duty, and
my duty is only too clear. I abhor your infamous calling; I shudder at the
thought that I have ever been mixed up with it; but duty is before all – at any
price I will do my duty. 235

KING. Bravely spoken! Come, you are one of us once more.

FRED. Lead on, I follow. (*Suddenly.*) Oh, horror!

KING. ⎫
RUTH. ⎭ What is the matter?

FRED. Ought I to tell you? No, no, I cannot do it; and yet, as one of
your band — 240

KING. Speak out, I charge you by that sense of conscientiousness to
which we have never yet appealed in vain.

FRED. General Stanley, the father of my Mabel —

KING. ⎫
RUTH. ⎭ Yes, yes!

FRED. He escaped from you on the plea that he was an orphan! 245

KING. He did!

FRED. It breaks my heart to betray the honoured father of the girl I
adore, but as your apprentice I have no alternative. It is my duty to tell you
that General Stanley is no orphan!

255 *Tremorden Castle*: This is a fictitious location, but a perfectly plausible name for a place in Cornwall. The Cornish word *tre* means hamlet or homestead and is found at the beginning of many place names in the county. There is a village of Tremore, for example, four miles west of Bodmin.

260 *This very night*: Gilbert originally wrote 'this very day', once again forgetting the lines he had given Frederic only a few pages earlier which suggested it was not yet eleven in the evening. It was changed to 'night' for the same reason that Mabel's phrase 'The midnight hour' was changed to 'The twilight hour' (line 17).

KING.
RUTH. } What!   250

FRED. More than that, he never was one!

KING. Am I to understand that, to save his contemptible life, he dared
to practise on our credulous simplicity? (FREDERIC *nods as he weeps.*) Our
revenge shall be swift and terrible. We will go and collect our band and
attack Tremorden Castle this very night.   255

FRED. But – stay —

KING. Not a word! He is doomed!

TRIO.

KING *and* RUTH.   FRÉDERIC.

Away, away! my heart's on fire,   Away, away! ere I expire –
  I burn this base deception to repay,   I find my duty hard to do to-day!
This very night my vengeance dire   My heart is filled with anguish dire,   260
  Shall glut itself in gore. Away, away!   It strikes me to the core. Away, away!

KING.

With falsehood foul
He tricked us of our brides.
  Let vengeance howl;
The Pirate so decides.   265
  Our nature stern
He softened with his lies,
  And, in return,
To-night the traitor dies.

ALL.   Yes, yes! to-night the traitor dies.   270

RUTH.   To-night he dies!

KING.   Yes, or early to-morrow.

FRED.   His girls likewise?

RUTH.   They will welter in sorrow.

KING.   The one soft spot   275

FRED.   In their natures they cherish –

RUTH.   And all who plot

KING.   To abuse it shall perish!

ALL.   To-night he dies, etc.

(*Exeunt* KING *and* RUTH.)   280

(*Enter* MABEL.)

292 *till 1940*: Another paradox, of which Gilbert may or may not have been aware. Frederic has a birthday every four years. Therefore he will not reach his twenty-first birthday until he is, in fact, eighty-four. On the face of it, if he is to reach the age of eighty-four in 1940, he must have been born on 29 February 1856, and *The Pirates of Penzance* must therefore be set in 1877 (two years before its first performance), when Frederic reaches his twenty-first year.

However, the Astronomer Royal has another trick up his sleeve. We have already noted that it is not exactly a full quarter day which needs to be added to each year to bring it in line with the time taken for the earth to revolve round the sun, but rather a fraction below that amount – 0.242 days, to be exact, rather than 0.25. The addition of one full day to the calendar every leap year, therefore, makes up more 'lost' time than it should (four times 0.25 days rather than four times 0.242 days, i.e. 24 hours rather than 23 hours, 4 minutes and 36 seconds). To compensate for this inaccuracy, leap days are only taken in century years which are exactly divisible by four. Thus while 1600 was a leap year, and 2000 will be one, 1700, 1800 and, most important for our present calculations, 1900 were not. Frederic therefore faces one eight-year gap between birthdays (from 1896 to 1904). This means that to be twenty-one in 1940 he must, in fact, have been born four years earlier than we first supposed, in 1852. In that case the action of *The Pirates* takes place in 1873, six years before the opera was written and first performed. Alternatively, if the play is set in 1877, and Frederic was born in 1856, he will not reach his twenty-first birthday until 1944. All this may seem of purely academic interest, but it is on such points as these that Gilbert and Sullivan fans love to speculate, and, after all, it cannot have been entirely of academic interest to Mabel to know whether she had to wait until her lover was a ripe old eighty-eight or whether he would be hers at the tender age of eighty-four.

RECITATIVE – Mabel.

All is prepared, your gallant crew await you.
My Frederic in tears? It cannot be
That lion-heart quails at the coming conflict?

FRED.   No, Mabel, no. A terrible disclosure   285
Has just been made! Mabel, my dearly-loved one,
I bound myself to serve the pirate captain
Until I reached my one-and-twentieth birthday –

MABEL.   But you *are* twenty-one?

FRED.   I've just discovered   290
That I was born in leap-year, and that birthday
Will not be reached by me till 1940.

MABEL.   Oh, horrible! catastrophe appalling!

FRED.   And so, farewell!

MABEL.   No, no! Ah, Frederic, hear me.   295

DUET – Mabel *and* Frederic.

MABEL.   Stay, Frederic, stay!
      They have no legal claim,
      No shadow of a shame
      Will fall upon thy name.
   Stay, Frederic, stay!   300

FRED.   Nay, Mabel, nay!
      To-night I quit these walls,
      The thought my soul appals,
      But when stern Duty calls,
   I must obey.   305

MABEL.   Stay, Frederic, stay!
FRED.   Nay, Mabel, nay!
MABEL.   They have no claim –
FRED.   But Duty's name!
      The thought my soul appals,   310
      But when stern Duty calls,
   I must obey.

DUET – Mabel *and* Frederic.

MABEL.   Ah, leave me not to pine
      Alone and desolate;
   No fate seemed fair as mine, –   315
      No happiness so great!

337-40 *Oh, here is love, and here is truth*

In early performances of *The Pirates*, including the Paignton and New York first nights, there was a second verse to this ensemble and an added recitative for Mabel:

What joy to know that though $\begin{Bmatrix} he \\ I \end{Bmatrix}$ must

Embrace piratical adventures,

$\begin{Bmatrix} He \\ She \end{Bmatrix}$ will be faithful to $\begin{Bmatrix} his \\ her \end{Bmatrix}$ trust

Till $\begin{Bmatrix} he\ is \\ I\ am \end{Bmatrix}$ out of $\begin{Bmatrix} his \\ my \end{Bmatrix}$ indentures!

FRED.	Farewell! Adieu!
MABEL.	The same to you!
BOTH.	Farewell! Adieu!

(FREDERIC *rushes to window and leaps out.*)

MABEL.   Distraction! Frederic! loved me! oh return! With love I burn
(*recollecting*)   Stay! I'm a Stanley! Even to the grave I will be brave.
                His conscience bids him give up love and all at duty's call;
                Mine teaches me that though I love him so,
                He is my foe.

In the Paignton performance, Mabel then had a full-scale aria about her family descent. This stirring number was not sung at either the New York or London premières:

When conquering William's legions came
To spoil our island dear
More likely someone of our name
Accompanied him here
But if with that great conqueror
That somebody arrived
Great Shade, if thou hadst being then
Such was thy modesty
Thy name the dread of Saxon men
Historians have passed by
But though to Norman blood my claim
Rests on hypothesis
Yet if with him the Stanleys came
I'm very sure of this
Although he loved his mistress much
He loved his duty more
And I will not discredit such
A glorious ancestor
Ancestral hero deathless shade
(If such a shade there be)
With strength inspire a simple maid
Great Possibility

Mabel's recitative about her family descent then followed (lines 341-4). In early productions this began 'Yes, I am brave' instead of the later form, 'No, I'll be brave'.

And nature, day by day,
  Has sung, in accents clear,
This joyous roundelay,
    'He loves thee – he is here.   320
    Fa-la, la, la, Fal-la, la, la.'

FRED.   Ah, must I leave thee here
  In endless night to dream,
Where joy is dark and drear,
  And sorrow all supreme!   325
Where nature, day by day,
  Will sing, in altered tone,
This weary roundelay,
    'He loves thee - he is gone.
    Fa-la, la, la, Fal-la, la, la.'   330

FRED.   In 1940 I of age shall be,
           I'll then return, and claim you – I declare it.
MABEL.   It seems so long!
FRED.   Swear that, till then, you will be true to me.
MABEL.   Yes, I'll be strong!   335
           By all the Stanleys dead and gone, I swear it.

ENSEMBLE.

Oh, here is love, and here is truth,
  And here is food for joyous laughter.
He   }   { his
          will be faithful to   sooth
She }   { her
Till we are wed, and even after.   (*Exit* FREDERIC.) 340

MABEL (*almost fainting*). No, I'll be brave! Oh, family descent,
    How great thy charm, thy sway how excellent!
    Come, one and all, undaunted men in blue,
    A crisis, now, affairs are coming to!

(*Enter Police, marching in single file.*)   345

SERGEANT *with* POLICE.

Though in body and in mind,
         Tarantara, tarantara!
We are timidly inclined,
         Tarantara!
And anything but blind,   350
         Tarantara, tarantara!

363 *That is not a pleasant way of putting it*: This, and the policemen's subsequent lines, are traditionally sung in plainsong as though they are the verses of a psalm. Shades of Sullivan's policemen's church choir again.

371 *endeared him to me tenfold*: In early performances of *The Pirates* Mabel had an extra sentence at this point: 'But if it is his duty to constitute himself my foe, it is likewise my duty to regard him in that light.' She continued 'He has done his duty' etc. as now.

374 *Right oh*: Gilbert originally wrote 'Very well' here but altered it for the 1900 revival of *The Pirates*, possibly at the request of Walter Passmore, who took over the role of the Sergeant, originally played in London by Rutland Barrington. Certainly 'Right oh' fits better into the rhythm of the policemen's chanting of their responses.

387-424 *When a felon's not engaged in his employment*
One of the most popular of all Gilbert and Sullivan's songs and the favourite party piece of many a beery bass in the public bar near closing time. It is almost invariably encored. Rutland Barrington was even moved to ask Gilbert to give him an extra verse to use when the audience shouted for more. 'Encore means sing it again' was the librettist's brusque reply.

The policemen's song has been parodied many times. Sydney Dark and Rowland Gray's book *W. S. Gilbert: His Life and Letters* (Methuen, 1923) even quotes a Latin version, the first verse by Dr Arthur Chilton, then prebendary of St Paul's Cathedral, and later rector of Colne Engaine, Essex, and the second by the then suffragan bishop of Southampton.

It begins:

> *Ubi fraudibus fraudator abrogatis*
> > *Abrogatis*
> *Secum mediatur nil nefarii*
> > *'arii*
> *Innocentis erit capax voluptatis*
> > *Voluptatis*
> *Sicut ego, sicut tu et ceteri*
> > *Ceteri.*

387 *felon*: One who has committed a felony, i.e. an offence, such as murder or burglary, which is in a graver category than mere misdemeanours. In early English law a felony was punishable by loss of life or limb or forfeiture of goods and chattels.

To the danger that's behind,
> Tarantara!
Yet, when the danger's near,
> Tarantara, tarantara!   355
We manage to appear,
> Tarantara!
As insensible to fear
As anybody here.
> Tarantara, tarantara-ra-ra-ra-ra!   360

MABEL. Sergeant, approach! Young Frederic was to have led you to
death and glory.
ALL. That is not a pleasant way of putting it.
MABEL. No matter; he will not so lead you, for he has allied himself
once more with his old associates.   365
ALL. He has acted shamefully!
MABEL. You speak falsely. You know nothing about it. He has acted
nobly.
ALL. He has acted nobly!
MABEL. Dearly as I loved him before, his heroic sacrifice to his sense of   370
duty has endeared him to me tenfold. He has done his duty. I will do mine.
Go ye and do yours.

> (*Exit* MABEL.)

ALL. Right oh!
SERG. This is perplexing.   375
ALL. We cannot understand it at all.
SERG. Still, as he is actuated by a sense of duty —
ALL. That makes a difference, of course. At the same time we repeat,
we cannot understand it at all.
SERG. No matter; our course is clear. We must do our best to capture   380
these pirates alone. It is most distressing to us to be the agents whereby our
erring fellow-creatures are deprived of that liberty which is so dear to all —
but we should have thought of that before we joined the Force.
ALL. We should!
SERG. It is too late now!   385
ALL. It is!

SONG – SERGEANT.

SERG.   When a felon's not engaged in his employment –
ALL.   His employment,
SERG.   Or maturing his felonious little plans –
ALL.   Little plans,   390

414 *coster*: A shortened form of 'costermonger', i.e. a street salesman selling fruit, vegetables or fish from a barrow. Costermongers had a reputation for rough behaviour.

430 *the manor*: A slang word for a police district. Gilbert must have been among the first to use it, since the first appearance in print recorded by the *Oxford English Dictionary* is not until 1924 when a book on *The Human Side of Crook and Convict Life* noted: 'There are straight crooks and crooked crooks on the "Manor" of a detective, and he gets to know them apart'.

SERG.	His capacity for innocent enjoyment –
ALL.	'Cent enjoyment
SERG.	Is just as great as any honest man's –
ALL.	Honest man's.
SERG.	Our feelings we with difficulty smother –
ALL.	'Culty smother
SERG.	When constabulary duty's to be done –
ALL.	To be done.
SERG.	Ah, take one consideration with another –
ALL.	With another,
SERG.	A policeman's lot is not a happy one.
ALL.	Ah! When constabulary duty's to be done –
	To be done,
	The policeman's lot is not a happy one –
	Happy one.
SERG.	When the enterprising burglar's not a-burgling –
ALL.	Not a-burgling,
SERG.	When the cut-throat isn't occupied in crime –
ALL.	'Pied in crime,
SERG.	He loves to hear the little brook a-gurgling –
ALL.	Brook a-gurgling,
SERG.	And listen to the merry village chime –
ALL.	Village chime.
SERG.	When the coster's finished jumping on his mother –
ALL.	On his mother,
SERG.	He loves to lie a-basking in the sun –
ALL.	In the sun.
SERG.	Ah, take one consideration with another –
ALL.	With another,
SERG.	The policeman's lot is not a happy one.
ALL.	When constabulary duty's to be done –
	To be done,
	The policeman's lot is not a happy one –
	Happy one.

395

400

405

410

415

420

(*Chorus of Pirates without, in the distance.*)   425

A rollicking band of pirates we,
Who, tired of tossing on the sea,
Are trying their hand at a burglaree,
    With weapons grim and gory.

SERG.   Hush, hush! I hear them on the manor poaching,   430
With stealthy step the pirates are approaching.

443 *They come in force*: The original version of these lines, sung at early performances, was:

> They come in force,
> The bold, burglarious elves;
> Our obvious course
> Is to conceal ourselves

459–63 *Come, friends, who plough the sea*
The tune of this song, which did not figure in the original Paignton performance and was not, in fact, added to the British libretto of the opera until 1914, is familiar to Americans, who have long used it for the chant:

> Hail! Hail! The Gang's all here.
> What the hell do we care?
> What the hell do we care?

The first known printing of this transatlantic version of the pirate's chorus dates from 1908. It was sung at a Democratic Party Convention in Saratoga early this century, and the words of the American version were copyrighted in 1917. Since then it has been sung thousands of times at gatherings of clubs, college alumni and servicemen's reunions.

465 *crowbar*: Bar made of iron, with one end bent and edged, used for levering open doors, windows and lids. An essential part of a burglar's tool kit.

centrebit: A drill which turns on a projecting centre point and is used for making cylindrical holes in wood or metal. A burglar would use it to cut into doors so as to open locks from the inside.

466 *life-preserver*: A stick or bludgeon loaded with lead and intended for self-defence. No wonder the unarmed policemen were rather nervous about going off to do battle with their pirate foes.

(*Chorus of Pirates, resumed nearer.*)

We are not coming for plate or gold –
A story General Stanley's told –
We seek a penalty fifty-fold,   435
For General Stanley's story.

POLICE.   They seek a penalty –
PIRATES (*without*).   Fifty-fold,
We seek a penalty –
POLICE.   Fifty-fold,   440
ALL.   We ⎫
                They ⎭ seek a penalty fifty-fold,
For General Stanley's story.
SERG.   They come in force, with stealthy stride,
Our obvious course is now – to hide.

(*Police conceal themselves. As they do so, the Pirates are seen appearing at ruined*   445
windows. They enter cautiously, and come down stage. SAMUEL *is laden with*
burglarious tools and pistols, etc.)

CHORUS – PIRATES (*very loud*).

With cat-like tread,
    Upon our prey we steal,
In silence dread   450
    Our cautious way we feel.
No sound at all,
    We never speak a word,
A fly's foot-fall
    Would be distinctly heard –   455
POLICE (*pianissimo*).   Tarantara, tarantara!
PIRATES.   So stealthily the pirate creeps,
While all the household soundly sleeps.
Come, friends, who plough the sea,
    Truce to navigation,   460
    Take another station;
Let's vary piracee
With a little burglaree!
POLICE (*pianissimo*).   Tarantara, tarantara!
SAM. (*distributing implements to various members of the gang*).
                Here's your crowbar and your centrebit,   465
                Your life-preserver – you may want to hit;

467 *silent matches*: Early matches were made by coating wooden sticks with sulphur and tipping them with chlorate of potash. The matches were ignited not, as now, by being struck against an abrasive surface, but by being dipped into a bottle of asbestos and sulphuric acid – a process which was at least silent if rather cumbersome.

468 *skeletonic keys*: Light keys with almost the whole substance of the bit (the part which engages with the levers of a lock) filed away. As a result, skeleton keys can fit many different locks and are therefore another popular item in the burglar's equipment.

In the original version of *The Pirates* performed at Paignton, and contained in the licence copy, the distribution of the burglarious tools was made by the Pirate King, who also handed out a revolver and a wedge while he sang that:

> It is my kingly privilege
> According to our pirate rules
> To carry these burglarious tools

before launching into yet another reprise of 'For I am a Pirate King'.

488 *No, all is still*: This line of General Stanley's following the *fortissimo* interruption by the chorus is reminiscent of the Countess Almaviva's remark 'I heard nothing' to her jealous husband just after her young admirer Cherubino has made a resounding thump off-stage in Act II of Mozart's *The Marriage of Figaro*.

That the latter half of the Second Act of *The Pirates* is a deliberate parody of Italian opera is confirmed in an interview which Sullivan gave to the London correspondent of *The New York Times* about his new work before leaving Britain in 1879:

> The notion chiefly develops a burlesque of Italian opera. It is a mere incident. An old gentleman returns home in the evening with his six daughters from a party. Nice bit of soft music takes them off for the night. Then a big orchestral crash, which introduces six burglars. They commence their knavish operations in a mysterious chorus, lights down. Presently, the old gentleman thinks he hears someone stirring; comes on; of course, sees nobody though the burglars are actively at work. The only noise is the sighing of the wind, or gentle evening breeze. The old gentleman and the burglars perform a bit of concerted music, and in due course the six ladies enter. The six burglars are struck by their beauty, forget their villainous purposes and make love . . . then there is a rescue by policemen and other numerous conceits of Gilbert's.

494–523 *Sighing softly to the river*
With the possible exception of Jack Point's 'I have a song to sing, O!' in *The Yeomen of the Guard*, this is the most moving and melodious song given to the comic lead in any of the Savoy Operas. It is said in some quarters that it was originally introduced in a rather malicious spirit for the fun that could be had out of George Grossmith, who created the role of the Major-General in London and who had a poor singing voice, trying to get his tongue round a serious ballad. Whatever the reason for its inclusion, however, it is a delightful number, for which Sullivan provided a particularly charming undulating accompaniment that imitates the rippling of the brook and the waving of the poplars.

As originally written, the song began:

> Softly sighing to the river
> Comes the lonely breeze

Your silent matches, your dark lantern seize,
Take your file and your skeletonic keys.

(*Enter* KING, FREDERIC, *and* RUTH.)

PIRATES (*fortissimo*).   With cat-like tread, etc.   470
POLICE (*pianissimo*).   Tarantara, tarantara!

RECITATIVE.

FRED.   Hush, hush, not a word! I see a light inside!
            The Major-General comes, so quickly hide!
PIRATES.   Yes, yes, the Major-General comes!

(PIRATES *conceal themselves. Exeunt* KING, FREDERIC,   475
                              SAMUEL, *and* RUTH.)

POLICE.   Yes, yes, the Major-General comes!
GEN. (*entering in dressing-gown, carrying a light*).
            Yes, yes, the Major-General comes!

SOLO – GENERAL.

Tormented with the anguish dread
     Of falsehood unatoned,   480
I lay upon my sleepless bed,
     And tossed and turned and groaned.
The man who finds his conscience ache
     No peace at all enjoys,
And as I lay in bed awake   485
     I thought I heard a noise.
PIRATES *and* POLICE.   He thought he heard a noise – ha! ha!
GEN.   No, all is still
                     In dale, on hill;
                     My mind is set at ease.   490
                     So still the scene –
                     It must have been
                     The sighing of the breeze.

BALLAD – GENERAL.

Sighing softly to the river
     Comes the loving breeze,   495
Setting nature all a-quiver,
     Rustling through the trees –

505 *River, river*: The D'Oyly Carte Opera Company sometimes cut the lines from 'River, river, little river' to 'Nobody can woo so well' (line 519).

524 *peignoirs*: A French word for women's dressing gowns.

ALL.   Through the trees.
GEN.   And the brook, in rippling measure,
                   Laughs for very love,   500
                 While the poplars, in their pleasure,
                   Wave their arms above.

POLICE   Yes, the trees, for very love,
  and   Wave their leafy arms above,
PIRATES.   River, river, little river,   505
                 May thy loving prosper ever.
                 Heaven speed thee, poplar tree,
                 May thy wooing happy be.

GEN.   Yet, the breeze is but a rover;
                   When he wings away,   510
                 Brook and poplar mourn a lover!
                   Sighing well-a-day!
ALL.   Well-a-day!
GEN.   Ah! the doing and undoing,
                   That the rogue could tell!   515
                 When the breeze is out a-wooing,
                   Who can woo so well?

POLICE   Shocking tales the rogue could tell,
  and   Nobody can woo so well.
PIRATES.   Pretty brook, thy dream is over,   520
                 For thy love is but a rover!
                 Sad the lot of poplar trees,
                 Courted by a fickle breeze!

(*Enter the* GENERAL'S *daughters led by Mabel, all in white peignoirs
     and night-caps, and carrying lighted candles.*)   525

GIRLS.   Now what is this, and what is that, and why
                   does father leave his rest
                At such a time of night as this, so very
                   incompletely dressed?
                Dear father is, and always was, the most
                   methodical of men!
                It's his invariable rule to go to bed at half-past
                   ten.
                What strange occurrence can it be that calls
                   dear father from his rest   530
                At such a time of night as this, so very
                   incompletely dressed?

533 *seize that General there*: In the New York first-night production, the Pirate King at this point had the additional line 'His life is over'. After the pirates' line 'Yes, we're the pirates, so despair!' they seized the Major-General, and the King went straight into his song 'With base deceit'. Then Frederic came forward with the echoing line 'Alas! alas! unhappy General Stanley', whereupon the General went on, as now, 'Frederic here? Oh joy! oh rapture!'

541 *I would if I could, but I am not able*: During one rehearsal for *The Pirates* in London, the tenor playing Frederic was temporarily absent from the stage at the time this section was being sung. After Mabel had delivered her line 'Frederic, save us!' Gilbert's voice was heard from the stalls, 'Beautiful Mabel, I'd sing if I could, but I am not able'.

551 *unshriven*: Without having made confession and received absolution of his sins. *unannealed*: Without having received extreme unction. The word should be spelt 'unaneled'; it comes from the verb to anele, meaning to anoint. Extreme unction is a sacrament of the Roman Catholic Church in which the dying are anointed by a priest. In Shakespeare's *Hamlet*, Act I, Scene 5, the Ghost speaks of dying 'Unhouseled, disappointed, unaneled'.

564 *the Central Criminal Court*: The Old Bailey, built in 1539 on Cheapside in the City of London, was used for many celebrated criminal trials. In 1834 the Central Criminal Court Act officially recognized it as the major criminal court in the land. The present court building, which is still known as the Old Bailey, was built between 1902 and 1907 on the site of the old Newgate Prison. The Old Bailey is also mentioned in the Judge's song in *Trial by Jury* ('And every day my voice was heard/At the Sessions or Ancient Bailey').

(*Enter* KING, SAMUEL, *and* FREDERIC.)

KING.   Forward, my men, and seize that General there!

(*They seize the* GENERAL.)

GIRLS.   The pirates! the pirates! Oh, despair!   535
PIRATES (*springing up*).   Yes, we're the pirates, so despair!
GEN.   Frederic here! Oh, joy! Oh, rapture!
              Summon your men and effect their capture!
MABEL.   Frederic, save us!
FRED.   Beautiful Mabel,   540
              I would if I could, but I am not able.
PIRATES.   He's telling the truth, he is not able.
KING.   With base deceit
                  You worked upon our feelings!
                  Revenge is sweet,   545
                    And flavours all our dealings!
                  With courage rare
                    And resolution manly,
                  For death prepare,
                    Unhappy General Stanley.   550

MABEL (*wildly*). Is he to die, unshriven – unannealed?
GIRLS.   Oh, spare him!
MABEL.   Will no one in his cause a weapon wield?
GIRLS.   Oh, spare him!
POLICE (*springing up*). Yes, we are here, though
                        hitherto concealed!   555
GIRLS.   Oh, rapture!
POLICE.   So to Constabulary, pirates, yield!
GIRLS.   Oh, rapture!

(*A struggle ensues between Pirates and Police. Eventually the Police are overcome,
    and fall prostrate, the Pirates standing over them with drawn swords.*)   560

CHORUS OF POLICE AND PIRATES.

$\left.\begin{array}{l}\text{You}\\ \text{We}\end{array}\right\}$ triumph now, for well we trow
                  Our mortal career's cut short,
                No pirate band will take its stand
                  At the Central Criminal Court.
SERG.   To gain a brief advantage you've contrived,   565

569 *in Queen Victoria's name*: For the 1908 revival of *The Pirates* Gilbert changed this line to 'We charge you yield, in good King Edward's name!' and the Pirate King's reply became:

> We yield at once, without a sting,
> Because with all our faults, we love our King.

In subsequent productions, the lines reverted to their original form.

Both the British and American first-night performances of *The Pirates* had finales very different from the present one. In the Paignton production the policemen's line 'We charge you yield, in Queen Victoria's name' was followed by:

RUTH.

> Alas, alas, we don't resist the claim
> All Britons bow to Queen Victoria's name.

KING.

> It is enough you've deftly played your cards
> That is a spell no Briton disregards.

> (*Pirates kneel – Police stand over them triumphantly*)

QUARTET – MABEL, KING, FREDERIC & RUTH *kneeling*.

> To Queen Victoria's name we bow
> As true born Britons should
> We can resist no longer now
> And would not if we could
> The man who dares to disregard
> A summons in that name
> We look on as a wretch ill-starred
> And lost to sense of shame.

ALL.

> We look on as a wretch, etc.

KING.

> We yield at once, with humble mien, etc.

The action then continued as it does now, with the pirates yielding and Ruth making her announcement that they are, in fact, all noblemen who have gone wrong. Then, after the girls' repetition of the line 'They are all noblemen who have gone wrong', both the Paignton and the New York first-night productions continued *Pinafore*-like as follows:

GENERAL. What all noblemen?

KING. Yes, all noblemen.

GENERAL. What, all?

KING. Well, nearly all.

ALL.

> They are nearly all noblemen who have gone wrong.
> Then give three cheers both loud and long
> For the twenty noblemen who have gone wrong,
> Then give three cheers both loud and long,
> For the noblemen who have gone wrong.

GENERAL.

> No Englishman unmoved that statement hears,
> Because, with all our faults, we love our House of Peers.

At this point, the two first-night versions diverged again. The Paignton production finished with the following 'Hymn to the Nobility':

But your proud triumph will not be long-lived.

KING. Don't say you are orphans, for we know that game.

SERG. On your allegiance we've a stronger claim –
We charge you yield, in Queen Victoria's name!

KING (*baffled*). You do! 570

POLICE. We do!
We charge you yield, in Queen Victoria's name!

(*Pirates kneel, Police stand over them triumphantly.*)

KING. We yield at once, with humbled mien,
Because, with all our faults, we love our Queen. 575

POLICE. Yes, yes, with all their faults, they love their Queen.

GIRLS. Yes, yes, with all, etc.

(*Police, holding Pirates by the collar, take out handkerchiefs and weep.*)

GEN. Away with them, and place them at the bar!

(*Enter* RUTH.) 580

RUTH. One moment! let me tell you who they are.
They are no members of the common throng;
They are all noblemen who have gone wrong!

GEN. No Englishman unmoved that statement hears,
Because, with all our faults, we love our House of Peers. 585

RECITATIVE – GENERAL.

I pray you, pardon me, ex-Pirate King,
Peers will be peers, and youth will have its fling.
Resume your ranks and legislative duties,
And take my daughters, all of whom are beauties.

FINALE.

MABEL. Poor wandering ones! 590
Though ye have surely strayed,
Take heart of grace,
Your steps retrace,
Poor wandering ones!

GENERAL.   Let foreigners look down with scorn
                    On legislators heaven-born;
                    We know what limpid wisdom runs
                    From Peers and all their eldest sons.
                    Enrapt the true-born Briton hears
                    The wisdom of his House of Peers

SERGEANT.   And if a noble lord should die
                    And leave no nearer progeny,
                    His twentieth cousin takes his place
                    And legislates with equal grace.

RUTH.   But should a son and heir survive,
                    Or other nearer relative,
                    Then twentieth cousins get you hence –
                    You're persons of no consequence.
                    When issue male their chances bar,
                    How paltry twentieth cousins are!

MABEL.   How doubly blest that glorious land
                    Where rank and brains go hand in hand,
                    Where wisdom pure and virtue hale
                    Obey the law of strict entail,
                    No harm can touch a country when
                    It's ruled by British noblemen.

CURTAIN

The American first-night production had a much shorter hymn to the nobility, sung by the entire company, following the General's line 'Because, with all our faults, we love our House of Peers':

Hail, ever hail, O House of Peers!
To wisdom that mankind reveres
We listen with respectful ears,
For oh! we love our House of Peers!

The General then had his recitative 'I pray you, pardon me, ex-Pirate King', as now. (During the 1908 revival of *The Pirates* at the Savoy Theatre, incidentally, Gilbert showed his low opinion of the female chorus, which for once he had played no part in selecting, by altering the last line in this recitative to 'And take my daughters, some of whom are beauties').

For the finale, the New York first-night production did not use the reprise of 'Poor wandering one' that is now sung but instead had the following variation on the Major-General's song. This is also used by Joseph Papp in the finale of his production:

RUTH.   At length we are provided, with unusual facility,
            To change piratic crime for dignified respectability.

KING.   Combined, I needn't say, with the unparalleled felicity
            Of what we have been longing for — unbounded domesticity.

MABEL.   Tomorrow morning early we will quickly be parsonified –
            Hymeneally coupled, conjugally matrimonified.

SERGEANT.   And this shall be accomplished by that doctor of divinity
            Who happily resides in the immediate vicinity.

CHORUS.   Who happily resides in the immediate vicinity, etc.

Poor wandering ones!   595
  If such poor love as ours
  Can help you find
  True peace of mind,
Why, take it, it is yours!

ALL.   Poor wandering ones! etc.   600

CURTAIN

GENERAL.   My military knowledge, though I'm plucky and adventury,
             Has only been brought down to the beginning of the century.
             But still, in getting off my daughters – eight or nine or ten in all,
             I've shown myself a model of a modern Major-General.

CHORUS.   His military knowledge etc.

DANCE

CURTAIN

IOLANTHE

OR

THE PEER AND THE PERI

DRAMATIS PERSONÆ

THE LORD CHANCELLOR
EARL OF MOUNTARARAT
EARL TOLLOLLER
PRIVATE WILLIS (*of the Grenadier Guards*)
STREPHON (*an Arcadian Shepherd*)
QUEEN OF THE FAIRIES
IOLANTHE (*a Fairy, Strephon's Mother*)
CELIA ⎤
LEILA ⎬ *Fairies*
FLETA ⎦
PHYLLIS (*an Arcadian Shepherdess and Ward in Chancery*)
Chorus of Dukes, Marquises, Earls, Viscounts, Barons, and Fairies.

ACT I. – An Arcadian Landscape.
ACT II. – Palace Yard, Westminster.

IOLANTHE

Iolanthe made theatrical history on 25 November 1882 when it became the first play ever to open in Britain and the United States on the same night. New Yorkers filing into the Standard Theater already knew of the show's success in London from a cable sent from the Savoy Theatre, where the first performance had ended barely an hour earlier.

As originally conceived by Gilbert, *Iolanthe* had a rather different plot from the one with which we are now familiar. He had first explored the comic possibilities of a marriage between a fairy and a mortal in his Bab Ballad 'The Fairy Curate'. In his preliminary notes for an opera based on the same theme, he first proposed that the fairy heroine should marry a prosaic solicitor aged forty-five. This was later changed to the rather grander idea that the entire female chorus of fairies should marry barristers of the Northern Circuit, with the action being set in a court of law, just like the first of Gilbert and Sullivan's collaborations for Richard D'Oyly Carte, *Trial by Jury*.

As he worked on the plot of the new opera Gilbert realized that he could have much more fun by switching from a legal to a political setting. He decided that the Fairy Queen should marry the Prime Minister (this was later changed to the Foreign Secretary), with the other principal fairies pairing off with the Home Secretary, the Attorney General, and other ministers of state. The scene was to be the House of Commons.

Finally Gilbert hit on a formula which satisfied him and which enabled him to produce a comic masterpiece. The setting of the opera would be the House of Lords, in its own way as romantic and as far removed from the real world as fairyland; the Fairy Queen would be set against the Lord Chancellor; and the chorus of fairies would fall in love with a chorus of peers. With the introduction of an Arcadian shepherdess and her shepherd lover to give a rustic and romantic note the plot was broadly complete.

The British House of Lords is an obvious subject for satirists and humorists. The idea of birth being the qualification for membership of the upper house of Parliament strongly appealed to Gilbert's sense of the

163

ridiculous. He had poked fun at it in *The Pirates of Penzance*, particularly in the finales of the original British and American versions, and was to do so again in *Utopia Limited*. *Iolanthe* gave him the opportunity to devote an entire opera to the gentle mockery of an institution for which, like most Englishmen, he, in fact, had a deep affection.

The power of the House of Lords was a highly topical issue in 1882. Resistance in the upper house to much of the reforming legislation of Gladstone's Liberal Government, which had been elected in 1880, led to a growing call for reform of the Lords and an end to their veto. Gilbert knew that his digs at the peerage would win ready applause from a contemporary audience, just as he could be sure of a cheer when he lampooned that other bogey of the British political tradition, the two-party system.

There have been some elaborate explanations of the contemporary political satire contained in *Iolanthe*. One of the most ingenious was made in an article in the *Daily Telegraph* on 23 January 1978 by Kenneth Baker, Conservative M.P. for Marylebone and St Pancras and now Minister for Information Technology in Mrs Thatcher's Government. He suggested that Gilbert clearly meant the Fairy Queen to be Queen Victoria, with Private Willis representing her faithful and manly ghillie John Brown. The Lord Chancellor, with his bad relations with the Queen and his nocturnal wanderings and eye for pretty young girls, was clearly Mr Gladstone, while Strephon was Lord Randolph Churchill, the quixotic exponent of Tory democracy whose so-called 'Fourth Party' of maverick Conservatives had already made the leaders of the established parties shake in their shoes.

It is an attractive theory and there may be some truth in it, although I doubt if Gilbert set out quite so deliberately to caricature the leading figures of the day. Certainly the satire in *Iolanthe* was sharp – too sharp, indeed, for contemporary tastes; two songs were cut from the opera because their biting social comment and angry political message were condemned by reviewers as being out of keeping with the gentle and humorous quality of the rest of the work.

The fact is that, like all the Savoy Operas, *Iolanthe* should not be taken too seriously. It is as much the vehicle for splendid pageantry – the entrance of the peers – and for parody of Wagnerian opera – the summoning of Iolanthe from the depths of the stream – as it is for political satire. After all, it is a fairy-tale opera, and that is the magic that weaves its spell over the audience. One of the girls who played a fairy in the original London run even won the heart of a real peer, who came night after night to see her tripping hither and thither around the stage.

Sullivan produced some of his most memorable melodies for *Iolanthe*, ranging from the triumphal march of the peers to the delicate 'None shall part us' duet for Strephon and Phyllis. In the music for Iolanthe herself there is also a haunting sadness which goes deeper than almost anything else in the Savoy Operas. The composer began work on the opera just a few days after his beloved mother died, and this almost certainly influenced the character of some of the music.

Iolanthe was the first of Gilbert and Sullivan's operas to open at the Savoy Theatre, which Richard D'Oyly Carte had built just off the Strand as the home for his company. It is, therefore, strictly speaking the first of the Savoy Operas. The theatre had opened in October 1881 with the transfer of *Patience* from the Opéra Comique. It was the first theatre in Britain to be lit by electricity. During the initial run of *Iolanthe* Carte made another innovation by introducing for the first time in Britain the French system of queuing for people waiting outside the theatre for unreserved seats. He was much commended for turning what had hitherto been an uncontrolled scramble into something 'dignified and stately'.

Iolanthe ran initially at the Savoy for 398 performances, more than *The Pirates of Penzance*, although not as many as *Patience*. It has continued to be very popular ever since, particularly in Britain. On 24 January 1962 it became the first Gilbert and Sullivan opera to receive a professional production out of copyright when it was put on by Sadler's Wells Opera Company. In the last few years it has acquired a new topicality. Since the British general election of May 1979 the line 'This comes of women interfering in politics' has taken on a new significance, while the determination of Mr Tony Benn (alias the 2nd Viscount Stansgate) and other members of the Labour Party to abolish the House of Lords if and when they next come to power has given an added urgency to Lord Mountararat's defence of the upper chamber in his stirring song 'When Britain really ruled the waves'. With her re-introduction of hereditary peerages following the 1983 election, Mrs Thatcher has taken us back once again into the fairy-tale world of the peers and peris.

1 *Scene*: In an early D'Oyly Carte prompt copy of *Iolanthe* the date of the action is given as between 1700 and 1882.

An Arcadian Landscape: Arcadia, a mountainous area of small valleys and villages in central Peloponnesus, was regarded by the ancient Greeks as the ideal region of rural contentment and pastoral simplicity. Sullivan composed the music for the First Act of *Iolanthe* while he was himself in the somewhat Arcadian landscape of Cornwall. He was staying at Pencarrow House, near Bodmin, the home of Sir William Molesworth.

2–3 *Leila, Celia, and Fleta*: Gilbert had originally intended calling his principal fairies Lola, Astarte and Lettie.

7 *our fairy ring*: This is, of course, also the term used to describe the rings in lawns or grassland formed by various species of mushroom.

8–15 *We are dainty little fairies*

Some of the critics who attended the London opening of *Iolanthe* felt that the fairies were not as dainty as they might be, musically speaking at least. *The Times* ventured the opinion that

> In the first scene of the play Mr Sullivan has somewhat neglected what was, perhaps, his best opportunity for musical development. His fairy revels are of the tamest. There is here nothing of the brightness and lightness which Weber and Mendelssohn would have given to such a scene. But then, it should be remembered that Mr Gilbert's fairies are very different from those of *Oberon* and *A Midsummer Night's Dream*. Here, as in so many occasions in these operettas, the chances of the musician have been sacrificed to the humour of the poet.

ACT I

Scene. – An Arcadian Landscape. A river runs around the back of the stage. A rustic bridge crosses the river. Enter Fairies, led by Leila, Celia, *and* Fleta. *They trip around the stage, singing as they dance.*

Chorus.

Tripping hither, tripping thither,
Nobody knows why or whither;   5
We must dance and we must sing
Round about our fairy ring!

SOLO – Celia.

We are dainty little fairies,
  Ever singing, ever dancing;
We indulge in our vagaries   10
  In a fashion most entrancing.
If you ask the special function
  Of our never-ceasing motion,
We reply, without compunction,
  That we haven't any notion!   15

Chorus.

No, we haven't any notion!
  Tripping hither, etc.

SOLO – Leila.

If you ask us how we live,
Lovers all essentials give –
  We can ride on lovers' sighs,   20

39 *Something awful*: Gilbert originally intended that Leila should have a song at this point. It is printed in the copy of the libretto sent to the Lord Chamberlain for licensing purposes and follows Fleta's question, 'What could she have done to have deserved such a terrible punishment?' Leila responds: 'Something too shocking – too terrible – too dreadful to be told. I'll tell it to you':

SONG – LEILA.

Five and twenty years ago
She, a fairy,
All unwary,
To a man of mortal clay
Gave her foolish heart away.
They were wed for weal or woe
Five and twenty years ago!

By a law that fairies prize
(Arbitrary
  For a fairy)
She who marries mortal, dies –
Heedless of her heart-drawn cries
We prepared the fatal blow
Five and twenty years ago!

But our Queen, whose heart was rent
By her wailing
Unavailing,
Changed her doom to banishment,
With a merciful intent
And politely told her so
Five and twenty years ago!

44 *Enter Fairy Queen*: The Fairy Queen is one of the great contralto roles in the Savoy Operas, 'great' being used in all senses of the word. In early performances the Queen, whom Gilbert had originally intended should have the name Varine, was dressed to look like Brünnhilde, the formidable chief of the Valkyries and favourite daughter of Wotan in Wagner's *Ring* cycle of operas. Alice Barnett, who created the role, wore a winged helmet and silver mail armour. As we will see, there are other touches of Wagner in both the First and Second Acts of *Iolanthe*.

48–9 *on her head*: 'On your head' was a familiar Victorian catch-phrase meaning 'with ease'. It is still used in the form 'You can do it standing on your head'. Gilbert's use of it here seems rather unnecessary.

Warm ourselves in lovers' eyes,
Bathe ourselves in lovers' tears,
Clothe ourselves with lovers' fears,
Arm ourselves with lovers' darts,
Hide ourselves in lovers' hearts. 25
When you know us, you'll discover
That we almost live on lover!

CHORUS.

Yes, we live on lover!
Tripping hither, etc.

(*At the end of Chorus, all sigh wearily.*) 30

CELIA. Ah, it's all very well, but since our Queen banished Iolanthe, fairy revels have not been what they were!

LEILA. Iolanthe was the life and soul of Fairyland. Why, she wrote all our songs and arranged all our dances! We sing her songs and we trip her measures, but we don't enjoy ourselves! 35

FLETA. To think that five-and-twenty years have elapsed since she was banished! What could she have done to have deserved so terrible a punishment?

LEILA. Something awful! She married a mortal!

FLETA. Oh! Is it injudicious to marry a mortal? 40

LEILA. Injudicious? It strikes at the root of the whole fairy system! By our laws, the fairy who marries a mortal dies!

CELIA. But Iolanthe didn't die!

(*Enter* FAIRY QUEEN.)

QUEEN. No, because your Queen, who loved her with a surpassing 45
love, commuted her sentence to penal servitude for life, on condition that she left her husband and never communicated with him again!

LEILA. That sentence of penal servitude she is now working out, on her head, at the bottom of that stream!

QUEEN. Yes, but when I banished her, I gave her all the pleasant 50
places of the earth to dwell in. I'm sure I never intended that she should go and live at the bottom of a stream! It makes me perfectly wretched to think of the discomfort she must have undergone!

LEILA. Think of the damp! And her chest was always delicate.

QUEEN. And the frogs! Ugh! I never shall enjoy any peace of mind 55
until I know why Iolanthe went to live among the frogs!

FLETA. Then why not summon her and ask her?

62 *Who taught me to curl myself inside a buttercup*: This is one of the prettiest passages which Gilbert ever wrote and shows that inside the satirist's skin there was a delicate lyric poet trying to get out. It has faint echoes of Ariel's song in Shakespeare's *The Tempest*, Act V, Scene 1:

> Where the bee sucks, there suck I.
> In a cowslip's bell I lie;
> There I couch when owls do cry.

73–94 *Invocation – Queen*

This scene, in which Iolanthe rises from the depths of the stream in response to the Queen's command, has a distinctly Wagnerian atmosphere. It has obvious similarities with Scene I of *Das Rheingold*, the first opera in the *Ring* cycle, which is set at the bottom of the River Rhine. The music played while Iolanthe rises from her watery prison bears a close resemblance to the theme 'Die alte Weise' from the Third Act of Wagner's opera *Tristan und Isolde*, which was itself partially set in Cornwall.

81 *Iolanthe*: During rehearsals both the opera and the character now known as *Iolanthe* were called *Perola*. At the final run-through at the Savoy, Sullivan told the company: 'You have been rehearsing *Perola*, but when the curtain goes up the opera will be called *Iolanthe*. Will you please change the name Perola to Iolanthe throughout.'

In fact, Gilbert and Sullivan had always intended to call their new work *Iolanthe*, but this title had leaked out, and to confuse would-be competitors and pirates they had changed the name to *Perola* for the duration of rehearsals.

There may also have been some concern about possible copyright complications in using the name *Iolanthe*. It was already the title of a lyrical drama by the Danish playwright Henrik Hertz based on an old story about a blind princess called Yolande. In 1880 an English translation of Hertz's play by W. G. Wills opened in London with the same title and with Ellen Terry and Henry Irving in the leading roles. In a letter written on 13 October 1882, just six weeks before the opera was due to open, Gilbert asked D'Oyly Carte to request permission to use the name from Irving, to whom Wills had sold the rights.

QUEEN. Why? Because if I set eyes on her I should forgive her at once!
CELIA. Then why not forgive her? Twenty-five years – it's a long time!
LEILA. Think how we loved her! 60
QUEEN. Loved her? What was your love to mine? Why, she was invaluable to me! Who taught me to curl myself inside a buttercup? Iolanthe! Who taught me to swing upon a cobweb? Iolanthe! Who taught me to dive into a dewdrop – to nestle in a nutshell – to gambol upon gossamer? Iolanthe! 65
LEILA. She certainly did surprising things!
FLETA. Oh, give her back to us, great Queen, for your sake if not for ours! (*All kneel in supplication.*)
QUEEN (*irresolute*). Oh, I should be strong, but I am weak! I should be marble, but I am clay! Her punishment has been heavier than I intended. I 70 did not mean that she should live among the frogs – and – well, well, it shall be as you wish – it shall be as you wish!

INVOCATION – QUEEN.

Iolanthe!
From thy dark exile thou art summoned!
Come to our call – 75
Come, come, Iolanthe!

CELIA. Iolanthe!
LEILA. Iolanthe!
ALL. Come to our call, Iolanthe!
Iolanthe, come! 80

(IOLANTHE *rises from the water. She is clad in water-weeds. She approaches the* QUEEN *with head bent and arms crossed.*)

IOLANTHE. With humbled breast
And every hope laid low,
To thy behest, 85
Offended Queen, I bow!

QUEEN. For a dark sin against our fairy laws
We sent thee into life-long banishment;
But mercy holds her sway within our hearts –
Rise – thou art pardoned! 90
IOL. Pardoned!
ALL. Pardoned!

(*Her weeds fall from her, and she appears clothed as a fairy. The* QUEEN *places a diamond coronet on her head, and embraces her. The others also embrace her.*)

105 *my son, Strephon*: The character of Strephon, half fairy and half mortal, is based on an idea originally developed by Gilbert in his Bab Ballad 'The Fairy Curate', which begins, rather like the song originally intended for Leila in *Iolanthe*:

> Once a fairy
> Light and airy
> Married with a mortal.

The ballad goes on to describe the circumstances of the marriage, with the fairy flying down to Ealing, where she meets and later weds an attorney. Their son, Georgie, becomes a curate in the Church of England but falls prey to High Church practices and ritualism to an extent which alarms his mother. She flies down to Ealing again to have words with him, only to be confronted by his Bishop, who refuses to believe she is his mother (see the note to line 558). The ballad ends with poor Georgie changing religion and becoming a Mormon.

118–19 *a Ward in Chancery* (also referred to as 'Ward of Chancery' and 'Ward of Court'): A minor whose guardianship is vested in the Court of Chancery for various legal reasons, often in cases of broken or difficult homes or where a dispute has arisen over property or inheritance. It is contempt of court to marry a Ward of Chancery without the court's consent. Major-General Stanley's daughters in *The Pirates of Penzance* are all wards of Chancery.

In the copy of the libretto sent to the Lord Chamberlain this line read 'and he loves Phyllis, a Ward in Chancery, who owns this farm'.

121 *a fairy down to the waist*: This same imagery is used about mermaids in Act I of *The Pirates of Penzance* when Kate says that they 'are only human beings down to the waist'.

127 *Enter Strephon. . . playing on a flageolet*: Gilbert had originally intended to call his shepherd hero Corydon. This name, used by the classical authors Virgil (in his *Eclogues*) and Theocritus (in his *Idylls*), became conventional in pastoral poetry. Corydon's name was traditionally linked with that of Phyllis, the ideal shepherdess. In John Milton's poem *L'Allegro* (1632), for example, Phyllis is described as giving dinner to Corydon and his fellow shepherd Thyrsis. However, Gilbert later decided to break with the convention and call his hero Strephon, a name he had already used in an earlier play (see the note to lines 229–44).

The flageolet, on which Strephon accompanies himself (as does Phyllis, at her entrance a little later in this act), is a small wind instrument similar to a flute, with a mouthpiece at one end, six principal holes and sometimes keys as well. Strephon and Phyllis are not the only characters in the Savoy Operas to come on stage playing a flageolet. Dr Daly, the vicar of Ploverleigh, does so in the Second Act of *The Sorcerer* before singing his haunting song 'Oh, my voice is sad and low'. Like Strephon's 'Good morrow, good mother!' that song has the most beautiful flageolet accompaniment, played, of course, from the orchestra pit rather than the stage.

CHORUS.

Welcome to our hearts again,   95
  Iolanthe! Iolanthe!
We have shared thy bitter pain,
  Iolanthe! Iolanthe!
Every heart and every hand
In our loving little band   100
Welcomes thee to Fairyland,
  Iolanthe!

QUEEN. And now, tell me, with all the world to choose from, why on earth did you decide to live at the bottom of that stream?

IOL. To be near my son, Strephon.   105

QUEEN. Bless my heart, I didn't know you had a son.

IOL. He was born soon after I left my husband by your royal command – but he does not even know of his father's existence.

FLETA. How old is he?

IOL. Twenty-four.   110

LEILA. Twenty-four! No one, to look at you, would think you had a son of twenty-four! But that's one of the advantages of being immortal. We never grow old! Is he pretty?

IOL. He's extremely pretty, but he's inclined to be stout.

ALL (*disappointed*). Oh!   115

QUEEN. I see no objection to stoutness, in moderation.

CELIA. And what is he?

IOL. He's an Arcadian shepherd – and he loves Phyllis, a Ward in Chancery.

CELIA. A mere shepherd! and he half a fairy!   120

IOL. He's a fairy down to the waist – but his legs are mortal.

ALL. Dear me!

QUEEN. I have no reason to suppose that I am more curious than other people, but I confess I should like to see a person who is a fairy down to the waist, but whose legs are mortal.   125

IOL. Nothing easier, for here he comes!

(*Enter* STREPHON, *singing and dancing and playing on a flageolet. He does not see the Fairies, who retire up stage as he enters.*)

SONG – STREPHON.

Good morrow, good mother!
  Good mother, good morrow!   130
By some means or other,
  Pray banish your sorrow!

141 *the Lord Chancellor*: The highest judicial functionary in England, the Lord Chancellor ranks in order of precedence above all peers, except princes of the blood (i.e. the Royal Family) and the Archbishop of Canterbury. He acts as Speaker of the House of Lords and presides over the Chancery Division of the Supreme Court of Judicature.

146 *the Bar*: A collective noun for the whole profession of barristers. The word is derived from the barrier or partition which used to separate the seats of benchers and readers (i.e. senior and fully established members) of one of the Inns of Court from those of the students who sat in the rest of the hall. When fully qualified, the students were called to this barrier to take part in the 'mootings' and business of the Inn – hence the expression still used to describe qualification as a barrister, 'called to the Bar'.

147 *A servile usher*: The usher is the officer who acts as doorkeeper in a court of law, showing persons to their seats and leading those of rank, like judges, into the court. In *Trial by Jury* the usher is given a solo part, although any pretensions above his station which this elevation might give him are dispelled when the judge contemptuously yells:

> Gentle, simple-minded Usher,
> Get you, if you like, to Russher!

crumpled bands: Bands are the strips of white cloth, normally cotton, which are worn hanging from the neck by clergymen and lawyers. An usher would not normally wear bands.

148 *rusty bombazine*: Bombazine is the black material from which legal and clerical gowns are made.

Chancery Lane: The street which goes through the heart of legal London, joining Gray's Inn to the north with Fleet Street (the Law Courts and the Middle and Inner Temples) to the south. Before the present Law Courts came into use – they were opened just a month after *Iolanthe* was first performed – Chancery cases were sometimes heard in the hall of Lincoln's Inn or in the Old Rolls Court of the now demolished Clifford's Inn, both of which were off Chancery Lane. The street also makes an appearance in Act II of *Patience* when Archibald Grosvenor, newly transformed from aesthete into matter-of-fact young man, proclaims himself 'A Chancery Lane young man'.

159 *My dear aunt*: This line was introduced by Gilbert for the 1907 revival of *Iolanthe* at the Savoy Theatre. The fairies' line 'Poor fellow!' (line 167) was also added at the same time.

169–70 *I've a borough or two at my disposal*: In early-nineteenth-century Britain, up to 200 parliamentary seats were in the private patronage of wealthy and influential individuals. These were the so-called pocket boroughs, where there was often only a handful of electors, and where the local landowner could get his own nominee into the House of Commons without any difficulty. Although most pocket boroughs were abolished by the Great Reform Act of 1832, there were still about sixty M.P.s who were nominated by individuals, mostly peers. Sir Joseph Porter in *H.M.S. Pinafore*, it may be remembered, was returned to Parliament for a pocket borough.

174 *confounded Radicals*: In the 1880s the word 'Radicals' was associated with advanced and left-wing members of the Liberal Party who stressed the need for social and economic reform. In 1885 Joseph Chamberlain, the acknowledged leader of this group, issued the *Radical Programme* (also known as the Unauthorized Programme), which called for much greater government intervention in social and economic matters and seemed to more traditional Liberals to come dangerously near to advocating socialism.

For the 1901 revival of *Iolanthe*, at the height of the war between Britain and the South African Boers, Gilbert changed this line to 'my legs are a couple of confounded Radicals, but this one is a pro-Boer'. The Liberal Party, and left-wing opinion in general, was split in its attitude to the war.

With joy beyond telling
My bosom is swelling,
So join in a measure   135
Expressive of pleasure,
For I'm to be married to-day – to-day –
Yes, I'm to be married to-day!

CHORUS (*aside*). Yes, he's to be married to-day – to-day –
Yes, he's to be married to-day!   140

IOL. Then the Lord Chancellor has at last given his consent to your
marriage with his beautiful ward, Phyllis?
STREPH. Not he, indeed. To all my tearful prayers he answers me, 'A
shepherd lad is no fit helpmate for a Ward of Chancery.' I stood in court, and
there I sang him songs of Arcadee, with flageolet accompaniment – in vain.   145
At first he seemed amused, so did the Bar; but quickly wearying of my song
and pipe, bade me get out. A servile usher then, in crumpled bands and
rusty bombazine, led me, still singing, into Chancery Lane! I'll go no more;
I'll marry her to-day, and brave the upshot, be it what it may! (*Sees Fairies.*)
But who are these?   150
IOL. Oh, Strephon! rejoice with me, my Queen has pardoned me!
STREPH. Pardoned you, mother? This is good news indeed.
IOL. And these ladies are my beloved sisters.
STREPH. Your sisters! Then they are – my aunts!
QUEEN. A pleasant piece of news for your bride on her wedding day!   155
STREPH. Hush! My bride knows nothing of my fairyhood. I dare not
tell her, lest it frighten her. She thinks me mortal, and prefers me so.
LEILA. Your fairyhood doesn't seem to have done you much good.
STREPH. Much good! My dear aunt! it's the curse of my existence!
What's the use of being half a fairy? My body can creep through a keyhole,   160
but what's the good of that when my legs are left kicking behind? I can make
myself invisible down to the waist, but that's of no use when my legs remain
exposed to view! My brain is a fairy brain, but from the waist downwards I'm
a gibbering idiot. My upper half is immortal, but my lower half grows older
every day, and some day or other must die of old age. What's to become of   165
my upper half when I've buried my lower half I really don't know!
FAIRIES. Poor fellow!
QUEEN. I see your difficulty, but with a fairy brain you should seek an
intellectual sphere of action. Let me see. I've a borough or two at my
disposal. Would you like to go into Parliament?   170
IOL. A fairy Member! That would be delightful!
STREPH. I'm afraid I should do no good there – you see, down to the
waist, I'm a Tory of the most determined description, but my legs are a
couple of confounded Radicals, and, on a division, they'd be sure to take me

175 *the wrong lobby*: When a bell sounds indicating a division in the House of Commons, members have a few minutes in which to take their seats in the Chamber. Then the doors are locked and they file into one of two lobbies which run parallel to the Chamber. The 'Aye' lobby (for those in favour of the motion beng put to the vote) is entered to the right of the Speaker's chair, the 'No' lobby (for those against) to the left. Once in the lobbies members give their names to clerks and as they leave they are counted by tellers. Members wishing to abstain on the division remain seated in the Chamber.

177–8 *a Liberal-Conservative*: This phrase was also the object of alteration for topical purposes, being changed for a period to 'Liberal-Unionist'. The Liberal Unionists, led by Joseph Chamberlain and Lord Hartington, broke away from the Liberal Party in 1886 because they could not stomach its policy of Home Rule for Ireland. They remained as a separate political grouping until 1912, when they amalgamated with the Conservative Party, which has since then had the full title 'Conservative and Unionist Party'.

The change of 'Liberal-Conservative' to 'Liberal-Unionist' in the Fairy Queen's line presumably took place some time between 1886 and 1912, although it does not appear in print until the fifth edition of the *Iolanthe* libretto, which was published around 1920, some years after the Liberal Unionists had ceased to exist. It still appears in the current Macmillan edition of the Savoy Operas, but both the Chappell edition of the libretto and the Oxford University Press edition of the operas have reverted to the original 'Liberal-Conservative', which is now normally sung. Perhaps 'Social Democrat' would be more appropriate today.

194 *Good morrow, good lover*: After Phyllis's introductory song, Gilbert originally planned a passage of dialogue in which she would tell us more about herself, including why she is a ward of Chancery. It is printed in the licence copy of the libretto sent to the Lord Chamberlain but was cut before the opera's first performance. Here it is:

STREPHON. Is everything prepared?

PHYLLIS. Yes, and papa has arrived from Wellington barracks – on pass!

STREPHON. O, nice and sober?

PHYL. Quite sober, bless him. His regiment says it thinks it can manage without him for a whole day.

STREPH. Won't it cripple their movements?

PHYL. No – I think not. But oh, Strephon, I tremble at the step I'm taking! I believe it's penal servitude for life to marry a Ward in Chancery without the Lord Chancellor's permission!

STREPH. And what right has he to refuse it? Because I'm only a shepherd. I'm a *decorative* shepherd.

PHYL. Anyway you're as good as I am. Papa's only a private soldier, and that's why they made me a Ward in Chancery – they said he wasn't fit to look after my money. And I shan't be of age for two years.

STREPH. Two years? I can't wait two years while half the House of Lords is sighing at your feet.

PHYL. The House of Lords is certainly extremely attentive.

The dialogue then continues as now (line 224).

into the wrong lobby. You see, they're two to one, which is a strong working   175
majority.

QUEEN. Don't let that distress you; you shall be returned as a Liberal-
Conservative, and your legs shall be our peculiar care.

STREPH. (*bowing*). I see your Majesty does not do things by halves.

QUEEN. No, we are fairies down to the feet.   180

ENSEMBLE.

QUEEN.	Fare thee well, attractive stranger.
FAIRIES.	Fare thee well, attractive stranger.
QUEEN.	Shouldst thou be in doubt or danger,
	Peril or perplexitee,
	Call us, and we'll come to thee!
FAIRIES.	Aye! Call us, and we'll come to thee!
	Tripping hither, tripping thither,
	Nobody knows why or whither;
	We must now be taking wing
	To another fairy ring!

185

190

(*Fairies and* QUEEN *trip off,* IOLANTHE, *who takes an
affectionate farewell of her son, going off last.*)

(*Enter* PHYLLIS, *singing and dancing, and accompanying herself on a flageolet.*)

SONG – PHYLLIS.

Good morrow, good lover!
  Good lover, good morrow!   195
I prithee discover,
  Steal, purchase, or borrow
    Some means of concealing
    The care you are feeling,
    And join in a measure   200
    Expressive of pleasure,
For we're to be married to-day – to-day!
  Yes, we're to be married to-day!

BOTH.   Yes, we're to be married, etc.

STREPH. (*embracing her*). My Phyllis! And to-day we are to be made   205
happy for ever.

PHYL. Well, we're to be married.

STREPH. It's the same thing.

PHYL. I suppose it is. But oh, Strephon, I tremble at the step I'm taking!

213 *Have you ever looked in the glass*: This line, and Phyllis's 'No, never', were added for the 1907 revival. It is somewhat reminiscent of the scene in the Second Act of *Patience* where Archibald Grosvenor enters gazing at his reflection in a hand-mirror. He later hands it to Reginald Bunthorne, who becomes equally obsessed with his own reflection.

225 *grass-plot*: A piece of ground covered with turf, and sometimes also with ornamental flower-beds, generally found around large country houses. Possession of such land seems to place Phyllis in a rather higher social station than that of a mere army private's daughter, or indeed an Arcadian shepherdess.

228 *delays are dangerous*: In the licence copy the duet 'If we're weak enough to tarry', now sung in Act II, follows at this point. This line of dialogue makes a much more natural introduction to that song than it does to 'None shall part us', which was hastily written and slotted in here shortly before the first performance.

229–44 *None shall part us from each other*
This delightful duet, with its charming metaphors drawn from rural life, firmly establishes Phyllis and Strephon as the perfect fairy-tale shepherd and shepherdess. For many years in D'Oyly Carte Company productions they were made to look like eighteenth-century Dresden figurines with powdered wigs, faces made up to give the impression of porcelain, and shiny satin clothes patterned with flowers.

Ten years before writing *Iolanthe* Gilbert had caricatured the idyllic pastoral couple whom he was to re-create for the opera. His play *Happy Arcadia* (1872), set to music by Fred Clay, has among its cast of characters Strephon, 'a happy Arcadian betrothed to Chloe', and Chloe, 'a happy Arcadian betrothed to Strephon'. He is fed up with the pipes he has to play every day, and she is equally bored with the little lamb she is forced to go around with. In *Iolanthe* he drops his cynicism and pokes only the most gentle fun at the conventions of pastoral poetry.

I believe it's penal servitude for life to marry a Ward of Court without the   210
Lord Chancellor's consent! I shall be of age in two years. Don't you think you
could wait two years?

STREPH. Two years. Have you ever looked in the glass?

PHYL. No, never.

STREPH. Here, look at that (*showing her a pocket mirror*), and tell me if   215
you think it rational to expect me to wait two years?

PHYL. (*looking at herself*). No. You're quite right – it's asking too much.
One must be reasonable.

STREPH. Besides, who knows what will happen in two years? Why,
you might fall in love with the Lord Chancellor himself by that time!   220

PHYL. Yes. He's a clean old gentleman.

STREPH. As it is, half the House of Lords are sighing at your feet.

PHYL. The House of Lords are certainly extremely attentive.

STREPH. Attentive? I should think they were! Why did five-and-twenty
Liberal Peers come down to shoot over your grass-plot last autumn? It   225
couldn't have been the sparrows. Why did five-and-twenty Conservative
Peers come down to fish your pond? Don't tell me it was the gold-fish! No,
no – delays are dangerous, and if we are to marry, the sooner the better.

DUET – STREPHON *and* PHYLLIS.

PHYLLIS.   None shall part us from each other,
        One in life and death are we: 230
    All in all to one another –
        I to thee and thou to me!

BOTH.   Thou the tree and I the flower –
        Thou the idol; I the throng –
    Thou the day and I the hour –   235
        Thou the singer; I the song!

STREPH.   All in all since that fond meeting
        When, in joy, I woke to find
    Mine the heart within thee beating,
        Mine the love that heart enshrined!   240

BOTH.   Thou the stream and I the willow –
        Thou the sculptor; I the clay –
    Thou the ocean; I the billow –
        Thou the sunrise; I the day!

(*Exeunt* STREPHON *and* PHYLLIS *together.*)   245

(*March. Enter Procession of Peers.*)

247–61 *Loudly let the trumpet bray*

The entrance of the peers in *Iolanthe* is undoubtedly the most spectacular scene in any of the Savoy Operas. Indeed it must rank alongside the triumphal march in Verdi's *Aïda* and the procession of apprentices and masters in the last act of Wagner's *Die Meistersinger* as one of the greatest processional scenes in the entire world of opera.

In several D'Oyly Carte productions, including the first night at the Savoy, the peers were led on to the stage by a section of the band of the Grenadier Guards. Gilbert's stage direction reads: 'Band cross bridge in double rank from left to right. Enter peers on bridge marching with great state in single rank and somewhat swaggering gesture, as fancying themselves, basses leading and tenors last'. At the phrases 'ye lower middle classes' and 'ye tradesmen' and 'ye masses', he notes that the peers should 'point imperiously to the ground'.

No expense was spared in dressing the peers. Their robes were specially made by Messrs Ede and Sons, robemakers to Queen Victoria's Court, and they wore the full insignia of Britain's highest orders of chivalry. Richard D'Oyly Carte was worried that this might cause offence in high circles. He wrote to his secretary 'If it gets over to the Lord Chamberlain's office that the sacred orders of the Garter, Thistle, Patrick and Bath are going on the stage the office may come down bang and forbid it being done'. However, although Queen Victoria is reported not to have been amused in general by *Iolanthe*, no royal complaint was received on that particular point.

Gilbert had a rather different concern about the possible reaction to the gorgeous spectacle that he was putting on stage. He remarked on the eve of the first night 'Some of our American friends who will be seeing *Iolanthe* in New York tomorrow will probably imagine that British lords are to be seen walking about our streets garbed in this fashion'. Certainly it is reported that the opera's New York run led to a greatly increased demand among American heiresses for eligible members of the British aristocracy.

Gilbert also decided that for added effect the peers should be completely shaven, except for a single tuft under their chins and mutton-chop whiskers. Under their coronets their heads were to be completely bald. 'Let your coronets remain off longer, gentlemen', he said at one rehearsal. 'There is £12's worth of bald heads on the stage and we must make the most of them'.

263–95 *The Law is the true embodiment*

This is the one song in the Savoy Operas where Sullivan's indication of speed has traditionally been ignored in D'Oyly Carte Opera Company performances. In the vocal score it is marked *Allegro vivace*, but it is generally sung at the slightly slower speed of *Allegro non troppo*. In his book *W. S. Gilbert, Stage Director* (1977) William Cox-Ife, chorus director of the D'Oyly Carte Company from 1950 to 1968, says that Sullivan's *Allegro vivace* was almost certainly a slip of the pen, understandable in view of the short time in which he completed the *Iolanthe* score.

Cox-Ife also maintains that 'there is incontrovertible proof that the speed at which this song is sung in the D'Oyly Carte performances is the one agreed upon by both Gilbert and Sullivan'. He points out that Martyn Green, whom he first heard singing it, took the song at the same speed as his predecessor in the comic roles, Sir Henry Lytton. Lytton, who first played the Lord Chancellor in a touring company in 1891 and took over the role in the main D'Oyly Carte Company in 1909, was personally directed by Gilbert, and so it is highly unlikely that he would have changed the speed of a song in a way not intended by the composer and librettist. However, in an early D'Oyly Carte recording C. H. Workman sings the number *Allegro vivace*, as marked, so it is just possible that Cox-Ife was wrong.

When George Grossmith appeared on stage to sing this song on the first night of *Iolanthe* at the Savoy Theatre, there was naturally much speculation in the audience as

CHORUS.

Loudly let the trumpet bray!
  Tantantara!
Proudly bang the sounding brasses!
    Tzing! Boom!   250
As upon its lordly way
  This unique procession passes,
    Tantantara! Tzing! Boom!
Bow, bow, ye lower middle classes!
Bow, bow, ye tradesmen, bow, ye masses!   255
Blow the trumpets, bang the brasses!
  Tantantara! Tzing! Boom!
We are peers of highest station,
Paragons of legislation,
Pillars of the British nation!   260
  Tantantara! Tzing! Boom!

(*Enter the* LORD CHANCELLOR, *followed by his train-bearer.*)

SONG – LORD CHANCELLOR.

The Law is the true embodiment
Of everything that's excellent.
It has no kind of fault or flaw,   265
And I, my Lords, embody the Law.
The constitutional guardian I
Of pretty young Wards in Chancery,
All very agreeable girls – and none
Are over the age of twenty-one.   270
    A pleasant occupation for
  . A rather susceptible Chancellor!

ALL.   A pleasant, etc.

But though the compliment implied
Inflates me with legitimate pride,   275
It nevertheless can't be denied
That it has its inconvenient side.
For I'm not so old, and not so plain,
And I'm quite prepared to marry again,
But there'd be the deuce to pay in the Lords   280
If I fell in love with one of my Wards!
  Which rather tries my temper, for
  I'm *such* a susceptible Chancellor!

to which well-known contemporary figure Gilbert had chosen as the model for his latest comic lead. There did not seem to be any close similarities between the stage Lord Chancellor and his real-life contemporary counterpart, Lord Selborne, who held the office in Gladstone's 1880–85 Government. Indeed the general view was that this time Gilbert had gone back into history and had loosely based his Lord Chancellor on Lord Lyndhurst (1772–1863), one of the most distinguished holders of the office in the nineteenth century. Lyndhurst, a Boston American by birth, was Lord Chancellor from 1827 to 1830 and was known for the mastery of his judicial summings-up and his ability to digest a mass of evidence.

301 *her cottage*: Gilbert seems to be a trifle uncertain about Phyllis's exact station in life. First, in his original version of the *Iolanthe* libretto, we are told that she owns the farm on which Act I is set (see the note to lines 118–19). That information is later cut out, as is the subsequent and rather conflicting intelligence that she is the daughter of a private stationed at the Wellington barracks. Next, Strephon informs us that she has both a grass-plot and a fish-pond, yet here we are told that she lives in a cottage. It is all rather confusing.

317–18 *contempt of . . . Court*: Action of any kind which interferes with the proper administration of justice. It includes any disobedience to the rules, orders or process of a court and any gross display of disrespect to the judge or officials.

318 *counsel*: The name given to a barrister or barristers when engaged in the direction or conduct of a case in court.

320 *woolsack*: A square couch said to have been originally placed in the House of Lords in the reign of Edward III and stuffed with wool clippings as a reminder of England's staple trade. It is now filled with a blend of wool from Britain and the Commonwealth. When the House of Lords is sitting, the woolsack is the seat of the Lord Chancellor. However, it is technically outside the precincts of the House, so when he wishes to address his fellow peers he has to stand aside from the woolsack and so 'enter' the chamber.

ALL. Which rather, etc.

> And every one who'd marry a Ward   285
> Must come to me for my accord,
> And in my court I sit all day,
> Giving agreeable girls away,
> With one for him – and one for he –
> And one for you – and one for ye –   290
> And one for thou – and one for thee –
> But never, oh, never a one for me!
>   Which is exasperating for
>   A highly susceptible Chancellor!

ALL. Which is, etc.   295

(*Enter* LORD TOLLOLLER.)

LORD TOLL. And now, my Lords, to the business of the day.

LORD CH. By all means. Phyllis, who is a Ward of Court, has so powerfully affected your Lordships, that you have appealed to me in a body to give her to whichever one of you she may think proper to select, and a   300
noble Lord has just gone to her cottage to request her immediate attendance. It would be idle to deny that I, myself, have the misfortune to be singularly attracted by this young person. My regard for her is rapidly undermining my constitution. Three months ago I was a stout man. I need say no more. If I could reconcile it with my duty, I should unhesitatingly award her to myself,   305
for I can conscientiously say that I know no man who is so well fitted to render her exceptionally happy. (PEERS: Hear, hear!) But such an award would be open to misconstruction, and therefore, at whatever personal inconvenience, I waive my claim.

LORD TOLL. My Lord, I desire, on the part of this House, to express   310
its sincere sympathy with your Lordship's most painful position.

LORD CH. I thank your Lordships. The feelings of a Lord Chancellor who is in love with a Ward of Court are not to be envied. What is his position? Can he give his own consent to his own marriage with his own Ward? Can he marry his own Ward without his own consent? And if he   315
marries his own Ward without his own consent, can he commit himself for contempt of his own Court? And if he commit himself for contempt of his own Court, can he appear by counsel before himself, to move for arrest of his own judgement? Ah, my Lords, it is indeed painful to have to sit upon a woolsack which is stuffed with such thorns as these!   320

(*Enter* LORD MOUNTARARAT.)

LORD MOUNT. My Lord, I have much pleasure in announcing that I

323–4 *the Bar of this House*: This is a completely different Bar from that referred to in line 146 above. In both the House of Commons and the House of Lords, a barrier separates from the main chamber a space near the door to which non-members may be admitted for business purposes. In the House of Lords the Bar consists of two rods which can be drawn across the end of the rows of benches. Offenders appealing to the Lords appear before the Bar, where they must traditionally kneel, and it is also the point to which the Speaker and members of the House of Commons come when they attend the monarch's opening of Parliament.

330–49 *Of all the young ladies I know*
The predicament of Phyllis, pursued by two peers of the realm as well as by the humble Strephon, is anticipated in Gilbert's Bab Ballad 'The Periwinkle Girl'. This tells the story of Mary, a winkle seller, who is eagerly sought after by two dukes, Duke Bailey and Duke Humphy, as well as by an earl, a less exalted member of the peerage. As these concluding verses show, Mary was initially attracted by the ducal overtures, but they were to prove less appealing on closer examination:

> 'Two Dukes would Mary make a bride,
> And from her foes defend her' –
> 'Well, not exactly that,' they cried,
> 'We offer guilty splendour.

> 'We do not promise marriage rite,
> So please dismiss the notion!'
> 'Oh dear,' said she, 'that alters quite
> The state of my emotion.'

> The Earl he ups and says, says he,
> 'Dismiss them to their orgies,
> For I am game to marry thee
> Quite reg'lar at St George's.'

> He'd had, it happily befell,
> A decent education,
> His views would have befitted well
> A far superior station.

> His sterling worth had worked a cure,
> She never heard him grumble;
> She saw his soul was good and pure,
> Although his rank was humble.

> Her views of earldoms and their lot,
> All underwent expansion –
> Come, Virtue in an earldom's cot!
> Go, Vice in ducal mansion.

351 *tabors*: Small drums.

have succeeded in inducing the young person to present herself at the Bar
of this House.

(Enter PHYLLIS.) 325

RECITATIVE – PHYLLIS.

My well-loved Lord and Guardian dear,
You summoned me, and I am here!

CHORUS OF PEERS.

Oh, rapture, how beautiful!
How gentle – how dutiful!

SOLO – LORD TOLLOLLER.

Of all the young ladies I know 330
  This pretty young lady's the fairest;
Her lips have the rosiest show,
  Her eyes are the richest and rarest.
Her origin's lowly, it's true,
  But of birth and position I've plenty; 335
I've grammar and spelling for two,
  And blood and behaviour for twenty!
    Her origin's lowly, it's true,
    I've grammar and spelling for two;

CHORUS. Of birth and position he's plenty, 340
With blood and behaviour for twenty!

SOLO – LORD MOUNTARARAT.

Though the views of the House have diverged
  On every conceivable motion,
All questions of Party are merged
  In a frenzy of love and devotion; 345
If you ask us distinctly to say
  What Party we claim to belong to,
We reply, without doubt or delay,
  The Party we're singing this song to!

SOLO – PHYLLIS.

I'm very much pained to refuse, 350
  But I'll stick to my pipes and my tabors;
I can spell all the words that I use,
  And my grammar's as good as my neighbours'.

362 *Nay, tempt me not*: In the original version of *Perola* there was a lengthy series of couplets and a longer recitative for Phyllis between the end of the repetition of the last part of her song (line 361) and the beginning of Lord Tolloller's ballad (line 368). They are printed in the licence copy:

LORD CH.   Nay, do not recklessly refuse their proffer.
            Attend to the advantages they offer.

COUPLETS.

LORD CH.   On you they'd set
            A coronet.
PHYL.   Oh, a coronet.
LORD CH.   What joy to be a noble's pet,
            And walk about in a coronet!
CHORUS.   What joy, etc.
LORD TOLL. You'll breathe the air of Grosvenor Square.
PHYL.   Oh Grosvenor, Grosvenor Square.
LORD TOLL. What joy to breathe the balmy air
            Of Grosvenor Square, of Grosvenor Square.
ALL.   What joy, etc.
LORD MOUNT. On every lip
            'Your ladyship!'
PHYL.   Oh lady – ladyship!
LORD MOUNT. What joy to hear on every lip
            'Your ladyship', 'Your ladyship!'
ALL.   What joy, etc.
LORD CH.   There'll be no dearth
            Of clothes from Worth!
PHYL. (*aside*). Oh, tasty tempting Worth!
LORD CH.   Oh, is there purer joy on earth
            Than to be dressed by Mister Worth!
ALL.   Oh, is there, etc.
LORD MOUNT. With footmen rare
            In powdered hair!
PHYL. (*aside*). Oh, powdered – powdered hair!
LORD MOUNT. What joy to drive through Vanity Fair
            With footmen rare in powdered hair!
ALL.   What joy, etc.
LORD TOLL. With a coachman big
            In a curly wig!
PHYL. (*aside*). Oh, a curly, curly wig!
LORD TOLL. What joy to drive about full fig,
            With a coachman big
            In a curly wig!
ALL.   What joy, etc.

PEERS.	PHYLLIS.
You'll breathe the air	I do not care
Of Grosvenor Square,	For Grosvenor Square;
There'll be no dearth	And who on earth
Of clothes from Worth,	Is Mister Worth?
With footmen rare	So bait no snare
In powdered hair,	With footmen rare,
And a coachman big	Or a coachman big
In a curly wig!	In a curly wig,
What joy to drive about full fig	Indeed, I do not care a fig
With a coachman big in a curly wig!	For a coachman big in a curly wig!

As for birth – I was born like the rest,
  My behaviour is rustic but hearty, 355
And I know where to turn for the best,
  When I want a particular Party!

PHYLLIS, LORD TOLL., *and* LORD MOUNT.

Though $\begin{Bmatrix} \text{my} \\ \text{her} \end{Bmatrix}$ station is none of the best,

I suppose $\begin{Bmatrix} \text{I} \\ \text{she} \end{Bmatrix}$ was born like the rest;

And $\begin{Bmatrix} \text{I know} \\ \text{she knows} \end{Bmatrix}$ where to look for $\begin{Bmatrix} \text{my} \\ \text{her} \end{Bmatrix}$ hearty, 360

When $\begin{Bmatrix} \text{I want} \\ \text{she wants} \end{Bmatrix}$ a particular Party!

RECITATIVE – PHYLLIS.

Nay, tempt me not.
  To rank I'll not be bound;
In lowly cot
  Alone is virtue found! 365

CHORUS. No, no; indeed high rank will never hurt you,
The Peerage is not destitute of virtue.

BALLAD – LORD TOLLOLLER.

Spurn not the nobly born
  With love affected,
Nor treat with virtuous scorn 370
  The well-connected.
High rank involves no shame –
We boast an equal claim
With him of humble name
  To be respected! 375
Blue blood! blue blood!
  When virtuous love is sought
  Thy power is naught,
Though dating from the Flood,
  Blue blood! Ah, blue blood! 380

CHORUS.   When virtuous love is sought, etc.

Spare us the bitter pain
  Of stern denials,

RECITATIVE - PHYLLIS.
No, no! it may not be, though I may mention,
I much appreciate your condescension,
I am a girl of lowly education,
And should disgrace your elevated station!

ALL.   No, no, despite defects of education
You would adorn our elevated station.

There then follows Lord Tolloller's ballad, 'Spurn not the nobly born'.

363 *To rank I'll not be bound*: In the vocal score and the Chappell edition of the libretto this is printed 'To wealth I'll not be bound'.

366 *No, no; indeed high rank will never hurt you*: In the first edition of the libretto this line was sung as 'Nay, do not shrink from us – we will not hurt you'.

387 *Belgrave Square*: One of the grandest squares in London, situated between Knightsbridge and Victoria, which gets its name from one of the titles of the ground landlord, the Duke of Westminster. The surrounding area, known as Belgravia, is a favourite location for embassies. In *Utopia Limited* the King, boasting about his successful attempt to anglicize his country, sings'

> Our city we have beautified – we've done it willy-nilly –
> And all that isn't Belgrave Square is Strand and Piccadilly.

389 *Seven Dials*: A point in Monmouth Street, north of Leicester Square and south of High Holborn in the centre of London, where seven streets converge. During Charles II's reign a doric pillar was erected at the crossroads with sundials facing the seven streets. The area came to be notorious for squalor and crime, and as the headquarters of London's street ballad printers and sellers. Now, however, with the 'trendification' of nearby Covent Garden it has become positively fashionable.

394 *Blue blood*: High or noble birth. The phrase is of Spanish origin and derives from the fact that the veins of pure-blooded Spanish aristocrats, untainted by any Moorish influences, were more blue than the veins of those with mixed ancestry.

Gilbert's prompt copy of *Iolanthe* indicates that during the music following Lord Tolloller's ballad 'the peers take out handkerchiefs, wipe right eye, left eye, *nose* and throw handkerchiefs into coronets at last note, and resume coronets'.

412 *Of Arcadee*: This spelling of Arcady for the purpose of rhyming also occurs in the first line of a song in Gilbert and Sullivan's first joint work, *Thespis*, 'Little maid of Arcadee'. Reference to Arcady, or Arcadia, as it is more often called, also occurs in *Trial by Jury* in the Counsel for the Plaintiff's line 'Camberwell became a bower,/Peckham an Arcadian vale'.

Nor with low-born disdain
    Augment our trials.   385
Hearts just as pure and fair
May beat in Belgrave Square
As in the lowly air
    Of Seven Dials!
Blue blood! blue blood!   390
    Of what avail art thou
    To serve us now?
Though dating from the Flood,
    Blue blood! Ah, blue blood!

CHORUS.   Of what avail art thou, etc.   395

RECITATIVE – PHYLLIS.

My Lords, it may not be.
    With grief my heart is riven!
You waste your time on me,
    For ah! my heart is given!

ALL.   Given!   400
PHYL.   Yes, given!
ALL.   Oh, horror! ! !

RECITATIVE – LORD CHANCELLOR.

And who has dared to brave our high displeasure,
And thus defy our definite command?

(*Enter* STREPHON.)   405

STREPH. 'Tis I – young Strephon! mine this priceless treasure!
    Against the world I claim my darling's hand!
        (PHYLLIS *rushes to his arms.*)
    A shepherd I –
ALL.   A shepherd he!   410
STREPH. Of Arcady –
ALL.   Of Arcadee!
STREPH. Betrothed are we!
ALL.   Betrothed are they –
STREPH. And mean to be –   415
ALL.   Espoused to-day!

438–9 *Manent Lord Chancellor and Strephon*: In this stage direction Gilbert shows that, like the fairies and peers, he has had a good classical education. *Manent* is from the Latin word *maneo*, meaning 'remain'. It is a standard stage direction.

441 *Court of Chancery*: Now one of the divisions of the High Court of Justice, the Court of Chancery has traditionally dealt with cases involving equity and also with the wardship of infants.

442–61 *I go by Nature's Acts of Parliament*: In this passage, reminiscent of Ralph Rackstraw's 'simple eloquence' to Josephine in *H.M.S. Pinafore* and of some of Frederic's musings in *The Pirates of Penzance*, Strephon proves that, just like these other Gilbertian heroes, his humble origins have not prevented him from developing impressive powers of expression. In its review of the London first night of *Iolanthe*, the *Sunday Times* described the ensuing dialogue between Strephon and the Lord Chancellor as 'one of the most comical bits in the piece'.

Some other papers, however, were distinctly critical of this passage. Both the *Whitehall Review* and *Punch*, which generally took a low view of Gilbert's work, perhaps not unconnected with the fact that his Bab Ballads had appeared in the pages of its great rival *Fun*, detected more than a hint of plagiarism. They suggested that the Lord Chancellor's rejection of Strephon's eloquent testimony from nature on the grounds that it was not evidence (line 458) was borrowed directly from the passage in Charles Dickens's *The Pickwick Papers* where Sam Weller is rebuked by Mr Justice Stareleigh for spicing his evidence with the phrase 'as the soldier said'. Stareleigh retorted 'You must not tell us what the soldier, or any other man, said, sir. . . it's not evidence.'

Whether or not Gilbert did borrow from Dickens, this remains a superb piece of comic dialogue. It is important not to 'ham' it, as is clear from the following extract from *The Secrets of a Savoyard*, the memoirs of Sir Henry Lytton, the D'Oyly Carte Company's principal exponent of the comic roles from 1908 to 1934:

> Now if an actor in these operas has to be careful of one thing above everything else, it is that of avoiding forcing a point. . . The lines must be declaimed in deadly seriousness just as if the actor believes absolutely in the fanciful and extravagant thing he is saying. I can think of no better illustration of this than the scene in *Iolanthe* where Strephon rejects recourse to the Chancery Court and says his code of conduct is regulated only by 'Nature's Acts of Parliament'. The Lord Chancellor then talks about the absurdity of 'an affidavit from a thunderstorm or a few words on oath from a heavy shower'.
>
> What a typical Gilbertian fancy! Well, you know how the 'comic' man would say that, how he would whip up his coat collar and shiver at the suggestion of rain, and how he would do his poor best to make it sound and look 'funny'. And the result would be that he would kill the wittiness of the lines by burlesque. The Lord Chancellor says the words as if he believed an affidavit from a thunderstorm was at least a possibility, and the suggestion that he does think it possible makes the very idea, in the audience's mind, more whimsical still.

ENSEMBLE.

STREPH.	THE OTHERS.	
A shepherd I	A shepherd he	
Of Arcady,	Of Arcadee,	
Betrothed are we,	Betrothed are they,	
And mean to be	And mean to be	420
Espoused to-day!	Espoused to-day!	

DUET – LORD MOUNTARARAT *and* LORD TOLLOLLER
(*aside to each other*).

'Neath this blow,
　　Worse than stab of dagger –
Though we mo-
　　Mentarily stagger,　　　　　　　　　　　　425
In each heart
　　Proud are we innately –
Let's depart,
　　Dignified and stately!
ALL.　　Let's depart,　　　　　　　　　　　　　　430
　　Dignified and stately!

CHORUS OF PEERS.

Though our hearts she's badly bruising,
In another suitor choosing,
Let's pretend it's most amusing.
　　Ha! ha! ha! Tan-ta-ra!　　　　　　　　　　435

(*Exeunt all the Peers, marching round stage with much dignity.*
LORD CHANCELLOR *separates* PHYLLIS *from* STREPHON
and orders her off. She follows Peers. Manent LORD
　　　　　　　　CHANCELLOR *and* STREPHON.)

LORD CH. Now, sir, what excuse have you to offer for having　440
disobeyed an order of the Court of Chancery?
STREPH. My Lord, I know no Courts of Chancery; I go by Nature's
Acts of Parliament. The bees – the breeze – the seas – the rooks – the brooks
– the gales – the vales – the fountains and the mountains cry, 'You love this
maiden – take her, we command you!' 'Tis writ in heaven by the bright　445
barbèd dart that leaps forth into lurid light from each grim thundercloud.
The very rain pours forth her sad and sodden sympathy! When chorused
Nature bids me take my love, shall I reply, 'Nay, but a certain Chancellor
forbids it'? Sir, you are England's Lord High Chancellor, but are you

458 *an affidavit from a thunderstorm*: An affidavit is a statement made in writing, and confirmed on oath, which is intended to be used in court.

465–96 *When I went to the Bar as a very young man*
This song has been sung by at least two real Lord Chancellors as well as by the stage variety. Sir Henry Lytton in his autobiography recalls a word-perfect rendering from memory by Lord Birkenhead, Lord Chancellor from 1919 to 1922. More recently, in December 1978, Lord Elwyn-Jones, who held the office from 1974 to 1979, performed the song as a duet with John Reed of the D'Oyly Carte Company at a special performance of the Bar Musical Society before the Queen Mother in the hall of the Middle Temple.

Gilbert's Lord Chancellor has, in fact, endeared himself to many of those who have held the office in real life. Lord Sankey, Lord Chancellor from 1929 to 1935, told Lytton, 'There is no doubt about it that Lytton's Lord Chancellor has given more pleasure to the public than mine . . . Ordinary Lord Chancellors go in and out with their governments, but you are a permanent official'. Lord Elwyn-Jones expressed similar sentiments to James Conroy-Ward, the last D'Oyly Carte principal comedian, when he met a deputation from the company outside the House of Lords in the summer of 1981.

'When I went to the Bar' has close similarities with the judge's song in *Trial by Jury*, 'When I, good friends, was called to the Bar'. Gilbert probably put a bit of himself into both songs. He himself was called to the Bar in 1864, having been a student at the Inner Temple. He practised as a barrister for four years but was singularly unsuccessful, making only £75 in that period. It was in the long waits for clients that he started writing humorous articles and began to realize where his true talents lay.

Punch, needless to say, in reviewing *Iolanthe*, found another example of Gilbertian plagiarism in this song. It suggested that the idea was taken from an old song, 'Says I to myself as I walked by myself,/And myself says again to me'.

471 *attorney*: Until 1873 those lawyers, other than barristers, who dealt in equity cases were known as solicitors and those who dealt in common law cases were called attorneys. The Judicature Act of that year brought the two groups together under the single title of Solicitors of the Supreme Court. Sir Joseph Porter, the First Lord of the Admiralty in *H.M.S. Pinafore*, began his legal career as office boy to an attorney's firm. The term is, of course, still used in the United States.
brief: A summary of the facts of a case, with reference to the points of law applicable to them, drawn up by a solicitor for the instruction of counsel conducting the case in court. The phrase 'to take a brief' means to accept the conduct of a case.

481 *throw dust in a juryman's eyes*: To throw dust in someone's eyes is to mislead him. The phrase is said to derive from the dust thrown up into the eyes of runners in a race from the heels of the leading runner. Mohammedans are said to have made a practice of casting dust into the air to confound their enemies.

486 *Exchequer, Queen's Bench, Common Pleas, or Divorce*: The courts of Exchequer, Common Pleas and Queen's (or King's) Bench were separate common law courts which traced their origins back to the reign of Edward I. The first decided revenue cases, the second civil actions between subject and subject, and the third, which was originally presided over by the sovereign, criminal actions. The Judicature Act of 1873 merged these three courts together into the Queen's Bench division of the Supreme Court of Judicature, or the High Court. It also brought together into a second division three special courts – the High Court of Admiralty, the Court of Probate, and the Court for Divorce and Matrimonial Causes. The third division created by the Act, which was the work of Lord Selborne, the Lord Chancellor of England at the time that *Iolanthe* was written and first performed, was that of Chancery. The effect of the Act was to bring together England's two legal traditions, common law and equity, into a single system.

487 *Have perjured themselves*: To perjure is to swear falsely or break one's oath.

Chancellor of birds and trees, King of the winds and Prince of   450
thunderclouds?

LORD CH. No. It's a nice point. I don't know that I ever met it before.
But my difficulty is that at present there's no evidence before the Court that
chorused Nature has interested herself in the matter.

STREPH. No evidence! You have my word for it. I tell you that she   455
bade me take my love.

LORD CH. Ah! but, my good sir, you mustn't tell us what she told you
– it's not evidence. Now an affidavit from a thunderstorm, or a few words on
oath from a heavy shower, would meet with all the attention they deserve.

STREPH. And have you the heart to apply the prosaic rules of evidence   460
to a case which bubbles over with poetical emotion?

LORD CH. Distinctly. I have always kept my duty strictly before my
eyes, and it is to that fact that I owe my advancement to my present
distinguished position.

SONG – LORD CHANCELLOR.

When I went to the Bar as a very young man,   465
    (Said I to myself – said I),
I'll work on a new and original plan,
    (Said I to myself – said I),
I'll never assume that a rogue or a thief
Is a gentleman worthy implicit belief,   470
Because his attorney has sent me a brief,
    (Said I to myself – said I!).

Ere I go into court I will read my brief through
    (Said I to myself – said I),
And I'll never take work I'm unable to do   475
    (Said I to myself – said I),
My learned profession I'll never disgrace
By taking a fee with a grin on my face,
When I haven't been there to attend to the case
    (Said I to myself – said I!).   480

I'll never throw dust in a juryman's eyes
    (Said I to myself – said I),
Or hoodwink a judge who is not over-wise
    (Said I to myself – said I),
Or assume that the witnesses summoned in force   485
In Exchequer, Queen's Bench, Common Pleas, or Divorce,
Have perjured themselves as a matter of course
    (Said I to myself – said I!).

516 *Finale*: In a interview with the magazine *Home News*, in 1889, Sullivan said 'I think *Iolanthe* contained the longest finale I ever wrote. Goodness knows how many pages of the score it covered'. In fact, the First Act finale of *Iolanthe* runs to thirty-five pages in the vocal score, beating by just one page the next longest finale in the Savoy Operas, that of Act I of *The Grand Duke*.

In other professions in which men engage
    (Said I to myself – said I),   490
The Army, the Navy, the Church, and the Stage
    (Said I to myself – said I),
Professional licence, if carried too far,
Your chance of promotion will certainly mar –
And I fancy the rule might apply to the Bar   495
    (Said I to myself – said I!).

                    (*Exit* LORD CHANCELLOR.)

                  (*Enter* IOLANTHE.)

STREPH. Oh, Phyllis, Phyllis! To be taken from you just as I was on the point of making you my own! Oh, it's too much – it's too much!   500

IOL. (*to* STREPHON, *who is in tears*). My son in tears – and on his wedding day!

STREPH. My wedding day! Oh, mother, weep with me, for the Law has interposed between us, and the Lord Chancellor has separated us for ever!   505

IOL. The Lord Chancellor! (*Aside.*) Oh, if he did but know!

STREPH. (*overhearing her*). If he did but know what?

IOL. No matter! The Lord Chancellor has no power over you. Remember you are half a fairy. You can defy him – down to the waist.

STREPH. Yes, but from the waist downwards he can commit me to   510 prison for years! Of what avail is it that my body is free, if my legs are working out seven years' penal servitude?

IOL. True. But take heart – our Queen has promised you her special protection. I'll go to her and lay your peculiar case before her.

STREPH. My beloved mother! how can I repay the debt I owe you?   515

                FINALE – QUARTET.

(*As it commences, the Peers appear at the back, advancing unseen and on tiptoe.* LORD MOUNTARARAT *and* LORD TOLLOLLER *lead* PHYLLIS *between them, who listens in horror to what she hears.*)

STREPH. (*to* IOLANTHE). When darkly looms the day,
           And all is dull and grey,   520
           To chase the gloom away,
             On thee I'll call!

PHYL. (*speaking aside to* LORD MOUNTARARAT). What was that?

LORD MOUNT. (*aside to* PHYLLIS).
           I think I heard him say,

530 *thy bark*: Nothing to do with dogs, but a word derived from the French *barque*, meaning a small sailing boat.

537 *St James's Park*: Lying behind Whitehall, between the Mall and Birdcage Walk, St James's Park is the oldest of the six Royal Parks in central London. It was originally established by Henry VIII in 1532, when he took swampy ground which had previously belonged to the Sisters of St James in the Field and built St James's Palace at its western end. The park was opened to the public in the seventeenth century, and in 1828 it was remodelled by John Nash for George III. In the nineteenth century it had something of a reputation as a haunt for prostitutes.

That on a rainy day, 525
To while the time away,
On her he'd call!

CHORUS.   We think we heard him say, etc.

(PHYLLIS *much agitated at her lover's supposed faithlessness.*)

IOL. (to STREPHON). When tempests wreck thy bark, 530
And all is drear and dark,
If thou shouldst need an Ark,
I'll give thee one!

PHYL. (*speaking aside to* LORD TOLLOLLER). What was that?

LORD TOLL. (*aside to* PHYLLIS).
I heard the minx remark, 535
She'd meet him after dark,
Inside St James's Park,
And give him one!

CHORUS.   We heard the minx remark, etc.

PHYL., IOL., LORD TOLL., STREPH.

The prospect's $\begin{Bmatrix} \text{very} \\ \text{not so} \end{Bmatrix}$ bad, 540

$\begin{matrix} \text{My} \\ \text{Thy} \end{matrix} \Big\}$ heart so sore and sad

May very soon be glad
As summer's sun;

For when the sky is dark

And tempests wreck $\begin{Bmatrix} \text{his} \\ \text{thy} \\ \text{my} \end{Bmatrix}$ bark, 545

If $\begin{Bmatrix} \text{he should} \\ \text{thou shouldst} \\ \text{I should} \end{Bmatrix}$ need an Ark,

$\begin{matrix} \text{She'll} \\ \text{I'll} \end{matrix} \Big\}$ give $\begin{Bmatrix} \text{him} \\ \text{thee} \\ \text{me} \end{Bmatrix}$ one!

558 *This lady's his what*: The peers' incredulity at the idea that Strephon, at nearly twenty-five, can have a mother of seventeen echoes the reaction of the Bishop in Gilbert's Bab Ballad 'The Fairy Curate' when he is confronted with Georgie's fairy mother (see the note to line 105):

> 'Who is this, sir,
> Ballet miss, sir?'
> Said the Bishop coldly.
> ''Tis my mother
> And no other,'
> Georgie answered boldly.
> 'Go along sir!
> You are wrong, sir,
> You have years in plenty;
> While this hussy
> (Gracious mussy!)
> Isn't two and twenty!'

564 *Enter Lord Chancellor*: Gilbert's own stage direction at this point reads: 'Lord Chancellor enters over style and stands on step of style during his recitative "What means this mirth unseemly?"'

571 *dolce far niente*: Gilbert makes much use of the rhyming possibilities of foreign phrases, particularly here in the Act I finale of *Iolanthe*. *Dolce far niente* is an Italian expression meaning literally 'sweet doing nothing', i.e. delightful idleness. Appropriately, it is used again in *The Gondoliers*, where Fiametta and Vittoria bid Antonio 'enjoy your *dolce far niente*', and in the chorus 'Quaff the nectar' in Act I of *Utopia Limited*, when the guards, nobles and dancing girls 'Sing the songs of *far niente*'.

577 *festina lente*: a Latin expression meaning to make haste slowly, picked up in the English saying 'The more haste, the less speed'.

PHYL. (*revealing herself*). Ah!

(IOLANTHE *and* STREPHON *much confused.*)

PHYL.   Oh, shameless one, tremble!   550
                Nay, do not endeavour
                Thy fault to dissemble,
                We part – and for ever!
                I worshipped him blindly
                He worships another –   555
STREPH.   Attend to me kindly,
                This lady's my mother!
TOLL.   This lady's his *what*?
STREPH.   This lady's my mother!
TENORS.   This lady's his *what*?   560
BASSES.   He says she's his mother!

(*They point derisively to* IOLANTHE, *laughing heartily
at her. She goes for protection to* STREPHON.)

(*Enter* LORD CHANCELLOR. IOLANTHE *veils herself.*)

LORD CH.   What means this mirth unseemly,   565
                That shakes the listening earth?

LORD TOLL.   The joke is good extremely,
                And justifies our mirth.

LORD MOUNT.   This gentleman is seen,
                With a maid of seventeen,   570
             A-taking of his *dolce far niente*;
                And wonders he'd achieve,
                For he asks us to believe
      She's his mother – and he's nearly five-and-twenty!

LORD CH. (*sternly*). Recollect yourself, I pray,   575
                And be careful what you say –
           As the ancient Romans said, *festina lente*.
                For I really do not see
                How so young a girl could be
        The mother of a man of five-and-twenty.   580

ALL.   Ha! ha! ha! ha! ha!

STREPH.   My Lord, of evidence I have no dearth –
        She is – has been – my mother from my birth!

584–91 *In babyhood*

Both *The Times* and the *Standard* reviewers of the first-night performance ventured the suggestion that this pretty ballad was inspired by the air *Sonst spielt ich mit Szepter und Kron* ('In childhood with crown and sceptre I played') from the opera *Zar und Zimmermann (Tsar and Carpenter)* by the German composer Gustav Lortzing (1801–51).

587 *Moistenèd my clay*: To moisten one's clay is to drink. The word clay in this context means the human body. It derives from the biblical statement that earth was the original material for the human body, an idea still preserved, of course, in the Christian burial service with its phrase 'dust to dust, ashes to ashes'. The word occurs with a slightly different connotation in the Fairy Queen's phrase 'I should be marble, but I am clay' early on in the opera (lines 69–70).

BALLAD.

In babyhood
Upon her lap I lay,   585
  With infant food
She moistenèd my clay;
  Had she withheld
The succour she supplied,
  By hunger quelled,   590
Your Strephon might have died!

LORD CH. (*much moved*).
        Had that refreshment been denied,
        Indeed our Strephon might have died!

ALL (*much affected*).
        Had that refreshment been denied,
        Indeed our Strephon might have died!   595

LORD MOUNT.   But as she's not
        His mother, it appears,
          Why weep these hot
        Unnecessary tears?
          And by what laws   600
        Should we so joyously
          Rejoice, because
        Our Strephon did not die?
        Oh rather let us pipe our eye
        Because our Strephon did not die!   605

ALL.   That's very true – let's pipe our eye
        Because our Strephon did not die!

(*All weep.* IOLANTHE, *who has succeeded in hiding her face from* LORD
                CHANCELLOR, *escapes unnoticed.*)

PHYL.   Go, traitorous one – for ever we must part: 610
        To one of you, my Lords, I give my heart!
ALL.   Oh, rapture!
STREPH.   Hear me, Phyllis, ere you leave me.
PHYL.   Not a word – you did deceive me.
ALL.   Not a word – you did deceive her.   615

                        (*Exit* STREPHON.)

620 *swain*: An archaic word, suitable for an Arcadian fairy story, for a shepherd or countryman. In his poem *The Faerie Queene* Edmund Spenser writes of 'The gentle Shepeard swaynes, which sat keeping their fleecie flockes'.

631 *As this couple of lords*: Once again, this song directly echoes the Bab Ballad 'The Periwinkle Girl' (see the note to lines 330–49).

635 *To you I give my heart so rich*: In the copy of *Perola* (as it was then called) sent to the Lord Chancellor, this song was repeated by the peers, with the tenors and basses taking alternate lines. Thus, after Phyllis's final 'I do not care', the tenors began 'To them she gives her heart so rich', with the basses coming in 'To which?', the tenors replying 'She does not care' and so on.

650 *'Countess' is the title*: Although there are no counts in England, there are countesses; the term is used for the wives of earls, and, as we know from the list of *Dramatis personæ*, that is the rank of both Lords Tolloller and Mountararat.

BALLAD – Phyllis.

For riches and rank I do not long –
   Their pleasures are false and vain;
I gave up the love of a lordly throng
   For the love of a simple swain.   620
But now that simple swain's untrue,
With sorrowful heart I turn to you –
     A heart that's aching,
     Quaking, breaking,
As sorrowful hearts are wont to do!   625

The riches and rank that you befall
   Are the only baits you use,
So the richest and rankiest of you all
   My sorrowful heart shall choose.
As none are so noble – none so rich   630
As this couple of lords, I'll find a niche
     In my heart that's aching,
     Quaking, breaking,
For one of you two – and I don't care which!

ENSEMBLE.

PHYL. (*to* LORD MOUNTARARAT *and* LORD TOLLOLLER).
    To you I give my heart so rich!   635
ALL (*puzzled*).   To which?
PHYL.   I do not care!
    To you I yield – it is my doom!
ALL.   To whom?
PHYL.   I'm not aware!   640
    I'm yours for life if you but choose.
ALL.   She's whose?
PHYL.   That's your affair!
    I'll be a countess, shall I not?
ALL.   Of what?   645
PHYL.   I do not care!
ALL.   Lucky little lady!
    Strephon's lot is shady;
    Rank, it seems, is vital,
    'Countess' is the title,   650
    But of what I'm not aware!

(*Enter* STREPHON.)

668 *young Strephon is a rogue*: This is one of the several instances where Sullivan changed a line of Gilbert's for musical reasons. He added the word 'young' before Strephon to give a more pleasing flow to the melody. 'Our' was added for the same reason in lines 676, 691 and 700.

670 *Taradiddle, taradiddle, tol lol lay*: 'Taradiddle' is a slang word for a lie or fib. The line 'Tol the riddle, lol the riddle, lol lol lay' is sung by the chorus in *The Grand Duke*.

681 *And she's but seventeen*: Clearly a favourite age for Gilbert. In the First Act of *The Pirates of Penzance* Frederic tells Ruth that 'A lad of twenty-one usually looks for a wife of seventeen'. In *Ages Ago*, a play written by Gilbert in 1869 and set to music by Fred Clay, the idea of paintings which come to life, later developed in *Ruddigore*, is employed to produce a situation where Lord Carnaby Poppytop, painted in 1713 at the age of sixty-five, is attracted to his grandmother, Lady Maud, painted at the age of seventeen in the fifteenth century. This produces the rather *Iolanthe*-like verse:

> So strange a meeting ne'er was seen
> For sure as I'm alive,
> His grandmama is seventeen,
> And he is sixty-five.

686 *repente*: A word found in both Latin and Italian meaning suddenly, unexpectedly, all of a sudden.

STREPH.   Can I inactive see my fortune fade?
            No, no!
PEERS.   Ho, ho!   655
STREPH.   Mighty protectress, hasten to my aid!

    (*Enter Fairies, tripping, headed by* CELIA, LEILA, *and*
       FLETA, *and followed by* QUEEN.)

           CHORUS OF FAIRIES.

Tripping hither, tripping thither.
Nobody knows why or whither;   660
Why you want us we don't know,
But you've summoned us, and so
   Enter all the little fairies
     To their usual tripping measure!
To oblige you all our care is –   665
   Tell us, pray, what is your pleasure!

STREPH. The lady of my love has caught me talking to another –
PEERS.   Oh, fie! young Strephon is a rogue!
STREPH. I tell her very plainly that the lady is my mother –
PEERS.   Taradiddle, taradiddle, tol lol lay!   670
STREPH. She won't believe my statement, and declares we must
      be parted,
     Because on a career of double-dealing I have started,
     Then gives her hand to one of these, and leaves me
      broken-hearted –
PEERS.   Taradiddle, taradiddle, tol lol lay!

QUEEN. Ah, cruel ones, to separate two lovers from each other! 675
FAIRIES.   Oh, fie! our Strephon's not a rogue!
QUEEN. You've done him an injustice, for the lady *is* his mother!
FAIRIES.   Taradiddle, taradiddle, tol lol lay!
LORD CH. That fable perhaps may serve his turn as well as any other.
 (*Aside.*) I didn't see her face, but if they fondled one another, 680
     And she's but seventeen – I don't believe it was his mother!
     Taradiddle, taradiddle.
ALL.   Tol lol lay!

LORD TOLL. I have often had a use
     For a thorough-bred excuse   685
Of a sudden (which is English for '*repente*'),
    But of all I ever heard
    This is much the most absurd,
For she's seventeen, and he is five-and-twenty!

694 *contradicente*: From the Latin word *contradico*, meaning to contradict, gainsay or deny. The phrase *nem. con.*, short for *nemine contradicente*, is used in legal and political circles to mean unanimously, without opposition.

699 *To say she is his mother*: During the singing of this line at a performance of *Iolanthe* which he was attending, Lytton Strachey, the author of *Eminent Victorians*, turned to his neighbour, Maurice Baring, and said 'That's what I call poetry'. He added that he thought the most enduring achievement of the Victorian age would be Gilbert and Sullivan and predicted that their work would be remembered long after that of Gladstone and Disraeli had been forgotten.

703 *could be reckoned as injurious*: This was originally written as 'could be construed as injurious', but 'construed' proved difficult to sing and it was changed to 'reckoned'.

707–57 *Go away, madam*

This verbal passage of arms between the Lord Chancellor and the Fairy Queen was one of the main pieces of evidence cited by Kenneth Baker to support his argument that Gilbert had based the former character on William Ewart Gladstone and the latter on Queen Victoria (see page 164). There is no doubt that relations were strained between the Queen and Gladstone, who was Prime Minister when *Iolanthe* was written and first performed. Unlike his Conservative opponent Disraeli, who often addressed her as the Fairy Queen, Gladstone did not believe in flattering his sovereign. Indeed, he became positively impatient with her for continuing her retreat from public life and official duties long after the death of her beloved husband Prince Albert. For her part, the Queen complained that the Liberal leader addressed her as though she were a public meeting. Perhaps Gilbert had this in mind when he put these lines in the mouth of his Fairy Queen:

> Oh! Chancellor unwary,
> It's highly necessary
> Your tongue to teach
> Respectful speech.

There is no direct evidence that Gilbert modelled his Lord Chancellor and Fairy Queen on the Prime Minister and monarch of the day. We know that Victoria was not greatly amused by *Iolanthe*. Gladstone rather enjoyed the piece, telling Sullivan 'Nothing, I thought, could be happier than the manner in which the comic strain of this piece was blended with its harmonies of sight and sound, so good in taste and so admirable in execution from beginning to end.' There is no indication, however, that either of them recognized themselves in the characters on stage, nor indeed that any of their contemporaries did.

ALL.   Though she is seventeen, and he is only five-and-twenty!   690
                Oh, fie! our Strephon's not a rogue!

LORD MOUNT. Now, listen, pray, to me,
                For this paradox will be
                Carried, nobody at all *contradicente.*
                Her age, upon the date   695
                Of his birth, was *minus* eight,
                If she's seventeen, and he is five-and-twenty!

PEERS *and* FAIRIES. If she is seventeen, and he is only five-and-twenty.

ALL.   To say she is his mother is an utter bit of folly!
             Oh, fie! our { Strephon is / Strephon's not } a rogue!   700
        Perhaps his brain is addled, and it's very melancholy!
             Taradiddle, taradiddle, tol lol lay!
             I wouldn't say a word that could be reckoned as injurious,
             But to find a mother younger than her son is very curious,
             And that's a kind of mother that is usually spurious.   705
             Taradiddle, taradiddle, tol lol lay!

LORD CH.   Go away, madam;
             I should say, madam,
             You display, madam,
                Shocking taste.   710

             It is rude, madam,
             To intrude, madam,
             With your brood, madam,
                Brazen-faced!

             You come here, madam,   715
             Interfere, madam,
             With a peer, madam.
                (I am one.)

             You're aware, madam,
             What you dare, madam,   720
             So take care, madam,
                And begone!

FAIRIES (*to* QUEEN). Let us stay, madam;
             I should say, madam,

In a long letter to me full of interesting comments, Keith Peterson of New York points out the close similarity between the tune to this song and a theme in Beethoven's Tempest Sonata.

753 *badinage*: A French word meaning light trifling raillery or humorous banter.

They display, madam,   725
    Shocking taste.

It is rude, madam,
To allude, madam,
To your brood, madam,
    Brazen-faced!   730

We don't fear, madam,
Any peer, madam,
Though, my dear madam,
    This is one.

They will stare, madam,   735
When aware, madam,
What they dare, madam –
    What they've done!

QUEEN   Bearded by these puny mortals!
  (*furious*).   I will launch from fairy portals   740
       All the most terrific thunders
       In my armoury of wonders!

PHYL. (*aside*).   Should they launch terrific wonders,
       All would then repent their blunders.
       Surely these must be immortals.   745

ENSEMBLE.

PEERS.	FAIRIES.
Go away, madam, etc.	Let us stay, madam, etc.

                                   (*Exit* PHYLLIS.)

QUEEN.   Oh! Chancellor unwary,
       It's highly necessary
         Your tongue to teach   750
         Respectful speech –
       Your attitude to vary!

Your badinage so airy,
Your manner arbitrary,
     Are out of place   755
     When face to face
With an influential Fairy.

761 *vagary*: Digression, rambling from the subject, frolic or prank.
762 *quandary*: State of uncertainty or perplexity.

767 *Andersen's library*: This is a reference to the well-known Danish writer of fairy-tales, Hans Christian Andersen, who lived from 1805 to 1875.

770 *a Ladies' Seminary*: Gilbert and Sullivan's next Savoy Opera after *Iolanthe*, *Princess Ida*, was to be partly set in a ladies' seminary. It tells the story of a trio of young men who dress up as women to gain entrance to the all-female establishment and allows Gilbert ample scope for digs at the idea of women's education.

780 *Take down our sentence as we speak it*: Gilbert's direction in his original prompt-book at this point reads: 'Peers get out notebooks and write with book on knees, for Queen's dictation (they turn backs to Queen as they write in stooping attitude)'. D'Oyly Carte performances traditionally maintained this bit of business.

ALL THE PEERS   We never knew
(*aside*).   We were talking to
          An influential Fairy!   760

LORD CH.   A plague on this vagary,
          I'm in a nice quandary!
          Of hasty tone
          With dames unknown
          I ought to be more chary;   765
          It seems that she's a fairy
          From Andersen's library,
          And I took her for
          The proprietor
          Of a Ladies' Seminary!   770

PEERS.   We took her for
          The proprietor
          Of a Ladies' Seminary!

QUEEN.   When next your Houses do assemble,
          You may tremble!   775

CELIA.   Our wrath, when gentlemen offend us,
          Is tremendous!

LEILA.   They meet, who underrate our calling,
          Doom appalling!

QUEEN.   Take down our sentence as we speak it,   780
          And *he* shall wreak it!   (*Indicating* STREPHON.)

PEERS.   Oh, spare us!

QUEEN.   Henceforth, Strephon, cast away
          Crooks and pipes and ribbons so gay –
          Flocks and herds that bleat and low;   785
          Into Parliament you shall go!

ALL.   Into Parliament he shall go!
          Backed by our supreme authority,
          He'll command a large majority;
          Into Parliament he shall go!   790

QUEEN.   In the Parliamentary hive,
          Liberal or Conservative –

793 *Whig or Tory*: Both these terms had effectively been superseded by the more modern 'Liberal' and 'Conservative' by 1882, but then, as now, 'Tory' was a common nickname for Conservatives, and there were more Whigs around than there are now. A word on the origins of the party labels may be of interest here. 'Whig' is almost certainly a shortened form of 'whiggamore', a term used for the adherents of the Presbyterian cause in Scotland who marched on Edinburgh in 1648. Later in the seventeenth century it came to be applied to those who opposed the Stuart cause, and particularly to those unhappy at the accession to the British throne in 1679 of the Roman Catholic, James, Duke of York. The 'glorious revolution' of 1685–8 which brought the Protestant William of Orange to the throne is normally seen as a triumph for the Whigs and their notion of limited constitutional monarchy. Whigs dominated politics under the Hanoverian kings of the eighteenth century, when they stood broadly for political reform and religious toleration. In the mid-nineteenth century they gradually gave way to the less oligarchic and more middle-class Liberal Party which took over as the main party of progress. Gladstone is generally seen as the first distinctly Liberal Prime Minister in Great Britain, but his Cabinets contained several men who still regarded themselves as Whigs, and the word did not die out until the end of the nineteenth century.

The word Tory also dates from the seventeenth century and was originally applied to dispossessed Irishmen who became outlaws. It later came to be used for all Irish Catholics and Royalists in arms, and specifically to those who supported James, Duke of York's accession to the throne. The Tories dominated British politics in the aftermath of the Stuart restoration in 1660 and again in the late eighteenth and early nineteenth centuries, when they were led by the younger Pitt and Lord Liverpool. The change of the party's name to Conservative is normally dated to 1833 and is credited to the journalist and politician J. W. Croker. The Conservative leader at the time when *Iolanthe* was first performed was Lord Salisbury, who had taken over after the death of Benjamin Disraeli, Earl of Beaconsfield, in 1881.

802 *Through the grouse and salmon season*: Acts of Parliament regulate the periods during which game and fish can be caught in Britain, the so-called 'open season'. The open season for shooting grouse begins on 12 August (known as 'the glorious twelfth') and ends on 10 December. The open season for salmon fishing begins on 1 February and ends on 31 August. The grouse moors continued to be a traditional haunt of politicians, particularly Conservatives, well into the twentieth century.

804–5 *the cherished rights. . . on Friday nights*: When Gilbert originally wrote these lines, the cherished rights were enjoyed on Wednesday, not Friday. Between 1852 and 1902 that was the so-called short sitting day in Parliament, when the Commons sat from 12 noon until 6 p.m. instead of its usual time of from 3 p.m. until late in the evening. The Lords very seldom sat at all on Wednesdays during this period, and if they did it was only for judicial business. So for most peers Wednesday as a whole was a day of rest. One particular cherished right that the Fairy Queen must surely have had on her little list for Strephon to end was the Lords' practice of never sitting on the first Wednesday in June – Derby Day. That persisted until the First World War.

In 1902 Arthur Balfour, the Conservative Prime Minister, introduced a series of reforms in parliamentary procedure which included changing the short sitting day from Wednesday to Friday, where it has remained ever since. The *Iolanthe* libretto was altered accordingly. In 1980 the Commons' hours of sitting on Fridays were made even earlier, from 9.30 a.m. to 3 p.m., to give M.P.s plenty of time to travel to their constituencies for the weekend. Friday sittings in the Commons are generally very sparsely attended. The Lords meet very rarely on a Friday, having had only thirteen sittings on that day in 1980 and eleven in 1981.

808 *Marriage with deceased wife's sister*: Many Liberals, including Mr Gladstone, supported the campaign to allow a man to marry his deceased wife's sister, which was led by the Marriage Law Reform Association after such a union had been included in the

Whig or Tory – I don't know –
But into Parliament you shall go!

ALL.   Into Parliament, etc.   795

QUEEN (*speaking through music*).

Every Bill and every measure
That may gratify his pleasure,
Though your fury it arouses,
Shall be passed by both your Houses!

PEERS.   Oh!   800

QUEEN.   You shall sit, if he sees reason,
Through the grouse and salmon season;

PEERS.   No!

QUEEN.   He shall end the cherished rights
You enjoy on Friday nights: 805

PEERS.   No!

QUEEN.   He shall prick that annual blister,
Marriage with deceased wife's sister:

PEERS.   Mercy!

QUEEN.   Titles shall ennoble, then,   810
All the Common Councilmen:

PEERS.   Spare us!

QUEEN.   Peers shall teem in Christendom,
        And a Duke's exalted station
Be attainable by Com-   815
        Petitive Examination!

PEERS.   FAIRIES *and* PHYLLIS.

Oh, horror!   Their horror
                        They can't dissemble
          Nor hide the fear that makes them
                        tremble!

Church's list of prohibited marriages in 1835. As the Fairy Queen's remark indicates, the subject was constantly coming up in Parliament. The Liberals' enthusiasm for promoting legislation on it was mocked by Matthew Arnold, who suggested that, 'the Liberal party must supplement that Bill by two others: one enabling people to marry their brothers' and sisters' children, the other enabling a man to marry his brother's wife'. The reformers, however, contented themselves with the matter of the deceased wife's sister and finally secured victory for their cause in 1907.

In the original version of the opera, contained in the licence copy and in the first American libretto (which was published before the British one), the Fairy Queen had two additional horrors with which to frighten the peers at this point:

> He shall offer to the many
> Peerages at three a penny

and, after the lines still sung about the Common Councilmen:

> Earldoms shall be sold apart
> Daily at the auction-mart.

811 *Common Councilmen*: Representatives of the population of a municipality. The City of London was traditionally governed by a Lord Mayor, aldermen and common councilmen.

815–16 *Competitive Examination*: Gladstonian Liberals had a passion for competitive examination, which they had already introduced as the main means of recruitment into the Civil Service, and the idea that the principle should now be extended to entry into the peerage would have tickled an audience in the 1880s. Gilbert himself had obtained his first job by passing a competitive examination at the age of twenty-one in 1857. It secured him a post as assistant clerk in the education department of the Privy Council, for which he received the princely salary of £120 a year. 'It was one of the worst bargains any Government ever made', he commented later. He hated the job but held it down for four years before a legacy from an aunt enabled him to read for the Bar.

849 *canaille*: Rabble or riff-raff.

853 *plebs*: The name given to the general body of Roman citizens who did not fall into the privileged category of patricians. In the later Roman Republic the word 'plebeian' became a rather derogatory term for those in the lower social orders. It is still used in that sense today.

ENSEMBLE.

Peers.	Fairies, Phyllis, *and* Strephon.	
Young Strephon is the kind of lout	With Strephon for your foe, no doubt,	820
We do not care a fig about!	A fearful prospect opens out,	
We cannot say	And who shall say	
What evils may	What evils may	
Result in consequence.	Result in consequence?	
But lordly vengeance will pursue	A hideous vengeance will pursue	825
All kinds of common people who	All noblemen who venture to	
Oppose our views,	Oppose his views,	
Or boldly choose	Or boldly choose	
To offer us offence.	To offer him offence.	

FAIRIES.

'Twill plunge them into grief and shame; 830
His kind forbearance they must claim,
 If they'd escape
 In any shape
A very painful wrench.

PEERS.

Your powers we dauntlessly pooh-pooh: 835
A dire revenge will fall on you,
 If you besiege
 Our high *prestige*

FAIRIES.

(The word *'prestige'* is French).

Peers.	Fairies *and* Queen.	
Your powers we dauntlessly pooh-pooh:	Although our threats you now pooh-pooh,	840
A dire revenge will fall on you.	A dire revenge will fall on you.	
Young Strephon is the kind of lout	With Strephon for your foe, no doubt	
We do not care a fig about!	A fearful prospect opens out,	
We cannot say	And who shall say	
What evils may	What evils may	845
Result in consequence.	Result in consequence?	

PEERS.

Our lordly style
 You shall not quench
With base *canaille*!

FAIRIES.

 (That word is French.) 850

PEERS.

Distinction ebbs
 Before a herd
Of vulgar *plebs*!

FAIRIES.

 (A Latin word.)

PEERS.

'Twould fill with joy, 855
 And madness stark

857 οἱ πολλοὶ: Pronounced 'hoi polloi', this phrase is the Greek equivalent of the Latin 'plebs'. Literally meaning 'the many', it has come to be used in the same rather slighting sense as 'plebs' to mean the unenlightened masses.

879 *Fairies threaten Peers with their wands*: It seems that this direction was followed by the D'Oyly Carte fairies rather too enthusiastically on the opening night of *Iolanthe* at the Savoy Theatre. Gilbert had to tell the ladies of the chorus the following day: 'You must not bang your wands on the stage, ladies. The diamonds in the heads drop out. The stage was strewn with diamonds last night.'

	The οἱ πολλοί!	
FAIRIES.	(A Greek remark.)	

PEERS.　　　　One Latin word, one Greek remark,
　　　　　　And one that's French.　　　　　　　　860

FAIRIES.　　　　Your lordly style
　　　　　　　　We'll quickly quench
　　　　　　　　With base *canaille*!
PEERS.　　　　　(That word is French.)
FAIRIES.　　　Distinction ebbs　　　　　　　　865
　　　　　　　Before a herd
　　　　　　　Of vulgar *plebs*!
PEERS.　　　　　(A Latin word.)
FAIRIES.　　　'Twill fill with joy
　　　　　　　And madness stark　　　　　　　870
　　　　　　　The οἱ πολλοί!
PEERS.　　　　　(A Greek remark.)

FAIRIES.　　　One Latin word, one Greek remark,
　　　　　　And one that's French.

PEERS.	FAIRIES.
You needn't wait:	We will not wait:　875
Away you fly!	We go sky-high!
Your threatened hate	Our threatened hate
We thus defy!	You won't defy!

(*Fairies threaten Peers with their wands. Peers kneel as begging for mercy.* PHYLLIS *implores* STREPHON *to relent. He casts her from him, and she falls* 880 *fainting into the arms of* LORD MOUNTARARAT *and* LORD TOLLOLLER.)

END OF ACT I

1 *Scene*: Palace Yard is the open court-yard at the eastern (Whitehall) end of the Houses of Parliament into which M.P.s drive on their way into the Commons. It was recently remodelled to allow the building of an underground car park and now has a fine fountain in the centre. It is closed to the public, who gain admission to the House of Commons further west at St Stephen's entrance.

As the stage directions indicate, Palace Yard is bounded on one side by Westminster Hall, the only substantial part of the old medieval Palace of Westminster to survive the disastrous fire of 1834, and on the other, at the rear, by the clock tower better known as Big Ben. In its review of the opening night of *Iolanthe* at the Savoy, the *Morning Post* noted two points which were inconsistent with the 'otherwise excellent realisation of the scene. The House is supposed to be sitting, yet there is no light in the tower, and the clock persistently pointed to a time nearly half an hour after midnight. This may have been a satirical allusion – the want of progress in the House shown by the unmoving hands of the dial'.

Gilbert obviously took the criticism to heart, for, at the time of the 1901 revival of the opera, he wrote to Mrs Helen D'Oyly Carte (who had taken over the running of the company on her husband's death) suggesting that the clock should have a real mechanism and should show the correct time throughout the performance of Act II. I have not been able to discover whether the suggestion was taken up.

A more serious inaccuracy in the setting of Act II of *Iolanthe* was overlooked by many reviewers. The Houses of Parliament are not guarded by soldiers, but rather by policemen. Strictly speaking, Private Willis should be replaced by one of the constabulary from *The Pirates of Penzance*. However, he makes a more colourful figure to be set in front of the slightly sombre background of Sir Charles Barry's great neo-Gothic building, which was only completed five years before *Iolanthe* was written.

Willis may have been in the wrong uniform, but he certainly had the right rifle. The first-night review in the *Echo* commented: 'At many theatres he would have been armed with a "property" musket, with old bayonet. Mr Gilbert's sentry is correct to attention, and he shoulders properly a Martini-Henry rifle with the long bayonet of the newest pattern'.

15 *Is either a little Liberal*: Private Willis's well-known reflections on the rigidity of the British two-party system have never been revised to take account of the rise of the Labour Party. Substitution of 'a little Socialist' for 'a little Liberal' would have provided a more accurate description of the prevailing political climate for most of the twentieth century, although in our present era of mould-breaking goodness knows what a modern Private Willis should sing. Perhaps it is best, after all, to leave him in those happy days when there were just Liberals and Conservatives.

The British party system comes under further scrutiny in Gilbert and Sullivan's penultimate opera, *Utopia Limited*, and in a song from *Ruddigore*, rarely performed nowadays, in which Sir Ruthven Murgatroyd casts scorn on:

> Ye supple M.P.s who go down on your knees,
> Your precious identity sinking,
> And vote black or white as your leaders indite
> (Which saves you the trouble of thinking).

19 *cerebellum*: A Latin word used to describe the back part of the brain which is concerned with the co-ordination of movement and the maintenance of equilibrium.

ACT II

SCENE. – *Palace Yard, Westminster. Westminster Hall,* L. *Clock tower up,*
R.C. PRIVATE WILLIS *discovered on sentry,* R. *Moonlight.*

SONG – PRIVATE WILLIS.

When all night long a chap remains
   On sentry-go, to chase monotony
He exercises of his brains,   5
   That is, assuming that he's got any.
Though never nurtured in the lap
   Of luxury, yet I admonish you,
I am an intellectual chap,
   And think of things that would astonish you.   10
      I often think it's comical – Fal, lal, la!
      How Nature always does contrive – Fal, lal, la!
        That every boy and every gal
         That's born into the world alive
        Is either a little Liberal   15
         Or else a little Conservative!
          Fal, lal, la!

When in that House M.P.s divide,
   If they've a brain and cerebellum, too,
They've got to leave that brain outside,   20
   And vote just as their leaders tell 'em to.
But then the prospect of a lot
   Of dull M.P.s in close proximity,
All thinking for themselves, is what
   No man can face with equanimity.   25
      Then let's rejoice with loud Fal la – Fal lal la!
      That Nature always does contrive – Fal lal la!
        That every boy and every gal

33 *Enter . . . Celia, Leila, and Fleta*: The Act II entrance of the three principal fairies caused great excitement on the opening night at the Savoy Theatre as they were wearing electric star lights on their heads. The Fairy Queen was also kitted out with one of these lamps, which were made by the Swan United Electric Company and worked off a battery carried on the shoulder and hidden by the fairies' long flowing hair. Most of the audience were enchanted by the effect created by the fairy lights on the dimly lit stage. Not so the reviewer from the *Figaro*, however, who wrote: 'The light dazzled the eyes and gave rise to an uncomfortable suspicion of possible danger. For, although the wires are doubtless completely insulated, yet a facture or a rub would imply instant death to the unhappy lady who wears the lamp'. Mercifully, no such mishaps seem to have occurred.

35–59 *Strephon's a Member of Parliament*
Punch regarded this chorus as the best number in *Iolanthe*. Gilbert's original version, printed in the licence copy, differs considerably from the present one:

FAIRIES.	Strephon's a Member of Parliament!
	All his measures have our assent!
	We've been slighted –
	We'll be righted –
	Strephon's a Member of Parliament!
LEILA.	Strephon every measure carries!
	Strephon every question parries!
	All the Peers are down in the blues –
	Strephon makes them shake in their shoes!
ALL.	Shake in their shoes!
	Shake in their shoes!
	All his measures have our assent –
	Strephon's a Member of Parliament!
PEERS.	Here's a pretty kettle of fish!
	For that Member most mysterious
	Carries every Bill he may wish!
	Really it's extremely serious!
LORD MOUNT.	Tells the House to pass his Bill –
	What is more surprising still,
	They obey his tone imperious –
	Really it's extremely serious!
PEERS *and*	Carries every Bill he may wish –
FAIRIES.	Here's a pretty kettle of fish!
LORD TOLL.	Fairy Queen her threat fulfils,
	All support against their wills,
	All his measures deleterious!
	Really it's extremely serious!
CHORUS.	Carries every Bill he may wish, etc.

56 *a pretty kettle of fish*: An awkward state of affairs, a mess, or a muddle. The phrase may possibly derive from the old Border expression 'a kettle of fish' to describe a riverside picnic where a newly caught salmon was boiled and eaten – a messy if otherwise pleasant sort of occasion.

That's born into the world alive
Is either a little Liberal   30
Or else a little Conservative!
        Fal lal la!

(*Enter Fairies, with* CELIA, LEILA, *and* FLETA.
        They trip round stage.)

CHORUS OF FAIRIES.

Strephon's a Member of Parliament!   35
Carries every Bill he chooses.
To his measures all assent –
    Showing that fairies have their uses.
        Whigs and Tories
            Dim their glories,   40
Giving an ear to all his stories –
Lords and Commons are both in the blues!
Strephon makes them shake in their shoes!
        Shake in their shoes!
        Shake in their shoes!   45
Strephon makes them shake in their shoes!

(*Enter Peers from Westminster Hall.*)

CHORUS OF PEERS.

    Strephon's a Member of Parliament!
        Running a-muck of all abuses.
    His unqualified assent   50
        Somehow nobody now refuses.
            Whigs and Tories
                Dim their glories,
    Giving an ear to all his stories –
    Carrying every Bill he may wish: 55
    Here's a pretty kettle of fish!
            Kettle of fish!
            Kettle of fish!
    Here's a pretty kettle of fish!

(*Enter* LORD MOUNTARARAT *and* LORD TOLLOLLER   60
        from Westminster Hall.)

CELIA. You seem annoyed.

67–8 *Parliamentary Pickford*: Pickfords are a famous firm of carriers and removers. The slogan on their vans used to be 'We carry everything'. They are also mentioned in one of Gilbert's early plays, *No Cards*, when one of the characters, Mrs Penrose, says 'Bless me, if I'm run over by a Pickford's van in Fleet Street, is that any reason why you should never go east of Charing Cross?'

79–80 *a House of Peers composed exclusively of people of intellect*: Gilbert toyed with this idea again in *Utopia Limited*. King Paramount proudly sings:

> Our Peerage we've remodelled on an intellectual basis,
> Which certainly is rough on our hereditary races.

At the time *Iolanthe* was written, the House of Lords was almost entirely composed of hereditary members who sat there by virtue of belonging to noble families. The Appellate Jurisdiction Act of 1876 allowed certain eminent judges to be created lords of appeal with a seat in the House of Lords for life, and there were, of course, also bishops in the Upper House; but it was not until half-way through the twentieth century (1958) that the Crown was empowered to confer life peerages on any man or woman. As presently constituted, the House of Lords is a mixture of hereditary and life peers. Lords Mountararat and Tolloller would still be quite at home there – it is not yet composed exclusively of people of intellect.

86–109 *When Britain really ruled the waves*
One of the most popular of Gilbert's patriotic songs, this very seldom fails to secure an encore in performances of *Iolanthe*. Remarkably, Sullivan composed the music for it, as well as for three other songs originally intended for Act II ('Fold your flapping wings', 'Heigho, love is a thorn', and 'He loves'), in the space of a single night. He started work after dinner and finished at five in the morning.

91 *bays*: Wreaths for conquerors and heroes, made from the leaves of the laurel or bay-tree.

94 *When Wellington thrashed Bonaparte*: This was, of course, at the battle of Waterloo (1815), which also gets a mention in *The Pirates of Penzance* as one of the 'fights historical' quoted by Major-General Stanley.

100 *good King George*: The particular King George on the throne at the time of Waterloo was George III.

LORD MOUNT. Annoyed! I should think so! Why, this ridiculous *protégé* of yours is playing the deuce with everything! To-night is the second reading of his Bill to throw the Peerage open to Competitive Examination!   65
LORD TOLL. And he'll carry it, too!
LORD MOUNT. Carry it? Of course he will! He's a Parliamentary Pickford – he carries everything!
LEILA. Yes. If you please, that's our fault!
LORD MOUNT. The deuce it is!   70
CELIA. Yes; we influence the members, and compel them to vote just as he wishes them to.
LEILA. It's our system. It shortens the debates.
LORD TOLL. Well, but think what it all means. I don't so much mind for myself, but with a House of Peers with no grandfathers worth   75
mentioning, the country must go to the dogs!
LEILA. I suppose it must!
LORD MOUNT. I don't want to say a word against brains – I've a great respect for brains – I often wish I had some myself – but with a House of Peers composed exclusively of people of intellect, what's to become of the   80
House of Commons?
LEILA. I never thought of that!
LORD MOUNT. This comes of women interfering in politics. It so happens that if there is an institution in Great Britain which is not susceptible of any improvement at all, it is the House of Peers!   85

SONG – LORD MOUNTARARAT.

> When Britain really ruled the waves –
>   (In good Queen Bess's time)
> The House of Peers made no pretence
> To intellectual eminence,
>   Or scholarship sublime;   90
> Yet Britain won her proudest bays
> In good Queen Bess's glorious days!

CHORUS.   Yes, Britain won, etc.

> When Wellington thrashed Bonaparte,
>   As every child can tell,   95
> The House of Peers, throughout the war,
> Did nothing in particular,
>   And did it very well:
> Yet Britain set the world ablaze
> In good King George's glorious days!   100

CHORUS.   Yes, Britain set, etc.

102–9 *And while the House of Peers withholds*: In 1909 some of the Liberals campaigning against the House of Lords' power of veto after its rejection of Lloyd George's radical budget of that year asked Gilbert for permission to quote this verse. He replied rather pepperily: 'I cannot permit the verses from *Iolanthe* to be used for electioneering purposes. They do not at all express my own view. They are supposed to be the views of the wrong-headed donkey who sings them.' With or without the help of *Iolanthe*, however, the Liberal reformers achieved their aims and in 1911 the Parliament Act was passed, curtailing the House of Lords' power to veto legislation already passed by the Commons. Since then noble statesmen have largely withheld their legislative hand and contented themselves with moving amendments to Bills sent up from the Lower House.

113 *a British Representative Peer*: Before the establishment of the Irish Free State in 1922, twenty-eight Irish peers were elected for life to sit in the House of Lords as representatives of the entire Irish peerage. Until 1963, sixteen Scottish peers were elected by their fellow peers each Parliament to serve a similar function. There are no longer any representative peers in the upper chamber.

118–49 *In vain to us you plead*
This delightful song, in which the fairies cannot conceal their infatuation with the peers, for all their angry words, won considerable praise from the reviewers when it was first performed at the Savoy. The *Advertiser* singled out for particular mention its 'charmingly fanciful and piquant accompaniment for the strings pizzicato'.

The lines of the second verse must have had a special significance for one real-life noble lord who was often to be found in the Savoy stalls during the initial run of *Iolanthe*. Lord Garmoyle, later to become the 2nd Earl Cairns, was captivated by Miss May Fortescue, who created the part of Celia. Eventually they became engaged, but he later jilted her, proving that make-believe peers are to be preferred to real ones.

And while the House of Peers withholds
      Its legislative hand,
And noble statesmen do not itch
To interfere with matters which   105
      They do not understand,
As bright will shine Great Britain's rays
As in King George's glorious days!
CHORUS.   As bright will shine, etc.

LEILA (*who has been much attracted by the Peers during this song*). Charm-   110
ing persons, are they not?
   CELIA. Distinctly. For self-contained dignity, combined with airy
condescension, give me a British Representative Peer!
   LORD TOLL. Then pray stop this *protégé* of yours before it's too late.
Think of the mischief you're doing!   115
   LEILA (*crying*). But we *can't* stop him now. (*Aside to* CELIA.) Aren't
they lovely! (*Aloud.*) Oh, why did you go and defy us, you great geese!

                  DUET – LEILA *and* CELIA.

LEILA.   In vain to us you plead –
                        Don't go!
                  Your prayers we do not heed –   120
                        Don't go!
                        It's true we sigh,
                        But don't suppose
                        A tearful eye
                        Forgiveness shows.   125
                        Oh, no!
                  We're very cross indeed –
                  Yes, very cross,
                        Don't go!

FAIRIES.   It's true we sigh, etc.   130

CELIA.   Your disrespectful sneers –
                        Don't go!
                  Call forth indignant tears –
                        Don't go!
                        You break our laws –   135
                        You are our foe:
                        We cry because
                        We hate you so!
                        You know!
                  You very wicked Peers!   140

150 *Exeunt Lord Mountararat, Lord Tolloller*: During the scene just ended, and for their other appearances in the Second Act of *Iolanthe*, Mountararat and Tolloller were originally dressed in D'Oyly Carte productions in plain court dress (dark velvet jackets and breeches). In a letter to Mrs Helen D'Oyly Carte at the time of the 1901 revival, however, Gilbert suggested something more fancy:

> We were *quite wrong* in putting the two Earls, in Act II, into plain Court dress. That is the dress of men who have no rank above baronets – or at all events who are not peers and knights of orders. A GCB or KG would never appear in velvet court dress – he would be certain to hold some appointment that would give him the right to wear a uniform. I should say that it would be best to put them into Lords Lieutenants dress (red coats, silver striped trousers, general's gold belt and cocked hat). These are posts that are (with one or two exceptions) held by peers of considerable landed property and would be perfectly suitable to these two earls – who ought also to wear the *star* of the order of knighthood assigned to them in Act I. Plain Court dress would be impossible for such howling swells.

In fact, D'Oyly Carte stuck to velvet court dress for the two principal Earls and did not adopt Gilbert's gaudier and more expensive alternative. His suggestion of letting them wear the stars of their respective orders of knighthood in the Second Act was, however, accepted.

163–4 *1st Grenadier Guards*: The First Regiment of Foot Guards in Britain, the Grenadiers are traditionally known for their height, physique and general discipline. As their name implies, the grenadiers were originally those soldiers equipped with grenades for throwing in battle. They are commemorated in the well-known song, dating from the sixteenth century, *The British Grenadiers*.

You wicked Peers!
Don't go!

FAIRIES.	LORDS MOUNT. *and* TOLL.	
You break our laws –	Our disrespectful sneers,	
You are our foe:	Ha, ha!	
We cry because	Call forth indignant tears,	145
We hate you so!	Ha, ha!	
You know!	If that's the case, my dears –	
You very wicked Peers!	FAIRIES. Don't go!	
Don't go!	PEERS. We'll go!	

(*Exeunt* LORD MOUNTARARAT, LORD TOLLOLLER, *and*   150
Peers. Fairies gaze wistfully after them.)

(*Enter* FAIRY QUEEN.)

QUEEN. Oh, shame – shame upon you! Is this your fidelity to the laws
you are bound to obey? Know ye not that it is death to marry a mortal?
LEILA. Yes, but it's not death to *wish* to marry a mortal!   155
FLETA. If it were, you'd have to execute us all!
QUEEN. Oh, this is weakness! Subdue it!
CELIA. We know it's weakness, but the weakness is so strong!
LEILA. We are not all as tough as you are!
QUEEN. Tough! Do you suppose that I am insensible to the effect of   160
manly beauty? Look at that man! (*Referring to Sentry.*) A perfect picture! (*To
Sentry.*) Who are you, sir?
WILLIS (*coming to 'attention'*). Private Willis, B Company, 1st Grenadier
Guards.
QUEEN. You're a very fine fellow, sir.   165
WILLIS. I am generally admired.
QUEEN. I can quite understand it. (*To Fairies.*) Now here is a man
whose physical attributes are simply godlike. That man has a most
extraordinary effect upon me. If I yielded to a natural impulse, I should fall
down and worship that man. But I mortify this inclination; I wrestle with it,   170
and it lies beneath my feet! That is how I treat my regard for that man!

SONG – FAIRY QUEEN.

Oh, foolish fay,
  Think you, because
His brave array
  My bosom thaws,   175
I'd disobey

185 *Type of Ovidius Naso*: A reference to the Latin amatory poet Ovid (43 B.C.–A.D. 17), who was nicknamed 'Naso' because of his big nose. He likened himself to a dove, hence the Fairy Queen's allusion here. Ovid also gets a mention in *Princess Ida*, the next Savoy Opera after *Iolanthe*, when Lady Psyche tells Melissa that if she wishes to succeed in Classics she must read Ovid's *Metamorphoses*. In *Ruddigore* Robin Oakapple compares his own talents as a poet to those of Ovid, greatly to the disadvantage of the latter, in his boasting song 'If you wish in the world to advance'.

201 *A Captain Shaw*: Captain Eyre Massey Shaw was chief of the Metropolitan Fire Brigade from 1861 to 1891. During that time he transformed London's old independent fire-fighting teams, financed by insurance companies, into the country's first public fire brigade. The fire-boat *Massey Shaw*, which was named after him, is now in the collection of historic vessels in St Katharine's Dock near the Tower of London.

Captain Shaw was sitting in the middle of the stalls at the first-night performance of *Iolanthe* at the Savoy Theatre to hear the Fairy Queen's tribute to him. A few nights later he was at the nearby Alhambra Theatre in a rather different capacity, fighting a fire which caused severe damage. A special matinée of *Iolanthe* was put on at the Savoy to benefit those who had lost their livelihood as a result of the fire.

In a note in his collection of *Iolanthe* material in the Pierpont Morgan Library, New York, Reginald Allen suggests that the Fairy Queen's description of Captain Shaw as 'Type of true love kept under' may be a reference to a scandal details of which were going round the drawing rooms of Mayfair at the time *Iolanthe* was being written. The wife of Lord Colin Campbell, a notorious profligate and bully, apparently sought consolation by striking up close friendships with a number of other men, including Captain Shaw. In 1884 Lady Campbell won a separation from her husband, but in revenge he brought a case naming four prominent figures, including Shaw, with whom she was alleged to have had relationships. When he gave evidence in this case, Shaw is reported to have 'burned with love for the lady but never declared himself'. Shaw's descendants told Reginald Allen that they were sure the Fairy Queen's remark about 'true love kept under' referred to the circumstances which led up to this case.

210 *I can't think why I'm not in better spirits*: In the original libretto of *Perola*, as printed in the licence copy but cut before the first performance, Phyllis has a ballad after this passage of dialogue and while she is still on her own on the stage:

> My love for him is dead,
>   And yet I sigh!
> My eyes are very red:
>   I wonder why?
> Love fills my heart no more,
> I've turned it out of door –
> And yet my heart is sore!
>   I wonder why!
> His falsehood I detest:
>   From him I fly,
> And yet I know no rest –
>   I wonder why!
> Maybe in spite of ill
> The heart subdues the will –
> Maybe I love him still!
>   I wonder why!

Our fairy laws?
Because I fly
In realms above,
In tendency   180
To fall in love,
Resemble I
The amorous dove?

(*Aside.*)   Oh, amorous dove!
Type of Ovidius Naso!   185
This heart of mine
Is soft as thine,
Although I dare not say so!

CHORUS.   Oh, amorous dove, etc.

On fire that glows   190
With heat intense
I turn the hose
Of common sense,
And out it goes
At small expense!   195
We must maintain
Our fairy law;
That is the main
On which to draw –
In that we gain   200
A Captain Shaw!

(*Aside.*)   Oh, Captain Shaw!
Type of true love kept under!
Could thy Brigade
With cold cascade   205
Quench my great love, I wonder!

CHORUS.   Oh, Captain Shaw! etc.

(*Exeunt Fairies and* FAIRY QUEEN, *sorrowfully.*)

(*Enter* PHYLLIS.)

PHYL. (*half crying*). I can't think why I'm not in better spirits. I'm   210
engaged to two noblemen at once. That ought to be enough to make any girl
happy. But I'm miserable! Don't suppose it's because I care for Strephon, for
I hate him! No girl *could* care for a man who goes about with a mother
considerably younger than himself!

(*Enter* LORD MOUNTARARAT *and* LORD TOLLOLLER.)   215

216 *Phyllis! My darling*: In the first performances in both London and New York, Mountararat alone came on to the stage at this point. He had the following conversation with Phyllis before launching into another song about the peerage:

LORD MOUNT. Phyllis! My own!

PHYL. Don't! How dare you! But perhaps you are one of the noblemen I am engaged to.

MOUNT. I am one of them.

PHYL. Oh! But how come *you* to have a peerage?

MOUNT. It's a prize for being born first.

PHYL. A kind of Derby Cup.

MOUNT. Not exactly. I'm of a very old and distinguished family.

PHYL. And you're proud of your race? Of course you are – you won it. But why are people *made* peers?

MOUNT. The principle is not easy to explain. I'll give you an example.

> De Belville was regarded as the Crichton of his age:
> His tragedies were reckoned much too thoughtful for the stage:
> His poems held a noble rank – although it's very true
> That, being very proper, they were read by very few.
> He was a famous painter, too, and shone upon the Line,
> And even Mister Ruskin came and worshipped at his shrine:
> But, alas, the school he followed was heroically high –
> The kind of Art men rave about, but very seldom buy.
> > And everybody said,
> > 'How can he be repaid –
> > This very great – this very good – this very gifted man?'
> > But nobody could hit upon a practicable plan!
>
> He was a great Inventor, and discovered, all alone,
> A plan for making everybody's fortune but his own;
> For in business an Inventor's little better than a fool,
> And my highly gifted friend was no exception to the rule.
> His poems – people read 'em in the sixpenny Reviews;
> His pictures – they engraved 'em in the *Illustrated News*;
> His inventions – they perhaps might have enriched him by degrees,
> But all his little income went to Patent Office fees!
> > So everybody said
> > 'How can he be repaid –
> > This *very* great – this *very* good – this *very* gifted man?'
> > But nobody could hit upon a practicable plan!
>
> At last the point was given up in absolute despair,
> When a distant cousin died, and he became a millionaire!
> With a county seat in Parliament, a moor or two of grouse,
> And a taste for making inconvenient speeches in the House.
> *Then*, Government conferred on him the highest of rewards –
> They took him from the Commons and they put him in the Lords!
> And who so fit to sit in it, deny it if you can,
> As this very great – this very good – this very gifted man?
> > Though I'm more than half afraid
> > That it sometimes may be said
> That we never should have revelled in that source of proper pride –
> However great his merits – if his cousin hadn't died!

At the London first night of *Iolanthe* the above verses were recited, rather than sung, by Rutland Barrington. He omitted the second verse entirely, much to the

LORD MOUNT. Phyllis! My darling!

LORD TOLL. Phyllis! My own!

PHYL. Don't! How dare you? Oh, but perhaps you're the two noblemen I'm engaged to?

LORD MOUNT. I am one of them.   220

LORD TOLL. I am the other.

PHYL. Oh, then, my darling! (*to* LORD MOUNTARARAT). My own! (*to* LORD TOLLOLLER). Well, have you settled which it's to be?

LORD TOLL. Not altogether. It's a difficult position. It would be hardly delicate to toss up. On the whole we would rather leave it to you.   225

PHYL. How can it possibly concern me? You are both Earls, and you are both rich, and you are both plain.

LORD MOUNT. So we are. At least I am.

LORD TOLL. So am I.

LORD MOUNT. No, no!   230

LORD TOLL. I am indeed. Very plain.

LORD MOUNT. Well, well – perhaps you are.

PHYL. There's really nothing to choose between you. If one of you would forgo his title, and distribute his estates among his Irish tenantry, why, then, I should then see a reason for accepting the other.   235

LORD MOUNT. Tolloller, are you prepared to make this sacrifice?

LORD TOLL. No!

LORD MOUNT. Not even to oblige a lady?

LORD TOLL. No! not even to oblige a lady.

LORD MOUNT. Then, the only question is, which of us shall give way   240
to the other? Perhaps, on the whole, she would be happier with me. I don't know. I may be wrong.

LORD TOLL. No. I don't know that you are. I really believe she would. But the awkward part of the thing is that if you rob me of the girl of my heart, we must fight, and one of us must die. It's a family tradition that I have   245
sworn to respect. It's a painful position, for I have a very strong regard for you, George.

LORD MOUNT. (*much affected*). My dear Thomas!

LORD TOLL. You are very dear to me, George. We were boys together – at least *I* was. If I were to survive you, my existence would be hopelessly   250
embittered.

LORD MOUNT. Then, my dear Thomas, you must not do it. I say it again and again – if it will have this effect upon you, you must not do it. No, no. If one of us is to destroy the other, let it be me!

LORD TOLL. No, no!   255

LORD MOUNT. Ah, yes! – by our boyish friendship I implore you!

LORD TOLL. (*much moved*). Well, well, be it so. But, no – no! – I cannot consent to an act which would crush you with unavailing remorse.

LORD MOUNT. But it would not do so. I should be very sad at first –

disappointment of the *Advertiser*, which commented that 'not a line of so good a thing should be lost'. Many critics, however, took a very different view and complained that the song held up the action and was rather too heavy in its message. Gilbert and Sullivan responded by cutting it early on in the Savoy run. In New York, however, where it was sung to a tune described by one reviewer as 'not altogether free from the influence of Mozart', it survived rather longer. Gilbert included the song in the 1897 edition of the *Bab Ballads*, giving it the title 'The Reward of Merit'. Sadly, the music does not survive.

After the 'De Belville' song, Lord Tolloller appeared on stage with the greeting 'Phyllis, my darling!' Phyllis then asked the two Earls whether they had settled which it was to be, and the dialogue continued very much as it does now (from line 224).

267 *it would not last a day*: Another 'lost' song occurred at this point in Gilbert's original *Perola* libretto:

> PHYL. *(coming down).* Oh dear, I'm a very wretched girl, to be the cause of so much misery! Why can't people fall in love with people that want to be fallen in love with? There are plenty of them about. I'm sure I don't want either of you!

TRIO. PHYLLIS, LORD MOUNTARARAT *and* LORD TOLLOLLER.

PHYL.	I dislike you both extremely!
(Crying.)	Boo, hoo! boo, hoo! boo, hoo, hoo!
	To distinguish were unseemly –
(Crying.)	Boo, hoo! boo, hoo! boo, hoo, hoo!
	I regret my explanation
	Ends in sad ejaculation,
	But in such a situation
	It would be sheer affectation
	To sing tra, la, la, la, la! *(wild dance)*
	To sing tra, la, la, la, etc.
	(After dance, all burst out crying.)
TOLL.	Though our lives we dearly cherished –
(Crying.)	Boo, hoo! boo, hoo! boo, hoo, hoo!
	Clearly one of us must perish.
(Crying.)	Boo, hoo! boo, hoo! boo, hoo, hoo!
	Fate with mortals never fences;
	We obey her exigences
	With such dismal consequences,
	No one in his sober senses
	Would sing tra la la, etc.
	(Dance as before, ending with Boo, hoo.)
MOUNT.	You'll regret it, if you lose me,
(Crying.)	Boo, hoo! boo, hoo! boo, hoo, hoo!
	I can't help it – pray excuse me!
(Crying.)	Boo, hoo! boo, hoo! boo, hoo, hoo!
	If to perish you elect me,
	At post mortem they'll dissect me,
	With such horrors to deject me,
	Surely no one will expect me
	To sing tra, la, la etc.

> *(Dance as before, ending with Boo, hoo, etc. At the end exeunt* PHYLLIS, LORD MOUNTARARAT *and* LORD TOLLOLLER.)

The quartet 'Though p'r'aps I may incur your blame' was substituted for the above trio some time before the first performance of *Iolanthe*.

oh, who would not be? – but it would wear off. I like you *very much* – but not,   260
perhaps, as much as you like me.

LORD TOLL. George, you're a noble fellow, but that tell-tale tear
betrays you. No, George; you are very fond of me, and I cannot consent to
give you a week's uneasiness on my account.

LORD MOUNT. But, dear Thomas, it would not last a week!   265
Remember, you lead the House of Lords! On your demise I shall take your
place! Oh, Thomas, it would not last a day!

PHYL. (*coming down*). Now, I do hope you're not going to fight about
me, because it's really not worth while.

LORD TOLL. (*looking at her*). Well, I don't believe it is!   270

LORD MOUNT. Nor I. The sacred ties of Friendship are paramount.

QUARTET – LORD MOUNTARARAT,
LORD TOLLOLLER, PHYLLIS, *and* PRIVATE WILLIS.

LORD TOLL.   Though p'r'aps I may incur your blame,
               The things are few
               I would not do
               In Friendship's name!   275

LORD MOUNT. And I may say I think the same;
               Not even love
               Should rank above
               True Friendship's name!

PHYL.   Then free me, pray; be mine the blame;   280
               Forget your craze
               And go your ways
               In Friendship's name!

ALL.   Oh, many a man, in Friendship's name,
               Has yielded fortune, rank, and fame!
               But no one yet, in the world so wide,   285
               Has yielded up a promised bride!

WILLIS.   Accept, O Friendship, all the same,

ALL.   This sacrifice to thy dear name!

(*Exeunt* LORD MOUNTARARAT *and* LORD TOLLOLLER,   290
lovingly, in one direction, and PHYLLIS *in another. Exit Sentry.*)

293–6 *Love, unrequited, robs me of my rest*
This recitative was cited by Kenneth Baker in his article suggesting that the character of the Lord Chancellor was based on W. E. Gladstone (see page 164) and the note to Act I, lines 707-57). The Liberal Prime Minister was well-known for his nocturnal ramblings through London in search of prostitutes to redeem and convert from their wicked ways. It was hardly a case of unrequited love robbing him of his rest, however.

297–328 *When you're lying awake with a dismal headache*
The nightmare song, as this is called, is perhaps the most brilliant of all Gilbert and Sullivan's patter songs. It is certainly the longest and fastest, and woe betide the singer who stumbles over a phrase half-way through.

    Punch accused Gilbert of taking the idea for the song from a comic recitation by the dramatist James Robinson Planché (1796–1880), which began 'I'm in such a flutter, I can scarcely utter'. However, it is much more likely to have been a Gilbertian original. He had, in fact, experimented with the metre later used for the nightmare song in a poem entitled 'Sixty-Three and Sixty-Four' which appeared in *Fun* in 1864 and which began:

> Oh, you who complain that the drawing's insane, or too much for your noodles have found it,
> But listen a minute, I'll tell you what's in it – completely explain and expound it.

302 *ticking*: A case or cover containing feathers or other stuffing to form a mattress or a pillow.
307 *tossing about in a steamer from Harwich*: Strictly speaking, steamers from Harwich cross the southern part of the North Sea rather than the English Channel. The main routes from the Essex port are to the Netherlands and Denmark.

    An earlier poem by Gilbert, 'The Return from My Berth', which appeared in *Punch* in October 1864, gives a more lurid account of a Channel crossing:

> The big Channel steamer is rolling,
> Frenchmen around me are bilious and fat
> And prone on the floor are behaving unheedingly,
> It's a 'sick transit', but never mind that!

In the early 1960s the American comedian and singer Danny Kaye recorded a transatlantic version of the nightmare song with new words written by his wife, Sylvia Fine. The lines about crossing the Channel became:

> For you dream that you're ill, having swallowed a pill,
> That was made out of ossified onyx
> And that doctor you've found, he is trav'ling around,
> On a subway that's bound for the Bronnyx.

308 *bathing machine*: A portable changing room, resembling a horse-drawn gipsy caravan, which could be towed out into the sea to allow modest Victorians to take to the water without anyone seeing them in their bathing apparel.
310 *Sloane Square and South Kensington Stations*: These are adjacent stations on the District Line of the London Underground, which was opened in 1868. In a letter to me Kenneth Baker suggested that this line referred to two well-known Radical politicians, Sir Charles Dilke, who lived in Sloane Street and was M.P. for Chelsea, and Joseph Chamberlain, who lived just off Exhibition Road, South Kensington. Both men were certainly something of a nightmare for Mr Gladstone.
311 *attorney*: See the note to Act I, line 473.
313 *a four-wheeler*: A four-wheeled hackney carriage. There is a celebrated story about the occasion when Gilbert was mistaken for a doorman by someone emerging from the

(*Enter* Lord Chancellor, *very miserable.*)

RECITATIVE – Lord Chancellor.

Love, unrequited, robs me of my rest:
Love, hopeless love, my ardent soul encumbers:
Love, nightmare-like, lies heavy on my chest,   295
And weaves itself into my midnight slumbers!

SONG – Lord Chancellor.

When you're lying awake with a dismal headache, and repose is taboo'd by
  anxiety,
I conceive you may use any language you choose to indulge in, without
  impropriety;
For your brain is on fire – the bedclothes conspire of usual slumber to
  plunder you:
First your counterpane goes, and uncovers your toes, and your sheet slips
  demurely from under you;   300
Then the blanketing tickles – you feel like mixed pickles – so terribly sharp
  is the pricking,
And you're hot, and you're cross, and you tumble and toss till there's
  nothing 'twixt you and the ticking.
Then the bedclothes all creep to the ground in a heap, and you pick 'em all
  up in a tangle;
Next your pillow resigns and politely declines to remain at its usual angle!
Well, you get some repose in the form of a doze, with hot eye-balls and head
  ever aching.   305
But your slumbering teems with such horrible dreams that you'd very much
  better be waking;
For you dream you are crossing the Channel, and tossing about in a steamer
  from Harwich –
Which is something between a large bathing machine and a very small
  second-class carriage –
And you're giving a treat (penny ice and cold meat) to a party of friends and
  relations –
They're a ravenous horde – and they all came on board at Sloane Square and
  South Kensington Stations.   310
And bound on that journey you find your attorney (who started that
  morning from Devon);
He's a bit undersized, and you don't feel surprised when he tells you he's
  only eleven.
Well, you're driving like mad with this singular lad (by the by, the ship's
  now a four-wheeler),

Haymarket Theatre, who went up to him and said 'Call me a cab!' 'Very well,' Gilbert replied, 'you're a four-wheeler.' 'What on earth do you mean by that?' was the man's startled response. 'Well, sir,' said Gilbert, 'you asked me to call you a cab, and I certainly couldn't call you "Hansom".'

314 *ties pay the dealer*: In games such as pontoon and blackjack a player loses to the dealer (who holds the 'bank') if he has a lower, or even an equal, hand of cards (i.e. if he ties with the dealer).

321 *boot-tree*: A shaped block inserted into a boot to stretch it.

324 *cherry brandy*: This may seem an odd commodity for a pastrycook to sell, but it was in fact served in some such establishments in Victorian times to provide a refined tipple for ladies, who would not venture into a public house or hotel bar.
three-corners: Triangular Danish pastries.
Banburys: Banbury cakes have a filling of currants and spice encased in pastry. They take their name from the Oxfordshire town of Banbury.

325 *Rothschild and Baring*: Two of the leading banking houses in Victorian Britain, both of which are still going strong today. The Rothschilds are, of course, the most famous of all the European banking families; at the time of *Iolanthe* the head of the firm in Britain was Sir Nathan Meyer Rothschild, who in 1885 became the 1st Baron Rothschild. He is remembered particularly for having helped Disraeli to get Britain a controlling interest in the Suez Canal in 1875. The name also occurs in *Utopia Limited* in a song for Mr Goldbury, the company promoter.

Barings was founded in 1770 by two brothers, John and Francis Baring, sons of a cloth manufacturer who had emigrated to London from Germany. The head of the firm at the time of *Iolanthe* was Edward Charles Baring, who, like Rothschild, was raised to the peerage in 1885.

327 *needles and pins*: This uncomfortable condition is also mentioned in Gilbert's earlier poem 'The Return from My Berth' in the verse:

> There's pleasure in feeling so coldly and clammily
> Joy in the needles and pins in my leg;
> Pleasure in watching that foreigner's family
> Eating stick chocolate mixed with hard egg.

328 *ditto ditto my song*: At almost every performance the nightmare song is not too long for the audience, who invariably demand an encore from the exhausted Lord Chancellor. The D'Oyly Carte practice was to start the encore at 'And he and the crew are on bicycles too' (line 317).

And you're playing round games, and he calls you bad names when you tell
    him that 'ties pay the dealer';
But this you can't stand, so you throw up your hand, and you find you're as
    cold as an icicle,   315
In your shirt and your socks (the black silk with gold clocks), crossing
    Salisbury Plain on a bicycle:
And he and the crew are on bicycles too – which they've somehow or other
    invested in –
And he's telling the tars all the particu*lars* of a company he's interested in –
It's a scheme of devices, to get at low prices all goods from cough mixtures
    to cables
(Which tickled the sailors), by treating retailers as though they were all
    vege*tab*les –   320
You get a good spadesman to plant a small tradesman (first take off his boots
    with a boot-tree),
And his legs will take root, and his fingers will shoot, and they'll blossom
    and bud like a fruit-tree –
From the greengrocer tree you get grapes and green pea, cauliflower,
    pineapple, and cranberries,
While the pastrycook plant cherry brandy will grant, apple puffs, and three-
    corners, and Banburys –
The shares are a penny, and ever so many are taken by Rothschild and
    Baring,   325
And just as a few are allotted to you, you awake with a shudder despairing –
You're a regular wreck, with a crick in your neck, and no wonder you snore,
    for your head's on the floor, and you've needles and pins from your
    soles to your shins, and your flesh is a-creep, for your left leg's asleep,
    and you've cramp in your toes, and a fly on your nose, and some fluff
    in your lung, and a feverish tongue, and a thirst that's intense, and a
    general sense that you haven't been sleeping in clover;
But the darkness has passed, and it's daylight at last, and the night has been
    long – ditto ditto my song – and thank goodness they're both of them
    over!

      (LORD CHANCELLOR *falls exhausted on a seat.*)

      (*Enter* LORDS MOUNTARARAT *and* TOLLOLLER.)   330

   LORD MOUNT. I am much distressed to see your Lordship in this
condition.
   LORD CH. Ah, my Lords, it is seldom that a Lord Chancellor has
reason to envy the position of another, but I am free to confess that I would
rather be two Earls engaged to Phyllis than any other half-dozen noblemen   335
upon the face of the globe.

343 *in six-eight time*: Whether by accident or design, Gilbert hit on an appropriate figure here. Six-eight is the time signature both for the nightmare song and for 'The Law is the true embodiment'. It is indeed the most common time signature in *Iolanthe*, being used for nine of the songs and for the overture.

361–97 *If you go in*
This exuberant trio, traditionally much encored, and finally ending in D'Oyly Carte performances with the Lord Chancellor dancing into Private Willis's sentry box to take refuge, ranks with 'Things are seldom what they seem' from Act II of *H.M.S. Pinafore* in its use of old proverbs and sayings. By my calculations, the *Pinafore* duet wins, with sixteen identifiable proverbs against eleven in this song.

367 *Faint heart never won fair lady*: According to the *Oxford Dictionary of English Proverbs* the first recorded use of this saying was in 1569, when it appeared in the form 'Faint hearts faire ladies never win'.

370 *Every journey has an end*: This is an original Gilbertianism, if the word original can be applied to such an obvious truism.

372 *Dark the dawn when day is nigh*: The earliest recorded version of this saying, 'The darkest hour is that before the dawn', dates from 1650.

373 *don't say die*: Curiously, the first use of this expression recorded in the *Oxford Dictionary of English Proverbs* is as late as 1837, in Charles Dickens's *The Pickwick Papers*, where it occurs in the form 'Never say die'.

LORD TOLL. (*without enthusiasm*). Yes. It's an enviable position when you're the only one.

LORD MOUNT. Oh yes, no doubt – most enviable. At the same time, seeing you thus, we naturally say to ourselves, 'This is very sad. His 340 Lordship is constitutionally as blithe as a bird – he trills upon the bench like a thing of song and gladness. His series of judgements in F sharp minor, given *andante* in six-eight time, are among the most remarkable effects ever produced in a Court of Chancery. He is, perhaps, the only living instance of a judge whose decrees have received the honour of a double *encore*. How can 345 we bring ourselves to do that which will deprive the Court of Chancery of one of its most attractive features?'

LORD CH. I feel the force of your remarks, but I am here in two capacities, and they clash, my Lords, they clash! I deeply grieve to say that in declining to entertain my last application to myself, I presumed to address 350 myself in terms which render it impossible for me ever to apply to myself again. It was a most painful scene, my Lords – most painful!

LORD TOLL. This is what it is to have two capacities! Let us be thankful that we are persons of no capacity whatever.

LORD MOUNT. Come, come. Remember you are a very just and kindly 355 old gentleman, and you need have no hesitation in approaching yourself, so that you do so respectfully and with a proper show of deference.

LORD CH. Do you really think so?

LORD MOUNT. I do.

LORD CH. Well, I will nerve myself to another effort, and, if that fails, 360 I resign myself to my fate!

> TRIO – LORD CHANCELLOR, LORDS MOUNTARARAT
> *and* TOLLOLLER.

LORD MOUNT.   If you go in
                  You're sure to win –
              Yours will be the charming maidie:
                  Be your law   365
                  The ancient saw,
              'Faint heart never won fair lady!'

ALL.   Never, never, never,
              Faint heart never won fair lady!

                  Every journey has an end –   370
                  When at the worst affairs will mend –
                  Dark the dawn when day is nigh –
                  Hustle your horse and don't say die!

LORD TOLL.   He who shies
                  At such a prize   375

376 *a maravedi*: A Spanish copper coin minted in 1848, with a value of only about one thirteenth of an English penny. This saying is, I think, a Gilbertian original.

382 *While the sun shines make your hay*: The first recorded appearance in print was in 1546 in the form 'Whan the sunne shinth make hay'. It is more normally inverted: 'Make hay while the sun shines'.

383 *Where a will is, there's a way*: Usually found in the form 'Where there's a will, there's a way'. The first recorded appearance is in 1836.

384 *Beard the lion in his lair*: Originally biblical, deriving from the well-known story of Daniel in the lion's den (Daniel 6.11–23). It means to tackle the enemy in his stronghold.

385 *None but the brave deserve the fair*: The only saying which occurs in both the *Iolanthe* trio and the *Pinafore* duet. It is found in John Dryden's ode *Alexander's Feast* (1697).

394 *Nothing venture, nothing win*: First recorded use 1668.

395 *Blood is thick, but water's thin*: Normally used in the form 'Blood is thicker than water', meaning that the ties of family and kinship are stronger than any others. Its first recorded use is in Sir Walter Scott's *Guy Mannering* (1815).

396 *In for a penny, in for a pound*: First recorded use 1695.

397 *It's Love that makes the world go round*: Some commentators, including Harry Benford in his *Gilbert and Sullivan Lexicon*, have suggested that this was Gilbert's own creation, involving a paraphrase of the old saying 'It's drink that makes the world go round'. In fact, the phrase 'Love makes the world go round' was well-known in nineteenth-century England. It occurs in Charles Dickens's *Our Mutual Friend* (1865). A French version, *C'est l'amour, l'amour qui fait le monde à la ronde*, is recorded as early as 1700.

399 *Enter Strephon, in very low spirits*: In early performances of *Iolanthe* in both London and New York, Strephon entered at this point to sing the following recitative and aria:

RECITATIVE.

My Bill has now been read a second time:
His ready vote no member now refuses;
In verity I wield a power sublime,
And one that I can turn to mighty uses.
What joy to carry, in the very teeth
Of Ministry, Cross-Bench and Opposition,
Some rather urgent measures – quite beneath
The ken of patriot and politician!

SONG.

Fold your flapping wings,
    Soaring Legislature!
Stoop to little things –
    Stoop to Human Nature!
Never need to roam,
    Members patriotic,
Let's begin at home –
    Crime is no exotic!
        Bitter is your bane –
            Terrible your trials –
        Dingy Drury Lane!
            Soapless Seven Dials!

Is not worth a maravedi,
Be so kind
To bear in mind –
Faint heart never won fair lady!

ALL. Never, never, never, 380
Faint heart never won fair lady!

While the sun shines make your hay –
Where a will is, there's a way –
Beard the lion in his lair –
None but the brave deserve the fair! 385

LORD CH. I'll take heart
And make a start –
Though I fear the prospect's shady –
Much I'd spend
To gain my end – 390
Faint heart never won fair lady!

ALL. Never, never, never,
Faint heart never won fair lady!

Nothing venture, nothing win –
Blood is thick, but water's thin – 395
In for a penny, in for a pound –
It's Love that makes the world go round!
(*Dance, and exeunt arm-in-arm together.*)

(*Enter* STREPHON, *in very low spirits.*)

STREPH. I suppose one ought to enjoy oneself in Parliament, when one 400
leads both Parties, as I do! But I'm miserable, poor, broken-hearted fool that
I am! Oh, Phyllis, Phyllis! —

(*Enter* PHYLLIS.)

PHYL. Yes.
STREPH. (*surprised*). Phyllis! But I suppose I should say 'My Lady'. I 405
have not yet been informed which title your ladyship has pleased to select?
PHYL. I – I haven't quite decided. You see, *I* have no *mother* to advise
me!
STREPH. No. I have.
PHYL. Yes; a *young* mother. 410
STREPH. Not very – a couple of centuries or so.
PHYL. Oh! She wears well.
STREPH. She does. She's a fairy.
PHYL. I beg your pardon – a what?
STREPH. Oh, I've no longer any reason to conceal the fact – she's a 415
fairy.

Take a tipsy lout
　Gathered from the gutter –
Hustle him about –
　Strap him to a shutter:
What am I but he,
　Washed at hours stated –
Fed on filigree –
　Clothed and educated?
　　　He's a mark of scorn –
　　　　I might be another,
　　　　If I had been born
　　　　Of a tipsy mother!

Take a wretched thief
　Through the city sneaking,
Pocket handkerchief
　Ever, ever seeking:
What is he but I
　Robbed of all my chances –
Picking pockets by
　Force of circumstances?
　　　I might be as bad –
　　　　As unlucky, rather –
　　　　If I'd only had
　　　　Fagin for a father!

'Fold your flapping wings' came in for considerable criticism in some of the first-night reviews. The magazine *Truth* complained that 'to eke out the time, the clown, now a Member of Parliament, has to sing a lengthy ditty, in which he ponderously explains that he never sees a criminal without thinking that it might have been himself'. The *Theatre* reviewer commented:

> The libretto of *Iolanthe* has been utilized by its author as the vehicle for conveying to society at large a feeling protest on behalf of the indigent, and a scathing satire upon the hereditary moiety of our Legislature. Advocacy and denunciation of this sort are all very well in melodrama, where telling 'points' may always be made with the unmerited wrongs of the poor and the reprehensible uselessness of the aristocracy. But they jar upon the ear and taste alike when brought to bear upon us through the medium of a song sung by half a fairy in a professedly comic opera.

Gilbert took this criticism to heart, and 'Fold your flapping wings' was cut during the initial Savoy run. It was, however, printed in both the first and second British editions of the libretto and in the first American edition of the vocal score, from which we can discover that it had an appealing waltz-time tune.

427–8 *half a dozen I don't*: For the 1907 revival of *Iolanthe* Phyllis was given an extra line at this point, 'Half a mortal's better than no bread'. This rather corny addition to the original libretto, apparently approved by Gilbert, was cut again in 1914 and has not been used in subsequent performances. Strephon's earlier line 'Don't do that' (line 423) was also added in 1907, as were the words 'I hate that sort of thing' immediately after it. The second part of the line was cut in 1914 to leave the present version.

442–65 *If we're weak enough to tarry*
As previously mentioned (see the note to Act I, line 228), this song was originally intended for Act I. In the licence copy of the *Perola* libretto, the dialogue between Strephon and Phyllis continues straight from 'I think we shall be very happy!' (line 436) to 'But does your mother know' (line 466).

PHYL. A fairy! Well, but – that would account for a good many things! Then – I suppose *you're* a fairy?

STREPH. I'm half a fairy.

PHYL. Which half? 420

STREPH. The upper half – down to the waistcoat.

PHYL. Dear me! (*Prodding him with her fingers.*) There is nothing to show it!

STREPH. Don't do that.

PHYL. But why didn't you tell me this before?

STREPH. I thought you would take a dislike to me. But as it's all off, 425
you may as well know the truth – I'm only half a mortal!

PHYL. (*crying*). But I'd rather have half a mortal I do love, than half a dozen I don't!

STREPH. Oh, I think not – go to your half-dozen.

PHYL. (*crying*). It's only two! and I hate 'em! Please forgive me! 430

STREPH. I don't think I ought to. Besides, all sorts of difficulties will arise. You know, my grandmother looks quite as young as my mother. So do all my aunts.

PHYL. I quite understand. Whenever I see you kissing a very young lady, I shall know it's an elderly relative. 435

STREPH. You will? Then, Phyllis, I think we shall be very happy! (*Embracing her.*)

PHYL. We won't wait long.

STREPH. No. We might change our minds. We'll get married first.

PHYL. And change our minds afterwards? 440

STREPH. That's the usual course.

DUET – STREPHON *and* PHYLLIS.

STREPH.   If we're weak enough to tarry
              Ere we marry,
                You and I,
              Of the feeling I inspire 445
                You may tire
                  By and by.
              For peers with flowing coffers
                Press their offers –
                  That is why 450
              I am sure we should not tarry
                Ere we marry,
                  You and I!

PHYL.   If we're weak enough to tarry
              Ere we marry,
                You and I, 455

466 *But does your mother know*: This was a well-known catch-phrase among the Victorian working classes, particularly in the form 'Does your mother know you're out?'

477 *You know not what you ask*: After delivering this line Iolanthe/Perola has the following song in the licence copy:

SONG – PEROLA.

A fairy once, as well you know
(Heigho, love is a thorn)
She loved a mortal years ago –
(And it's oh my beating heart!)
They married were, this foolish pair,
And then was born a son and heir,
I'm sure of my facts, for I was there!
(And it's oh for my beating heart!)

ALL.   Heigho, love is a thorn,
And it's oh my beating heart!

I was that fond and foolish fay
(Heigho, etc.)
That you were the son, I need not say.
(And it's oh, etc.)
The mortal – your progenitor –
Whom I give up my freedom for –
He is the present Lord Chancellor!
And it's oh my beating heart!

ALL.   Heigho, love is a thorn,
And it's oh my beating heart!

The dialogue then continued:

STREPH. The Lord Chancellor my father! But he knows nothing of this?
PEROLA. No, by our Queen's command, I quitted him shortly after our marriage. He believes me to be dead: and, dearly as I love him, I am bound, under penalty of death, never to undeceive him.
STREPH. Then, Phyllis, I really don't see what is to become of us.
PEROLA. Nay, there is hope. I will disguise myself, and plead your case as best I may. He comes! This veil will conceal my face. Oh that I could so easily veil my trembling voice!

(Enter LORD CHANCELLOR.)

With a more attractive maiden,
 Jewel-laden,
  You may fly.
If by chance we should be parted,   460
 Broken-hearted
  I should die –
So I think we will not tarry
 Ere we marry,
  You and I.   465

PHYL. But does your mother know you're – I mean, is she aware of our engagement?

(Enter IOLANTHE.*)*

IOL. She is; and thus she welcomes her daughter-in-law! *(Kisses her.)*
PHYL. She kisses just like other people! But the Lord Chancellor?   470
STREPH. I forgot him! Mother, none can resist your fairy eloquence; you will go to him and plead for us?
IOL. *(much agitated).* No, no; impossible!
STREPH. But our happiness – our very lives – depend upon our obtaining his consent!   475
PHYL. Oh, madam, you cannot refuse to do this!
IOL. You know not what you ask! The Lord Chancellor is – my husband!
STREPH. *and* PHYL. Your husband!
IOL. My husband and your father! *(Addressing* STREPHON, *who is much*   480
moved.)
PHYL. Then our course is plain; on his learning that Strephon is his son, all objection to our marriage will be at once removed!
IOL. No; he must never know! He believes me to have died childless, and, dearly as I love him, I am bound, under penalty of death, not to   485
undeceive him. But see – he comes! Quick – my veil!
(IOLANTHE *veils herself.* STREPHON *and* PHYLLIS *go off on tiptoe.)*

(Enter LORD CHANCELLOR.*)*

LORD CH. Victory! Victory! Success has crowned my efforts, and I may consider myself engaged to Phyllis! At first I wouldn't hear of it – it was out   490
of the question. But I took heart. I pointed out to myself that I was no stranger to myself; that, in point of fact, I had been personally acquainted with myself for some years. This had its effect. I admitted that I had watched my professional advancement with considerable interest, and I handsomely added that I yielded to no one in admiration for my private and professional   495
virtues. This was a great point gained. I then endeavoured to work upon my

505–20 *He loves! If in the bygone years*

Gilbert wrote the part of Iolanthe specially for Jessie Bond, the D'Oyly Carte's leading mezzo-soprano, who had joined the company to sing the role of Hebe in the first production of *H.M.S. Pinafore*. At the time *Iolanthe* was being written, she was incapacitated by a serious accident which made any vigorous movement impossible. Gilbert told her 'You will not have to dance and hardly to move, and as you are always laughing, I have written a song to show you can be serious when you have the chance'. The song was, of course, 'He loves', which is one of the saddest and most moving in all the Savoy Operas.

In setting 'He loves' to music, Sullivan must surely have been profoundly influenced by the death of his mother, which had occurred only a few days before he started work on the *Iolanthe* score. The line 'Sad thoughts of her arise' must have had particularly poignant echoes for the composer, who was deeply distraught at the loss of one to whom he had always been very close. Perhaps indeed he even saw this song as standing in some way as a memorial to her, just as his overture *In Memoriam* (1866) was written as a memorial to his father, and his famous song *The Lost Chord* (1877) was inspired by the death of his brother.

feelings. Conceive my joy when I distinctly perceived a tear glistening in my own eye! Eventually, after a severe struggle with myself, I reluctantly – most reluctantly – consented.

(Iolanthe comes down veiled.)

500

RECITATIVE – Iolanthe (kneeling).

My lord, a suppliant at your feet I kneel,
Oh, listen to a mother's fond appeal!
Hear me to-night! I come in urgent need –
'Tis for my son, young Strephon, that I plead!

BALLAD – Iolanthe.

He loves! If in the bygone years   505
    Thine eyes have ever shed
Tears – bitter, unavailing tears,
    For one untimely dead –
If, in the eventide of life,
    Sad thoughts of her arise,   510
Then let the memory of thy wife
    Plead for my boy – he dies!

He dies! If fondly laid aside
    In some old cabinet,
Memorials of thy long-dead bride   515
    Lie, dearly treasured yet,
Then let her hallowed bridal dress –
    Her little dainty gloves –
Her withered flowers – her faded tress –
    Plead for my boy – he loves!   520

(The Lord Chancellor *is moved by this appeal. After a pause.*)

Lord Ch.   It may not be – for so the fates decide!
            Learn thou that Phyllis is my promised bride.
Iol. (*in horror*).   Thy bride! No! no!
Lord Ch.   It shall be so!   525
            Those who would separate us woe betide!
Iol.   My doom thy lips have spoken –
                            I plead in vain!
Chorus of Fairies (*without*).   Forbear! forbear!

545 *Willahalah! Willaloo*: Another Wagnerian touch; the fairies' chorus is reminiscent of the wailing of the Rhinedaughters in *Das Rheingold*: 'Wag-a-la-weia, Wa-la-la, Wei-la-la, Weia'.

561 *Equity draftsman*: An old name given to a barrister practising in the Court of Chancery who drafted pleadings to be heard in that court.

562 *The subtleties of the legal mind*: The legal mind receives another 'puff' in *The Grand Duke* when the notary says: 'It is always amusing to the legal mind to see a parcel of laymen bothering themselves about a matter which to a trained lawyer presents no difficulty whatever.'

567 *Private Willis*: In the 1907 revival, the Fairy Queen at this point had the extra line, reminiscent of Captain Corcoran's command to Ralph Rackstraw in *H.M.S. Pinafore*, 'Three paces to the front'. It was cut again in 1914.

IOL.	A vow already broken	530
	I break again!	

CHORUS OF FAIRIES (*without*).   Forbear! forbear!

IOL.   For him – for her – for thee
                I yield my life.
            Behold – it may not be!   535
                I am thy wife.

CHORUS OF FAIRIES (*without*).   Aiaiah! Aiaiah! Willaloo!

LORD CH. (*recognizing her*).   Iolanthe! thou livest?

IOL.   Aye!
            I live! Now let me die!   540

(*Enter* FAIRY QUEEN *and Fairies.* IOLANTHE *kneels to her.*)

QUEEN.   Once again thy vows are broken:
            Thou thyself thy doom hast spoken!

CHORUS OF FAIRIES.   Aiaiah! Aiaiah!
                        Willahalah! Willaloo!   545
                        Willahalah! Willaloo!

QUEEN.   Bow thy head to Destiny:
            Death thy doom, and thou shalt die!

CHORUS OF FAIRIES.   Aiaiah! Aiaiah! etc.

(*Peers and Sentry enter. The* QUEEN *raises her spear.*)   550

LEILA. Hold! If Iolanthe must die, so must we all; for, as she has sinned, so have we!

QUEEN. What?

CELIA. We are all fairy duchesses, marchionesses, countesses, viscountesses, and baronesses.   555

LORD MOUNT. It's our fault. They couldn't help themselves.

QUEEN. It seems they *have* helped themselves, and pretty freely, too! (*After a pause.*) You have all incurred death; but I can't slaughter the whole company! And yet (*unfolding a scroll*) the law is clear – every fairy must die who marries a mortal!   560

LORD CH. Allow me, as an old Equity draftsman, to make a suggestion. The subtleties of the legal mind are equal to the emergency. The thing is really quite simple – the insertion of a single word will do it. Let it stand that every fairy shall die who *doesn't* marry a mortal, and there you are, out of your difficulty at once!   565

QUEEN. We like your humour. Very well! (*Altering the MS. in pencil.*) Private Willis!

SENTRY (*coming forward*). Ma'am!

QUEEN. To save my life, it is necessary that I marry at once. How should you like to be a fairy guardsman?   570

572 *ill-convenience*: In the manner of the Victorian lower classes, Private Willis pronounces his 'v's as 'w's. The word is, indeed, printed as 'inconwenience' in several editions of the libretto.

582 *Wings spring from shoulders of Peers*: Gilbert's note in his prompt-book reads: 'At "off we go to Fairyland", each principal pulls a string which is fastened to the pin which keeps his wings down. On release, the wings fly up. The soldier's wings have appeared on his shoulder before this – that is to say when the Fairy Queen says, "You are a fairy from this moment".'

602 *House of Peris*: Peris originally appeared in Persian mythology as a race of beautiful but malevolent fairy-like creatures who were descended from fallen angels and excluded from Paradise until they had completed their penance. They were held responsible for comets, eclipses of the sun and moon, and the failure of crops. Later the word came to be used more generally for fairies and, indeed, for any beautiful girl.

SENTRY. Well, ma'am, I don't think much of the British soldier who wouldn't ill-convenience himself to save a female in distress.

QUEEN. You are a brave fellow. You're a fairy from this moment. (*Wings spring from Sentry's shoulders.*) And you, my Lords, how say you, will you join our ranks?   575

(*Fairies kneel to Peers and implore them to do so.*)

(PHYLLIS *and* STREPHON *enter.*)

LORD MOUNT. (*to* LORD TOLLOLLER). Well, now that the Peers are to be recruited entirely from persons of intelligence, I really don't see what use *we* are, down here, do you, Tolloller?   580

LORD TOLL. None whatever.

QUEEN. Good! (*Wings spring from shoulders of Peers.*) Then away we go to Fairyland.

FINALE.

PHYL.   Soon as we may,
                Off and away!   585
                We'll commence our journey airy –
                Happy are we –
                As you can see,
                Every one is now a fairy!

ALL.   Every, every, every,   590
                Every one is now a fairy!

IOL., QUEEN,   Though as a general rule we know
  and PHYL.   Two strings go to every bow,
                Make up your minds that grief 'twill bring
                If you've two beaux to every string.   595

ALL.   Though as a general rule, etc.

LORD CH.   Up in the sky,
                Ever so high,
                Pleasures come in endless series;
                  We will arrange   600
                  Happy exchange –
                House of Peers for House of Peris!

ALL.   Peris, Peris, Peris,
                      House of Peers for House of Peris!

LORDS CH.,   Up in the air, sky-high, sky-high,   605
MOUNT.,   Free from Wards in Chancery,
and TOLL.   I ⎫
                He ⎬ will be surely happier, for
                    ⎭

                  I'm ⎫
                  He's ⎬ such a susceptible Chancellor.
ALL.   Up in the air, etc.

CURTAIN

THE MIKADO

OR

THE TOWN OF TITIPU

DRAMATIS PERSONÆ

THE MIKADO OF JAPAN
NANKI-POO (*his Son, disguised as a wandering minstrel, and in love with* YUM-YUM)
KO-KO (*Lord High Executioner of Titipu*)
POOH-BAH (*Lord High Everything Else*)
PISH-TUSH (*a Noble Lord*)
GO-TO (*a Noble Lord*)
YUM-YUM
PITTI-SING } *Three Sisters – Wards of* KO-KO
PEEP-BO
KATISHA (*an elderly Lady, in love with* NANKI-POO)
Chorus of School-girls, Nobles, Guards, and Coolies.

ACT I. – Courtyard of Ko-Ko's Official Residence.
ACT II. – Ko-Ko's Garden.

THE MIKADO

The Mikado has almost certainly been performed more times than any other Gilbert and Sullivan opera. Its initial run at the Savoy Theatre of 672 performances stretched for very nearly two years. It has continued ever since to delight audiences all over the world in productions in many different languages and styles. In 1939 it became the first Savoy Opera to be filmed, and more recently it has been presented on television in several countries.

Surprisingly, perhaps, *The Mikado* was written at a time when the spirits of Gilbert and Sullivan were at a low ebb and when relations between the two men, which were never too good at the best of times, were particularly strained. By the late spring of 1884 audiences for their latest work, *Princess Ida*, were dropping off, and Richard D'Oyly Carte was demanding a new opera to revive the flagging fortunes of the company. Gilbert responded by resurrecting a rather fanciful idea for a plot based on a magic lozenge which Sullivan had turned down two years earlier. The composer once again rejected the idea, telling Gilbert in no uncertain terms that he was fed up with ridiculous plots and topsy-turvy situations and wanted a more straightforward libretto, where the music would not just have to be subordinate to the words but could stand on its own.

Gilbert took this response as a personal slight and wrote back 'I cannot consent to construct another plot for the next opera'. Sullivan, equally emphatically, replied 'The tone of your letter convinces me that your decision is final and therefore further discussion is useless'. D'Oyly Carte desperately tried to mediate between his two protégés, but his efforts were unsuccessful and it began to look very much as though the partnership which had produced seven very successful comic operas had now come to an end.

The situation was saved by a dramatic accident which could have inflicted a much more tragic and conclusive blow to the partnership. As Gilbert was pacing up and down the library of his new house in Harrington Gardens, Kensington, one day in May 1884 – and no doubt brooding about the sorry state of affairs – a large Japanese executioner's sword fell from its mounting on the wall and crashed to the floor. This inspired the dramatist with the idea of a possible plot for a new opera. Why not set it in Japan and make the leading characters the emperor of that country and his public executioner? On that basis he was able to write a libretto free of the absurd topsy-turvydom that Sullivan so disliked but still rich in humour, and composer and librettist were once again reconciled.

Things Japanese were all the rage in England in the mid-1880s. Oriental prints and ceramics were on sale in the most fashionable West End stores. Liberty's was enjoying a spectacular success with its Japanese-style fabrics and dresses. There was even a Japanese village which had been set up in Knightsbridge, complete with real geisha girls serving tea in the traditional manner. So Gilbert was developing a fashionable contemporary theme in setting his new opera in the far-away Pacific islands, which were beginning to be washed by the strong currents of Western influence.

The location of *The Mikado* was to lead to a typically Gilbertian piece of official silliness early in the twentieth century. Shortly before the official visit to Britain of Crown Prince Fushimi of Japan in 1907, the Lord Chamberlain announced an indefinite ban on all performances of the opera on the grounds that it was offensive to the Japanese. Several M.P.s protested about the ban; one asked whether it applied to military bands playing excerpts from *The Mikado* (it apparently did), while another pointed out that as Shakespeare's *Hamlet* portrayed the King of Denmark as a murderer, and as Denmark was a friendly power, presumably it should be banned for the same reason. In the event the ban lasted for six weeks before it was withdrawn by the Home Secretary. Gilbert, who was honoured with a knighthood shortly afterwards, commented that before long 'we shall probably be at war with Japan about India, and they will offer me a high price to permit *The Mikado* to be played.'

It was, of course, absurd to ban *The Mikado* on the grounds that it might offend the Japanese. Despite its setting, the opera is quite clearly about Britain, and its satire is directed at domestic rather than foreign targets. There is nothing very Japanese about the pluralist Pooh-Bah, with his offices *(inter alia)* of Archbishop, Paymaster-General and Lord Chief Justice, or about a Mikado whose ideas of suitable punishments for criminals include sending them to Madame Tussaud's or making them ride on the buffers of Parliamentary trains. As G. K. Chesterton observed, 'I doubt if there is a single joke in the whole play that fits the Japanese. But all the jokes in the play fit the English.'

Certainly the music for *The Mikado* could hardly have been more English. It is true that there are one or two Japanese touches like the use of the pentatonic scale for the opening chorus and the quotation of the Imperial marching song 'Miya sama'. But the dominant musical influence is the English folk-song tradition, seen particularly in Nanki-Poo's opening number, 'A wandering minstrel I', the madrigal 'Brightly dawns our wedding day' and the delightful duet 'The flowers that bloom in the spring'.

Even the entrance of the Lord High Executioner is set to a tune remarkably similar to the traditional air 'A Fine Old English Gentleman'.

More than any other of the Savoy Operas, *The Mikado* has been the subject of changes and widely different interpretations in the twentieth century. Several of the 'gags' introduced in early performances by Rutland Barrington when he was playing Pooh-Bah are still used today although they failed to secure Gilbert's approval. In 1948 two of the best-loved songs in the opera, Ko-Ko's 'I've got a little list' and the Mikado's 'My object all sublime', had to be altered when it was found that the word 'nigger' caused offence to American audiences.

Foreign productions have sometimes taken *The Mikado* a long way from the original intentions of its librettist and composer. A jazz version performed in Berlin in 1927 had Nanki-Poo doing the charleston in Oxford bags and double-breasted blazer, and Yum-Yum singing 'The sun whose rays' while naked in her bath! The Americans have had *The Swing Mikado* (an all-black version produced in Chicago in 1938), *The Hot Mikado* (New York, 1939) and *The Black Mikado* (1975). There has also been a *Cool Mikado* – a film made in 1962 and starring Frankie Howerd.

The Mikado has, indeed, been particularly popular in the United States from the very beginning. Richard D'Oyly Carte tried to beat the many pirate companies which were putting on unauthorized productions by secretly assembling a company and shipping it incognito on a Cunard liner from Liverpool to New York. Its authentic *Mikado* opened at the Fifth Avenue Theater on 19 August 1885, just five months after the London opening. The opera was so popular that on one evening in 1886 there were said to have been 170 separate performances across the States, no doubt including at least one in the city of Mikado, Michigan, which was so named in that year. Richard D'Oyly Carte at one stage had five companies touring North America, four in Britain and another touring Europe. He didn't send one to Japan, but the opera became well enough known there for its music to be in the regular repertoire of the bands of the Imperial Army and Navy by 1907 – just as it was being banned in Britain for fear of giving offence.

1 *Scene*: Having decided to set his new opera in Japan, Gilbert told a reporter of the *New York Tribune* in 1885:

> the next thing was to decide upon two scenes, which should be characteristic and effective. The respective advantages of a street in Nagasaki, a Japanese market-place, a wharf with shipping, a Japanese garden, a seaside beach, and the courtyard of a Japanese palace were duly weighed; and the courtyard and the Japanese garden were finally decided upon.

3–16 *If you want to know who we are*
Considerable care was taken by both Gilbert and Sullivan to give their opening chorus an authentic Japanese atmosphere. The nobles were clad in splendid printed silk robes based on original oriental designs, and they were schooled in traditional Japanese movements and gestures. The opening vocal phrases of the chorus are confined to the pentatonic scale, a scale of five notes without semitones on which oriental music was traditionally based.

Sullivan's autograph score has a different version of the second verse:

> Polite etiquette demands,
>   That persons of either sex,
> Shall suffer cramp in the hand
>   And a crick in their outstretched necks.
>   When suffering from constraint,
>   We're always allowed to faint,
>   You're wrong if you think we mayn't, oh!

18 *obi*: A brightly coloured sash worn, like a cummerbund, round the waist, but usually by Japanese women and children rather than men. In most editions of the libretto, this stage direction has been changed to '*in his hand*'.

ACT I

SCENE. – *Courtyard of* KO-KO's *Palace in Titipu. Japanese nobles discovered standing and sitting in attitudes suggested by native drawings.*

CHORUS OF NOBLES.

If you want to know who we are,
　　We are gentlemen of Japan:
On many a vase and jar –　　　　　　　　　　　　5
　　On many a screen and fan,
　　　We figure in lively paint:
　　　Our attitude's queer and quaint –
　　　You're wrong if you think it ain't, oh!

If you think we are worked by strings,　　　　　　10
　　Like a Japanese marionette,
You don't understand these things:
　　It is simply Court etiquette.
　　　Perhaps you suppose this throng
　　　Can't keep it up all day long?　　　　　　　15
　　　If that's your idea, you're wrong, oh!

(*Enter* NANKI-POO *in great excitement. He carries a native guitar on his back and a bundle of ballads in his obi.*)

RECITATIVE – NANKI-POO.

Gentlemen, I pray you tell me
Where a gentle maiden dwelleth,　　　　　　　　20
Named Yum-Yum, the ward of Ko-Ko?
In pity speak – oh, speak, I pray you!

A NOBLE.　　Why, who are you who ask this question?

25–72 *A wandering minstrel I*
   With its double change of mood from romantic ballad to rousing martial tune to
   rollicking sea shanty, this is one of the best-known and best-loved of all Gilbert and
   Sullivan's songs. Its first line was used by Sir Henry Lytton, a member of the D'Oyly
   Carte Opera Company for almost forty-five years, as the title of his autobiography. It
   could equally well apply to the company as a whole, faithful guardian of the Savoy
   Opera tradition for more than a century until its sad demise at the beginning of 1982.
   From the very start the D'Oyly Carte was first and foremost a touring company, on the
   road for thirty-five weeks a year and taking the works of Gilbert and Sullivan to towns
   as far apart as Inverness and Torquay. It was, indeed, this wandering minstrel
   existence, unique in British theatrical or musical life, which ultimately led to the
   company's downfall. The high costs of touring proved impossible to meet from box-
   office revenue and, denied any public financial support in England, the D'Oyly Carte
   was forced to close. Oh, sorrow, sorrow!

35 *Oh, sorrow*: Gilbert originally wrote this line, and the subsequent lines 38 and 43, as
   'Oh, willow'. They appear in that form in early editions of the libretto, but not in any
   vocal scores.

44 *if patriotic sentiment is wanted*: This phrase was used by Decca Records as the title for a
   long-playing record and cassette, now sadly deleted, featuring all the patriotic songs
   from the Savoy Operas, sung by members of the D'Oyly Carte Opera Company.

56 *a-trip*: Clear of mud and ready to be hauled aboard.
   a-lee: Away from the wind. In other words, the helm has been placed to bring the
   rudder to leeward and to swing the ship's bow into the wind ready to make sail.

NANK.   Come gather round me, and I'll tell you.

SONG and CHORUS – NANKI-POO.

A wandering minstrel I –   25
  A thing of shreds and patches,
  Of ballads, songs and snatches,
And dreamy lullaby!

My catalogue is long,
  Through every passion ranging,   30
  And to your humours changing
I tune my supple song!

    Are you in sentimental mood?
      I'll sigh with you,
        Oh, sorrow,   35
    On maiden's coldness do you brood?
      I'll do so, too –
        Oh, sorrow, sorrow!
    I'll charm your willing ears
    With songs of lovers' fears,   40
    While sympathetic tears
      My cheeks bedew –
        Oh, sorrow, sorrow!

But if patriotic sentiment is wanted,
  I've patriotic ballads cut and dried;   45
For where'er our country's banner may be planted,
  All other local banners are defied!
Our warriors, in serried ranks assembled,
  Never quail – or they conceal it if they do –
And I shouldn't be surprised if nations trembled   50
  Before the mighty troops of Titipu!

CHORUS. We shouldn't be surprised, etc.

NANK.   And if you call for a song of the sea,
  We'll heave the capstan round,
With a yeo heave ho, for the wind is free,   55
Her anchor's a-trip and her helm's a-lee,
  Hurrah for the homeward bound!

CHORUS.   Yeo-ho – heave-ho –
Hurrah for the homeward bound!

60 *lay aloft*: Climb into the rigging to raise or lower sails.

70 *rumbelow*: A meaningless combination of syllables or words, like 'yeo heave ho', used as a refrain by sailors when rowing or performing some other routine and rhythmical task. In some editions of the libretto the phrase is altered to 'a rum below'.

73 *Enter Pish-Tush*: Gilbert had first invented the names he was to give to two of his noble lords in *The Mikado* in his Bab Ballad 'King Borria Bungalee Boo', which first appeared in the magazine *Fun* in July 1886:

> There was haughty PISH-TUSH-POOH-BAH,
> There was lumbering DOODLE-DUM-DEH. . .

For the opera, of course, the name was split and Pish-Tush and Pooh-Bah are separate characters.

78 *Ko-Ko*: Apart from the Emperor himself, Ko-Ko is the only one of the characters in *The Mikado* to have a real Japanese name. According to a Japanese-speaking friend of mine, the word Ko-Ko has no fewer than thirty-seven different meanings, depending on how it is pronounced. As pronounced in *The Mikado* (i.e. with the vowels long so that it sounds like 'cocoa'), it can mean pickles, filial piety, succeeding clause, grammar school, navigation, mineshaft or pithead, estuary, prince and marquess, month, trussed girder, bright, or so-and-so. Perhaps the first and last terms are most appropriate for the cheap tailor turned Lord High Executioner.

86–133 *Our great Mikado, virtuous man*

This song, with its mockery of the Mikado of Japan and the practices of his country, was no doubt one which the British Government felt would cause offence to Crown Prince Fushimi and which led to the ban on all performances of *The Mikado* around the time of his state visit in 1907 (see page 258). Although most people felt that the ban was ridiculous, a small minority agreed that the opera was offensive to the Japanese. Mr Joseph Longford, who had been British consul in Japan for thirty-three years, wrote to *The Times* calling for a permanent ban on the grounds that 'the production of *The Mikado* was from the first an insult to the most sacred sentiments of the Japanese, galling and humiliating in every way'.

To lay aloft in a howling breeze   60
   May tickle a landsman's taste,
But the happiest hour a sailor sees
   Is when he's down
   At an inland town,
With his Nancy on his knees, yeo-ho!   65
And his arm around her waist!

CHORUS.   Then man the capstan – off we go,
                As the fiddler swings us round,
                With a yeo heave ho,
                And a rumbelow,   70
                  Hurrah for the homeward bound!

        A wandering minstrel I, etc.

        (*Enter* PISH-TUSH.)

PISH. And what may be your business with Yum-Yum?

NANK. I'll tell you. A year ago I was a member of the Titipu town   75
band. It was my duty to take the cap round for contributions. While
discharging this delicate office, I saw Yum-Yum. We loved each other at
once, but she was betrothed to her guardian Ko-Ko, a cheap tailor, and I saw
that my suit was hopeless. Overwhelmed with despair, I quitted the town.
Judge of my delight when I heard, a month ago, that Ko-Ko had been   80
condemned to death for flirting! I hurried back at once, in the hope of finding
Yum-Yum at liberty to listen to my protestations.

PISH. It is true that Ko-Ko was condemned to death for flirting, but he
was reprieved at the last moment, and raised to the exalted rank of Lord
High Executioner under the following remarkable circumstances: 85

    SONG – PISH-TUSH *and* CHORUS.

    Our great Mikado, virtuous man,
    When he to rule our land began,
        Resolved to try
        A plan whereby
        Young men might best be steadied.   90
    So he decreed, in words succinct,
    That all who flirted, leered or winked
    (Unless connubially linked),
        Should forthwith be beheaded.

Lord de Saumarez, a former secretary to the British legation in Tokyo, argued in similar terms, maintaining that 'the very name given to this play is most offensive to the feelings of every Japanese, whatever disclaimer any individual Japanese, actuated by the national somewhat exaggerated politeness, may verbally make when assailed by an interested interviewer'. He went on to point out that in Japan the Mikado was invested with a religious character, and he asked what the feelings of Roman Catholics would be if a comic opera entitled 'The Pope of Rome' was put on the stage, 'and the sacred office of the Pope were made the subject of burlesque'.

108 *non-connubial*: Not directed to a married partner, out of wedlock (from the Latin word *connubium*, meaning 'marriage').

124 *decapited*: The word is, of course, 'decapitated' but Gilbert shortened it for the purposes of scansion.

And I expect you'll all agree 95
That he was right to so decree.
 And I am right,
 And you are right,
And all is right as right can be!

CHORUS.   And you are right, 100
      And we are right, etc.

This stern decree, you'll understand,
Caused great dismay throughout the land!
 For young and old
 And shy and bold 105
Were equally affected.
The youth who winked a roving eye,
Or breathed a non-connubial sigh,
Was thereupon condemned to die –
 He usually objected. 110

And you'll allow, as I expect,
That he was right to so object.
 And I am right,
 And you are right,
And everything is quite correct! 115

CHORUS.   And you are right,
      And we are right, etc.

And so we straight let out on bail
A convict from the county jail,
 Whose head was next 120
 On some pretext
Condemnëd to be mown off,
And made *him* Headsman, for we said,
'Who's next to be decapited
Cannot cut off another's head 125
 Until he's cut his own off.'

And we are right, I think you'll say,
To argue in this kind of way;
 And I am right,
 And you are right, 130
And all is right – too-looral-lay!

135 *Enter Pooh-Bah*: In an article written at the time of the 1907 ban, G. K. Chesterton described Pooh-Bah as 'the great creation' of *The Mikado*. He went on to argue that this character above all others showed that the play was a satire on the English rather than the Japanese. Pluralism, he wrote, was not specially a vice of the East, yet

> about England Pooh-Bah is something more than a satire; he is the truth. It is true of British politics (probably not of Japanese) that we meet the same man twenty times as twenty different officials. There is a quarrel between a landlord, Lord Jones, and a railway company presided over by Lord Smith. Strong comments are made on the case by a newspaper (owned by Lord Brown), and after infinite litigation, it is sent up to the House of Lords, that is, Lords Jones, Smith, and Brown. Generally the characters are more mixed. The landlord cannot live by land, but does live as director of the railway. The railway lord is so rich that he buys up the newspaper. The general result can be expressed only in the two syllables (to be uttered with the utmost energy of the lungs): Pooh-Bah.

145 *of pre-Adamite ancestral descent*: As well as making Pooh-Bah the archetypal pluralist and corrupt official, Gilbert also uses him to poke some fun at the controversy over the theory of evolution which raged so passionately in the latter half of the nineteenth century following the publication of Charles Darwin's *Origin of Species*. Accepting Darwin's theory that man did not appear fully formed on earth, as the Bible says, but rather derived originally from 'a protoplasmal primordial atomic globule', Gilbert turns it with characteristic wit and skill into a source of great pride to Pooh-Bah, neatly reversing the anti-evolutionists' cry that such a descent greatly demeaned the dignity of man.

153–6 *as First Lord of the Treasury. . .*: It has been suggested that Gilbert got the idea for Pooh-Bah from the Victorian humorist and dramatist James Robinson Planché, whose play *The Sleeping Beauty* (1840) included the following lines for the Lord Factotum:

> As Lord High Chamberlain, I slumber never;
> As Lord High Steward, in a stew I'm ever;
> As Lord High Constable, I watch all day;
> As Lord High Treasurer, I've the deuce to pay;
> As Great Grand Cup-bearer, I'm handled queerly,
> As Great Grand Carver, I'm cut up severely.
> In other states, the honours are divided,
> But here, they're one and all to me confided.

161 *I dance at cheap suburban parties*: Rutland Barrington, who created the role of Pooh-Bah, was an arch ad-libber and introduced into his performance numerous gags which Gilbert had not originally intended. After delivering this line, for example, he gave a brief display of a dancing Pooh-Bah. A pencilled note in Helen D'Oyly Carte's copy of the libretto records: 'This was not objected to by the author'.

165 *Another insult, and, I think, a light one*: Another of Barrington's gags came at this point. He turned to Pish-Tush and asked 'Do you want it?' This one, however, was not approved by Gilbert.

CHORUS.   And you are right,
                     And we are right, etc.

                                    (*Exeunt* CHORUS.)

                       (*Enter* POOH-BAH.)   135

NANK. Ko-Ko, the cheap tailor, Lord High Executioner of Titipu! Why, that's the highest rank a citizen can attain!

POOH. It is. Our logical Mikado, seeing no moral difference between the dignified judge who condemns a criminal to die, and the industrious mechanic who carries out the sentence, has rolled the two offices into one,   140 and every judge is now his own executioner.

NANK. But how good of you (for I see that you are a nobleman of the highest rank) to condescend to tell all this to me, a mere strolling minstrel!

POOH. Don't mention it. I am, in point of fact, a particularly haughty and exclusive person, of pre-Adamite ancestral descent. You will understand 145 this when I tell you that I can trace my ancestry back to a protoplasmal primordial atomic globule. Consequently, my family pride is something inconceivable. I can't help it. I was born sneering. But I struggle hard to overcome this defect. I mortify my pride continually. When all the great officers of State resigned in a body, because they were too proud to serve 150 under an ex-tailor, did I not unhesitatingly accept all their posts at once?

PISH. And the salaries attached to them? You did.

POOH. It is consequently my degrading duty to serve this upstart as First Lord of the Treasury, Lord Chief Justice, Commander-in-Chief, Lord High Admiral, Master of the Buckhounds, Groom of the Back Stairs, 155 Archbishop of Titipu, and Lord Mayor, both acting and elect, all rolled into one. And at a salary! A Pooh-Bah paid for his services! I a salaried minion! But I do it! It revolts me, but I do it!

NANK. And it does you credit.

POOH. But I don't stop at that. I go and dine with middle-class people 160 on reasonable terms. I dance at cheap suburban parties for a moderate fee. I accept refreshment at any hands, however lowly. I also retail State secrets at a very low figure. For instance, any further information about Yum-Yum would come under the head of a State secret. (NANKI-POO *takes the hint, and gives him money.*) (*Aside.*) Another insult, and, I think, a light one! 165

SONG – POOH-BAH *with* NANKI-POO *and* PISH-TUSH.

               Young man, despair,
                  Likewise go to,
              Yum-Yum the fair
                 You must not woo.
                 It will not do: 170

172 *ablutioner*: Presumably one who performs the act of ablution, or washing. There is, in fact, no such word as 'ablutioner' in the dictionary, but what else – apart, of course, from 'diminutioner' – rhymes with 'executioner'?

185 *With the Lord High Executioner!*: Gilbert originally added another two lines to Poo-Bah's verse here:

> From what I say you may infer
> It's as good as a play for him and her.

They occur in the original libretto, but were apparently never used or set by Sullivan.

207 *The fact appears to be as you've recited*: This was the cue for another unauthorized gag introduced by Rutland Barrington. After 'you've recited' he added the line 'Good morning!', and at the end of the next line he turned to Nanki-Poo and asked 'Got any more money?', to which the reply from the wandering minstrel was 'No! Certainly not!'

I'm sorry for you,
You very imperfect ablutioner!
This very day
From school Yum-Yum
Will wend her way,   175
And homeward come,
With beat of drum
And a rum-tum-tum,
To wed the Lord High Executioner!
And the brass will crash,   180
And the trumpets bray,
And they'll cut a dash
On their wedding day.
She'll toddle away, as all aver,
With the Lord High Executioner!   185

NANK. *and* PISH.   And the brass will crash, etc.
ALL.   She'll toddle away, etc.

It's a hopeless case,
As you may see,
And in your place   190
Away I'd flee;
But don't blame me –
I'm sorry to be
Of your pleasure a diminutioner.
They'll vow their pact   195
Extremely soon,
In point of fact
This afternoon.
Her honeymoon
With that buffoon   200
At seven commences, so *you* shun her!

NANK. *and* PISH.   And the brass will crash, etc.
ALL.   She'll toddle away, etc.   (*Exit* PISH-TUSH.)

RECITATIVE – NANKI-POO *and* POOH-BAH.

NANK.   And I have journeyed for a month, or nearly,
         To learn that Yum-Yum, whom I love so dearly,   205
         This day to Ko-Ko is to be united!
POOH.   The fact appears to be as you've recited:
         But here he comes, equipped as suits his station;
         He'll give you any further information.

212–17 *Behold the Lord High Executioner*
This chorus recalls the tune of the old English air 'A Fine Old English Gentleman'.

218 *Enter Ko-Ko attended*: When George Grossmith made his entrance as Ko-Ko on the opening night of *The Mikado* at the Savoy Theatre on 14 March 1885, he carried the Japanese executioner's sword which, at least according to popular legend, had fallen from the wall of Gilbert's study and inspired the writing of the opera. In subsequent productions, Ko-Ko was attended by a sword-bearer. It was in that role that Sir Malcolm Sargent, the great British conductor, made his stage debut at the age of thirteen in a production of the Stamford Amateur Operatic Society in 1908. Sargent went on to have a life-long association with Gilbert and Sullivan, conducting the D'Oyly Carte Opera Company first in 1926 and last in 1964, three years before his death.

221 *bail*: Security given by or on behalf of an accused person, who would otherwise be kept in prison, that he or she will appear for trial at a particular place and time in return for being allowed free in the interim.

222 *recognizances*: Bond by which a person engages before a court or magistrate to observe some condition, such as paying a debt or keeping the peace.

234–8 *Gentlemen, I'm much touched by this reception*: In the first-night performance, Ko-Ko's 'little list' song came later in Act I (see the note to line 551). Ko-Ko's speech at this point did not contain the sentence beginning 'If I should ever be called upon' but instead went on to announce the imminent arrival of Yum-Yum, Pitti-Sing and Peep-Bo and then continued with the words addressed to Pooh-Bah about the festivities in connection with the approaching marriage which now appear at line 276.

239–74 *As some day it may happen that a victim must be found*
Ko-Ko's 'little list' song has almost certainly been altered more than any other number in the Savoy Operas. Gilbert originally wrote it to be sung much later in Act I, after the trio 'To sit in solemn silence', and it appears there in the licence copy sent to the Lord Chamberlain. For the opening performance it was moved slightly forward so that it came after Yum-Yum and Nanki-Poo's duet 'Were you not to Ko-Ko plighted'. However, after only a few performances it was moved again to its present position, with the words being considerably altered.

Apart from these changes, Gilbert also made several alterations to the song during his lifetime, substituting various topical allusions for the phrase 'lady novelist' and adding a whole new verse in 1908. The practice of introducing up-to-date references has continued ever since, and in 1948 the D'Oyly Carte Opera Company felt obliged to make a change to the wording of the second verse for reasons of taste (see the note to line 251).

As originally written, when it was conceived that Ko-Ko would sing the song after receiving word from the Mikado that he must carry out an execution within a month, the first verse began:

> As it seems to be essential that a victim must be found,
>   I've got a little list – I've got a little list
> Of social offenders who might well be underground,
>   And who never would be missed – who never would be missed!

That version was sung by George Grossmith on the opening night but was changed soon after to the present opening when the song was moved.

(*Exeunt* POOH-BAH *and* NANKI-POO.) 210

(*Enter* CHORUS OF NOBLES.)

Behold the Lord High Executioner!
A personage of noble rank and title –
A dignified and potent officer,
   Whose functions are particularly vital! 215
   Defer, defer,
To the Lord High Executioner!

(*Enter* KO-KO *attended.*)

SOLO – KO-KO.

Taken from the county jail
   By a set of curious chances; 220
Liberated then on bail,
   On my own recognizances;
Wafted by a favouring gale
   As one sometimes is in trances,
To a height that few can scale, 225
   Save by long and weary dances;
Surely, never had a male
   Under such-like circumstances
So adventurous a tale,
   Which may rank with most romances. 230

CHORUS.   Taken from the county jail, etc.
        Defer, defer,
     To the Lord High Executioner, etc.

  KO. Gentlemen, I'm much touched by this reception. I can only trust
that by strict attention to duty I shall ensure a continuance of those favours 235
which it will ever be my study to deserve. If I should ever be called upon to
act professionally, I am happy to think that there will be no difficulty in
finding plenty of people whose loss will be a distinct gain to society at large.

SONG – KO-KO *with* CHORUS OF MEN.

As some day it may happen that a victim must be found,
   I've got a little list – I've got a little list 240
Of society offenders who might well be underground,
   And who never would be missed – who never would be missed!
There's the pestilential nuisances who write for autographs –

The licence copy contains an early version of the rest of the first verse which also appears in the full score published in Leipzig in 1898:

> There's the Income Tax Commissioners with all their prying clerks,
> And vulgar little streetboys who are rude in their remarks,
> All persons with presentiments, a very wholesome rule,
> And next-door neighbours everywhere, and boys at home from school,
> All men who bite their nails, all people who revoke at whist.

251 *the banjo serenader*: Until 1948 the phrase always sung at this point was 'the nigger serenader'. The word 'nigger' also occurred in the Mikado's song 'My object all sublime' (see the note to Act II, line 358). In a letter to *The Times* on 28 May of that year Rupert D'Oyly Carte wrote:

> We found recently in America that much objection was taken by coloured persons to a word used twice in *The Mikado*, a word which I will not quote but which your readers may easily guess. Many protests and letters were received, and we consulted the witty writer on whose shoulders the lyrical mantle of Gilbert may be said to have fallen. He made several suggestions, one of which we adopted in America, and it seems well to continue doing so in the British Empire. Gilbert would surely have approved, and the alteration will be heard during our season at Sadler's Wells.

The witty writer mentioned by Carte was the late A. P. Herbert and it was he who came up with the substitute 'banjo serenader', which has been used ever since and now appears in all libretti and vocal scores.

252 *the piano-organist*: Piano organs were similar to barrel organs, played in the streets often by men accompanied by monkeys.

258 *doesn't think she dances*: This was originally written as 'doesn't think she waltzes'. As far as I can discover, it was changed to 'dances' in 1923, presumably on the grounds that even ladies from the provinces were no longer waltzing. The current Macmillan edition of the libretto still has 'waltzes', but both the Chappell libretto and the 1963 Oxford University Press edition of the operas prepared by Dame Bridget D'Oyly Carte have 'dances'.

259 *the lady novelist*: Even within Gilbert's lifetime there ceased to be anything either singular or anomalous about the lady novelist (if indeed there ever had been), and for Edwardian revivals he variously substituted 'the critic dramatist', 'the scorching bicyclist' and 'the scorching motorist'. Throughout the 1920s and the early 1930s Sir Henry Lytton sang of 'that singular anomaly, the prohibitionist', while in 1942 it became 'the clothing rationist'. In the 1950s Peter Pratt sang of 'The televisionist', and in 1975, when Britain's future membership of the E.E.C. was being decided by referendum, John Reed referred to 'the referendumist'. On the opening day of the 1980 Olympic Games James Conroy-Ward sang of 'The Olympic boycott-ist'.

263 *Nisi Prius*: A Latin term literally meaning 'unless before' and formerly used in law for civil actions heard in local assize courts when they should technically have been heard in London. Such actions were entered for hearing at the Royal Courts of Justice 'unless heard before'. Assize judges were known as *'nisi prius'* judges, and it is to the humorous qualities of these individuals that Ko-Ko is presumably referring in the next line.

267 *apologetic statesmen*: For the 1908 revival Gilbert changed this to 'Little England statesmen', showing his own sympathies in the contemporary political debate between Imperialists and 'Little Englanders'.

Several well-known politicians have found themselves caricatured over the years during the singing of this last part of Ko-Ko's song. George Grossmith helped the first-night audience in their task of filling up the blanks by successively donning the large

All people who have flabby hands and irritating laughs –
All children who are up in dates, and floor you with 'em flat –   245
All persons who in shaking hands, shake hands with you like *that* –
And all third persons who on spoiling *tête-à-têtes* insist –
    They'd none of 'em be missed – they'd none of 'em be missed!

CHORUS. He's got 'em on the list – he's got 'em on the list;
        And they'll none of 'em be missed – they'll none of 'em
        be missed.   250

There's the banjo serenader, and the others of his race,
    And the piano-organist – I've got him on the list!
And the people who eat peppermint and puff it in your face,
    They never would be missed – they never would be missed!
Then the idiot who praises, with enthusiastic tone,   255
All centuries but this, and every country but his own;
And the lady from the provinces, who dresses like a guy,
And who 'doesn't think she dances, but would rather like to try';
And that singular anomaly, the lady novelist –
    I don't think she'd be missed – I'm *sure* she'd not be missed!   260

CHORUS. He's got her on the list – he's got her on the list;
        And I don't think she'll be missed – I'm *sure* she'll not
        be missed!

And that *Nisi Prius* nuisance, who just now is rather rife,
    The Judicial humorist – I've got *him* on the list!
All funny fellows, comic men, and clowns of private life –   265
    They'd none of 'em be missed – they'd none of 'em be missed.
And apologetic statesmen of a compromising kind,
Such as – What d'ye call him – Thing'em-bob, and likewise – Never-mind,
And 'St – 'st – 'st – and What's-his-name, and also You-know-who –
The task of filling up the blanks I'd rather leave to *you*.   270
But it really doesn't matter whom you put upon the list,
    For they'd none of 'em be missed – they'd none of 'em be missed!

CHORUS. You may put 'em on the list – you may put 'em on the list;
        And they'll none of 'em be missed – they'll none of 'em
        be missed!   (*Exeunt* CHORUS.)

(*Enter* POOH-BAH.)   275

KO. Pooh-Bah, it seems that the festivities in connection with my
approaching marriage must last a week. I should like to do it handsomely,
and I want to consult you as to the amount I ought to spend upon them.

collars always worn by Mr Gladstone, beards similar to those worn by Lord Salisbury and the Marquess of Hartington, and the monocle and floral button-hole that were the trade-mark of Joseph Chamberlain. Subsequent Ko-Kos have imitated the golf stroke of David Lloyd George, the pipe-lighting of Stanley Baldwin, and the distinctive shoulder-hunching laugh of Edward Heath.

In 1908 Gilbert wrote an extra verse of the 'little list' to be used as an encore:

> That well-intentioned lady who's too bulky for her boots,
> The lovely suffragist – I've got her on the list.
> That single-minded patriot, who doesn't bank with Coutts,
> The red hot Socialist – I don't think he'd be missed.
> All those who hold that publicans it's virtuous to fleece,
> And impose a heavy war tax in these piping times of peace,
> And preach the code that moralists like Robin Hood held true,
> That to benefit the pauper you must rob the well-to-do,
> That peculiar variety of sham philanthropist,
> I don't think he'd be missed, I'm sure he'd not be missed.

A year later Gilbert produced yet more verses for a special children's version of the opera:

> There's the nursemaid who each evening in curlpapers does your hair,
> With an aggravating twist – *she* never would be missed –
> And tells you that you mustn't cough or sneeze or yawn or stare,
> She never would be missed – I'm sure she'd not be missed.
> All those who hold that children shouldn't have too much to eat,
> And think cold suet pudding a delicious birthday treat,
> Who say that little girls to bed at seven should be sent,
> And consider pocket-money isn't given to be spent,
> And doctors who on giving you unpleasant draughts insist –
> They never would be missed – they'd none of them be missed.
>
> Then the teacher who for hours keeps you practising your scales,
> With an ever-aching wrist – she never would be missed.
> And children, too, who out of school are fond of telling tales,
> They never would be missed – I'm sure they'd not be missed.
> All people who maintain (in solemn earnest – not in joke)
> That quantities of sugar-plums are bad for little folk,
> And those who hold the principle, unalterably fixed,
> That instruction with amusement should most carefully be mixed;
> All these (and many others) I have placed upon the list,
> For they never would be missed – never, never would be missed.

312 *they wouldn't be sufficiently degraded*: Gilbert originally wrote this and the next line in the first person, but Rutland Barrington changed it to the third, and there it has remained ever since.

317 *No money – no grovel*: Another of Barrington's gags. Gilbert refused to authorize it, but it has nonetheless passed into general use and is to be found in both the current Chappell libretto and the 1963 Oxford University Press edition, although not in the modern Macmillan version. A handwritten note in Helen D'Oyly Carte's copy of the 1908 libretto suggests that the gag was originally much longer and went as follows (after Ko-Ko's 'would be esteemed a favour'):

POOH. Certainly. In which of my capacities? As First Lord of the Treasury, Lord Chamberlain, Attorney-General, Chancellor of the Exchequer, Privy 280
Purse, or Private Secretary?

KO. Suppose we say as Private Secretary.

POOH. Speaking as your Private Secretary, I should say that, as the city will have to pay for it, don't stint yourself, do it well.

KO. Exactly – as the city will have to pay for it. That is your advice. 285

POOH. As Private Secretary. Of course you will understand that, as Chancellor of the Exchequer, I am bound to see that due economy is observed.

KO. Oh! But you said just now 'Don't stint yourself, do it well'.

POOH. As Private Secretary. 290

KO. And now you say that due economy must be observed.

POOH. As Chancellor of the Exchequer.

KO. I see. Come over here, where the Chancellor can't hear us. (*They cross the stage.*) Now, as my Solicitor, how do you advise me to deal with this difficulty? 295

POOH. Oh, as your Solicitor, I should have no hesitation in saying 'Chance it —'

KO. Thank you. (*Shaking his hand.*) I will.

POOH. If it were not that, as Lord Chief Justice, I am bound to see that the law isn't violated. 300

KO. I see. Come over here where the Chief Justice can't hear us. (*They cross the stage.*) Now, then, as First Lord of the Treasury?

POOH. Of course, as First Lord of the Treasury, I could propose a special vote that would cover all expenses, if it were not that, as Leader of the Opposition, it would be my duty to resist it, tooth and nail. Or, as 305
Paymaster-General, I could so cook the accounts that, as Lord High Auditor, I should never discover the fraud. But then, as Archbishop of Titipu, it would be my duty to denounce my dishonesty and give myself into my own custody as First Commissioner of Police.

KO. That's extremely awkward. 310

POOH. I don't say that all these distinguished people couldn't be squared; but it is right to tell you that they wouldn't be sufficiently degraded in their own estimation unless they were insulted with a very considerable bribe.

KO. The matter shall have my careful consideration. But my bride and her sisters approach, and any little compliment on your part, such as an abject 315
grovel in a characteristic Japanese attitude, would be esteemed a favour.

POOH. No money – no grovel!

(*Exeunt together.*)

(*Enter procession of* YUM-YUM's *schoolfellows, heralding* YUM-YUM, PEEP-
BO, *and* PITTI-SING.) 320

POOH. Grovels is an extra.

KO. Throw in a grovel, Pooh-Bah.

POOH. No money, no grovel.

KO. You will be grossly insulted as usual.

321–36 *Comes a train of little ladies*
For the opening performance at the Savoy, the female chorus was splendidly attired in Japanese silk kimonos made specially by Liberty's, the Regent Street fashion house. There was a certain amount of consternation when it was discovered that Japanese women did not wear petticoats. In the interests of modesty, and of warmth, the D'Oyly Carte ladies wore special 'combinations' of chamois leather and thin silk.

Gilbert had taken great pains to school both the male and female chorus in the niceties of Japanese etiquette. The girls came on with short, shuffling steps and fluttered their fans with a precision that would have delighted a regimental sergeant-major. The magazine *Moonshine* commented in its review of the first night: 'Society will discover a new source of entertainment after witnessing the fan operations. There will be "fan drill" at boarding schools. Present fans! unfurl fans! flutter fans! recover fans!'

333 *eighteen and under*: In an interesting article in the January 1978 issue of *The Savoyard*, Stephen J. Baston pointed out that in the autograph vocal score this phrase appeared as 'sixteen and under' and suggested that this was Gilbert's original intention. Certainly, that would seem to square with Nanki-Poo's later comment (lines 469–70) that in Japan 'from seventeen to forty-nine are considered years of indiscretion', which seems to suggest that the school-leaving age and the age of Yum-Yum are both sixteen.

337–60 *Three little maids from school are we*
This has always been a show-stopper. Rutland Barrington noted after the first night that it 'was received with such enthusiasm and insistent encores as no musical number in my experience, or I believe anyone else's, has ever equalled.' The song has recently achieved wide exposure in the award-winning British film *Chariots of Fire* about the 1924 Olympic gold medallist Harold Abrahams. In the film, Abrahams marries Sybil Gordon, principal soprano with the D'Oyly Carte Opera Company in the 1920s, whom he first sees when she is playing the part of Yum-Yum at the Savoy Theatre. The film has a scene in which Alice Krige, playing the part of Sybil Gordon, sings 'Three little maids' with Lorraine Daniels and Roberta Morrell of the D'Oyly Carte Company. Unfortunately, *Chariots of Fire* is inaccurate on this point – it was not Sybil Gordon whom Abrahams married in real life but rather Sybil Evers, who was a minor soprano with the D'Oyly Carte from March 1930 to September 1931 and who never played Yum-Yum, except possibly as an understudy. Still, it makes a more romantic story the way the film tells it.

'Three little maids' was the first of the songs in *The Mikado* which Sullivan set to music. He composed it on 21 December 1884. The bassoon 'gurgle' which follows the line 'Freed from its genius tutelary' was added much later, possibly at a rehearsal in 1895.

To coach the three little maids in their movements, Gilbert hired a geisha girl from the Japanese village in Knightsbridge. She was responsible for getting Yum-Yum, Peep-Bo and Pitti-Sing to giggle in an appropriately Japanese way and to use their fans properly. The tutor became known as 'the sixpence girl' since her only two words of English were 'sixpence, please', the price of a cup of tea at the village.

346 *a ladies' seminary*: This phrase also occurs in *Iolanthe*, when the Lord Chancellor mistakes the Fairy Queen for the proprietor of a ladies' seminary.

347 *tutelary*: Having the status of protector or guardian.

CHORUS OF GIRLS.

Comes a train of little ladies
   From scholastic trammels free,
Each a little bit afraid is,
   Wondering what the world can be!

Is it but a world of trouble –   325
   Sadness set to song?
Is its beauty but a bubble
   Bound to break ere long?

Are its palaces and pleasures
   Fantasies that fade?   330
And the glory of its treasures
   Shadow of a shade?

Schoolgirls we, eighteen and under,
   From scholastic trammels free,
And we wonder – how we wonder! –   335
   What on earth the world can be!

TRIO.

YUM-YUM, PEEP-BO, *and* PITTI-SING, *with* CHORUS OF GIRLS.

THE THREE. Three little maids from school are we,
            Pert as a school-girl well can be
            Filled to the brim with girlish glee,
               Three little maids from school!   340
YUM-YUM. Everything is a source of fun. (*Chuckle.*)
PEEP-BO. Nobody's safe, for we care for none! (*Chuckle.*)
PITTI-SING. Life is a joke that's just begun! (*Chuckle.*)
THE THREE.   Three little maids from school!
ALL (*dancing*).   Three little maids who, all unwary,   345
            Come from a ladies' seminary,
            Freed from its genius tutelary –
THE THREE (*suddenly demure*). Three little maids from school!

YUM-YUM. One little maid is a bride, Yum-Yum –
PEEP-BO. Two little maids in attendance come –   350
PITTI-SING. Three little maids is the total sum.
THE THREE.   Three little maids from school!
YUM-YUM. From three little maids take one away.
PEEP-BO. Two little maids remain, and they –

363 *You're not going to kiss me before all these people*: In 1907 Gilbert agreed to an ad-lib which had been introduced at this point, once again probably at the instigation of Rutland Barrington. Ko-Ko replied to Yum-Yum 'Well, I'm certainly not going to kiss you after them'. This line was dropped again in 1914.

370 *Eh, Lord Chamberlain*: For the 1908 revival, this line was changed to 'Eh, Licenser of Plays?' and Pooh-Bah's reply became 'I have known it done. I have not blue-pencilled it yet'. These additions appear in Helen D'Oyly Carte's copy of the 1908 libretto, which was approved by Gilbert, but they were dropped again in 1914.

376–84 *Oh, I'm so glad. . .*: In the licence copy submitted by Gilbert to the Lord Chamberlain before the first performance, the speeches delivered simultaneously at this point are longer than in the final version:

> YUM. Oh, I'm so glad! I haven't seen you for ever so long, and you can't imagine how often I've thought of you, and it is nice to come upon you in this unexpected way, and I'm right at the top of the school, etc.
> PEEP. And how have you been and have you got an engagement? Yum-Yum's got one, but she don't like it at all, it's to old Ko-Ko, and she's going to be married to him, and I think she'd ever so much rather it was you, and I expect I shall be married soon. I've come home for good, etc.
> PITTI. Now tell us all the news, because you go about everywhere and we've been shut up in a stupid old school, learning ridiculous lessons that will never be the least use to us afterwards, but thank goodness, etc.

393 *On the Marine Parade*: Little can Gilbert have realized when he wrote this line how apt it was to be and how many bandstands on real marine parades and coastal promenades would be echoing to the strains of *The Mikado* for a century and more to come.

PITTI-SING. Won't have to wait very long, they say –   355
THE THREE.   Three little maids from school!
ALL (*dancing*).   Three little maids who, all unwary,
                    Come from a ladies' seminary,
                    Freed from its genius tutelary –
THE THREE (*suddenly demure*). Three little maids from school!   360

(*Enter* KO-KO *and* POOH-BAH.)

KO. At last, my bride that is to be! (*About to embrace her.*)
YUM. You're not going to kiss me before all these people?
KO. Well, that was the idea.
YUM. (*aside to* PEEP-BO). It seems odd, doesn't it?   365
PEEP. It's rather peculiar.
PITTI. Oh, I expect it's all right. Must have a beginning, you know.
YUM. Well, of course I know nothing about these things; but I've no
objection if it's usual.
KO. Oh, it's quite usual, I think. Eh, Lord Chamberlain? (*Appealing to* 370
POOH-BAH.)
POOH. I have known it done. (KO-KO *embraces her.*)
YUM. Thank goodness that's over! (*Sees* NANKI-POO, *and rushes to him.*)
Why, that's never you? (*The Three Girls rush to him and shake his hands, all*
speaking at once.)   375

    YUM. Oh, I'm so glad! I haven't seen you for ever so long, and I'm
right at the top of the school, and I've got three prizes, and I've come
home for good, and I'm not going back any more!

    PEEP. And have you got an engagement? – Yum-Yum's got one, but
she doesn't like it, and she'd ever so much rather it was you! I've come   380
home for good, and I'm not going back any more!

    PITTI. Now tell us all the news, because you go about everywhere,
and we've been at school, but, thank goodness, that's all over now, and
we've come home for good, and we're not going back any more!

(*These three speeches are spoken together in one breath.*)   385

KO. I beg your pardon. Will you present me?
YUM.   ⎰ Oh, this is the musician who used –
PEEP. ⎱ Oh, this is the gentleman who used –
PITTI. ⎱ Oh, it is only Nanki-Poo who used –
KO. One at a time, if you please.   390
YUM. Oh, if you please he's the gentleman who used to play so
beautifully on the – on the —
PITTI. On the Marine Parade.
YUM. Yes, I think that was the name of the instrument.

403 *That is a Tremendous Swell*: The *Oxford English Dictionary* defines 'swell' in its colloquial sense as 'a fashionably or stylishly dressed person; hence, a person of good social position, a highly distinguished person'. It is in that latter sense that Ko-Ko applies the term to Pooh-Bah, although he is probably rather cheekily thinking also of the more usual meaning of 'swell' as 'the condition of being swollen, distended, or increased in bulk'. Pooh-Bah is always played as a large gentleman, and even some of the more well-endowed bass-baritones in the D'Oyly Carte Company have had to be padded out with cushions to produce the desired effect. The word 'swell' also occurs in Gilbert and Sullivan's last joint work, *The Grand Duke*, when Ben Hashbaz, a costumier, says 'Oh, he's a swell – he's the Duke of Riviera!'

404 *Oh, it's alive*: This line was added, with Gilbert's approval, early on in the original run. Helen D'Oyly Carte's copy of the libretto has the stage note at this point: 'Pitti-Sing prods Pooh-Bah with fan, he flicks his fan'.

422 *he can't help it*: Another line added for the 1908 revival, as was a subsequent line, later cut, for the three little maids: 'Poor fellow', which followed 'he's under treatment for it'.

NANK. Sir, I have the misfortune to love your ward, Yum-Yum – oh, I   395
know I deserve your anger!

Ko. Anger! not a bit, my boy. Why, I love her myself. Charming little
girl, isn't she? Pretty eyes, nice hair. Taking little thing, altogether. Very glad
to hear my opinion backed by a competent authority. Thank you very much.
Good-bye. (*To* PISH-TUSH.) Take him away. (PISH-TUSH *removes him.*)   400

PITTI. (*who has been examining* POOH-BAH). I beg your pardon, but
what is this? Customer come to try on?

Ko. That is a Tremendous Swell.

PITTI. Oh, it's alive. (*She starts back in alarm.*)

POOH. Go away, little girls. Can't talk to little girls like you. Go away,   405
there's dears.

Ko. Allow me to present you, Pooh-Bah. These are my three wards.
The one in the middle is my bride elect.

POOH. What do you want me to do to them? Mind, I *will not* kiss them.

Ko. No, no, you shan't kiss them; a little bow – a mere nothing – you   410
needn't mean it, you know.

POOH. It goes against the grain. They are not young ladies, they are
young persons.

Ko. Come, come, make an effort, there's a good nobleman.

POOH. (*aside to* Ko-Ko). Well, I shan't mean it. (*With a great effort.*)   415
How de do, little girls, how de do? (*Aside.*) Oh, my protoplasmal ancestor!

Ko. That's very good. (*Girls indulge in suppressed laughter.*)

POOH. I see nothing to laugh at. It is very painful to me to have to say
'How de do, little girls, how de do?' to young persons. I'm not in the habit
of saying 'How de do, little girls, how de do?' to anybody under the rank of   420
a Stockbroker.

Ko. (*aside to girls*). Don't laugh at him, he can't help it – he's under
treatment for it. (*Aside to* POOH-BAH.) Never mind them, they don't
understand the delicacy of your position.

POOH. We know how delicate it is, don't we?   425

Ko. I should think we did! How a nobleman of your importance can do
it at all is a thing I never can, never shall understand.

(Ko-Ko *retires up and goes off.*)

QUARTET AND CHORUS OF GIRLS.

YUM-YUM, PEEP-BO, PITTI-SING, *and* POOH-BAH.

YUM., PEEP.   So please you, sir, we much regret
and PITTI.   If we have failed in etiquette   430
          Towards a man of rank so high –
          We shall know better by and by.

439 *If we're inclined to dance and sing*: In the licence copy and the early vocal scores this line ran 'If we're designed to dance and sing' and in early editions of the libretto 'If we're disposed to dance and sing'. Here's a pretty mess!

455 *Exeunt all but Yum-Yum*: In the first-night performance, Yum-Yum sang 'The sun, whose rays' at this point, having first had the following soliloquy:

> YUM. How pitiable is the condition of a young and innocent child brought from the gloom of a ladies' academy into the full-blown blaze of her own marriage ceremony; and with a man for whom I care nothing! True, he loves me, but everybody does that. Sometimes I sit and wonder, etc.

Her speech continued as now in Act II, lines 26–30. 'The sun, whose rays', which then followed, was moved to its present position in Act II only a few days into the first London run.

463 *Modified rapture*: In the original libretto this line was simply 'Rapture!' At an early rehearsal Gilbert had to check Durward Lely, the tenor playing the part of Nanki-Poo, for the vehemence with which he spoke the word. 'Modified rapture', Gilbert called from his seat in the stalls. 'Modified rapture', retorted the actor from the stage, and so it has remained ever since.

471 *plays a wind instrument*: Like the reference to the piano-organist in Ko-Ko's 'little list' song (see the note to line 252), Sullivan might well have felt this line was a little too close to home. His own father had started his working life playing the clarinet in the orchestra at the Surrey Theatre, London, for a guinea a week. He later rose to become a professor at the Army's School of Music at Kneller Hall.

YUM.   But youth, of course, must have its fling,
                  So pardon us,
                  So pardon us,   435
PITTI.   And don't, in girlhood's happy spring,
                  Be hard on us,
                  Be hard on us,
                  If we're inclined to dance and sing.
                  Tra la la, etc. (*Dancing.*)   440
CHORUS OF GIRLS. But youth, of course, etc.

POOH.   I think you ought to recollect
                  You cannot show too much respect
                  Towards the highly titled few;
                  But nobody does, and why should you?   445
                  That youth at us should have its fling,
                  Is hard on us,
                  Is hard on us;
                  To our prerogative we cling –
                  So pardon us,   450
                  So pardon us,
                  If we decline to dance and sing.
                  Tra la la, etc. (*Dancing.*)
CHORUS OF GIRLS. But youth, of course, must have its fling, etc.
                              (*Exeunt all but* YUM-YUM.)   455
                  (*Enter* NANKI-POO.)

NANK. Yum-Yum, at last we are alone! I have sought you night and
day for three weeks, in the belief that your guardian was beheaded, and I
find that you are about to be married to him this afternoon!
YUM. Alas, yes!   460
NANK. But you do not love him?
YUM. Alas, no!
NANK. Modified rapture! But why do you not refuse him?
YUM. What good would that do? He's my guardian, and he wouldn't
let me marry you!   465
NANK. But I would wait until you were of age!
YUM. You forget that in Japan girls do not arrive at years of discretion
until they are fifty.
NANK. True; from seventeen to forty-nine are considered years of
indiscretion.   470
YUM. Besides – a wandering minstrel, who plays a wind instrument
outside tea-houses, is hardly a fitting husband for the ward of a Lord High
Executioner.
NANK. But — (*Aside.*) Shall I tell her? Yes! She will not betray me!
(*Aloud.*) What if it should prove that, after all, I am no musician?   475

485 *Lucius Junius Brutus*: The first consul of Rome, who in 509 B.C. sentenced his own
sons to death for their part in a conspiracy to restore the Tarquins.
487 *a Second Trombone*: It has been suggested that Gilbert was poking a little gentle fun at
his collaborator here. Most theatre orchestras had only one trombone, and Sullivan
was always grumbling about the effects of this restriction on his composing. He finally
won a second trombone from Richard D'Oyly Carte for *The Yeomen of the Guard*.
493 *To flirt is capital*: Neither this line nor the next one appeared in the original libretto,
which simply had Yum-Yum saying: 'To flirt is illegal and we must obey the law'.
However, the form of words now used was obviously introduced at an early stage. A
note in 1907 by Helen D'Oyly Carte against the modern version records: 'This has
always been said'. Gilbert agreed to the change.

515–36 *Were you not to Ko-Ko plighted*
The licence copy, the autograph score and the first-night performance of *The Mikado* all
had a different version of this song to the one now sung:

YUM.
Were I not to Ko-Ko plighted
I would say in tender tone,
'Loved one, let us be united –
Let us be each other's own!'
I would say 'Oh gentle stranger,
Press me closely to thy heart,
Sharing ev'ry joy and danger,
We will never, never part!'

BOTH.
We will never, never part!

YUM.
But as I'm to marry Ko-Ko,
To express my love *'con fuoco'*
Would distinctly be no *gioco*,
And for yam I should get toco!

BOTH.
Toco, toco, toco, toco!

YUM.
So I will not say 'Oh stranger,
Press me closely to thy heart,
Sharing ev'ry joy and danger,
We will never, never part!'
Clearly understand, I pray,
This is what I never say –
This – oh, this – oh, this – oh, this –
This is what I'll never say.

NANKI.
Were you not to Ko-Ko plighted
I should thrill at words like those,
Joy of joys is love requited,
Love despised is woe of woes.
I would merge all rank and station,
Worldly sneers are nought to us,
And, to mark my admiration,
I would kiss you fondly thus –

Yum. There! I was certain of it, directly I heard you play!

Nank. What if it should prove that I am no other than the son of his Majesty the Mikado?

Yum. The son of the Mikado! But why is your Highness disguised? And what has your Highness done? And will your Highness promise never to do it again? 480

Nank. Some years ago I had the misfortune to captivate Katisha, an elderly lady of my father's Court. She misconstrued my customary affability into expressions of affection, and claimed me in marriage, under my father's law. My father, the Lucius Junius Brutus of his race, ordered me to marry her within a week, or perish ignominiously on the scaffold. That night I fled his Court, and, assuming the disguise of a Second Trombone, I joined the band in which you found me when I had the happiness of seeing you! (*Approaching her.*) 485

Yum. (*retreating*). If you please, I think your Highness had better not come too near. The laws against flirting are excessively severe. 490

Nank. But we are quite alone, and nobody can see us.

Yum. Still, that doesn't make it right. To flirt is capital.

Nank. It *is* capital!

Yum. And we must obey the law. 495

Nank. Deuce take the law!

Yum. I wish it would, but it won't!

Nank. If it were not for that, how happy we might be!

Yum. Happy indeed!

Nank. If it were not for the law, we should now be sitting side by side, like that. (*Sits by her.*) 500

Yum. Instead of being obliged to sit half a mile off, like that. (*Crosses and sits at other side of stage.*)

Nank. We should be gazing into each other's eyes, like that. (*Gazing at her sentimentally.*) 505

Yum. Breathing sighs of unutterable love – like that. (*Sighing and gazing lovingly at him.*)

Nank. With our arms round each other's waists, like that. (*Embracing her.*)

Yum. Yes, if it wasn't for the law.

Nank. If it wasn't for the law. 510

Yum. As it is, of course we couldn't do anything of the kind.

Nank. Not for worlds!

Yum. Being engaged to Ko-Ko, you know!

Nank. Being engaged to Ko-Ko!

DUET – Yum-Yum *and* Nanki-Poo.

Nank.   Were you not to Ko-Ko plighted, 515
        I would say in tender tone,

The duet then continued as it does now. The original, longer version was reduced to the present shorter one in the second edition of the libretto.

525 *con fuoco*: An Italian term meaning 'passionately' (literally, 'with fire').

526 *giuoco*: Another Italian word, meaning 'joke' or 'jest'. In many editions of the libretto and vocal score it is spelt *gioco*.

527 *And for yam I should get toko*: The yam is a sweet potato, found mostly in tropical countries. Toko (also spelt 'toco') was a Victorian schoolboys' expression, derived from Hindu, for punishment, in the form either of a beating or of a diet of bread and water. The sense of this line, therefore, appears to be 'Instead of something sweet, I would get something nasty'. In one edition of the libretto – that published by Macmillan in 1926 – I have found the line printed 'And for jam I should get toko'. Although this makes it more intelligible to the average Englishman, I fear it is a misprint.

537 *Exeunt in opposite directions*: In the licence copy, Yum-Yum and Nanki-Poo's duet is followed immediately by the entrance of the nobles and Pish-Tush:

CHORUS OF NOBLES.

Fire and thunder,
For a wonder,
We have made a serious blunder!
Chopped asunder,
Statute under,
Short'ly,
Mort'lly,
We shall be.

KO-KO (*entering*).

Will you kindly be explicit
As to this informal visit,
What the dooce (or dickens) is it?
Rude t'you –
Who do you
Wish to see?

PISH. (*reading document*).

Here's a note from our Mikado,
Which in spite of all bravado,
Comes on us like a tornado,
Rushingly,
Crushingly,
So say we!

CHORUS.

Fire and thunder, etc.

Pooh-Bah then delivers the lines now given to Ko-Ko about the Mikado being struck by the fact that no executions have taken place (lines 547–50), and the dialogue continues as now.

543 *an apostrophe*: An exclamatory address, in the course of a public speech or a poem, to a particular person or object. There is a good example in *The Sorcerer*, where both Sir Marmaduke Pointdextre and Lady Sangazure sing 'I find some satisfaction/In apostrophe like this' before enthusiastically addressing their respective loves.

551 *irretrievable ruin*: In the very earliest productions of *The Mikado* Ko-Ko's 'little list' song followed at this point, cued in by this speech:

KO. Yes – somebody will have to suffer. Send the Recorder to me. (*Exit* PISH-TUSH.) I expected something of this sort! I knew it couldn't go on! Well, they've brought it on themselves, and the only question is, who shall it be? Fortunately, there will be no difficulty in pitching upon somebody whose death will be a distinct gain to society.

'Loved one, let us be united –
  Let us be each other's own!'
I would merge all rank and station,
  Worldly sneers are nought to us,   520
And, to mark my admiration,
  I would kiss you fondly thus – (*Kisses her.*)

BOTH. ${I \atop He}$ would kiss ${you \atop me}$ fondly thus – (*Kiss.*)

YUM.   But as I'm engaged to Ko-Ko,
  To embrace you thus, *con fuoco*,   525
Would distinctly be no *giuoco*,
  And for yam I should get toko –

BOTH.   Toko, toko, toko, toko!

NANK.   So, in spite of all temptation,
  Such a theme I'll not discuss,   530
And on no consideration
  Will I kiss you fondly thus – (*Kissing her.*)
Let me make it clear to you,
This is what I'll never do!
  This, oh, this, oh, this, oh, this – (*Kissing her.*)   535

TOGETHER.   This, oh, this, etc.

                     (*Exeunt in opposite directions.*)

(*Enter* KO-KO.)

KO. (*looking after* YUM-YUM). There she goes! To think how entirely
my future happiness is wrapped up in that little parcel! Really, it hardly   540
seems worth while! Oh, matrimony! – (*Enter* POOH-BAH *and* PISH-
TUSH.) Now then, what is it? Can't you see I'm soliloquizing? You have
interrupted an apostrophe, sir!

PISH. I am the bearer of a letter from his Majesty the Mikado.

KO. (*taking it from him reverentially*). A letter from the Mikado! What in   545
the world can he have to say to me? (*Reads letter.*) Ah, here it is at last! I
thought it would come sooner or later! The Mikado is struck by the fact that
no executions have taken place in Titipu for a year, and decrees that unless
somebody is beheaded within one month the post of Lord High Executioner
shall be abolished, and the city reduced to the rank of a village!   550

PISH. But that will involve us all in irretrievable ruin!

KO. Yes. There is no help for it, I shall have to execute somebody at
once. The only question is, who shall it be?

POOH. Well, it seems unkind to say so, but as you're already under
sentence of death for flirting, everything seems to point to *you*.   555

KO. To me? What are you talking about? I can't execute myself.

POOH. Why not?

The song then followed with its original opening ('As it seems to be essential that a victim must be found' – see the note to lines 239–74). The first edition of the libretto also includes the following additional refrain for Ko-Ko at the end of each verse:

> As a victim must be found,
> If you'll only look around,
> There are criminals at large
> (And enough to fill a barge),
> Whose swift decapitation
> Would be hailed with acclamation,
> If accomplished by the nation
> At a reasonable charge.

It is doubtful if this refrain was, in fact, ever sung. The 'little list' song was revised and moved to its present position earlier in the act only a few days after the opening night.

566–7 *that would be something*: This was the cue for another gag introduced in early productions. Ko-Ko responded to Pish-Tush's remark by saying 'Really! You don't say so! how awfully jolly!' Gilbert, however, vetoed this addition, and it was cut in the 1908 revival.

579 *Lord High Substitute*: Gilbert originally wrote this simply as 'my substitute'.

582–608 *My brain it teems/I am so proud/I heard one day*
On 9 December 1884 Gilbert wrote to Sullivan 'I send a trio for Ko-Ko, Pooh-Bah, and Pish-Tush. I think it ought to be quaint and effective. I have put the three verses side by side for convenience' sake, but, of course, they will be sung separately. I fancy the metre admits of each verse being set differently from the others, but I may be wrong in this.'
Sullivan did indeed set the three verses to different tunes which match the different moods of the characters singing them. Ko-Ko's 'My brain it teems' is distracted and confused, Pooh-Bah's 'I am so proud' is haughty and pompous, and Pish-Tush's 'I heard one day' is bright and carefree. Set against each other, as they are in the reprise, the verses have a striking effect comparable to that achieved in the quartet 'In a contemplative fashion' in *The Gondoliers*.

Ko. Why not? Because, in the first place, self-decapitation is an extremely difficult, not to say dangerous, thing to attempt; and, in the second, it's suicide, and suicide is a capital offence. 560

Pooh. That is so, no doubt.

Pish. We might reserve that point.

Pooh. True, it could be argued six months hence, before the full Court.

Ko. Besides, I don't see how a man *can* cut off his own head.

Pooh. A man might try. 565

Pish. Even if you only succeeded in cutting it half off, that would be something.

Pooh. It would be taken as an earnest of your desire to comply with the Imperial will.

Ko. No. Pardon me, but there I am adamant. As official Headsman, my 570
reputation is at stake, and I can't consent to embark on a professional operation unless I see my way to a successful result.

Pooh. This professional conscientiousness is highly creditable to *you*, but it places us in a very awkward position.

Ko. My good sir, the awkwardness of your position is grace itself 575
compared with that of a man engaged in the act of cutting off his own head.

Pish. I am afraid that, unless you can obtain a substitute —

Ko. A substitute? Oh, certainly – nothing easier. (*To* Pooh-Bah.) Pooh-Bah, I appoint you Lord High Substitute.

Pooh. I should be delighted. Such an appointment would realize my fond- 580
est dreams. But no, at any sacrifice, I must set bounds to my insatiable ambition!

TRIO.

Ko-Ko.	Pooh-Bah.	Pish-Tush.	
My brain it teems	I am so proud,	I heard one day	
With endless schemes	If I allowed	A gentleman say	
Both good and new	My family pride	That criminals who	
For Titipu;	To be my guide,	Are cut in two	585
But if I flit,	I'd volunteer	Can hardly feel	
The benefit	To quit this sphere	The fatal steel,	
That I'd diffuse	Instead of you,	And so are slain	
The town would lose!	In a minute or two.	Without much pain.	
Now every man	But family pride	If this is true,	590
To aid his clan	Must be denied,	It's jolly for you;	
Should plot and plan	And set aside,	Your courage screw.	
As best he can,	And mortified.	To bid us adieu,	
And so,	And so,	And go	
Although	Although	And show	595
I'm ready to go,	I wish to go,	Both friend and foe	
Yet recollect	And greatly pine	How much you dare.	
'Twere disrespect	To brightly shine,	I'm quite aware	
Did I neglect	And take the line	It's your affair,	
To thus effect	Of a hero fine,	Yet I declare	600
This aim direct,	With grief condign	I'd take your share,	
So I object –	I must decline –	But I don't much care –	
So I object –	I must decline –	I don't much care –	
So I object –	I must decline –	I don't much care –	

605–8 *To sit in solemn silence in a dull, dark dock*
This is the only substantial piece of alliteration to occur in a song in the Savoy Operas, although there are several alliterative passages of dialogue. Perhaps the best occurs early in Act II of *The Yeomen of the Guard*, when Jack Point, the strolling player, addresses Wilfred Shadbolt, head jailer of the Tower of London: 'Ha! friend jailer! Jailer that wast – jailer that never shalt be more! Jailer that jailed not, or that jailed, if jail he did, so unjailerly that 'twas by jerry-jailing, or jailing in joke – though no joke to him who, by unjailerlike jailing, did so jeopardize his jailership.'
Gilbert anticipated the distinctive rhythm of this song in an Indian trio which he wrote for *Princess Toto*, an early work with music by Fred Clay:

> With feathers, paint and patches and a tom, tom, tom,
> That with our colour matches, with a tom, tom, tom.

609 *Exeunt Pooh. and Pish.*: Gilbert's very first intention was to have Ko-Ko sing his 'little list' song at this point in the opera. The licence copy has the following speech for Ko-Ko as a prelude to the original version of the song:

> Ko. This is exceedingly hard on me. It was distinctly stated, when I was asked to accept the post of Lord High Executioner, that the duties were purely nominal. And here I am, called upon to behead the very person of all others for whom I entertain the most affectionate regard, unless I can find a substitute within half an hour! If someone *must* be beheaded, why not choose somebody whose death would be a distinct gain to society? There are plenty of them about!

The 'little list' song then follows in its original version.
620 *to marry the girl I adore*: In early performances the dialogue continued as follows:

> Ko. And do you suppose that I am likely to stand quietly by while you deliberately take your life?
> NANK. Please yourself. You can withdraw if you prefer it.
> Ko. Withdraw if I prefer it! Are you aware, sir, that I am Lord High Executioner of this city, and that in that capacity, it is my duty to prevent unnecessary bloodshed?
> NANK. I know nothing about your capacity. I only know that I die to-day.
> Ko. Nonsense, sir, etc.

The dialogue continues as now from line 621.
625 *the Happy Despatch*: Japanese military and government officials who were in disgrace or whose honour had been seriously impugned traditionally committed suicide by disembowelling themselves. This practice was known as the Happy Despatch or, in Japanese, as *hara-kiri* (literally, 'cutting the belly'). It ceased to be obligatory in 1868.
629 *Substitute*: Although this word was said from very early on in performances, it was not actually in the original libretto. Gilbert authorized its inclusion at the time of the 1908 revival.

645 *bands*: When playing Ko-Ko, Sir Henry Lytton would at this point hold his nose and hum 'The Campbells are Coming', striking his throat with his other hand to produce the effect of bagpipes.

ALL.   To sit in solemn silence in a dull, dark dock,   605
        In a pestilential prison, with a life-long lock,
        Awaiting the sensation of a short, sharp shock,
        From a cheap and chippy chopper on a big black block!
                                    (*Exeunt* POOH: *and* PISH.)

KO. This is simply appalling! I, who allowed myself to be respited at   610
the last moment, simply in order to benefit my native town, am now
required to die within a month, and that by a man whom I have loaded
with honours! Is this public gratitude? Is this — (*Enter* NANKI-POO, *with
a rope in his hands.*) Go away, sir! How dare you? Am I never to be permitted to soliloquize?   615
    NANK. Oh, go on – don't mind me.
    KO. What are you going to do with that rope?
    NANK. I am about to terminate an unendurable existence.
    KO. Terminate your existence? Oh, nonsense! What for?
    NANK. Because you are going to marry the girl I adore.   620
    KO. Nonsense, sir. I won't permit it. I am a humane man, and if you
attempt anything of the kind I shall order your instant arrest. Come, sir,
desist at once, or I summon my guard.
    NANK. That's absurd. If you attempt to raise an alarm, I instantly
perform the Happy Despatch with this dagger.   625
    KO. No, no, don't do that. This is horrible! (*Suddenly.*) Why, you cold-
blooded scoundrel, are you aware that, in taking your life, you are
committing a crime which – which – which is — Oh! (*Struck by an idea.*)
Substitute!
    NANK. What's the matter?   630
    KO. Is it *absolutely certain* that you are resolved to die?
    NANK. Absolutely!
    KO. Will *nothing* shake your resolution?
    NANK. Nothing.
    KO. Threats, entreaties, prayers – all useless?   635
    NANK. All! My mind is made up.
    KO. Then, if you really mean what you say, and if you are absolutely
resolved to die, and if nothing whatever will shake your determination –
don't spoil yourself by committing suicide, but be beheaded handsomely at
the hands of the Public Executioner!   640
    NANK. I don't see how that would benefit me.
    KO. You don't? Observe: you'll have a month to live, and you'll live
like a fighting-cock at my expense. When the day comes there'll be a grand
public ceremonial – you'll be the central figure – no one will attempt
to deprive you of that distinction. There'll be a procession – bands – dead 645
march – bells tolling – all the girls in tears – Yum-Yum distracted – then,
when it's all over, general rejoicings, and a display of fireworks in the

658 *Life without Yum-Yum*: It sounds like an advertising slogan and, indeed, was used as such by one enterprising American entrepreneur in the 1880s. E. M. Statler, running a not very successful restaurant in Buffalo, New York State, decided that he could improve his business by cashing in on the *Mikado* craze then sweeping the States. So he advertised and served 'Yum-Yum' ice-cream shaped in the form of a Japanese lady with a paper parasol. As an added incentive to his customers, he put five-dollar pieces in some of the figures. Sales boomed, his business took off and with the profits he founded the well-known Statler hotel chain.

Characters from *The Mikado* were, in fact, used extensively in advertisements in the United States. Ko-Ko and Katisha appeared together on posters extolling the virtues of J. & P. Coats' thread, the three little maids from school advertised spool silk, dental cream, soap, cotton thread, Waterbury matches and corsets, while the Mikado himself promoted Lautz Brothers' 'Pure and Healthy Soap' and even had a kerosene stove named after him.

evening. *You* won't see them, but they'll be there all the same.

NANK. Do you think Yum-Yum would really be distracted at my death?

KO. I am convinced of it. Bless you, she's the most tender-hearted little   650
creature alive.

NANK. I should be sorry to cause her pain. Perhaps, after all, if I were
to withdraw from Japan, and travel in Europe for a couple of years, I might
contrive to forget her.

KO. Oh, I don't think you could forget Yum-Yum so easily; and, after   655
all, what is more miserable than a love-blighted life?

NANK. True.

KO. Life without Yum-Yum – why, it seems absurd!

NANK. And yet there are a good many people in the world who have
to endure it.   660

KO. Poor devils, yes! You are quite right not to be of their number.

NANK. (*suddenly*). I *won't* be of their number!

KO. Noble fellow!

NANK. I'll tell you how we'll manage it. Let me marry Yum-Yum to-
morrow, and in a month you may behead me.   665

KO. No, no. I draw the line at Yum-Yum.

NANK. Very good. If you can draw the line, so can I. (*Preparing rope.*)

KO. Stop, stop – listen one moment – be reasonable. How can I consent
to your marrying Yum-Yum if I'm going to marry her myself?

NANK. My good friend, she'll be a widow in a month, and you can   670
marry her then.

KO. That's true, of course. I quite see that. But, dear me! my position
during the next month will be most unpleasant – most unpleasant.

NANK. Not half so unpleasant as my position at the end of it.

KO. But – dear me! – well – I agree – after all, it's only putting off my   675
wedding for a month. But you won't prejudice her against me, will you? You
see, I've educated her to be my wife; she's been taught to regard me as a wise
and good man. Now I shouldn't like her views on that point disturbed.

NANK. Trust me, she shall never learn the truth from me.

FINALE.

(*Enter* CHORUS, POOH-BAH, *and* PISH-TUSH.)   680

CHORUS.

With aspect stern
  And gloomy stride,
We come to learn
  How you decide.

705 *Take her – she's yours*: This line was the occasion for another ad-lib gag in early
productions. Taking his cue from Ko-Ko's 'Take her', Pitti-Sing came forward to grab
Nanki-Poo. Ko-Ko rebuffed her with the words 'Not you silly'. This phrase was
written into the 1914 D'Oyly Carte master copy of the libretto but then scratched out.
As far as I can establish, it has never appeared in any printed edition of the libretto,
although it was included in comparatively recent D'Oyly Carte productions.

707–22 *The threatened cloud has passed away*
In the original libretto the first ten lines of this song (everything from 'The threatened
cloud' to 'our brief career') were first given to Yum-Yum and Nanki-Poo, singing
together, with the chorus repeating everything from 'Then let the throng'. The lines
from 'A day, a week, a month, a year' to 'You'll live at least a honeymoon!' (lines
717–20) were given to Pitti-Sing as a solo, with all singing the refrain beginning 'Then
let the throng'. This seems to have been a piece of carelessness in the drafting of the
libretto and the musical lines written by Sullivan suggest that the ensemble was never
performed in this way.

          Don't hesitate   685
             Your choice to name,
          A dreadful fate
             You'll suffer all the same.

POOH. To ask you what you mean to do we punctually appear.
KO.   Congratulate me, gentlemen, I've found a Volunteer!   690
ALL.   The Japanese equivalent for Hear, Hear, Hear!
KO. (*presenting him*).   'Tis Nanki-Poo!
ALL.   Hail, Nanki-Poo!
KO.   I think he'll do?
ALL.   Yes, yes, he'll do!   695

KO.   He yields his life if I'll Yum-Yum surrender.
             Now I adore that girl with passion tender,
             And could not yield her with a ready will,
                Or her allot,
                If I did not   700
             Adore myself with passion tenderer still!

      (*Enter* YUM-YUM, PEEP-BO, *and* PITTI-SING.)

ALL.   Ah, yes!
             He loves himself with passion tenderer still!
KO. (*to* NANKI-POO). Take her – she's yours!   705
                                   (*Exit* KO-KO.)

                 ENSEMBLE.

NANKI-POO. The threatened cloud has passed away,
YUM-YUM.   And brightly shines the dawning day;
NANKI-POO. What though the night may come too soon,
YUM-YUM.   There's yet a month of afternoon!   710

NANKI-POO, POOH-BAH, PISH-TUSH, YUM-YUM, PITTI-SING, *and*
                  PEEP-BO.

          Then let the throng
            Our joy advance,
          With laughing song
          And merry dance,

CHORUS.   With joyous shout and ringing cheer,   715
             Inaugurate our brief career!
PITTI-SING. A day, a week, a month, a year —

723 *As in a month you've got to die*: Gilbert originally wrote 'As in three weeks you've got to die' but authorized the change to 'a month' at the time of the 1908 revival, presumably to tie in with the specific time-scale mentioned in Nanki-Poo's discussions with Ko-Ko in lines 642–79. Line 727 was also altered at the same time, but Pooh-Bah's toast was left, slightly incongruously, as 'three times three'.

730 *Long life to you*: This line is delivered by Pooh-Bah in the form of a very long and very impressive cadenza. Rutland Barrington was in the habit of breaking the cadenza up with the following gags:

> (*During cadenza* PITTI-SING, NANKI-POO *and* PISH-TUSH *laugh.*)
>
> POOH. I am addressing myself to you sir.
> NANK. I beg your pardon.
> POOH. I should think you did. (*Resumes cadenza.*)
> NANK. Thank you very much.
> POOH. I've not nearly finished. (POOH *finishes cadenza.*)

Gilbert approved this bit of business and it was included in the 1908 revival. However, it was cut again in 1914.

737 *Enter Katisha*: When Rosina Brandram entered as Katisha on the first night she was wearing a Japanese costume which was reputed to be 200 years old. Gilbert had also bought some antique Japanese armour for the male chorus, but it was found to be far too small and too heavy for any of the men to wear.

738–45 *Your revels cease! Assist me, all of you*
In the licence copy, Katisha is given the following lines after her entrance:

> Your revels cease – assist me, all of you,
> I come to claim my lover Nanki-Poo.
> I've sought him everywhere for nearly a year,
> And now I find him masquerading here.

Nanki-Poo then comes in with his line 'Ah!/'Tis Katisha' etc.

YUM.	Or far or near, or far or near,
POOH.	Life's eventime comes much too soon,
PITTI-SING.	You'll live at least a honeymoon!
ALL.	Then let the throng, etc.
CHORUS.	With joyous shout, etc.

720

SOLO – POOH-BAH.

As in a month you've got to die,
   If Ko-Ko tells us true,
'Twere empty compliment to cry
   'Long life to Nanki-Poo!'
But as one month you have to live
   As fellow-citizen,
This toast with three times three we'll give –
   'Long life to you – till then!'

725

730

(*Exit* POOH-BAH.)

CHORUS.   May all good fortune prosper you,
    May you have health and riches too,
    May you succeed in all you do!
       Long life to you – till then!

735

(*Dance.*)

(*Enter* KATISHA *melodramatically.*)

KAT.	Your revels cease! Assist me, all of you!
CHORUS.	Why, who is this whose evil eyes
	Rain blight on our festivities?
KAT.	I claim my perjured lover, Nanki-Poo!
	Oh, fool! to shun delights that never cloy!
CHORUS.	Go, leave thy deadly work undone!
KAT.	Come back, oh, shallow fool! come back to joy!
CHORUS.	Away, away! ill-favoured one!

740

745

NANK. (*aside to* YUM-YUM).   Ah!
       'Tis Katisha!
       The maid of whom I told you.   (*About to go.*)
KAT. (*detaining him*).   No!
       You shall not go,
       These arms shall thus enfold you!

750

759 *dole*: Not, in this case, unemployment benefit, but the original meaning of the word, which is a share or portion.

769 *Heroic nerves*: This line was originally written as 'Steel-tempered nerves', but was apparently changed to 'heroic nerves' before the opening night, probably because of the difficulty of singing the original.

771 *Lore-laden years*: Years filled with teaching and instruction.

772 *smooth tongue*: This appears in early vocal scores as 'sweet tongue'.

776 *knell*: The sound made by a bell when rung slowly and solemnly, as at a funeral, and therefore a sound announcing death. In *Princess Ida* King Hildebrand sings of King Gama:

> We'll shut him up in a dungeon cell,
> And toll his knell on a funeral bell.

SONG – KATISHA.

KAT. (*addressing* NANKI-POO).

Oh fool, that fleest
My hallowed joys!
Oh blind, that seest
No equipoise!   755
Oh rash, that judgest
From half, the whole!
Oh base, that grudgest
Love's lightest dole!
Thy heart unbind,   760
Oh fool, oh blind!
Give me my place,
Oh rash, oh base!

CHORUS.   If she's thy bride, restore her place,
        Oh fool, oh blind, oh rash, oh base!   765

KAT. (*addressing* YUM-YUM).

Pink cheek, that rulest
Where wisdom serves!
Bright eye, that foolest
Heroic nerves!
Rose lip, that scornest   770
Lore-laden years!
Smooth tongue, that warnest
Who rightly hears!
Thy doom is nigh,
Pink cheek, bright eye!   775
Thy knell is rung,
Rose lip, smooth tongue!

CHORUS.   If true her tale, thy knell is rung,
       Pink cheek, bright eye, rose lip, smooth tongue!

PITTI-SING.   Away, nor prosecute your quest –   780
       From our intention, well expressed,
          You cannot turn us!
       The state of your connubial views
       Towards the person you accuse
          Does not concern us!   785
       For he's going to marry Yum-Yum –
ALL.   Yum-Yum!

799 *There's lots of good fish in the sea*: This line is based on the old English saying 'There's as good fish in the sea as ever came out of it', meaning don't be disheartened if you have lost the chance of something good, because you'll soon get another. In the finale of Act I of *Patience*, the dragoons sing:

> There's fish in the sea, no doubt of it,
> As good as ever came out of it.

820 *O ni! bikkuri shakkuri to*: All sorts of translations have been offered for this line. Leslie Ayre in *The Gilbert and Sullivan Companion* (1972) agrees with the Oxford University Press edition of *The Savoy Operas* (1963) that it means 'O! he was frightened to death!' The glossary in D'Oyly Carte programmes for *The Mikado* gives 'O, no such thing, what a surprise and shock', while Harry Benford in his *Gilbert and Sullivan Lexicon* suggests: 'Oh! You she devil! We are so shocked by you it makes us hiccup. Bah!' The Japanese expert whom I have consulted says that a literal translation of the line would be 'surprise, with a hiccup', which seems a suitably Gilbertian phrase.

In early productions the line was first given to Nanki-Poo and Yum-Yum, with the chorus coming in for the repeats from line 823 onwards. In one early revival, instead of singing the Japanese words, Nanki-Poo drowned Katisha by producing his trombone and blowing fierce blasts into her face.

PITTI.	Your anger pray bury,	
	For all will be merry,	
	I think you had better succumb –	790
ALL.	Cumb – cumb!	
PITTI.	And join our expressions of glee.	
	On this subject I pray you be dumb –	
ALL.	Dumb – dumb.	
PITTI.	You'll find there are many	795
	Who'll wed for a penny –	
	The word for your guidance is 'Mum' –	
ALL.	Mum – mum!	
PITTI.	There's lots of good fish in the sea!	
ALL.	On this subject we pray you be dumb, etc.	800

SOLO – KATISHA.

The hour of gladness
  Is dead and gone;
In silent sadness
  I live alone!
The hope I cherished   805
  All lifeless lies,
And all has perished
  Save love, which never dies!
Oh, faithless one, this insult you shall rue!
In vain for mercy on your knees you'll sue.   810
I'll tear the mask from your disguising!

NANK. (*aside*).	Now comes the blow!	
KAT.	Prepare yourselves for news surprising!	
NANK. (*aside*).	How foil my foe?	
KAT.	No minstrel he, despite bravado!	815
YUM. (*aside, struck by an idea*).	Ha! ha! I know!	
KAT.	He is the son of your —	

(NANKI-POO, YUM-YUM, *and* CHORUS, *interrupting,*
  sing Japanese words, to drown her voice.)

	O ni! bikkuri shakkuri to!	820
KAT.	In vain you interrupt with this tornado!	
	He is the only son of your —	
ALL.	O ni! bikkuri shakkuri to!	

826 *gambado*: A word of Spanish origin, normally used in the plural, meaning a caper or sudden action.

843 *My wrongs with vengeance shall be crowned*: This line was originally written as 'And when he learns his son is found'. It was changed to its present form in the 1914 edition of the libretto, although the vocal score always had 'My wrongs with vengeance shall be crowned'.

KAT.	I'll spoil —	
ALL.	O ni! bikkuri shakkuri to!	825
KAT.	Your gay gambado!	
	He is the son —	
ALL.	O ni! bikkuri shakkuri to!	
KAT.	Of your —	
ALL.	O ni! bikkuri shakkuri to!	830
KAT.	The son of your —	
ALL.	O ni! bikkuri shakkuri to! oya! oya!	

ENSEMBLE.

KATISHA.		THE OTHERS.	
Ye torrents roar!		We'll hear no more,	
Ye tempests howl!		Ill-omened owl,	
Your wrath outpour	835	To joy we soar,	835
With angry growl!		Despite your scowl!	
Do ye your worst, my vengeance call		The echoes of our festival	
Shall rise triumphant over all!		Shall rise triumphant over all!	
Prepare for woe,	840	Away you go,	
Ye haughty lords,		Collect your hordes;	840
At once I go		Proclaim your woe	
Mikado-wards,		In dismal chords;	
My wrongs with vengeance shall be crowned!		We do not heed their dismal sound,	
My wrongs with vengeance shall be crowned!		For joy reigns everywhere around.	

(KATISHA *rushes furiously up stage, clearing the crowd away right and left,*   845
finishing on steps at the back of stage.)

END OF ACT I

10 *Emphasize the grace*: There was a feeling among some critics that, graceful as they undoubtedly were, the costumes worn by the girls' chorus in *The Mikado* did not sufficiently emphasize their femininity. Reginald Allen in his *First Night Gilbert and Sullivan* quotes one reviewer's complaint that 'they obliterate the natural distinction between the sexes, imparting to the prettiest girl's figure the seeming of a bolster loosely wrapped up in a dressing-gown'.

The *Daily News* reviewer, also quoted by Allen, was rather more enthusiastic:

> The Japanese gowns, with their delicate tints, their richly embroidered conceits and fantasies, and their ample sashes, lent not a little aid to the oddly pleasing effect. If the enthusiasm of the ladies among the audience may afford a token, sashes rising halfway from the waist to the shoulders and tied in huge double bows upon the backs of the wearers, may find a place ere long among the fashions of the day.

14 *Sit with downcast eye*: There was nothing very downcast, or modest, about the performance of the original Pitti-Sing, Miss Jessie Bond. Determining that she should be singled out from the other little maids, she persuaded the wardrobe mistress to give her an obi twice as big as the others, with an enormous bow at the back. 'I made the most of my big, big bow', she recalled in her memoirs, 'turning my back to the audience whenever I got the chance and waggling it. The gallery was delighted, but *I* nearly got the sack for that prank! However, I did get noticed, which was what I wanted.'

ACT II

SCENE. – KO-KO's *Garden*. YUM-YUM *discovered seated at her bridal toilet, surrounded by maidens, who are dressing her hair and painting her face and lips, as she judges of the effect in a mirror.*

SOLO – PITTI-SING *and* CHORUS OF GIRLS.

CHORUS.   Braid the raven hair –
                 Weave the supple tress –   5
                 Deck the maiden fair
                 In her loveliness –
                 Paint the pretty face –
                 Dye the coral lip – ·
                 Emphasize the grace   10
                 Of her ladyship!
                 Art and nature, thus allied,
                 Go to make a pretty bride.

SOLO – PITTI-SING.

Sit with downcast eye –
    Let it brim with dew –   15
Try if you can cry –
    We will do so, too.
When you're summoned, start
    Like a frightened roe –
Flutter, little heart,   20
    Colour, come and go!
Modesty at marriage-tide
Well becomes a pretty bride!

CHORUS.

Braid the raven hair, etc.

(*Exeunt* PITTI-SING, PEEP-BO, *and* CHORUS.)   25

31–62 *The sun, whose rays*
This song was originally designed to be sung in the First Act, following 'Three little maids from school' and the quartet 'So please you, sir, we much regret'. At a rehearsal the morning after the opening night, however, Miss Leonora Braham, who was playing Yum-Yum, told Sullivan that she had been too exhausted by the earlier two songs to do justice to her solo number. The composer agreed to move it to Act II to give her a breathing space.

A resemblance to the 'Song of the Bird' in Wagner's *Siegfried* has been detected by some critics. Whether he was influenced by Wagner or not, there is no doubt that Sullivan produced one of his loveliest tunes for this song and showed his supreme gift for melody. Dr Percy Buck, a former professor of music at London University, wrote in his book *The Scope of Music:*

> The writing of a learned eight-part fugue is within the power of any musician who cares to waste his time in learning how to do it; but if he tries to reset the words, 'The sun whose rays are all ablaze' and then compares his music to Sullivan's, he will have no doubts as to which is the more serious task.

In an early unauthorized version of *The Mikado* performed in Texas in 1888, the opening lines of this song became:

> The sun, whose rays
> Are all ablaze
>   With ever-living glory,
> Shines brightly forth
> On all Fort Worth,
>   And makes things hunki-dori!

Yum. Yes, I am indeed beautiful! Sometimes I sit and wonder, in my artless Japanese way, why it is that I am so much more attractive than anybody else in the whole world. Can this be vanity? No! Nature is lovely and rejoices in her loveliness. I am a child of Nature, and take after my mother.   30

SONG – YUM-YUM.

The sun, whose rays
Are all ablaze
  With ever-living glory,
Does not deny
His majesty –   35
  He scorns to tell a story!
He don't exclaim,
  'I blush for shame,
  So kindly be indulgent.'
But, fierce and bold,   40
In fiery gold
  He glories all effulgent!

I mean to rule the earth,
  As he the sky –
We really know our worth,   45
  The sun and I!

Observe his flame,
That placid dame,
  The moon's Celestial Highness;
There's not a trace   50
Upon her face
  Of diffidence or shyness:
She borrows light
That, through the night,
  Mankind may all acclaim her!   55
And, truth to tell,
She lights up well,
  So I, for one, don't blame her!

Ah, pray make no mistake,
  We are not shy;   60
We're very wide awake,
  The moon and I!

(*Enter* PITTI-SING *and* PEEP-BO.)

70–71 *It does seem to take the top off it, you know*: Another ad-lib gag not found in the original libretto but authorized by Gilbert in 1907.

79 *Go-To*: Go-To is not found in the list of *Dramatis personæ* in the original libretto and vocal score of *The Mikado*, nor, indeed, is the part included in the current Macmillan and Chappell editions of the libretto. It was, in fact, added during the opera's initial run at the Savoy Theatre. Frederick Bovill, who created the role of Pish-Tush, found that he was unable to reach the low bass notes of his part in the madrigal 'Brightly dawns our wedding day'. So Gilbert introduced the new character of Go-To simply to sing the bass line in the madrigal.

The D'Oyly Carte Opera Company generally thereafter kept Go-To as a separate character, giving him also the line in Act I 'Why, who are you who ask this question?' (line 23), which the libretto simply assigns to 'A Noble'. However, many amateur companies have dispensed with his services and allowed their Pish-Tushes to show their command of the lower reaches of the bass-baritone register in the madrigal.

93–4 *four hours and three-quarters*: For the 1908 revival, with Gilbert's approval, Pitti-Sing was given the extra line 'Silly little cuckoo' at this point. It was cut again in 1914.

Yum. Yes, everything seems to smile upon me. I am to be married to-day to the man I love best, and I believe I am the very happiest girl in Japan! 65
Peep. The happiest girl indeed, for she is indeed to be envied who has attained happiness in all but perfection.
Yum. In 'all but' perfection?
Peep. Well, dear, it can't be denied that the fact that your husband is to be beheaded in a month is, in its way, a drawback. It does seem to take the 70
top off it, you know.
Pitti. I don't know about that. It all depends!
Peep. At all events, *he* will find it a drawback!
Pitti. Not necessarily. Bless you, it all depends!
Yum. (*in tears*). I think it very indelicate of you to refer to such a subject 75
on such a day. If my married happiness *is* to be – to be —
Peep. Cut short.
Yum. Well, cut short – in a month, can't you let me forget it? (*Weeping.*)

(*Enter* Nanki-Poo, *followed by* Go-To.)

Nank. Yum-Yum in tears – and on her wedding morn! 80
Yum. (*sobbing*). They've been reminding me that in a month you're to be beheaded! (*Bursts into tears.*)
Pitti. Yes, we've been reminding her that you're to be beheaded. (*Bursts into tears.*)
Peep. It's quite true, you know, you *are* to be beheaded! (*Bursts into tears.*) 85
Nank. (*aside*). Humph! Now, some bridegrooms would be depressed by this sort of thing! (*Aloud.*) A month? Well, what's a month? Bah! These divisions of time are purely arbitrary. Who says twenty-four hours make a day?
Pitti. There's a popular impression to that effect.
Nank. Then we'll efface it. We'll call each second a minute – each 90
minute an hour – each hour a day – and each day a year. At that rate we've about thirty years of married happiness before us!
Peep. And, at that rate, this interview has already lasted four hours and three-quarters!

(*Exit* Peep-Bo.) 95

Yum. (*still sobbing*). Yes. How time flies when one is thoroughly enjoying oneself!
Nank. That's the way to look at it! Don't let's be downhearted! There's a silver lining to every cloud.
Yum. Certainly. Let's – let's be perfectly happy! (*Almost in tears.*) 100
Go. By all means. Let's – let's thoroughly enjoy ourselves.
Pitti. It's – it's absurd to cry! (*Trying to force a laugh.*)
Yum. Quite ridiculous! (*Trying to laugh.*)

(*All break into a forced and melancholy laugh.*)

105–28 *Brightly dawns our wedding day*
Nothing could be more thoroughly English than this charming madrigal. There is only one other song formally described as a madrigal in the Savoy Operas, 'When the buds are blossoming' from Act I of *Ruddigore*. However, both 'Strange adventure' in Act II of *The Yeomen of the Guard*, which is described as a quartet, and 'I hear the soft note of the echoing voice' in Act I of *Patience*, described as a sestet, conform to the dictionary definition of madrigal as a contrapuntal and largely unaccompanied part-song for several voices.

111 *tocsin*: A word of French origin meaning an alarm signal sounded by the ringing of a bell, and later extended to mean a bell used to sound an alarm.

132 *Go on – don't mind me*: In the licence copy there is a slightly different version of the ensuing dialogue between Ko-Ko, Nanki-Poo and Yum-Yum, as follows:

Ko. Well, I hope you are getting on pretty comfortably?
NANK. Oh yes! There's only one drawback to our happiness – the reflection that it can only be enjoyed at the expense of your peace of mind.
Ko. How good of you to think of that!
YUM. We can't help thinking how miserable we are making you. For instance, this sort of thing (*embracing* NANKI-POO), must be perfect torture to you.

MADRIGAL.

Yum-Yum, Pitti-Sing, Nanki-Poo, *and* Go-To.

Brightly dawns our wedding day;   105
  Joyous hour, we give thee greeting!
  Whither, whither art thou fleeting?
Fickle moment, prithee stay!
  What though mortal joys be hollow?
  Pleasures come, if sorrows follow: 110
Though the tocsin sound, ere long,
  Ding dong! Ding dong!
Yet until the shadows fall
Over one and over all,
Sing a merry madrigal –   115
Fal-la – fal-la! etc. (*Ending in tears.*)

Let us dry the ready tear,
  Though the hours are surely creeping
  Little need for woeful weeping,
Till the sad sundown is near.   120
  All must sip the cup of sorrow –
  I to-day and thou to-morrow;
This the close of every song –
  Ding dong! Ding dong!
What, though solemn shadows fall,   125
Sooner, later, over all?
Sing a merry madrigal –
Fal-la – fal-la! etc. (*Ending in tears.*)

(*Exeunt* Pitti-Sing *and* Go-To.)

(Nanki-Poo *embraces* Yum-Yum. *Enter* Ko-Ko. Nanki-Poo   130
releases Yum-Yum.)

Ko. Go on – don't mind me.

Nank. I'm afraid we're distressing you.

Ko. Never mind, I must get used to it. Only please do it by degrees.
Begin by putting your arm round her waist. (Nanki-Poo *does so.*) There; 135
let me get used to that first.

Yum. Oh, wouldn't you like to retire? It must pain you to see us so
affectionate together!

Ko. It's most unpleasant – *most* unpleasant.

Nank. I suppose we can't even sit like this without causing you serious inconvenience.

Ko. It's particularly disagreeable to me.

Nank. It must be! (*embracing* Yum-Yum) But come, look at its bright side. In a month she will be yours.

Yum. My darling! (*embracing* Nanki-Poo.)

Ko. Thank you, my boy, for the kind thought that prompted the suggestion; but it's no use deluding oneself with false hopes, etc.

The dialogue continues as now from line 145.

151 *I'm so glad*: This line, and Nanki-Poo's 'Like that' above (line 141) were added, with Gilbert's approval, in the libretto used for the 1908 revival.

177 *I call it a beast of a death*: This seems to have been another ad-lib which received official sanction from Gilbert. It first appears in the 1887 libretto as 'I call it a beastly death' and in its present form in 1914.

KO. No, I must learn to bear it! Now oblige me by allowing her head to rest on your shoulder. 140

NANK. Like that? (*He does so.* KO-KO *much affected.*)

KO. I am much obliged to you. Now – kiss her! (*He does so.* KO-KO *writhes with anguish.*) Thank you – it's simple torture!

YUM. Come, come, bear up. After all, it's only for a month.

KO. No. It's no use deluding oneself with false hopes. 145

NANK.⎱ What do you mean?
YUM. ⎰

KO. (*to* YUM-YUM). My child – my poor child! (*Aside.*) How shall I break it to her? (*Aloud.*) My little bride that was to have been —

YUM. (*delighted*). *Was* to have been?

KO. Yes, you never can be mine! 150

NANK.⎱ (*in ecstasy*). ⎰ What!
YUM. ⎰   ⎱ I'm so glad!

KO. I've just ascertained that, by the Mikado's law, when a married man is beheaded his wife is buried alive.

NANK.⎱ Buried alive! 155
YUM. ⎰

KO. Buried alive. It's a most unpleasant death.

NANK. But whom did you get that from?

KO. Oh, from Pooh-Bah. He's my Solicitor.

YUM. But he may be mistaken!

KO. So I thought; so I consulted the Attorney-General, the Lord Chief 160 Justice, the Master of the Rolls, the Judge Ordinary, and the Lord Chancellor. They're all of the same opinion. Never knew such unanimity on a point of law in my life!

NANK. But stop a bit! This law has never been put in force.

KO. Not yet. You see, flirting is the only crime punishable with 165 decapitation, and married men never flirt.

NANK. Of course they don't. I quite forgot that! Well, I suppose I may take it that my dream of happiness is at an end!

YUM. Darling – I don't want to appear selfish, and I love you with all my heart – I don't suppose I shall ever love anybody else half as much – but 170 when I agreed to marry you – my own – I had no idea – pet – that I should have to be buried alive in a month!

NANK. Nor I! It's the very first I've heard of it!

YUM. It – makes a difference, doesn't it?

NANK. It *does* make a difference, of course. 175

YUM. You see – burial alive – it's such a stuffy death!

NANK. I call it a beast of a death.

YUM. You see my difficulty, don't you?

NANK. Yes, and I see my own. If I insist on your carrying out your promise, I doom you to a hideous death; if I release you, you marry Ko-Ko at once! 180

181–206 *Here's a how-de-do*
One of the most encored numbers in *The Mikado*. In an article in the *Gilbert and Sullivan Journal* for January 1960, Colin Prestige calculated that Isidore Godfrey, musical director of the D'Oyly Carte Opera Company from 1929 to 1968, must have conducted it 13,000 times. Martyn Green, principal comedian with the company from 1934 to 1939 and from 1946 to 1951, used the first line of the song as the title for his memoirs, published in 1952.

The song has always offered plenty of opportunities for comic business on stage. At the final line, 'Here's a pretty how-de-do', Sir Henry Lytton snapped open a fan which promptly split in two. In encores he opened what was apparently the same fan, now miraculously intact. Martyn Green pulled out a different fan from his sleeve at every encore, each smaller than the previous one. It was also usual during encores for Ko-Ko to address a few words in 'Japanese' to a bewildered Yum-Yum.

TRIO – Yum-Yum, Nanki-Poo, *and* Ko-Ko.

Yum.

Here's a how-de-do!
If I marry you,
When your time has come to perish,
Then the maiden whom you cherish
   Must be slaughtered, too!   185
Here's a how-de-do!

Nank.

Here's a pretty mess!
In a month, or less,
I must die without a wedding!
Let the bitter tears I'm shedding   190
   Witness my distress,
Here's a pretty mess!

Ko.

Here's a state of things!
To her life she clings!
Matrimonial devotion   195
Doesn't seem to suit her notion –
   Burial it brings!
Here's a state of things!

ENSEMBLE.

Yum-Yum *and* Nanki-Poo.	Ko-Ko.	
With a passion that's intense	With a passion that's intense	
I worship and adore,	You worship and adore,	200
But the laws of common sense	But the laws of common sense	
We oughtn't to ignore.	You oughtn't to ignore.	
If what he says is true,	If what I say is true,	
'Tis death to marry you!	'Tis death to marry you!	
Here's a pretty state of things!	Here's a pretty state of things!	205
Here's a pretty how-de-do!	Here's a pretty how-de-do!	

                     (*Exit* Yum-Yum.)

Ko. (*going up to* Nanki-Poo). My poor boy, I'm really very sorry for you.

Nank. Thanks, old fellow. I'm sure you are.

Ko. You see I'm quite helpless.   210

Nank. I quite see that.

Ko. I can't conceive anything more distressing than to have one's marriage broken off at the last moment. But you shan't be disappointed of a wedding – you shall come to mine.

Nank. It's awfully kind of you, but that's impossible.   215

Ko. Why so?

Nank. To-day I die.

Ko. What do you mean?

228 *Now then, Lord Mayor, what is it*: When Pooh-Bah was played by the twenty-stone Fred Billington, who regularly took the role in D'Oyly Carte touring productions from the 1880s until his death in 1917, Ko-Ko changed this line to 'Now, feather-weight, what is it?' In a set of notes sent to Gilbert in 1907 about unauthorized changes to the libretto, Helen D'Oyly Carte commented: 'This seems to have been said recently only – in allusion to Mr Billington's size – it seems *undesirable*'. Gilbert agreed and the interpolation was forbidden.

229–30 *and will be here in ten minutes*: In another unauthorized ad-lib this line was altered to 'and they'll do it in eleven minutes'. In the set of notes referred to above, Helen D'Oyly Carte commented: 'I have had this omitted as soon as I heard of it', to which Gilbert added 'Quite right'.

232 *carried out*: At this point Pooh-Bah was wont to interject 'Yes, and you'll be carried out too, old chap'. Gilbert did not approve this gag, but it was nonetheless included in the libretto for the 1908 revival.

237 *What, now*: the cue for yet another ad-lib by Pooh-Bah: 'Cut it off, Ko-Ko, he don't want it'. Gilbert's comment on this one was 'Not authorised. Please omit'.

240 *I don't go about. . .*: This time an occasion for some ad-libbing by Ko-Ko, who changed this line to 'I don't go about prepared to execute orders while you wait'. According to Helen D'Oyly Carte, 'This appears to have crept in without authorisation – it is said to go well – but it is of course for Mr Gilbert's decision.' Mr Gilbert was adamant: 'Omit. It is a most impertinent alteration.'

242 *Still, as Lord High Executioner*: Nearly all of these unauthorized alterations to the libretto which were the subject of scrutiny by Gilbert and Mrs D'Oyly Carte in 1907 had originally been introduced by Rutland Barrington, who was to return to play the part of Pooh-Bah in the 1908 revival. This line he had altered to 'Still you know, Ko-Ko, as Lord High Bluebottle – I mean executioner'. This was one of the few Barrington gags which Gilbert did authorize, but, curiously, it does not appear in the copy of the libretto prepared by Helen D'Oyly Carte for the 1908 revival.

NANK. I can't live without Yum-Yum. This afternoon I perform the
Happy Despatch.   220
Ko. No, no – pardon me – I can't allow that.
NANK. Why not?
Ko. Why, hang it all, you're under contract to die by the hand of the
Public Executioner in a month's time! If you kill yourself, what's to become
of me? Why, I shall have to be executed in your place!   225
NANK. It would certainly seem so!

(*Enter* POOH-BAH.)

Ko. Now then, Lord Mayor, what is it?
POOH. The Mikado and his suite are approaching the city, and will be
here in ten minutes.   230
Ko. The Mikado! He's coming to see whether his orders have been
carried out! (*To* NANKI-POO.) Now look here, you know – this is getting
serious – a bargain's a bargain, and you really mustn't frustrate the ends of
justice by committing suicide. As a man of honour and a gentleman, you are
bound to die ignominiously by the hands of the Public Executioner.   235
NANK. Very well, then – behead me.
Ko. What, now?
NANK. Certainly; at once.
POOH. Chop it off! Chop it off!
Ko. My good sir, I don't go about prepared to execute gentlemen at a   240
moment's notice. Why, I never even killed a blue-bottle!
POOH. Still, as Lord High Executioner —
Ko. My good sir, as Lord High Executioner, I've got to behead him in a
month. I'm not ready yet. I don't know how it's done. I'm going to take
lessons. I mean to begin with a guinea pig, and work my way through the   245
animal kingdom till I come to a Second Trombone. Why, you don't suppose
that, as a humane man, I'd have accepted the post of Lord High Executioner
if I hadn't thought the duties were purely nominal? I *can't* kill you – I can't
kill anything! I can't kill anybody! (*Weeps.*)
NANK. Come, my poor fellow, we all have unpleasant duties to   250
discharge at times; after all, what is it? If I don't mind, why should you?
Remember, sooner or later it must be done.
Ko. (*springing up suddenly*). Must it? I'm not so sure about that!
NANK. What do you mean?
Ko. Why should I kill you when making an affidavit that you've been   255
executed will do just as well? Here are plenty of witnesses – the Lord Chief
Justice, Lord High Admiral, Commander-in-Chief, Secretary of State for the
Home Department, First Lord of the Treasury, and Chief Commissioner of
Police.
NANK. But where are they?   260
Ko. There they are. They'll all swear to it – won't you? (*To* POOH-BAH.)

271-2 *Commissionaire*: Helen D'Oyly Carte's marked copy of the 1908 libretto has 'District messenger' substituted at this point. 'Commissionaire' was restored in 1914. In 1975, at the last night of the D'Oyly Carte London season, always an occasion for high-jinks, Pooh-Bah made his entrance at line 274 wearing a Savoy Hotel commissionaire's cap. He had previously appeared, at line 227, with a lord mayor's top hat and chain of office, and at line 279 he changed to a bishop's mitre.

282-3 *Nanki-Poo will explain all*: The licence copy has the following extra lines for Ko-Ko at this point: 'I'll have a couple of horses ready for you at the back kitchen door, and, as soon as you're married, gallop away, and don't ever come back any more.'

292-6 *Miya sama, miya sama*
This is the one genuine Japanese song in *The Mikado*. Known as 'The Tokotonyare Song' after its chorus, it was composed by Masujiro Omura with words by Yajiro Shinagawa in the early years of the Meiji era, which began in 1868. It was a war song of the Japanese Imperial Army and was sung by the loyalist troops under Prince Arisugawa who put down a rebellion against the Mikado by the leaders of the old feudal order in 1877.

Translated, the first verse seems to mean: 'Your majesty, your majesty, what is it that flutters in front of the stallion?' The second verse of the song, which is not used here, answers this question: 'Do you not know that it is the imperial banner of silken brocade, signifying our intention to defeat the enemies of the Crown'.

There is some difficulty about translating the chorus '*Toko tonyaré tonyaré na*'. *Tokoton* is a slang word for 'the finish' in an idiom corresponding to 'a fight to the finish', but it also has obscene connotations. In his *The Gilbert and Sullivan Book* Leslie Baily writes:

> The legend has grown up that Sullivan did not know the meaning of these words and that it was only in later years that a Japanese told him it was 'the foulest song ever sung in the lowest tea-house in Japan'; it is a nice story, especially when one thinks of the innocent amateur societies who have chanted these 'foul words' so many thousands of times, but it isn't true.

I have myself been offered an obscene translation of this line, however, which I feel compelled to withhold from the eyes of my gentle readers.

Pooh. Am I to understand that all of us high Officers of State are required to perjure ourselves to ensure your safety?

Ko. Why not? You'll be grossly insulted, as usual.

Pooh. Will the insult be cash down, or at a date? 265

Ko. It will be a ready-money transaction.

Pooh. (*Aside.*) Well, it will be a useful discipline. (*Aloud.*) Very good. Choose your fiction, and I'll endorse it! (*Aside.*) Ha! ha! Family Pride, how do you like *that*, my buck?

Nank. But I tell you that life without Yum-Yum — 270

Ko. Oh, Yum-Yum, Yum-Yum! Bother Yum-Yum! Here, Commissionaire (*to* Pooh-Bah), go and fetch Yum-Yum. (*Exit* Pooh-Bah.) Take Yum-Yum and marry Yum-Yum, only go away and never come back again. (*Enter* Pooh-Bah *with* Yum-Yum.) Here she is. Yum-Yum, are you particularly busy? 275

Yum. Not particularly.

Ko. You've five minutes to spare?

Yum. Yes.

Ko. Then go along with his Grace the Archbishop of Titipu; he'll marry you at once. 280

Yum. But if I'm to be buried alive?

Ko. Now, don't ask any questions, but do as I tell you, and Nanki-Poo will explain all.

Nank. But one moment —

Ko. Not for worlds. Here comes the Mikado, no doubt to ascertain 285 whether I've obeyed his decree, and if he finds you alive I shall have the greatest difficulty in persuading him that I've beheaded you. (*Exeunt* Nanki-Poo *and* Yum-Yum, *followed by* Pooh-Bah.) Close thing that, for here he comes!

(*Exit* Ko-Ko.) 290

(*March – Enter procession, heralding* Mikado, *with* Katisha.)

> Entrance of Mikado *and* Katisha.
> ('*March of the Mikado's troops.*')

Chorus.   Miya sama, miya sama,
                   On n'm-ma no mayé ni
                   Pira-Pira suru no wa
                   Nan gia na   295
                   Toko tonyaré tonyaré na?

DUET – Mikado *and* Katisha.

Mik.   From every kind of man
                   Obedience I expect;
                   I'm the Emperor of Japan –

312 *In a fatherly kind of way*: This is, perhaps, an appropriate point at which to look at the situation of the real Mikado of Japan at the time the opera was written. The word 'Mikado' is, incidentally, a perfectly respectable Japanese 'elevated' expression for the Emperor – its literal meaning is 'Honourable Gate'.

In 1885 the Emperor of Japan was indeed governing his country in a fatherly kind of way. The Meiji Restoration seventeen years earlier had brought back direct imperial rule to the country after a long period where effective power had rested with the feudal lords, or *shoguns*, led by the Tokugawa family.

The Emperor Mutsuhito, whose reign from 1867 to 1912 inaugurated the Meiji era, transformed Japan from a feudal oligarchy into a Western-style constitutional monarchy. He introduced strong centralized government and in 1889 established a two-chamber legislature based on the British model.

There is, of course, still an Emperor of Japan, who is the current representative of the longest reigning imperial dynasty in the world. However, since 1946 he has had no power and has been simply a figurehead. In 1885 he was still a force to be reckoned with, even if he was a more humane, and a more Westernized Mikado than had ever existed before.

327–88 *A more humane Mikado*

Unbelievable as it may seem, the famous song in which the Mikado tries to make the punishment fit the crime was very nearly struck out of the opera and never performed. Gilbert announced his decision to cut it at the dress rehearsal, and only a last-minute deputation from the chorus led him to change his mind and keep it in.

KAT.   And I'm his daughter-in-law elect!   300
                        He'll marry his son
                        (He's only got one)
                        To his daughter-in-law elect!

MIK.   My morals have been declared
                        Particularly correct;   305

KAT.   But they're nothing at all, compared
                        With those of his daughter-in-law elect!
                        Bow – Bow –
                        To his daughter-in-law elect!

ALL.   Bow – Bow –   310
                        To his daughter-in-law elect.

MIK.   In a fatherly kind of way
                        I govern each tribe and sect,
                        All cheerfully own my sway –

KAT.   Except his daughter-in-law elect!   315
                        As tough as a bone,
                        With a will of her own,
                        Is his daughter-in-law elect!

MIK.   My nature is love and light –
                        My freedom from all defect –   320

KAT.   Is insignificant quite,
                        Compared with his daughter-in-law elect!
                        Bow – Bow –
                        To his daughter-in-law elect!

ALL.   Bow – Bow –   325
                        To his daughter-in-law elect!

SONG – MIKADO *and* CHORUS.

A more humane Mikado never
Did in Japan exist,
      To nobody second,
      I'm certainly reckoned   330

Since its first-night performance by Richard Temple it has, of course, been one of the most popular numbers in the entire Gilbert and Sullivan repertoire. Its greatest exponent was almost certainly Darrel Fancourt, who played the role of the Mikado more than 3,000 times in D'Oyly Carte productions between 1920 and 1953, and who developed the blood-curdling laugh between verses which had been introduced by earlier performers and which has been a feature of D'Oyly Carte Mikados ever since.

Gilbert originally wrote a different version of the first verse from the one now sung. It is in the licence copy:

> All men who give indifferent dinners,
>> And poison their friends and mine
>>> With two shilling sillery
>>> Stand in a pillory
>>> Every day at nine.
> All prosy dull society sinners
>> Who chatter and bleat and bore,
>>> Are sent to hear sermons
>>> From mystical Germans
>>> Who preach from ten till four.
> And every big and bulky fellow,
>> Of elephantine weights,
>>> Is made to run races
>>> On gravelly places
>>> In eighteenpenny skates.

348 *mystical Germans*: This is thought to be a reference to a group of zealous, and evidently rather long-winded, Lutheran evangelists, who had recently been over in England on a preaching tour.

354 *Madame Tussaud's waxwork*: Madame Tussaud came to England in the early 1800s from her native France, where she had been compelled to make wax casts of the heads of victims of the guillotine. She toured the country with her waxworks exhibition and finally established a permanent museum in Baker Street, London. Madame Tussaud's moved to its present site in the Marylebone Road in 1884. She also gets a mention in Colonel Calverley's list of 'all the remarkable people in history' in Act I of *Patience*.

358 *Is painted with vigour*: Until 1948 this line was sung 'Is blacked like a nigger' (with the next line continuing 'With permanent walnut juice'). In that year it was amended for the same reason as 'the nigger serenader' in Ko-Ko's 'little list' song (see the note to Act I, line 251). A. P. Herbert, who provided the new line, offered two other alternatives to Rupert D'Oyly Carte, which would have involved more extensive alteration of Gilbert's original and were, therefore, rejected:

> (1) The lady who dyes a chemical yellow
>> Or stains her grey hair green,
>>> Is taken to Dover
>>> And painted all over
>>> A horrible ultramarine.

> (2) The lady who dyes a chemical yellow
>> Or stains her grey hair puce,
>>> Is made to wear feathers
>>> In all the worst weathers
>>> And legibly labelled 'Goose'.

364 *Parliamentary trains*: An Act of 1844 had compelled railway companies to run at least one train a day on all lines which stopped at every station with a fare of one penny a mile. These came to be known as Parliamentary trains and brought the benefits of rail

A true philanthropist.
It is my very humane endeavour
To make, to some extent,
   Each evil liver
   A running river   335
Of harmless merriment.

   My object all sublime
   I shall achieve in time –
   To let the punishment fit the crime –
      The punishment fit the crime;   340
   And make each prisoner pent
   Unwillingly represent
   A source of innocent merriment!
   Of innocent merriment!

All prosy dull society sinners,   345
   Who chatter and bleat and bore,
   Are sent to hear sermons
   From mystical Germans
Who preach from ten till four.
The amateur tenor, whose vocal villainies   350
   All desire to shirk,
   Shall, during off-hours,
   Exhibit his powers
To Madame Tussaud's waxwork.

The lady who dyes a chemical yellow   355
   Or stains her grey hair puce,
   Or pinches her figger,
   Is painted with vigour
And permanent walnut juice.
The idiot who, in railway carriages,   360
   Scribbles on window-panes,
   We only suffer
   To ride on a buffer
In Parliamentary trains.

   My object all sublime, etc.   365

CHORUS.   His object all sublime, etc.

The advertising quack who wearies
   With tales of countless cures,

travel, albeit at a rather slow speed, to the working classes. In 1962 Donald Adams, principal bass with the D'Oyly Carte Company from 1953 to 1969, substituted 'slow suburban trains', although he reverted to the original phrase for the 1965 recording and at performances in the mid-1960s.

374 *By Bach*: At this point Sullivan introduced into his orchestration the first twelve notes of Bach's *Fugue in G minor*, to be played by bassoon and clarinet.

376 *Monday Pops*: Forerunners of the modern-day Promenade Concerts, the Monday Pops were weekly concerts of classical music organized by Chappells, the music publishers. They began in 1859 in the St James's Hall, on the site of the present Piccadilly Hotel, and continued there until 1901, when they were transferred to the Queen's Hall. They are also mentioned in *Patience*, when Archibald Grosvenor portrays himself as an every-day young man

> Who thinks suburban 'hops'
> More fun than 'Monday Pops'.

377 *The billiard sharp*: Gilbert was himself something of a billiard sharp. In a letter sent to Sullivan when the composer was abroad, quoted in Leslie Ayre's *Gilbert and Sullivan Companion*, he wrote: 'I send you Cook on Billiards – the study of that work has made me what I am in Billiards, and if you devote six or eight hours a day to it regularly, you may hope to play up to my form when you return'.

381 *a spot that's always barred*: 'Spot' is the word used for the marked places on a billiard table where the balls are put, and particularly for the one where the red ball is placed.

His teeth, I've enacted,
Shall all be extracted   370
By terrified amateurs.
The music-hall singer attends a series
Of masses and fugues and 'ops'
By Bach, interwoven
With Spohr and Beethoven,   375
At classical Monday Pops.

The billiard sharp whom any one catches,
His doom's extremely hard –
He's made to dwell –
In a dungeon cell   380
On a spot that's always barred.
And there he plays extravagant matches
In fitless finger-stalls
On a cloth untrue,
With a twisted cue   385
And elliptical billiard balls!

My object all sublime, etc.

CHORUS.   His object all sublime, etc.

(*Enter* POOH-BAH, KO-KO, *and* PITTI-SING. *All kneel.*)

(POOH-BAH *hands a paper to* KO-KO.)   390

KO. I am honoured in being permitted to welcome your Majesty. I guess the object of your Majesty's visit – your wishes have been attended to. The execution has taken place.
MIK. Oh, you've had an execution, have you?
KO. Yes. The Coroner has just handed me his certificate.   395
POOH. I am the Coroner. (KO-KO *hands certificate to* MIKADO.)
MIK. And this is the certificate of his death. (*Reads.*) 'At Titipu, in the presence of the Lord Chancellor, Lord Chief Justice, Attorney-General, Secretary of State for the Home Department, Lord Mayor, and Groom of the Second Floor Front —'   400
POOH. They were all present, your Majesty. I counted them myself.
MIK. Very good house. I wish I'd been in time for the performance.
KO. A tough fellow he was, too – a man of gigantic strength. His struggles were terrific. It was really a remarkable scene.
MIK: Describe it.   405

414 *snickersnee*: A word of Dutch origin meaning a knife or dagger.

421–6 *We know him well*
    G. K. Chesterton, in an essay on Gilbert and Sullivan in *The Eighteen Eighties*, suggested that this chorus was written in mockery of the Victorians' absurdly exaggerated belief in the probity and gentlemanliness of their upper classes. A correct interpretation of these lines, according to this argument, would be 'This is a man belonging to a class so exquisitely well-bred that even when he tries to tell lies he cannot bring it off'. But this, as W. A. Darlington argued in his *The World of Gilbert and Sullivan*, is mistakenly to read deep social satire into what was simply a humorous chorus. Anyway, Ko-Ko could hardly be described as upper-class.

432 *he whistled an air*: At this point Sullivan added a suitable piccolo solo in the orchestral score. At first it was a snatch from the very popular 'Cotillion Waltz', but later a phrase from the traditional song 'The Girl I Left Behind Me' was substituted.

435 *His cervical vertebræ*: The seven bones forming the upper part of the spine, also known as the neck bones.

TRIO AND CHORUS.

KO-KO, PITTI-SING, POOH-BAH *and* CHORUS.

Ko.   The criminal cried, as he dropped him down,
In a state of wild alarm –
With a frightful, frantic, fearful frown,
I bared my big right arm.
I seized him by his little pig-tail,   410
And on his knees fell he,
As he squirmed and struggled,
And gurgled and guggled,
I drew my snickersnee!
Oh, never shall I   415
Forget the cry,
Or the shriek that shriekèd he,
As I gnashed my teeth,
When from its sheath
I drew my snickersnee!   420

CHORUS.

We know him well,
He cannot tell
Untrue or groundless tales –
He always tries
To utter lies,   425
And every time he fails.

PITTI.   He shivered and shook as he gave the sign
For the stroke he didn't deserve;
When all of a sudden his eye met mine,
And it seemed to brace his nerve;   430
For he nodded his head and kissed his hand,
And he whistled an air, did he,
As the sabre true
Cut cleanly through
His cervical vertebræ!   435
When a man's afraid,
A beautiful maid
Is a cheering sight to see;
And it's oh, I'm glad
That moment sad   440
Was soothed by sight of me!

452 *none of your impudent off-hand nods*: In another bit of Barrington-inspired business, Pitti-Sing touched Pooh-Bah during the singing of this line, and he said 'Go away'. According to Helen D'Oyly Carte, 'This was not objected to by WSG'.

456 *To a man of pedigree*: Cue for another ad-lib gag – Pooh-Bah is interrupted by Pitti-Sing while in the middle of singing the word 'pedigree' and says to her 'I'll give you such a Japanese smack in a minute'. In her notes Helen D'Oyly Carte wrote: 'This was never authorized. It seems to have sprung out of some "business" between Miss Bond and Mr Barrington, and he said something to this effect'. Gilbert's verdict was 'utterly stupid – please omit.'

CHORUS.

Her terrible tale
You can't assail,
With truth it quite agrees:
Her taste exact
For faultless fact
Amounts to a disease.

POOH.   Now though you'd have said that head was dead
    (For its owner dead was he),
    It stood on its neck, with a smile well-bred,
    And bowed three times to me!
    It was none of your impudent off-hand nods,
     But as humble as could be;
     For it clearly knew
     The deference due
    To a man of pedigree!
     And it's oh, I vow,
     This deathly bow
    Was a touching sight to see;
     Though trunkless, yet
     It couldn't forget
    The deference due to me!

CHORUS.

This haughty youth,
He speaks the truth
Whenever he finds it pays:
And in this case
It all took place
Exactly as he says!   (*Exeunt* CHORUS.)

MIK. All this is very interesting, and I should like to have seen it. But we came about a totally different matter. A year ago my son, the heir to the throne of Japan, bolted from our Imperial Court.

KO. Indeed! Had he any reason to be dissatisfied with his position?

KAT. None whatever. On the contrary, I was going to marry him – yet he fled!

POOH. I am surprised that he should have fled from one so lovely!

KAT. That's not true.

POOH. No!

KAT. You hold that I am not beautiful because my face is plain. But you know nothing; you are still unenlightened. Learn, then, that it is not in the face alone that beauty is to be sought. My face is unattractive!

487 *it is the largest in the world*: In early performances, Katisha had more anatomical delights
to reveal, as follows:

> KAT. Observe this ear.
> Ko. Large.
> KAT. Large? Enormous! But think of its delicate internal mechanism. It is fraught with
> beauty! As for this tooth, it almost stands alone. Many have tried to draw it, but in vain.

In the licence copy, Katisha's speech then continued:

> I took this young man in hand, and endeavoured to teach him my theory, but he was dull,
> and it took time. My theory is not learnt in a moment. It takes years to master. Just as the
> light was about to break upon this young man's darkened soul, he fled.

499 *Knightsbridge*: The reason for this apparently strange location was, of course, that it
was where the Japanese village had been erected in 1885. After the dismantling of the
village, the reference became somewhat obscure, and Gilbert took the unusual step of
telling Mrs D'Oyly Carte, at the time of the 1908 revival, 'the location in The Mikado
can be varied according to circumstances'. The D'Oyly Carte Company adopted
certain standard locations when it was on tour. Thus in Liverpool performances
Nanki-Poo's address was Wigan, in Manchester it was Oldham, and in Birmingham,
Small Heath.
    There were many other variations to suit topical events. A correspondent to *The
Times* in 1954 noted that in the 101 performances of *The Mikado* which he had seen
since 1913, there had been seventy different addresses for Nanki-Poo. They included
Croydon at the time of Amy Johnson's return from Australia to the airport there in
1930; Battersea Park and the South Bank at the time of the Festival of Britain; Epsom
on Derby Day; The Oval during cricket Test matches; Putney on Boat Race day; and
'he's gone down' in Oxford.

508 *I beg to offer an unqualified apology*: This and the next line were Barrington gags which
Gilbert did not approve but which nonetheless found their way into both the 1887
libretto and the edition authorized for the 1908 revival.

515 *thoroughly deserved all he got*: At this point Barrington was wont to remark 'He did, and
he got it'. Gilbert's comment on this gag was 'No. Please omit – it is idiotic'.

520 *who the gentleman really was*: Yet another Barrington alteration. The original line went
'We couldn't know that he was the Heir Apparent'. This time Gilbert authorized the
change.

POOH. It is.

KAT. But I have a left shoulder-blade that is a miracle of loveliness. People come miles to see it. My right elbow has a fascination that few can resist.

POOH. Allow me! 485

KAT. It is on view Tuesdays and Fridays, on presentation of visiting card. As for my circulation, it is the largest in the world.

KO. And yet he fled!

MIK. And is now masquerading in this town, disguised as a Second Trombone. 490

KO.
POOH. } A Second Trombone!
PITTI.

MIK. Yes; would it be troubling you too much if I asked you to produce him? He goes by the name of —

KAT. Nanki-Poo.

MIK. Nanki-Poo. 495

KO. It's quite easy. That is, it's rather difficult. In point of fact, he's gone abroad!

MIK. Gone abroad! His address.

KO. Knightsbridge!

KAT. (*who is reading certificate of death*). Ha! 500

MIK. What's the matter?

KAT. See here – his name – Nanki-Poo – beheaded this morning. Oh, where shall I find another? Where shall I find another?

(KO-KO, POOH-BAH *and* PITTI-SING *fall on their knees.*)

MIK. (*looking at paper*). Dear, dear, dear! this is very tiresome. (*To* KO- 505 KO.) My poor fellow, in your anxiety to carry out my wishes you have beheaded the heir to the throne of Japan!

KO. I beg to offer an unqualified apology.

POOH. I desire to associate myself with that expression of regret.

PITTI. We really hadn't the least notion — 510

MIK. Of course you hadn't. How could you? Come, come, my good fellow, don't distress yourself – it was no fault of yours. If a man of exalted rank chooses to disguise himself as a Second Trombone, he must take the consequences. It really distresses me to see you take on so. I've no doubt he thoroughly deserved all he got. (*They rise.*) 515

KO. We are infinitely obliged to your Majesty —

PITTI. Much obliged, your Majesty.

POOH. Very much obliged, your Majesty.

MIK. Obliged? not a bit. Don't mention it. How *could* you tell?

POOH. No, of course we couldn't tell who the gentleman really was. 520

526 *They drop down on their knees again*: It was at this point that a celebrated bit of business was first developed during the long initial run of *The Mikado*. While Pitti-Sing, Pooh-Bah and Ko-Ko were kneeling before the Mikado, Jessie Bond gave George Grossmith a push and he rolled right over. Gilbert was not amused and told Grossmith to cut out the gag. 'But I got a big laugh', the comic protested. 'So you would if you sat on a pork pie' was Gilbert's chilly reply.

Despite Gilbert's disapproval, variations on the gag continued. In 1907 Helen D'Oyly Carte noted that Pooh-Bah now rolled over Ko-Ko, with Pitti-Sing saying 'Pull him off quick'. Gilbert wrote against this note: 'No – there is too much clowning in this scene'. The business, however, continued. One night when Sir Henry Lytton was playing Ko-Ko he concealed a bladder under his costume so that when Fred Billington – all twenty stone of him – rolled over him there was a loud explosion. 'What's happened, Harry?' he whispered anxiously, 'what have I done?'

529 *either boiling oil or melted lead*: This line is said to have caused particular amusement to Queen Victoria during a special command performance of *The Mikado* which was given at Balmoral Castle in Scotland in September 1891.

556 *I don't want any lunch*: One of Barrington's more inspired additions to Gilbert's text, which the author agreed should be incorporated in the libretto. It appears in the 1887 libretto, where it is placed before the Mikado's line 'Then we'll make it after luncheon'.

PITTI. It wasn't written on his forehead, you know.

KO. It might have been on his pocket-handkerchief, but Japanese don't use pocket-handkerchiefs! Ha! ha! ha!

MIK. Ha! ha! ha! (*To* KATISHA.) I forget the punishment for compassing the death of the Heir Apparent.   525

KO.
POOH. } Punishment. (*They drop down on their knees again.*)
PITTI.

MIK. Yes. Something lingering, with boiling oil in it, I fancy. Something of that sort. I think boiling oil occurs in it, but I'm not sure. I know it's something humorous, but lingering, with either boiling oil or melted lead. Come, come, don't fret – I'm not a bit angry.   530

KO. (*in abject terror*). If your Majesty will accept our assurance, we had no idea —

MIK. Of course —

PITTI. I knew nothing about it.

POOH. I wasn't there.   535

MIK. That's the pathetic part of it. Unfortunately, the fool of an Act says 'compassing the death of the Heir Apparent.' There's not a word about a mistake —

KO., PITTI., *and* POOH. No!

MIK. Or not knowing —   540

KO. No!

MIK. Or having no notion —

PITTI. No!

MIK. Or not being there —

POOH. No!   545

MIK. There should be, of course —

KO., PITTI., *and* POOH. Yes!

MIK. But there isn't.

KO., PITTI., *and* POOH. Oh!

MIK. That's the slovenly way in which these Acts are always drawn.   550
However, cheer up, it'll be all right. I'll have it altered next session. Now, let's see about your execution – will after luncheon suit you? Can you wait till then?

KO., PITTI., *and* POOH. Oh, yes – we can wait till then!

MIK. Then we'll make it after luncheon.   555

POOH. I don't want any lunch.

MIK. I'm really very sorry for you all, but it's an unjust world, and virtue is triumphant only in theatrical performances.

GLEE.

PITTI-SING, KATISHA, KO-KO, POOH-BAH, *and* MIKADO.

559–86 *See how the Fates their gifts allot*
Gilbert uses the same device of letters of the alphabet standing for individuals in the second verse of Jack Point's song 'Oh! a private buffoon is a light-hearted loon' in Act II of *The Yeomen of the Guard*:

> What is all right for B would quite scandalize C
> (For C is so very particular);
> And D may be dull, and E's very thick skull
> Is as empty of brains as a ladle;
> While F is F sharp, and will cry with a carp
> That he's known your best joke from his cradle!

In the second verse of 'Were I a king in very truth' in Act I of *The Grand Duke* Ernest Dummkopf manages to get as far as the letter G:

> Both A and B rehearsal slight –
> They say they'll be 'all right at night'
> (They've both to go to school yet);
> C in each act *must* change her dress,
> D *will* attempt to 'square the press';
> E won't play Romeo unless
> His grandmother plays Juliet;
> F claims all hoydens as her rights
> (She's played them thirty seasons);
> And G must show herself in tights
> For two convincing reasons –
> Two very well-shaped reasons!

596 *But how about your big right arm*: Barrington changed this line to 'Yes, well; you can't say much, Ko-Ko; look at that rubbish about your big right arm, look at it'. Gilbert said in 1907 that this alteration was not authorized 'but it can remain'. It was not, however, included in the libretto for the 1908 revival.

MIK.   See how the Fates their gifts allot,
　　　For A is happy – B is not.　　　　　　　560
　　　Yet B is worthy, I dare say,
　　　Of more prosperity than A!
Ko., Pooh., *and* Pitti. *Is* B more worthy?
KAT.   　　　　　　　　I should say
　　　He's worth a great deal more than A.　　565
　　　┌　Yet A is happy!
　　　│　　Oh, so happy!
　　　│　Laughing, Ha! ha!
Ensemble. ┤　Chaffing, Ha! ha!
　　　│　Nectar quaffing, Ha! ha! ha!　　　　570
　　　│　Ever joyous, ever gay,
　　　└　Happy, undeserving A!
Ko., Pooh., *and* Pitti.
　　　If I were Fortune – which I'm not –
　　　B should enjoy A's happy lot,
　　　And A should die in miserie –　　　　575
　　　That is, assuming I am B.
MIK. *and* KAT. But *should* A perish?
Ko., Pooh., *and* Pitti.　　That should he
　　　(Of course, assuming I am B).
　　　B should be happy!　　　　　　　580
　　　　Oh, so happy!
　　　Laughing, Ha! ha!
　　　Chaffing, Ha! ha!
　　　Nectar quaffing, Ha! ha! ha!
　　　But condemned to die is he,　　　　585
　　　Wretched meritorious B!

(*Exeunt* MIKADO *and* KATISHA.)

Ko. Well, a nice mess you've got us into, with your nodding head and the deference due to a man of pedigree!

Pooh. Merely corroborative detail, intended to give artistic veri-   590
similitude to an otherwise bald and unconvincing narrative.

Pitti. Corroborative detail indeed! Corroborative fiddlestick!

Ko. And you're just as bad as he is with your cock-and-a-bull stories about catching his eye and his whistling an air. But that's so like you! You must put in your oar!   595

Pooh. But how about your big right arm?

Pitti. Yes, and your snickersnee!

Ko. Well, well, never mind that now. There's only one thing to be done. Nanki-Poo hasn't started yet – he must come to life again at once.

600 *Enter Nanki-Poo*: Traditionally, Nanki-Poo enters with a bundle of belongings tied on a pole which he carries over his shoulder. Miss Beti Lloyd-Jones, who joined the D'Oyly Carte Company in 1957 and was still singing contralto roles when it closed in 1982, has told me that one of the favourite 'dirty tricks' occasionally played on leading tenors was to load Nanki-Poo's bundle with a 56-lb. stage weight just before he shouldered it for this entrance.

632–55 *The flowers that bloom in the spring*
Another song that never fails to get an encore. It received a triple encore at the first-night performance, as did 'Three little maids'. Sullivan composed the music for 'The flowers that bloom in the spring' one evening between tea and dinner. .

In the licence copy the song is preceded by a short recitative for Nanki-Poo instead of the speech which he was later given in lines 629–31:

> Now hear my resolution – it's suggested by my wife –
> While Katisha is single I decline to come to life –
> When Katisha is married, that is quite another thing –
> Existence will be welcome as the flowers in the spring.

(*Enter* NANKI-POO *and* YUM-YUM *prepared for journey.*) Here he comes. 600
Here, Nanki-Poo, I've good news for you – you're reprieved.

NANK. Oh, but it's too late. I'm a dead man, and I'm off for my
honeymoon.

KO. Nonsense! A terrible thing has just happened. It seems you're the
son of the Mikado. 605

NANK. Yes, but that happened some time ago.

KO. Is this a time for airy persiflage? Your father is here, and with
Katisha!

NANK. My father! And with Katisha!

KO. Yes, he wants you particularly. 610

POOH. So does she.

YUM. Oh, but he's married now.

KO. But, bless my heart! what has that to do with it?

NANK. Katisha claims me in marriage, but I can't marry her because I'm
married already – consequently she will insist on my execution, and if I'm 615
executed, my wife will have to be buried alive.

YUM. You see our difficulty.

KO. Yes. I don't know what's to be done.

NANK. There's one chance for you. If you could persuade Katisha to
marry you, she would have no further claim on me, and in that case I could 620
come to life without any fear of being put to death.

KO. I marry Katisha!

YUM. I really think it's the only course.

KO. But, my good girl, have you seen her? She's something appalling!

PITTI. Ah! that's only her face. She has a left elbow which people come 625
miles to see!

POOH. I am told that her right heel is much admired by connoisseurs.

KO. My good sir, I decline to pin my heart upon any lady's right heel.

NANK. It comes to this: While Katisha is single, I prefer to be a
disembodied spirit. When Katisha is married, existence will be as welcome 630
as the flowers in spring.

DUET – NANKI-POO *and* KO-KO.

(*With* YUM-YUM, PITTI-SING, *and* POOH-BAH.)

NANK. The flowers that bloom in the spring,
 Tra la,
 Breathe promise of merry sunshine –
 As we merrily dance and we sing, 635
 Tra la,
We welcome the hope that they bring,
 Tra la,

During the first-night performance George Grossmith, who was notoriously nervous on such occasions, slipped and fell in the middle of this song. This was greeted by so much laughter from the audience that Gilbert told him to make a regular feature of it.

Another famous bit of D'Oyly Carte business also has its origins in an accident during the singing of 'The flowers that bloom in the spring'. While dancing around between verses, Sir Henry Lytton trod on a tack that had been left on the stage and drew his foot back with the pain. His autobiography records:

> From the audience there came a tremendous roar of laughter. For a moment I could not understand it at all. Looking down, however, I was amazed to find my big toe upright, almost at right angles to the rest of the foot. With my fan I pressed it down – then raised it again. This provoked such merriment among the audience that I did it a second time, and a third. All this time the theatre was convulsed. I confess that to myself it seemed jolly funny.

659–62 *Alone, and yet alive*
This recitative, and Katisha's subsequent solo, 'Hearts do not break', are sometimes cut.

663–81 *Hearts do not break*
The licence copy contains a second verse of this song, cut before the first performance:

> Hearts do not break!
> If I mistake
> Why sleep, and wake
> To life-long gloom?
> If love betrayed
> Can kill a maid
> As poets have said,
> Where is thy tomb?
> Oh, life-long gloom –
> Dark demon, whom
> In dread I shun
> Go, loathly one!
> Come, haven sure,
> Come, grave obscure,
> Come, relatively cheerful tomb!

Of a summer of roses and wine.
    And that's what we mean when we say that a thing   640
    Is welcome as flowers that bloom in the spring.
        Tra la la la la la, etc.

ALL.   Tra la la la, etc.

KO.   The flowers that bloom in the spring,
        Tra la,   645
    Having nothing to do with the case.
I've got to take under my wing,
        Tra la,
A most unattractive old thing,
        Tra la,   650
    With a caricature of a face,
    And that's what I mean when I say, or I sing,
    'Oh, bother the flowers that bloom in the spring.'
        Tra la la la la la, etc.

ALL.   Tra la la la, Tra la la la, etc.   655

(*Dance and exeunt* NANKI-POO, YUM-YUM, POOH-BAH,
        PITTI-SING, *and* KO-KO.)

(*Enter* KATISHA.)

RECITATIVE AND SONG – KATISHA.

Alone, and yet alive! Oh, sepulchre!
My soul is still my body's prisoner!   660
Remote the peace that Death alone can give –
My doom, to wait! my punishment, to live!

SONG.

Hearts do not break!
They sting and ache
For old love's sake,   665
    But do not die,
Though with each breath
They long for death
As witnesseth
    The living I!   670

706 *Darling*: This was added to the libretto at the time of the 1908 revival, although doubtless it had been said for some time before that.

713 *You know not what you say*: An almost identical phrase, 'You know not what you ask', occurs in *Iolanthe* and was originally the cue for the song 'A fairy once, as well you know' (see the note to line 477 on page 244).

Oh, living I!
Come, tell me why,
When hope is gone,
Dost thou stay on?
Why linger here,   675
Where all is drear?
Oh, living I!
Come, tell me why,
When hope is gone,
Dost thou stay on?   680
May not a cheated maiden die?

Ko. (*entering and approaching her timidly*). Katisha!
Kat. The miscreant who robbed me of my love! But vengeance pursues
– they are heating the cauldron!
Ko. Katisha – behold a suppliant at your feet! Katisha – mercy!   685
Kat. Mercy? Had you mercy on him? See here, you! You have slain my
love. He did not love *me*, but he would have loved me in time. I am an
acquired taste – only the educated palate can appreciate *me*. I was educating
his palate when he left me. Well, he is dead, and where shall I find another?
It takes years to train a man to love me. Am I to go through the weary round   690
again, and, at the same time, implore mercy for you who robbed me of my
prey – I mean my pupil – just as his education was on the point of
completion? Oh, where shall I find another?
Ko. (*suddenly, and with great vehemence*). Here! – Here!
Kat. What!!!   695
Ko. (*with intense passion*). Katisha, for years I have loved you with a
white-hot passion that is slowly but surely consuming my very vitals! Ah,
shrink not from me! If there is aught of woman's mercy in your heart, turn
not away from a love-sick suppliant whose every fibre thrills at your tiniest
touch! True it is that, under a poor mask of disgust, I have endeavoured to   700
conceal a passion whose inner fires are broiling the soul within me! But the
fire will not be smothered – it defies all attempts at extinction, and, breaking
forth, all the more eagerly for its long restraint, it declares itself in words that
will not be weighed – that cannot be schooled – that should not be too
severely criticized. Katisha, I dare not hope for your love – but I will not live   705
without it! Darling!
Kat. You, whose hands still reek with the blood of my betrothed,
dare to address words of passion to the woman you have so foully
wronged!
Ko. I do – accept my love, or I perish on the spot!   710
Kat. Go to! Who knows so well as I that no one ever yet died of a
broken heart!
Ko. You know not what you say. Listen!

714–37 *On a tree by a river a little tom-tit*
In *The Gilbert and Sullivan Book* Leslie Baily points to the close similarity between Gilbert's famous lines and verses by the poet Nicholas Rowe (1674–1718):

> To the Brook and the Willow that heard him complain,
> Ah Willow, Willow,
> Poor Colin sat weeping and told them his pain,
> Ah, Willow, Willow; ah Willow, Willow.
> Sweet stream, he cry'd sadly, I'll teach thee to flow;
> And the waters shall rise to the brink with my woe,
> Ah Willow, Willow.

There is, of course, an even earlier parallel to Ko-Ko's ditty in the Willow Song from Shakespeare's *Othello* for which Sullivan wrote a setting not wholly dissimilar from his tune for Tit Willow.

Students of Gilbert and Sullivan have been much exercised by what might be called the ornithological aspects of this song. A correspondent to *The Times* in May 1959 suggested that Gilbert must have been glancing through the index of a book on birds when he came across the entry 'Tit, willow' and was attracted by its rhythm. A pencilled note in the margin of the copy of G. E. Dunn's *A Gilbert and Sullivan Dictionary* in the music library on the Berkeley campus of the University of California reads 'the song is that of the American bob-white quail which Sullivan must have heard on his visit a few years earlier'. It also points out that true tits only very rarely eat worms.

There have been many parodies of the 'titwillow' song. One of the best, quoted in *The Gilbert and Sullivan Book,* appeared in a London newspaper in 1907 at the time of the ban on *The Mikado:*

> In a house by the River the stalls and the pit
> Wanted 'Willow, tit-willow, tit-willow.'
> But were told they'd no right to hear even a bit
> Of 'Willow, tit-willow, tit-willow.'
> 'Why this utter inanity?' every one cried,
> As they asked the Lord Chamberlain why he had shied
> At the musical play which alone can provide
> Us with 'Willow, tit-willow, tit-willow.'
>
> Is it true that Japan doesn't like us to sing
> 'Oh, willow – tit-willow, tit-willow'?
> For we're cutting 'The Flowers that Bloom in the Spring'
> Besides 'Willow, tit-willow, tit-willow.'
> We've lost the Mikado; the scenes we all know,
> Pooh-Bah and Yum-Yum and the schoolgirls must go,
> With Katisha and also the cheerful Ko-Ko
> Who sang 'Willow, tit-willow, tit-willow.'
>
> Now, the light-hearted natives of distant Japan
> Hearing 'Willow, tit-willow, tit-willow'
> Could scarcely do aught but respond, to a man,
> And 'Willow, tit-willow, tit-willow'.
> Might quickly become (I see no reason why
> Not) a joy to Japan; Japanese passers-by
> I can picture delightedly shouting 'Banzai!
> That's Willow, tit-willow, tit-willow.'

SONG – KO-KO.

On a tree by a river a little tom-tit
    Sang 'Willow, titwillow, titwillow!'   715
And I said to him, 'Dicky-bird, why do you sit
    Singing "Willow, titwillow, titwillow"?'
'Is it weakness of intellect, birdie?' I cried,
'Or a rather tough worm in your little inside?'
With a shake of his poor little head, he replied,   720
    'Oh, willow, titwillow, titwillow!'

He slapped at his chest, as he sat on that bough,
    Singing 'Willow, titwillow, titwillow!'
And a cold perspiration bespangled his brow,
    Oh, willow, titwillow, titwillow!   725
He sobbed and he sighed, and a gurgle he gave,
Then he plunged himself into the billowy wave,
And an echo arose from the suicide's grave –
    'Oh, willow, titwillow, titwillow!'

Now I feel just as sure as I'm sure that my name   730
    Isn't Willow, titwillow, titwillow,
That 'twas blighted affection that made him exclaim,
    'Oh, willow, titwillow, titwillow!'
And if you remain callous and obdurate, I
Shall perish as he did, and you will know why,   735
Though I probably shall not exclaim as I die,
    'Oh, willow, titwillow, titwillow!'

(*During this song* KATISHA *has been greatly affected, and at the end is almost in tears.*)

KAT. (*whimpering*). Did he really die of love?   740
KO. He really did.
KAT. All on account of a cruel little hen?
KO. Yes.
KAT. Poor little chap!
KO. It's an affecting tale, and quite true. I knew the bird intimately.   745
KAT. Did you? He must have been very fond of her.
KO. His devotion was something extraordinary.
KAT. (*still whimpering*). Poor little chap! And – and if I refuse you, will you go and do the same?
KO. At once.   750
KAT. No, no – you mustn't! Anything but that! (*Falls on his breast.*) Oh, I'm a silly little goose!
KO. (*making a wry face*). You are!

765 *the Congo or the Niger*: As a cheap tailor, Ko-Ko can, perhaps, be pardoned a serious lapse in his knowledge of geography and natural history here. Tigers are, of course, only found in Asia, while both the Congo and the Niger are in West Africa.

The Congo was much in the news at the time *The Mikado* was written. In 1878 the explorer H. M. Stanley had returned to Europe after establishing the source of the river, the longest in Africa. As a result of an agreement which he made with King Leopold II, Belgium acquired sovereignty over the surrounding territory. At the Berlin Conference in 1885 Belgium's sovereignty over the Congo was recognized by the other powers and Leopold II took the title of ruler of the Independent State of the Congo.

The upper reaches of the Niger river were also being extensively explored and opened up during the 1880s. The French gradually consolidated their hold on the surrounding territory and established the Federation of French West Africa in 1895.

784 *Do you fancy you are elderly enough*: Gilbert has sometimes been taken to task by critics for his morbid and most ungentlemanly obsession with the ageing of women and the decay of their attractive features. Compared to some of the other principal contraltos in the Savoy Operas, Katisha in fact comes off fairly lightly in this respect. Perhaps the cruellest song of all that a Gilbertian matron has to sing is Lady Jane's 'Silvered is the raven hair' at the beginning of Act II of *Patience:*

> Fading is the taper waist,
>   Shapeless grows the shapely limb,
> And although severely laced,
>   Spreading is the figure trim!
> Stouter than I used to be,
>   Still more corpulent grow I –
> There will be too much of me
>   In the coming by and by!

KAT. And you won't hate me because I'm just a little teeny weeny wee bit bloodthirsty, will you?   755

Ko. Hate you? Oh, Katisha! is there not beauty even in bloodthirstiness?

KAT. My idea exactly.

DUET – KATISHA *and* KO-KO.

KAT. There is beauty in the bellow of the blast,
  There is grandeur in the growling of the gale,   760
    There is eloquent outpouring
    When the lion is a-roaring,
  And the tiger is a-lashing of his tail!
Ko.   Yes, I like to see a tiger
    From the Congo or the Niger,   765
  And especially when lashing of his tail!
KAT. Volcanoes have a splendour that is grim,
  And earthquakes only terrify the dolts,
    But to him who's scientific
    There is nothing that's terrific   770
  In the falling of a flight of thunderbolts!
Ko.   Yes, in spite of all my meekness,
    If I have a little weakness,
  It's a passion for a flight of thunderbolts!
BOTH.   If that is so,   775
    Sing derry down derry!
      It's evident, very,
        Our tastes are one.
    Away we'll go,
      And merrily marry,   780
      Nor tardily tarry
        Till day is done!

Ko. There is beauty in extreme old age –
    Do you fancy you are elderly enough?
      Information I'm requesting   785
      On a subject interesting:
    Is a maiden all the better when she's tough?
KAT.   Throughout this wide dominion
        It's the general opinion
    That she'll last a good deal longer when she's tough.   790
Ko. Are you old enough to marry, do you think?
    Won't you wait until you're eighty in the shade?
      There's a fascination frantic

819 *Mercy even for Pooh-Bah*: This, I am sure, was another of Rutland Barrington's gags. Although it is not in the list drawn up in 1907 by Helen D'Oyly Carte to put to Gilbert for approval, it does not appear in the original libretto and is written in by hand in the master-copy of the libretto for the 1908 revival.

823 *We were married*: In another Barrington gag, Ko-Ko altered this line to 'We were married after lunch before the Registrar'. Gilbert approved this change in 1907. The 1908 libretto also changes Pooh-Bah's next line to 'I am the after luncheon Registrar'.

831 *seizing Ko-Ko*: As Katisha vigorously shook Ko-Ko, Rutland Barrington would call out 'Time'. Gilbert authorized this gag in 1907.

In a ruin that's romantic;
Do you think you are sufficiently decayed?   795
KAT.   To the matter that you mention
I have given some attention,
And I think I am sufficiently decayed.
BOTH.   If that is so,
Sing derry down derry!   800
It's evident, very,
Our tastes are one!
Away we'll go,
And merrily marry,
Nor tardily tarry   805
Till day is done!

(*Exeunt together.*)

(*Flourish. Enter the* MIKADO, *attended by* PISH-TUSH *and Court.*)

MIK. Now then, we've had a capital lunch, and we're quite ready. Have
all the painful preparations been made?   810
PISH. Your Majesty, all is prepared.
MIK. Then produce the unfortunate gentleman and his two well-
meaning but misguided accomplices.

(*Enter* KO-KO, KATISHA, POOH-BAH, *and* PITTI-SING. *They throw
themselves at the* MIKADO'S *feet.*)   815

KAT. Mercy! Mercy for Ko-Ko! Mercy for Pitti-Sing! Mercy even for
Pooh-Bah!
MIK. I beg your pardon, I don't think I quite caught that remark.
POOH. Mercy even for Pooh-Bah.
KAT. Mercy! My husband that was to have been is dead, and I have   820
just married this miserable object.
MIK. Oh! You've not been long about it!
KO. We were married before the Registrar.
POOH. *I* am the Registrar.
MIK. I see. But my difficulty is that, as you have slain the Heir   825
Apparent —

(*Enter* NANKI-POO *and* YUM-YUM. *They kneel.*)

NANKI. The Heir Apparent is *not* slain.
MIK. Bless my heart, my son!
YUM. And your daughter-in-law elected!   830
KAT. (*seizing* KO-KO). Traitor, you have deceived me!

846–77 *For he's gone and married Yum-Yum*
 In early editions of the libretto, the reprise of 'For he's gone and married Yum-Yum'
 was not sung and the finale simply consisted of 'The threatened cloud has passed
 away', arranged, as now, with Yum-Yum and Nanki-Poo singing the first four lines
 and everyone else singing the rest. It is very doubtful if this version was ever
 performed, however, as all editions of the vocal score have the present arrangement
 which was almost certainly produced before the opening night.
 The finale of the Texas version of *The Mikado* in 1888, mentioned above in the note
 to lines 31–62, went:

> For he's going to stay in Fort Worth –
> Fort Worth,
> Now pocket your malice
> And slip off to Dallas,
> Or come and partake of our mirth –
> Mirth – mirth,
> And join our expressions of glee.

MIK. Yes, you are entitled to a little explanation, but I think he will give it better whole than in pieces.

KO. Your Majesty, it's like this: It is true that I stated that I had killed Nanki-Poo — 835

MIK. Yes, with most affecting particulars.

POOH. Merely corroborative detail intended to give artistic veri-similitude to a bald and —

KO. *Will* you refrain from putting in your oar? (*To* MIKADO.) It's like this: When your Majesty says, 'Let a thing be done,' it's as good as done – 840 practically, it *is* done – because your Majesty's will is law. Your Majesty says, 'Kill a gentleman,' and a gentleman is told off to be killed. Consequently, that gentleman is as good as dead – practically, he *is* dead – and if he is dead, why not say so?

MIK. I see. Nothing could possibly be more satisfactory! 845

FINALE.

PITTI.	For he's gone and married Yum-Yum –
ALL.	Yum-Yum!
PITTI.	Your anger pray bury,
	For all will be merry,
	I think you had better succumb – 850
ALL.	Cumb – cumb.
PITTI.	And join our expressions of glee!
KO.	On this subject I pray you be dumb –
ALL.	Dumb – dumb!
KO.	Your notions, though many, 855
	Are not worth a penny,
	The word for your guidance is 'Mum' –
ALL.	Mum – mum!
KO.	You've a very good bargain in me.
ALL.	On this subject we pray you be dumb – 860
	Dumb – dumb!
	We think you had better succumb –
	Cumb – cumb!
	You'll find there are many
	Who'll wed for a penny, 865
	There are lots of good fish in the sea.
YUM. *and* NANK.	The threatened cloud has passed away,
	And brightly shines the dawning day;
	What though the night may come too soon,
	We've years and years of afternoon! 870

ALL.

> Then let the throng
>   Our joy advance,
> With laughing song
>   And merry dance,
> With joyous shout and ringing cheer,
> Inaugurate our new career!
>   Then let the throng, etc.

CURTAIN

875

THE GONDOLIERS

OR

THE KING OF BARATARIA

DRAMATIS PERSONÆ

THE DUKE OF PLAZA-TORO (*a Grandee of Spain*)
LUIZ (*his Attendant*)
DON ALHAMBRA DEL BOLERO (*the Grand Inquisitor*)
MARCO PALMIERI ⎫
GIUSEPPE PALMIERI │
ANTONIO   ⎬ (*Venetian Gondoliers*)
FRANCESCO   │
GIORGIO   │
ANNIBALE   ⎭
THE DUCHESS OF PLAZA-TORO
CASILDA (*her Daughter*)
GIANETTA ⎫
TESSA   │
FIAMETTA ⎬ (*Contadine*)
VITTORIA │
GIULIA   ⎭
INEZ (*the King's Foster-mother*)
Chorus of Gondoliers and Contadine, Men-at-Arms, Heralds, and Pages.

ACT I. – The Piazzetta, Venice.
ACT II. – Pavilion in the Palace of Barataria.

(*An interval of three months is supposed to elapse between Acts I and II.*)

Date – 1750.

THE GONDOLIERS

The Gondoliers is the twelfth opera on which Gilbert and Sullivan collaborated and the last of those which are regularly performed today. Although there were to be two later Savoy Operas, *Utopia Limited* and *The Grand Duke*, neither of them was very successful and they are only rarely staged. *The Gondoliers*, however, has consistently remained one of the most popular of all Gilbert and Sullivan's works, ranking second only to *The Mikado* in frequency of performance by both amateur and professional companies.

Its beginnings were hardly auspicious. Although *The Mikado* had been a great success and had reunited composer and librettist after their earlier quarrels, their next work, *The Yeomen of the Guard*, had a more mixed reception and had done rather sluggish business at the box office. For Sullivan, however, it had marked a distinct step forward from the pure comedy of the earlier Savoy Operas towards the world of grand opera. He made it known that henceforth he wanted to concentrate on composing serious operatic works, and Richard D'Oyly Carte obliged by agreeing to set up an English Opera Company and building a new opera house to be its home.

Sullivan approached Gilbert to write the libretto for the new grand opera, telling him that it must be a work 'where the music is to be the first consideration – where words are to suggest music, not govern it'. Gilbert did not take kindly to this suggestion and responded waspishly: 'If you are really under the astounding impression that you have been effacing yourself for the last twelve years . . . there is most certainly no "modus vivendi" to be found that shall be satisfactory to both of us. You are an adept in your profession, and I am an adept in mine. If we meet, it must be as master and master – not as master and servant'.

An acrimonious correspondence now ensued. Sullivan, writing by a curious coincidence from Venice, where Gilbert was already planning to set the next comic opera, told D'Oyly Carte that as far as he was concerned his relationship to Gilbert had always been that of servant and that 'excepting during the vocal rehearsals and the two orchestra rehearsals I am a cipher in the theatre'. This remark provoked further outbursts from Gilbert, and, not for the first time, D'Oyly Carte found himself using all his skills as a diplomatist in an effort to pacify and reconcile his two talented but sensitive partners.

His tactful diplomacy worked and in May 1889 Gilbert and Sullivan met and agreed to bury the hatchet. D'Oyly Carte had now commissioned a large-scale grand opera from Sullivan, and the composer agreed in addition to do another comic piece with Gilbert. He liked the idea of the Venetian plot and saw that it offered considerable scope for colourful and exciting music.

Both Gilbert and Sullivan spent longer on *The Gondoliers* than they had on their previous works. Gilbert took the best part of five months to write the libretto, a brilliant satire on the emerging enthusiasm for republicanism and egalitarianism, and Sullivan was occupied on the music for the whole of the summer of 1889, which he spent at Weybridge, Surrey. He received the songs to be set one or two a time, and numerous letters passed between composer and librettist about redrafting or dropping particular numbers once the overall structure of the work became clearer.

The comparatively long period of preparation did not prevent the run-up to the opening performance being a frantic rush. Sullivan did not have his first orchestral rehearsal until five days before the London first night. After taking the rehearsal, he dined at home and then sat down until three the following morning composing the overture. He was up again after only a few hours' sleep to agree with Gilbert the title of the piece, which had, characteristically, been left to the last minute. Two days later the dress rehearsal lasted for a marathon seven hours.

The Gondoliers opened at the Savoy Theatre on 7 December 1889 and ran for 559 performances until 20 June 1891. The critics were almost unanimous in their praise, and the audience's reaction was little short of ecstatic. In the United States, however, its reception was markedly cooler. A D'Oyly Carte company sailed out from Britain in secret to beat the pirates and opened at the Park Theater, New York, on 7 January 1890. Their lack of success at the box office earned the opera the nickname 'The Gone Dollars', and D'Oyly Carte himself came out to revamp the production. Even in its new form, it only ran until April, by which time no fewer than seven actors had been tried in the role of the Duke of Plaza-Toro. Meanwhile a pirate company in New Jersey was having rather more success with a hammed-up version in which the Grand Inquisitor dropped a real tear, with a splash worked from the wings, and Marco and Giuseppe were discovered on stage at the beginning of Act II busily ironing their shirts.

In some ways *The Gondoliers* stands as the supreme achievement of the distinct yet united talents of Gilbert and Sullivan. The libretto manages to pack a considerable satirical punch without being either heavy-handed or overtly silly. It also enabled Sullivan to achieve his object of making his music more dominant than it had been in earlier works. Of the forty-seven pages in the original edition of the libretto, only fourteen are dialogue. *The*

Gondoliers has the longest vocal score of any of the Savoy Operas, including the three-act *Princess Ida*.

It was not to be long, however, before the two men were at loggerheads again. Shortly after the opening of *The Gondoliers* Gilbert went off on a cruise to India with his wife. He was appalled to find when he returned home that £4,500 of the partners' money had been spent on preliminary expenses for the new work, including what he regarded as the outrageous sum of £500 for new carpets for the Savoy Theatre. He exploded at Carte, who responded by saying 'Very well then – you write no more for the Savoy Theatre.' This time it was Sullivan, who on the whole took Carte's side in the quarrel, who found himself trying to act as mediator.

In the event Richard D'Oyly Carte's wife, Helen, managed to patch up the quarrel and reconciled Gilbert and Sullivan once again. But it was to be three years before they worked together on another comic opera, and by then the old magic, and perhaps also the old motivation, had gone. Sullivan meanwhile concentrated on being a serious composer. His grand opera *Ivanhoe*, based on the novel by Sir Walter Scott, opened at Carte's new Royal English Opera House (now the Palace Theatre in Cambridge Circus) on 31 January 1891 and enjoyed a moderately successful if limited run.

So *The Gondoliers* must serve as the last great example of the genius of these two men, temperamentally so incompatible yet artistically so perfectly matched. Happily, its success inspired from both of them rare but heartfelt tributes to the talents of the other. Gilbert wrote to Sullivan the morning after the opening night: 'I must thank you for the magnificent work you have put into the piece. It gives one the chance of shining right through the twentieth century with a reflected light'. Sullivan replied 'Don't talk of reflected light. In such a perfect book as *The Gondoliers* you shone with an individual brilliancy which no other writer can hope to attain'. A case, for once, of a librettist and composer 'who act in perfect unity'!

1 *Scene*: The Piazzetta in Venice lies to the south-east of St Mark's Square and is one of the main tourist attractions in that most romantic of all European cities. Gilbert's stage direction establishes that the audience is looking at the Piazzetta from the north side, i.e. as though from St Mark's Square. On the left (stage right) is the famous Doge's Palace, built in the fourteenth and fifteenth centuries, faced with pink and white marble arranged in a diamond pattern, and with its two arcades of delicately traceried windows. In his book *The Stones of Venice*, published in 1853, the great Victorian art critic John Ruskin described the palace as the perfect union of Gothic and early Renaissance styles and 'the central building of the world'.

To be totally faithful to the location, the backcloth for this act should show the lagoon with the island of San Giorgio Maggiore in the distance and, in the foreground, the two great columns which were brought from the east in the twelfth century and erected at the top of the steps leading down to the water's edge. One is surmounted by a winged lion, the heraldic emblem of the Venetian Republic, and the other by a statue of St Theodore, the city's patron saint.

4–35 *List and learn, ye dainty roses*
This chorus begins a sequence of music which continues, unbroken by dialogue, for more than eighteen minutes. It is the longest opening sequence and very nearly the longest continuous passage of music in any of the Savoy Operas, being only marginally shorter than the Act I finale to *Iolanthe*.

There is some evidence that Gilbert had originally intended to have a very different style of opening chorus which would establish the political theme of the opera. He had apparently got the initial idea for *The Gondoliers* from a book on Venice in the fifteenth century which made much of the city's strong republicanism. Gilbert saw that a satire on republican ideas would have an appeal to a contemporary audience. More than fifty Republican Clubs had been established in Britain in the 1870s, and anti-monarchical and pro-egalitarian principles were also being vociferously championed by the various groups which grew up in the 1880s to propagate the new creed of socialism.

According to Leslie Baily in his *Gilbert and Sullivan Book*, Gilbert's original manuscript contained an opening chorus which introduced

> A people, dignified and polished,
> Who class-distinctions have abolished,
> And one and all with zeal combine
> To make their monarch toe the line.

I have not been able to trace this original manuscript, but it is interesting that the lines quoted by Baily occur in the song written for Pietro at the beginning of Act II but cut out before the first performance (see the note to Act II, lines 15–22). I wonder if, in fact, it was this number to which Leslie Baily was referring. It is, of course, quite

ACT I

SCENE. – THE PIAZZETTA, VENICE. *The Ducal Palace on the right.*
FIAMETTA, GIULIA, VITTORIA, *and other Contadine discovered, each tying a bouquet of roses.*

CHORUS OF CONTADINE.

List and learn, ye dainty roses,
  Roses white and roses red,   5
Why we bind you into posies
  Ere your morning bloom has fled.
By a law of maiden's making,
Accents of a heart that's aching,
Even though that heart be breaking,   10
  Should by maiden be unsaid:
Though they love with love exceeding,
They must seem to be unheeding –
Go ye then and do their pleading,
  Roses white and roses red!   15

FIAMETTA.

Two there are for whom, in duty,
  Every maid in Venice sighs –
Two so peerless in their beauty
  That they shame the summer skies.
We have hearts for them, in plenty,   20
  They have hearts, but all too few,
We, alas, are four-and-twenty!
  They, alas, are only two!
We, alas!
CHORUS.   Alas!   25
FIA.   Are four-and-twenty,
They, alas!
CHORUS.   Alas!
FIA.   Are only two.

possible that the lines were originally written for an opening chorus in Act I and later transferred to the song in Act II.

Either way, this seems to be the so-called 'growling chorus' to which Gilbert refers in a letter to Sullivan in August 1889. Sullivan did not like the chorus. If it was, indeed, written for the start of Act I one can see that he would feel that it jarred with the generally romantic and light-hearted atmosphere of the rest of the opera's opening. Gilbert, however, was unhappy about cutting it out:

> It seems to me that the piece as it stands at present wants it. The Venetians of the fifteenth century were red-hot Republicans. One of their party is made king and invites his friends to form a Court. They object because they are Republicans. He replies that he has considered that and proposed to institute a Court in which all people shall be equal, and to this they agree. In Act II the absurdity of this state of things is shown. Without the dissatisfaction expressed by the 'Growling' chorus (which can be rewritten if it won't do in its present form) the story would be unintelligible.

Sullivan had his way, however. The 'growling chorus' was cut and the republican theme overall was less emphasized than Gilbert had apparently first intended.

Gilbert's letter to Sullivan also shows that another major change was made to the overall structure of the opera during the summer months in which both composer and librettist worked on it. Gilbert apparently planned initially to set the action in the fifteenth century, when the Venetian Republic was at the height of its power and influence. However, he later shifted it to the mid-eighteenth century, by which time Venice was no longer of political importance. At the end of that century, indeed, it lost its independence, being handed over by Napoleon to the Austrians. It remained under Austrian rule for much of the nineteenth century, becoming part of the newly unified country of Italy in 1866. The reason for this shift in the dating of the opera is unclear. Apart from the Duke of Plaza-Toro's reference to Wesleyan Methodism (Act I, line 311), there is not very much in the libretto which is incompatible with a fifteenth-century setting. The Duke's status as a limited company would, of course, be somewhat anachronistic, but so it is in the present mid-eighteenth-century setting.

54 *dolce far niente*: The first of several genuine Italian expressions introduced into *The Gondoliers*. Its literal meaning is 'sweet doing nothing', i.e. delightful idleness. It also makes an appearance in Act I of *Iolanthe*, when Lord Mountararat sings of Strephon 'A-taking of his *dolce far niente*', and in Act I of *Utopia Limited*, where the guards, nobles and dancing girls 'Sing the songs of *far niente*'.

55 *contradicente*: From the Italian (and Latin) word *contradico*, meaning to contradict, gainsay or deny. It is used in Britain in the form *nemine contradicente*, usually shortened to *nem. con.*, to mean unanimously, with no dissent. The word also occurs in the Act I finale of *Iolanthe*.

CHORUS.	They, alas, are only two, alas!	30
	Now ye know, ye dainty roses,	
	Roses white and roses red,	
	Why we bind you into posies,	
	Ere your morning bloom has fled,	
	Roses white and roses red!	35

(*During this chorus* ANTONIO, FRANCESCO, GIORGIO, *and other Gondoliers have entered unobserved by the Girls – at first two, then two more, then four, then half a dozen, then the remainder of the Chorus.*)

SOLI.

FRANC.	Good morrow, pretty maids; for whom prepare ye	
	These floral tributes extraordinary?	40
FIA.	For Marco and Giuseppe Palmieri,	
	The pink and flower of all the Gondolieri.	
GIU.	They're coming here, as we have heard but lately,	
	To choose two brides from us who sit sedately.	
ANT.	Do all you maidens love them?	45
ALL.	Passionately!	
ANT.	These gondoliers are to be envied greatly!	
GIOR.	But what of us, who one and all adore you?	
	Have pity on our passion, we implore you!	
FIA.	These gentlemen must make their choice before you;	50
VIT.	In the meantime we tacitly ignore you.	
GIU.	When they have chosen two that leaves you plenty –	
	Two dozen we, and ye are four-and-twenty.	
FIA. *and* VIT.	Till then, enjoy your *dolce far niente*.	
ANT.	With pleasure, nobody *contradicente*!	55

SONG – ANTONIO *and* CHORUS.

For the merriest fellows are we, tra la,
That ply on the emerald sea, tra la;
    With loving and laughing,
    And quipping and quaffing,
We're happy as happy can be, tra la –   60
    With loving and laughing, etc.

With sorrow we've nothing to do, tra la,
And care is a thing to pooh-pooh, tra la;
    And Jealousy yellow,
    Unfortunate fellow,
We drown in the shimmering blue, tra la –   65
    And Jealousy yellow, etc.

71 *ben' venuti*: Welcome. The phrase derives from the words *bene,* meaning well, and the verb *venire,* to come.

75–95 *Buon' giorno, signorine*
The exchange in Italian between Marco and Giuseppe and the chorus of girls translates as follows:

MAR. *and* GIU. Good morning, young ladies!
GIRLS.   Dearest gondoliers!
                    We are country maidens!
MAR. *and* GIU. (*bowing*). Your humble servants!
                    For whom are these flowers –
                    These most beautiful flowers?
GIRLS.   For you, good gentlemen,
                    O most excellent!

(*The Girls present their bouquets to* MARCO *and* GIUSEPPE *, who are overwhelmed with them, and carry them with difficulty.*)

MAR. *and* GIU. (*their arms full of flowers*).   O heaven! O heaven!
GIRLS.   Good morning, cavaliers!
MAR. *and* GIU. (*deprecatingly*).   We are gondoliers.
    (*To* FIA. *and* VIT.)   Young lady, I love you!
GIRLS (*deprecatingly*).   We are country maidens.
MAR. *and* GIU.   Young ladies!
GIRLS (*deprecatingly*).   Country maidens!
    (*Curtseying to* MAR. *and* GIU.)   Cavaliers!
MAR. *and* GIU. (*deprecatingly*).   Gondoliers!
                                                Poor gondoliers!
CHORUS.   Good morning, young ladies, etc.

96–120 *We're called gondolieri*
Sullivan deliberately chose an Italian folk-song idiom for this seductively lazy and lilting song in which the two principal gondoliers introduce themselves. Its elongated cadences are, in fact, more reminiscent of the Neapolitan than the Venetian style.

FIA. (*looking off*). See, see, at last they come to make their choice –
    Let us acclaim them with united voice.

      (MARCO *and* GIUSEPPE *appear in gondola at back.*)   70

CHORUS (*Girls*). Hail, hail! gallant gondolieri, ben' venuti! ben' venuti!
    Accept our love, our homage, and our duty.
    Ben' venuti! ben' venuti!

    (MARCO *and* GIUSEPPE *jump ashore – the Girls salute them.*)

        DUET – MARCO *and* GIUSEPPE, *with*
          CHORUS OF GIRLS.

MAR. *and* GIU.   Buon' giorno, signorine!   75
GIRLS.   Gondolieri carissimi!
             Siamo contadine!
MAR. *and* GIU. (*bowing*).   Servitori umilissimi!
             Per chi questi fiori –
             Questi fiori bellissimi?   80
GIRLS.   Per voi, bei signori,
             O eccellentissimi!

(*The Girls present their bouquets to* MARCO *and* GIUSEPPE, *who are overwhelmed with them, and carry them with difficulty.*)

MAR. *and* GIU. (*their arms full of flowers*).   O ciel'! O ciel'!   85
GIRLS.   Buon' giorno, cavalieri!
MAR. *and* GIU. (*deprecatingly*).   Siamo gondolieri.
  (*To* FIA. *and* VIT.)   Signorina, io t' amo!
GIRLS (*deprecatingly*).   Contadine siamo.
MAR. *and* GIU.   Signorine!   90
GIRLS (*deprecatingly*).   Contadine!
  (*Curtseying to* MAR. *and* GIU.)   Cavalieri.
MAR. *and* GIU. (*deprecatingly*).   Gondolieri!
                Poveri gondolieri!
CHORUS.   Buon' giorno, signorine, etc.   95

        DUET – MARCO *and* GIUSEPPE.

    We're called *gondolieri*,
    But that's a vagary,
    It's quite honorary
        The trade that we ply.

The trade plied by Marco and Giuseppe is, of course, an old and distinguished one in the city of Venice with its twenty-eight miles of waterways. Gondolas have been in use there since the early Middle Ages, although it was not until the seventeenth century that they took on their present distinctive long, sleek, double-ended shape. In keeping with the Venetians' dislike of ostentation in civil dress and decoration, an ordinance of 1562 laid down that all gondolas should be painted black, and so they have remained ever since.

102 *To beauty devoted*: This line was originally 'To ladies devoted' and was changed in the third edition of the libretto. 'To beauty devoted' is, however, found in all editions of the vocal score.

126 *A bias to disclose*: Helen D'Oyly Carte's annotated copy of the libretto prepared for the 1907 revival has this line struck out and 'To pitch on these or those' substituted. The line also occurs in that form in Sullivan's autograph score and the prompt copy in the British Library. The present version was re-introduced in the libretto in 1914.

131 *Viva*: Hurrah.

For gallantry noted   100
Since we were short-coated,
To beauty devoted,
    Giuseppe } and I;
    Are Marco
When morning is breaking,
Our couches forsaking,   105
To greet their awaking
    With carols we come.
At summer day's nooning,
When weary lagooning,
Our mandolins tuning,   110
    We lazily thrum.
When vespers are ringing,
To hope ever clinging,
With songs of our singing
    A vigil we keep,   115
When daylight is fading,
Enwrapt in night's shading,
With soft serenading
    We sing them to sleep.
We're called *gondolieri*, etc.   120

RECITATIVE – Marco *and* Giuseppe.

MAR.   And now to choose our brides!
GIU.   As all are young and fair,
    And amiable besides,
BOTH.   We really do not care
    A preference to declare.   125
MAR.   A bias to disclose
    Would be indelicate –
GIU.   And therefore we propose
    To let impartial Fate
    Select for us a mate!   130
ALL.   Viva!
GIRLS. A bias to disclose
    Would be indelicate –
MEN.   But how do they propose
    To let impartial Fate   135
    Select for them a mate?
GIU. These handkerchiefs upon our eyes be good enough to bind,
MAR. And take good care that both of us are absolutely blind;

166–70 *My papa he keeps three horses*

Although this sounds like an old nursery rhyme, and Sullivan's tune is strongly reminiscent of a children's chant, I think the words are original to Gilbert. I can find no trace of them in either the *Oxford Dictionary of Nursery Rhymes* compiled by Iona and Peter Opie or the same authors' *Children's Games in Street and Playground*.

172 *Business of blind-man's buff*: This, by contrast, goes back long before Gilbert, of course. The Opies describe it as probably the best-known of all children's games in Britain and cite references to it dating back to the sixteenth century. They also point out that the game is known in Italian as *mosca cieca* ('blind fly'), which is, presumably, how Marco and Giuseppe would have known it.

Characteristically, Gilbert took immense trouble over this bit of business and he drilled the cast in it for three whole days before the opening performance. In a letter to Helen D'Oyly Carte in July 1898 he wrote: 'If you revive *The Gondoliers* I hope you will take care to have at least three chorus rehearsals for business. The ladies got fearfully slack towards the end of the run – in the blindfold scene they used to walk in circles instead of dancing.'

BOTH.   Then turn us round – and we, with all convenient despatch,
      Will undertake to marry any two of you we catch!   140
ALL.   Viva!

They undertake to marry any two of $\begin{cases} \text{us they catch!} \\ \text{them they catch!} \end{cases}$

(The Girls prepare to bind their eyes as directed.)

FIA. (*to* MARCO).   Are you peeping?
                          Can you see me?   145
MAR.   Dark I'm keeping,
                          Dark and dreamy!   (MARCO *slyly lifts bandage.*)
VIT. (*to* GIUSEPPE). If you're blinded
                          Truly, say so.
GIU.   All right-minded   150
                          Players play so!   (*slyly lifts bandage*).
FIA. (*detecting* MARCO). Conduct shady!
                          They are cheating!
                          Surely they de-
                          Serve a beating!   (*replaces bandage*). 155
VIT. (*detecting* GIUSEPPE). This too much is;
                          Maidens mocking –
                          Conduct such is
                          Truly shocking!   (*replaces bandage*).
GIRLS.   You can spy, sir!   160
                          Shut your eye, sir!
                          You may use it by and by, sir!
ALL.   You can see, sir!
                          Don't tell me, sir!
                          That will do – now let it be, sir!   165
CHORUS OF   My papa he keeps three horses,
GIRLS.   Black, and white, and dapple grey, sir;
          Turn three times, then take your courses,
           Catch whichever girl you may, sir!
CHORUS OF MEN. My papa, etc.   170

(MARCO *and* GIUSEPPE *turn round, as directed, and try to catch the girls. Business of blind-man's buff. Eventually* MARCO *catches* GIANETTA, *and* GIUSEPPE *catches* TESSA. *The two girls try to escape, but in vain. The two men pass their hands over the girls' faces to discover their identity.*)

GIU.   I've at length achieved a capture!   175
  (*Guessing.*) This is Tessa! (*removes bandage*). Rapture, rapture!
CHORUS.   Rapture, rapture!

205–16 *Thank you, gallant gondolieri*
On the opening night the chorus of girls did not simply repeat Gianetta's opening verse as they do now, but had their own slightly different version of the song:

> To these gallant *gondolieri,*
> > In a set and formal measure,
> It is scarcely necessary
> > To express their pride and pleasure.
> > Each of us to prove a treasure,
> Conjugal and monetary,
> > Gladly will devote her leisure,
> To the other *gondolieri!*
> Tra, la, la, la, la, la, etc.

219 *A gondola arrives at the Piazzetta steps*: In his autobiography, *A Wandering Minstrel*, Sir Henry Lytton recalls an opening night in New York when the D'Oyly Carte gondola had been lost in transit from Britain and a substitute had to be constructed out of soap boxes. It fell to pieces as it was being pulled across the back of the stage and so Lytton, playing the part of the Duke of Plaza-Toro, abandoned the presumably sinking craft and pretended to rescue his wife and daughter and swim ashore. As he made his way to the front of the stage to begin 'From the sunny Spanish shore', a voice from the audience cried 'You ain't very wet, mister.'

MAR. (*guessing*). To me Gianetta fate has granted! (*removes bandage*).
      Just the very girl I wanted!
CHORUS.   Just the very girl he wanted!   180
GIU. (*politely to* MAR.). If you'd rather change –
TESS.   My goodness!
      This indeed is simple rudeness.
MAR. (*politely to* GIU.). I've no preference whatever –
GIA.   Listen to him! Well, I never!   185

    (*Each man kisses each girl.*)

GIA.   Thank you, gallant *gondolieri*!
     In a set and formal measure
   It is scarcely necessary
     To express our pleasure.   190
     Each of us to prove a treasure,
   Conjugal and monetary,
     Gladly will devote our leisure,
   Gallant *gondolieri*.
     Tra, la, la, la, la, la, etc.   195
TESS.   Gay and gallant *gondolieri*,
     Take us both and hold us tightly,
   You have luck extraordinary;
     We might have been unsightly!
     If we judge your conduct rightly, 200
   'Twas a choice involuntary;
     Still we thank you most politely,
   Gay and gallant *gondolieri*!
     Tra, la, la, la, la, la, etc.
CHORUS OF Thank you, gallant *gondolieri*;   205
GIRLS.   In a set and formal measure,
   It is scarcely necessary
     To express our pleasure.
     Each of us to prove a treasure
     Gladly will devote our leisure,   210
   Gay and gallant *gondolieri*!
     Tra, la, la, la, la, la, etc.
ALL.   Fate in this has put his finger –
     Let us bow to Fate's decree,
   Then no longer let us linger,   215
     To the altar hurry we!

  (*They all dance off two and two –* GIANETTA *with* MARCO,
    TESSA *with* GIUSEPPE.)

224–43 *From the sunny Spanish shore*
The clear implication of this song is that the Duke of Plaza-Toro and his suite have made the entire journey from Spain to 'Venetia's shores' by sea, rather than taking the shorter route of sailing over to Genoa and then crossing to Venice by land. If that is indeed the case, then it is no wonder that they never want to cross the sea again.

The autograph score of *The Gondoliers* contains an earlier version of this song which began 'From the country of the Cid,/The Duke of Valladolid'. Gilbert rewrote it to produce the present version before the opening night.

234 *that Grandee from the Spanish shore*: 'Grandee' was the term used in Spain or Portugal for a nobleman of the highest rank, one of whose distinguishing privileges was that he could wear his hat in the presence of royalty. The Duke of Plaza-Toro later contradicts this exalted description of his position by telling us (line 245) that he is a hidalgo, i.e. a member of the lowest order of Spanish nobility. I suspect that the latter is a more truthful description of his status, but 'grandee' sounds good in the song.

243 *Cross the sea again*: In the licence copy sent to the Lord Chamberlain for vetting, there follows at this point a song which was cut out before the opening night and has never been performed.

SOLO – Duchess.

The Duke of Plaza-Tor'
    Though poor in purse and land,
He owns a goodly store
    Of condescension bland;
And that, when it comes from a Ducal chair,
Is a coin that's current everywhere.

ALL.
    Yes, everywhere!
    Yes, everywhere!
It's a coin that's current everywhere.

DUCH.
And of all the Dukes who have coin to spare,
That haughty Duke can alone declare
That he always pays his bills of fare
With a coin that is current everywhere!

ALL.
    With a coin, etc.

DUCH.
With words of gracious praise,
    And high-flown compliment,
And condescending ways,
    And bunkum eloquent,
And bows of stately etiquette,
He every day pays every debt.

ALL.
    Pays every debt!
    Pays every debt!
He every day pays every debt.

DUCH.
And of all the Dukes I have known as yet,
In our own exclusive high-born set,
He's the only Duke I've ever met
Who every day pays every debt.

ALL.
    And of all the Dukes, etc.

(*Flourish. A gondola arrives at the Piazzetta steps, from which enter the*
DUKE OF PLAZA-TORO, *the* DUCHESS, *their daughter* CASILDA, *and*   220
their attendant LUIZ, *who carries a drum. All are dressed in pompous but old and*
faded clothes.)

(*Entrance of* DUKE, DUCHESS, CASILDA, *and* LUIZ.)

DUKE.	From the sunny Spanish shore,
	The Duke of Plaza-Tor' –
DUCH.	And His Grace's Duchess true –
CAS.	And His Grace's daughter, too –
LUIZ.	And His Grace's private drum
	To Venetia's shores have come:
ALL.	If ever, ever, ever
	They get back to Spain,
	They will never, never, never
	Cross the sea again –
DUKE.	Neither that Grandee from the Spanish shore,
	The noble Duke of Plaza Tor' –
DUCH.	Nor His Grace's Duchess, staunch and true –
CAS.	You may add, His Grace's daughter, too –
LUIZ.	Nor His Grace's own particular drum
	To Venetia's shores will come:
ALL.	If ever, ever, ever
	They get back to Spain,
	They will never, never, never
	Cross the sea again!

225

230

235

240

DUKE. At last we have arrived at our destination. This is the Ducal
Palace, and it is here that the Grand Inquisitor resides. As a Castilian hidalgo   245
of ninety-five quarterings, I regret that I am unable to pay my state visit on
a horse. As a Castilian hidalgo of that description, I should have preferred to
ride through the streets of Venice; but owing, I presume, to an unusually wet
season, the streets are in such a condition that equestrian exercise is
impracticable. No matter. Where is our suite?   250
    LUIZ (*coming forward*). Your Grace, I am here.
    DUCH. Why do you not do yourself the honour to kneel when you
address His Grace?
    DUKE. My love, it is so small a matter! (*To* LUIZ.) Still, you may as
well do it. (LUIZ *kneels.*)   255
    CAS. The young man seems to entertain but an imperfect appreciation
of the respect due from a menial to a Castilian hidalgo.

245 *it is here that the Grand Inquisitor resides*: It is something of a mystery why the Grand Inquisitor of Spain (for so Don Alhambra is identified in line 484) should be residing in the Doge's Palace in Venice. The abduction of the young heir to the Baratarian throne, which originally brought him there, took place many years before the action of the opera. It is true that parts of Italy were under Spanish rule in the mid-eighteenth century, and therefore, presumably, under the jurisdiction of the Spanish Inquisition (on which see the note to line 427). They did not, however, include Venice, which retained its staunch republican independence. Indeed one would have thought that a Spanish Grand Inquisitor would not be at all welcome in that city. But perhaps Don Alhambra found the Doge's instruments of torture infinitely more exciting than those back home.

246 *of ninety-five quarterings*: 'Quarterings' are the divisions on a heraldic shield, each containing a different coat of arms and indicating the number of noble families from which the owner of the shield is descended. Plaza-Toro is here maintaining that his family has, over the years, married into ninety-five other blue-blooded families. In a version of *The Gondoliers* apparently adapted by Helen D'Oyly Carte in the 1900s for performance in the United States, this line was altered to 'possessing nineteen castles, all in Spain, and nearly all ruined'.

249 *the streets are in such a condition*: This line recalls the celebrated cable which the American humorist Robert Benchley (1889–1945) sent back to New York after arriving in Venice: 'Streets full of water. Please advise'. In the American version of the libretto mentioned above, this line is changed to 'The streets are so uncomfortably damp that equestrian exercise is impracticable'.

259 *I've no patience. . .*: Decima Moore, who was brought into the D'Oyly Carte Opera Company as a totally inexperienced newcomer at the age of eighteen to create the role of Casilda, later gave the following description of Gilbert's unique method of training his actors:

> Exact diction; every word to be heard at the back of the dress circle; the rhythm of the lines to be scrupulously followed. He would read a line of dialogue out, clapping his hands between the words to emphasize their rhythm, thus: 'I've no patience (clap) with the presumption (clap) of persons (clap) in his plebeian (clap) position.'

264 *halberdiers*: Soldiers, and in particular civic guards, who carry halberds, a combination of a spear and battle-axe consisting of a sharp-edged blade mounted on a handle, often as a badge of office.

278 *cornet-à-piston*: A brass instrument, more commonly known simply as a cornet, with valves or pistons for producing notes additional to the natural harmonics.

The exchange about the cornet-à-piston, and, indeed, everything from 'Well, let us hope' in line 277 to 'our suite's feelings' in line 286, were cut from many D'Oyly Carte productions, although they were reinstated shortly before the company's recent demise.

In the version of the libretto prepared for American audiences and mentioned above (in the note to line 246), this passage of dialogue was rewritten as follows:

> DUKE. Well, let us hope that the Grand Inquisitor may also prove to be a deaf gentleman. However a trumpeter to announce our approach appears essential. You do not happen to possess the accomplishment of ta-ran-ta-ra-ing like a trumpet?
>
> LUIZ. Alas, no, Your Grace! But my imitation of a cat is invariably received with great applause.
>
> DUKE. I don't see how that would help us, etc.

287–8 *the Duke of Plaza-Toro, Count Matadoro, Baron Picadoro*: All these titles are derived from the national Spanish sport of bull-fighting. Plaza-Toro means literally 'the place of the bull', i.e. the arena. The matador is the official who waves a red handkerchief in front of the bull to work up its anger, while the picador further torments the unfortunate creature by attacking it with a lance. The final assault is, of course, left to the toreador.

DUKE. My child, you are hard upon our suite.

CAS. Papa, I've no patience with the presumption of persons in his plebeian position. If he does not appreciate that position, let him be whipped   260
until he does.

DUKE. Let us hope the omission was not intended as a slight. I should be much hurt if I thought it was. So would he. (*To* LUIZ.) Where are the halberdiers who were to have had the honour of meeting us here, that our visit to the Grand Inquisitor might be made in becoming state?   265

LUIZ. Your Grace, the halberdiers are mercenary people who stipulated for a trifle on account.

DUKE. How tiresome! Well, let us hope the Grand Inquisitor is a blind gentleman. And the band who were to have had the honour of escorting us? I see no band!   270

LUIZ. Your Grace, the band are sordid persons who required to be paid in advance.

DUCH. That's so like a band!

DUKE (*annoyed*). Insuperable difficulties meet me at every turn!

DUCH. But surely they know His Grace?   275

LUIZ. Exactly – they know His Grace.

DUKE. Well, let us hope that the Grand Inquisitor is a deaf gentleman. A cornet-à-piston would be something. You do not happen to possess the accomplishment of tootling like a cornet-à-piston?

LUIZ. Alas, no, Your Grace! But I can imitate a farmyard.   280

DUKE (*doubtfully*). I don't see how that would help us. I don't see how we could bring it in.

CAS. It would not help us in the least. We are not a parcel of graziers come to market, dolt!

(LUIZ *rises*.)   285

DUKE. My love, our suite's feelings! (*To* LUIZ.) Be so good as to ring the bell and inform the Grand Inquisitor that his Grace the Duke of Plaza-Toro, Count Matadoro, Baron Picadoro –

DUCH. And suite –

DUKE. And suite – have arrived at Venice, and seek –   290

CAS. Desire –

DUCH. Demand!

DUKE. And demand an audience.

LUIZ. Your Grace has but to command.

DUKE (*much moved*). I felt sure of it – I felt sure of it! (*Exit* LUIZ *into*   295
Ducal Palace.) And now, my love – (*aside to* DUCHESS) Shall we tell her? I think so – (*aloud to* CASILDA) And now, my love, prepare for a magnificent surprise. It is my agreeable duty to reveal to you a secret which should make you the happiest young lady in Venice!

305 *Barataria*: Gilbert takes the name of his imaginary island 'That lies in a Southern sea' from Miguel De Cervantes' famous story *Don Quixote*. Readers of that work will recall that Barataria was the island 'surrounded by land' of which Don Quixote made his faithful companion Sancho Panza governor. The description of the latter's arrival in Barataria may also have influenced the passage in *The Gondoliers* in which the Duke of Plaza-Toro complains of the lack of ceremony attending his own arrival there (Act II, lines 707–23): 'As soon as he came to the gates the magistrates came out to receive him, the bells rang, and all the people gave demonstrations of joy.'

311 *a Wesleyan Methodist*: The King of Barataria must have been a remarkably early convert to Methodism. The action of *The Gondoliers* takes place in 1750. We are told here that the King became a Methodist shortly after the marriage of his infant son to the baby Casilda. That event must have taken place at least eighteen years or so before the conversation we are now witnessing, say around 1732. Yet the foundation in Oxford by John and Charles Wesley of the Holy Club, the group which is normally taken to be the precursor of the Methodists, had only taken place in 1729, and it was not until 1738 that John Wesley was converted to 'vital religion' and started to apply the term 'Methodist' to himself and his followers. The term 'Wesleyan Methodist', incidentally, used to identify those who saw themselves as belonging specifically to his church as distinct from other Methodist denominations, was of even later application, being first recorded in the United States in 1796 and in Britain not until 1858.

In the version of the opera adapted by Helen D'Oyly Carte for performance in America, the phrase 'became a Wesleyan Methodist' was changed to 'joined the Salvation Army'. In a production in Belfast at the time when the Revd Ian Paisley was beginning his rise to prominence in Northern Irish politics the Duke spoke of 'a Free Presbyterian of the most bigoted and persecuting type'.

314 *conveyed to Venice*: Venice seems a curious place for a Spanish Grand Inquisitor to take the infant son of the King of Barataria in an effort to prevent him falling victim to heresy. Although certainly free from Methodist influence, the home of red-hot republicanism was hardly the most fervent centre of Roman Catholicism in Europe. Why, one wonders, did Don Alhambra not take the baby back to Spain or at least to one of her Italian possessions?

329 *after allotment*: When a limited company is formed it issues a prospectus and invites investors to apply for shares. The company then allots the shares. In Britain the Duke of Plaza-Toro would not have been able to form himself into a limited company in 1750, but Venice may well have been more advanced in these matters (see the note to Act II, line 601). I have not, I fear, researched too deeply into Venetian company law!

For her American audience, Helen D'Oyly Carte altered this passage to read:

> DUKE. A joint stock company, under the title the Duke of Plaza-Toro, Limited, has been organized for the purpose of working me. An influential syndicate will supply the capital – and I shall supply myself.
>
> CAS. Am I to understand that the Queen of Barataria may be called upon at any time to hear her honoured sire quoted below par, or behold him in the hand of a receiver?
>
> DUCH. The speculation is not exempt from that drawback. If your father should stop, it will, of course, be necessary to wind him up.
>
> CAS. But it's so undignified – it's so degrading! A Grandee of Spain turned into a public corporation.
>
> DUKE. There is every reason to believe that I shall command a handsome premium. If I am issued as a first mortgage bond, that gratifying result is almost certain.
>
> CAS. But such a thing was never heard of!

CAS. A secret? 300

DUCH. A secret which, for State reasons, it has been necessary to preserve for twenty years.

DUKE. When you were a prattling babe of six months old you were married by proxy to no less a personage than the infant son and heir of His Majesty the immeasurably wealthy King of Barataria! 305

CAS. Married to the infant son of the King of Barataria? Was I consulted? (DUKE *shakes his head*.) Then it was a most unpardonable liberty!

DUKE. Consider his extreme youth and forgive him. Shortly after the ceremony that misguided monarch abandoned the creed of his 310 forefathers, and became a Wesleyan Methodist of the most bigoted and persecuting type. The Grand Inquisitor, determined that the innovation should not be perpetuated in Barataria, caused your smiling and unconscious husband to be stolen and conveyed to Venice. A fortnight since the Methodist Monarch and all his Wesleyan Court were killed in 315 an insurrection, and we are here to ascertain the whereabouts of your husband, and to hail you, our daughter, as Her Majesty, the reigning Queen of Barataria! (*Kneels*.)

(*During this speech* LUIZ *re-enters*.)

DUCH. Your Majesty! (*Kneels*.) (*Drum roll*.) 320

DUKE. It is at such moments as these that one feels how necessary it is to travel with a full band.

CAS. I, the Queen of Barataria! But I've nothing to wear! We are practically penniless!

DUKE. That point has not escaped me. Although I am unhappily in 325 straitened circumstances at present, my social influence is something enormous; and a Company, to be called the Duke of Plaza-Toro, Limited, is in course of formation to work me. An influential directorate has been secured, and I shall myself join the Board after allotment.

CAS. Am I to understand that the Queen of Barataria may be called 330 upon at any time to witness her honoured sire in process of liquidation?

DUCH. The speculation is not exempt from that drawback. If your father should stop, it will, of course, be necessary to wind him up.

CAS. But it's so undignified – it's so degrading! A Grandee of Spain turned into a public company! Such a thing was never heard of! 335

DUKE. My child, the Duke of Plaza-Toro does not follow fashions – he leads them. He always leads everybody. When he was in the army he led his regiment. He occasionally led them into action. He invariably led them out of it.

340–93 *In enterprise of martial kind*

There is no proper patter song in *The Gondoliers*. This is the nearest equivalent, but it is not really in quite the same genre as the songs given to the 'funny men' in the other Savoy Operas. The reason for this apparently strange omission may well be that for the first time since the opening of *The Sorcerer* in 1877 George Grossmith was not available to play the comic lead. He had left the D'Oyly Carte Company in the summer of 1889 to go back to his old job as a piano-entertainer. The role of the Duke of Plaza-Toro in the new opera was given to Frank Wyatt, a well-known actor in the straight theatre who had, however, no previous experience as a singer. Both Gilbert and Sullivan may well have felt that it would be very risky, and very unkind, to subject an untried newcomer to the rigours of a patter song.

SONG – DUKE OF PLAZA-TORO.

In enterprise of martial kind,   340
    When there was any fighting,
He led his regiment from behind –
    He found it less exciting.
But when away his regiment ran,
    His place was at the fore, O –   345
       That celebrated,
       Cultivated,
       Underrated
         Nobleman,
    The Duke of Plaza-Toro!   350

ALL.   In the first and foremost flight, ha, ha!
You always found that knight, ha, ha!
       That celebrated,
       Cultivated,
       Underrated   355
         Nobleman,
    The Duke of Plaza-Toro!

When, to evade Destruction's hand,
    To hide they all proceeded,
No soldier in that gallant band   360
    Hid half as well as he did.
He lay concealed throughout the war,
    And so preserved his gore, O!
       That unaffected,
       Undetected,   365
       Well-connected
         Warrior,
    The Duke of Plaza-Toro!

ALL.   In every doughty deed, ha, ha!
He always took the lead, ha, ha!   370
       That unaffected,
       Undetected,
       Well-connected
         Warrior,
    The Duke of Plaza-Toro!   375

When told that they would all be shot
    Unless they left the service,
That hero hesitated not,
    So marvellous his nerve is.

385 *Paladin*: Originally one of the twelve famous warriors of the Emperor Charlemagne's court, of whom the Count Palatine was the foremost. The word later came to be applied to any knightly hero or renowned champion.

397–415 *O rapture, when alone together*
In early performances, Casilda and Luiz sang both verses of this recitative as an ensemble rather than as two solos. It was then followed by a ballad for Luiz which was replaced early on in the original run by the duet 'Ah, well-beloved':

BALLAD – Luiz.

Thy wintry scorn I dearly prize,
    Thy mocking pride I bless;
Thy scorn is love in deep disguise,
    Thy pride is loneliness.
        Thy cold disdain,
        It gives no pain –
        'Tis mercy, played
        In masquerade.
        Thine angry frown
        Is but a gown
        That serves to dress
        Thy gentleness!

If angry frown and deep disdain
    Be love in masked array,
So much the bitterer their arraign,
    So much the sweeter they!
        With mocking smile
        My love beguile;
        With idle jest
        Appease my breast;
        With angry voice
        My soul rejoice;
        Beguile with scorn
        My heart forlorn!

Oh, happy he who is content to gain
Thy scorn, thine angry frown, thy deep disdain!

He sent his resignation in,   380
 The first of all his corps, O!
  That very knowing,
   Overflowing,
   Easy-going
    Paladin,   385
 The Duke of Plaza-Toro!

ALL.   To men of grosser clay, ha, ha!
 He always showed the way, ha, ha!
  That very knowing,
   Overflowing,   390
   Easy-going
    Paladin,
 The Duke of Plaza-Toro!

(*Exeunt* DUKE *and* DUCHESS *into Ducal Palace. As soon as*
they have disappeared, LUIZ *and* CASILDA *rush to*   395
each other's arms.)

RECITATIVE AND DUET – CASILDA AND LUIZ.

O rapture, when alone together
 Two loving hearts and those that bear them
May join in temporary tether,
 Though Fate apart should rudely tear them.   400

CAS.   Necessity, Invention's mother,
 Compelled me to a course of feigning –
But, left alone with one another,
 I will atone for my disdaining!

   Ah, well-beloved,   405
   Mine angry frown
   Is but a gown
   That serves to dress
   My gentleness!

LUIZ.   Ah, well-beloved,   410
   Thy cold disdain,
   It gives no pain –
   'Tis mercy, played
   In masquerade!

BOTH.   Ah, well-beloved, etc.   415

422 *Casilda*: Until shortly before the opening night, the Duke of Plaza-Toro's daughter was known as Carlotta. It is not clear why this was changed to Casilda at the last moment.

427 *the Inquisition*: The name given to the ecclesiastical courts set up in Roman Catholic countries in the Middle Ages to deal with the trial and prosecution of heretics. The Spanish Inquisition, established in 1479, was particularly brutal, and during the term of office of its first Grand Inquisitor, Torquemada, some two thousand heretics were burned alive. The Spanish Inquisition was abolished by Joseph Bonaparte in 1808, reintroduced in 1814 and finally terminated in 1834.

454 *Perhaps not*: At this point, the dialogue originally continued:

> CAS. We may recollect an embrace – I recollect many – but we must not repeat them.
> LUIZ. Then let us recollect a few!
> (*A moment's pause, as they recollect, then both heave a deep sigh.*)
> LUIZ. Ah, Casilda, you were to me as the sun is to the earth!
> CAS. A quarter of an hour ago?
> LUIZ. About that.
> CAS. And to think that, but for this miserable discovery, you would have been my own for life!
> LUIZ. Through life to death – a quarter of an hour ago!
> CAS. How greedily my thirsty ears would have drunk the golden melody of those sweet words a quarter – well it's now about twenty minutes since (*looking at her watch*).
> LUIZ. About that. In such a matter one cannot be too precise.

In its first-night review the *Daily News* commented that 'both the ballad of Luiz and the paradoxical dialogue in which the lady confesses how much she loved him "a quarter of an hour ago" somehow missed their point'. Gilbert accepted the criticism and both items were removed. They are, however, printed in several modern editions of the libretto and are performed by many amateur societies.

CAS. O Luiz, Luiz – what have you said? What have I done? What have I allowed you to do?

LUIZ. Nothing, I trust, that you will ever have reason to repent. (*Offering to embrace her.*)

CAS. (*withdrawing from him*). Nay, Luiz, it may not be. I have embraced you for the last time.   420

LUIZ (*amazed*). Casilda!

CAS. I have just learnt, to my surprise and indignation, that I was wed in babyhood to the infant son of the King of Barataria!   425

LUIZ. The son of the King of Barataria? The child who was stolen in infancy by the Inquisition?

CAS. The same. But, of course, you know his story.

LUIZ. Know his story? Why, I have often told you that my mother was the nurse to whose charge he was entrusted!   430

CAS. True. I had forgotten. Well, he has been discovered, and my father has brought me here to claim his hand.

LUIZ. But you will not recognize this marriage? It took place when you were too young to understand its import.

CAS. Nay, Luiz, respect my principles and cease to torture me with vain entreaties. Henceforth my life is another's.   435

LUIZ. But stay – the present and the future – *they* are another's; but the past – that at least is ours, and none can take it from us. As we may revel in naught else, let us revel in that!

CAS. I don't think I grasp your meaning.   440

LUIZ. Yet it is logical enough. You say you cease to love me?

CAS. (*demurely*). I say I *may* not love you.

LUIZ. Ah, but you do not say you *did* not love me?

CAS. I loved you with a frenzy that words are powerless to express – and that but ten brief minutes since!   445

LUIZ. Exactly. My own – that is, until ten minutes since, my own – my lately loved, my recently adored – tell me that until, say a quarter of an hour ago, I was all in all to thee! (*Embracing her.*)

CAS. I see your idea. It's ingenious, but don't do that. (*Releasing herself.*)   450

LUIZ. There can be no harm in revelling in the past.

CAS. None whatever, but an embrace cannot be taken to act retrospectively.

LUIZ. Perhaps not! Casilda, you were to me as the sun is to the earth!   455

CAS. And now our love, so full of life, is but a silent, solemn memory!

LUIZ. Must it be so, Casilda?

CAS. Luiz, it must be so!

481–2 *Don Alhambra del Bolero*: One of the great bass-baritone roles in the Savoy Operas, the
Grand Inquisitor was first played by W. H. Denny, whose appearance in the part was
thought by many to bear a striking resemblance to Lord Granville, Foreign Secretary
in Gladstone's first two governments.

Kenneth Sandford, who has played Don Alhambra in three different D'Oyly Carte
productions of *The Gondoliers* stretching over twenty-five years, told me that the role
has greatly changed in that period:

> In the old days a Grand Inquisitor was a Grand Inquisitor in name, bearing and looks.
> Now we have humanized the part. You accept the fact that you are a Grand Inquisitor, but
> the man is as normal as anyone else, and if he's tempted to look down the front of a lady's
> dress, it doesn't alter the fact that he's a Grand Inquisitor. In the old days that just wouldn't
> have been done. But now you can put a little light in your eye and enjoy it, as I'm quite sure
> Gilbert would have liked, because he was quite a boy.

Certainly Kenneth Sandford's lecherous portrayal of the Don was one of the delights
of the last days of the D'Oyly Carte Company.

488 *Jimp*: A word of Scandinavian origin meaning slender, slim, graceful or neat.

489 *Offers his hand*: The original stage direction at this point was 'Proceeds to inspect her'.
J. M. Gordon, stage director of the D'Oyly Carte Opera Company from 1907 to 1939,
altered it in 1914.

DUET – CASILDA *and* LUIZ.

LUIZ.　　　There was a time –　　　　　　　　　　　　　　460
　　　　　　　A time for ever gone – ah, woe is me!
　　　　It was no crime
　　　　　　　To love but thee alone – ah, woe is me!
　　　　One heart, one life, one soul,
　　　　　　　One aim, one goal –　　　　　　　　　　465
　　　　Each in the other's thrall,
　　　　　　　Each all in all, ah, woe is me!

BOTH.　　　Oh, bury, bury – let the grave close o'er
　　　　The days that were – that never will be more!
　　　　Oh, bury, bury love that all condemn,　　　　470
　　　　And let the whirlwind mourn its requiem!

CAS.　　　Dead as the last year's leaves –
　　　　　　　As gathered flowers – ah, woe is me!
　　　　Dead as the garnered sheaves,
　　　　　　　That love of ours – ah, woe is me!　　　475
　　　　Born but to fade and die
　　　　　　　When hope was high,
　　　　Dead and as far away
　　　　　　　As yesterday! – ah, woe is me!

BOTH.　　　Oh, bury, bury – let the grave close o'er, etc.　　480

(*Re-enter from the Ducal Palace the* DUKE *and* DUCHESS, *followed by* DON ALHAMBRA DEL BOLERO, *the Grand Inquisitor.*)

DUKE. My child, allow me to present to you His Distinction Don Alhambra del Bolero, the Grand Inquisitor of Spain. It was His Distinction who so thoughtfully abstracted your infant husband and brought him to Venice.　485

DON AL. So this is the little lady who is so unexpectedly called upon to assume the functions of Royalty! And a very nice little lady, too!

DUKE. Jimp, isn't she?

DON AL. Distinctly jimp. Allow me! (*Offers his hand. She turns away scornfully.*) Naughty temper!　490

DUKE. You must make some allowance. Her Majesty's head is a little turned by her access of dignity.

DON AL. I could have wished that Her Majesty's access of dignity had turned it in this direction.

DUCH. Unfortunately, if I am not mistaken, there appears to be some　495
little doubt as to His Majesty's whereabouts.

CAS. (*aside*). A doubt as to his whereabouts? Then we may yet be saved!

503–50 *I stole the Prince, and I brought him here*
Gilbert almost certainly took the idea for this song, and indeed the central theme of *The Gondoliers*, from an experience which had befallen him as a child. At the age of two he was taken by his parents on holiday to Naples. One afternoon he was out for a pram ride with his nurse when two Italians came up and told her that they had been sent by 'the Engleesh papa' to bring back 'dis lofly bambino'. The credulous nurse handed over the baby and a few hours later Gilbert's father received a ransom demand for £25. Happily for posterity, William Gilbert senior considered that his son was worth that amount and so redeemed him from the kidnappers.

507 *timoneer*: From the French word *timonier*, meaning helmsman or steersman.

508 *bratling*: A diminutive form of 'brat', a slightly contemptuous term for a child.

515 *But owing, I'm much disposed to fear*: This verse, and the next one, beginning 'Time sped', were transposed in early editions of the libretto.

530 *bier*: The movable stand on which a corpse is placed before burial and on which it is carried to the grave.

Don Al. A doubt? Oh dear, no – no doubt at all! He is here, in
Venice, plying the modest but picturesque calling of a gondolier. I can give
you his address – I see him every day! In the entire annals of our history   500
there is absolutely no circumstance so entirely free from all manner of doubt
of any kind whatever! Listen, and I'll tell you all about it.

SONG – Don Alhambra (*with* Duke, Duchess,
Casilda, *and* Luiz).

I stole the Prince, and I brought him here,
   And left him gaily prattling
With a highly respectable gondolier,   505
Who promised the Royal babe to rear,
And teach him the trade of a timoneer
   With his own beloved bratling.

      Both of the babes were strong and stout,
         And, considering all things, clever.   510
      Of that there is no manner of doubt –
      No probable, possible shadow of doubt –
         No possible doubt whatever.

All.   No possible doubt whatever.

But owing, I'm much disposed to fear,   515
   To his terrible taste for tippling,
That highly respectable gondolier
Could never declare with a mind sincere
Which of the two was his offspring dear,
   And which the Royal stripling!   520

      Which was which he could never make out
         Despite his best endeavour.
      Of *that* there is no manner of doubt –
      No probable, possible shadow of doubt –
         No possible doubt whatever.   525

All.   No possible doubt whatever.

Time sped, and when at the end of a year
   I sought that infant cherished,
That highly respectable gondolier
Was lying a corpse on his humble bier –   530
I dropped a Grand Inquisitor's tear –
   That gondolier had perished.

533 *combined with gout*: Little did Gilbert realize when he wrote this that he himself was to become crippled with gout within a few years. In a letter to Richard D'Oyly Carte in 1893 he wrote 'I have been laid up with a most violent attack of gout in both feet and in the right hand, so I have not been able to do anything but swear for the last eighteen days.'

559 *a Grand Inquisitor is always up to date*: This line was originally written: 'A Grand Inquisitor is a well informed personage'.

562 *Cordova*: A town on the Guadalquivir river in southern Spain. It is more usually spelt Cordoba.

A taste for drink, combined with gout,
   Had doubled him up for ever.
Of *that* there is no manner of doubt –   535
No probable, possible shadow of doubt –
   No possible doubt whatever.

ALL.   No possible doubt whatever.

The children followed his old career –
   (This statement can't be parried)   540
Of a highly respectable gondolier:
Well, one of the two (who will soon be here) –
But *which* of the two is not quite clear –
   Is the Royal Prince you married!

Search in and out and round about,   545
   And you'll discover never
A tale so free from every doubt –
All probable, possible shadow of doubt –
All possible doubt whatever!

ALL.   A tale so free from every doubt, etc.   550

CAS. Then do you mean to say that I am married to one of two gondoliers, but it is impossible to say which?

DON AL. Without any doubt of any kind whatever. But be reassured: the nurse to whom your husband was entrusted is the mother of the musical young man who is such a past-master of that delicately modulated   555 instrument (*indicating the drum*). She can, no doubt, establish the King's identity beyond all question.

LUIZ. Heavens, how did he know that?

DON AL. My young friend, a Grand Inquisitor is always up to date. (*To* CAS.) His mother is at present the wife of a highly respectable and old-   560 established brigand, who carries on an extensive practice in the mountains around Cordova. Accompanied by two of my emissaries, he will set off at once for his mother's address. She will return with them, and if she finds any difficulty in making up her mind, the persuasive influence of the torture chamber will jog her memory.   565

RECITATIVE – CASILDA *and* DON ALHAMBRA.

CAS.   But, bless my heart, consider my position!
         I am the wife of one, that's very clear;
      But who can tell, except by intuition,
         Which is the Prince, and which the Gondolier?

DON AL. Submit to Fate without unseemly wrangle: 570

572 *Life is one closely complicated tangle*: This line was the cue for a splendid bit of business
introduced by Anthony Besch in his 1968 D'Oyly Carte production. Shortly after the
entrance of the Duke and Duchess and Don Alhambra at line 481, a steaming bowl of
spaghetti was brought on to the stage. This the ducal party proceeded to devour while
Don Alhambra sang 'I stole the Prince'. The spaghetti became more and more tangled
up, and at the line 'Life is one closely complicated tangle' the Duke lifted the whole
glutinous and soggy mess with his fork and spoon.

Peter Riley, successively stage manager, stage director, technical director, company
manager and general manager of D'Oyly Carte, told me that he has spent many an
anxious time at the stage door waiting for that evening's consignment of spaghetti to
arrive. Normally, wherever the company was playing, there was an Italian restaurant
nearby. In the wilds of Wimbledon, however, there was apparently a dearth of such
establishments, and during a season there procuring the precious pasta involved a
five-mile taxi journey. 'We had to put it in a thermos flask,' Peter Riley recalls, 'and I
don't think it tasted very good by the time it reached the stage. One night it didn't
arrive at all so I sent a ham sandwich on instead. Dame Bridget D'Oyly Carte
suggested that it would be much easier to use false spaghetti made out of white
knitting wool but it wouldn't have been as realistic. Eventually we took to heating up
tins on a hot plate back-stage.'

598 *goes off in gondola*: At one rehearsal Gilbert, precise and meticulous as ever, told the
stage-hands: 'Please get the gondola off as quickly as can reasonably be expected, not
as fast as a steam launch, but as quickly as a normally active gondola.'

601–8 *Bridegroom and bride*
As sung in early performances, this chorus had a second verse and a different ending
to the first verse. After the second 'Bridegroom and bride!' (line 605), this original
version continued:

> Hail it with merriment;
> It's an experiment
> Frequently tried.

Such complications frequently occur –
Life is one closely complicated tangle:
Death is the only true unraveller!

QUINTET – Duke, Duchess, Casilda, Luiz,
and Grand Inquisitor.

ALL.	Try we life-long, we can never	
	Straighten out life's tangled skein,	575
	Why should we, in vain endeavour,	
	Guess and guess and guess again?	
LUIZ.	Life's a pudding full of plums,	
DUCH.	Care's a canker that benumbs.	
ALL.	Life's a pudding full of plums,	580
	Care's a canker that benumbs.	
	Wherefore waste our elocution	
	On impossible solution?	
	Life's a pleasant institution,	
	Let us take it as it comes!	585

Set aside the dull enigma,
    We shall guess it all too soon;
Failure brings no kind of stigma –
    Dance we to another tune!
        String the lyre and fill the cup,   590
        Lest on sorrow we should sup.
        String the lyre and fill the cup,
        Lest on sorrow we should sup.
Hop and skip to Fancy's fiddle,
Hands across and down the middle –   595
Life's perhaps the only riddle
    That we shrink from giving up!

(*Exeunt all into Ducal Palace except* LUIZ, *who goes off in gondola.*)

(*Enter Gondoliers and Contadine, followed by* MARCO,
    GIANETTA, GIUSEPPE, *and* TESSA.)   600

CHORUS.

Bridegroom and bride!
    Knot that's insoluble,
    Voices all voluble
Hail it with pride.
Bridegroom and bride!   605
    We in sincerity

> Bridegroom and bride!
>   Bridegrooms all joyfully,
>   Brides, rather coyfully,
> Stand at their side.
> Bridegroom and bride!
>   We in sincerity
>   Wish you prosperity,
> Bridegroom and bride!

Gilbert was upbraided by the *Globe* for using the word 'coyfully'. He replied:

> Your critic takes exception to it because one cannot be full of 'coy'. That is quite true; but
> is it a conclusive argument against the use of the word? We use the word 'manfully',
> though one cannot be full of 'man'. We use the word 'bashfully', though one cannot – at
> least I don't think one can – be full of 'bash'.

609–40 *When a merry maiden marries*
Several critics detected a strong resemblance between the opening bars of this song
and the chorus 'Just a song at twilight' from the popular Victorian parlour ballad
composed by James Molloy, 'Love's Old Sweet Song'. When this was put to him,
Sullivan responded 'I do not happen to have heard the song, but even if I had, you
must remember that Molloy and I had only seven notes on which to work between us'.

643 *And now our lives. . .:* The passage of dialogue which begins here and continues until
line 650 was one of several cut in performance by the D'Oyly Carte Opera Company
in recent years in an effort to speed up the long First Act of *The Gondoliers*. Other
passages generally cut were the cornet-à-piston exchange already mentioned in the
note to line 278, and lines 320-22, 330-35, 440-45, 449-50, and 719-23 inclusive.

Wish you prosperity,
Bridegroom and bride!

SONG – TESSA.

TESS.   When a merry maiden marries,
Sorrow goes and pleasure tarries;   610
Every sound becomes a song,
All is right, and nothing's wrong!
From to-day and ever after
Let our tears be tears of laughter.
Every sigh that finds a vent   615
Be a sigh of sweet content!
When you marry, merry maiden,
Then the air with love is laden;
Every flower is a rose,
Every goose becomes a swan,   620
Every kind of trouble goes
Where the last year's snows have gone!

CHORUS.   Sunlight takes the place of shade
When you marry, merry maid!

TESS.   When a merry maiden marries,   625
Sorrow goes and pleasure tarries;
Every sound becomes a song,
All is right, and nothing's wrong.
Gnawing Care and aching Sorrow,
Get ye gone until to-morrow;   630
Jealousies in grim array,
Ye are things of yesterday!
When you marry, merry maiden,
Then the air with joy is laden;
All the corners of the earth   635
Ring with music sweetly played,
Worry is melodious mirth,
Grief is joy in masquerade;

CHORUS.   Sullen night is laughing day –
All the year is merry May!   640

(*At the end of the song,* DON ALHAMBRA *enters at back. The Gondoliers and
Contadine shrink from him, and gradually go off, much alarmed.*)

GIU. And now our lives are going to begin in real earnest! What's a
bachelor? A mere nothing – he's a chrysalis. He can't be said to live – he exists.

MAR. What a delightful institution marriage is! Why have we wasted all   645
this time? Why didn't we marry ten years ago?

653 *Ceremony of some sort going on*: Gilbert originally wrote this line as 'Festivities of some sort going on?' It seems to have been altered at an early revival.

663 *Remarkably fine children*: This line was added in 1907.

680 *who led the last revolution*: There were not, as far as I can discover, any revolutions in Venice in the first half of the eighteenth century, although there was one in 1848, when Daniele Manin led a revolt against Austrian rule and proclaimed the re-establishment of the Venetian Republic. It was short-lived, and in 1849 the Austrians regained control of the city.

TESS. Because you couldn't find anybody nice enough.

GIA. Because you were waiting for *us*.

MAR. I suppose that *was* the reason. We were waiting for you without knowing it. (DON ALHAMBRA *comes forward*.) Hallo! 650

DON AL. Good morning.

GIU. If this gentleman is an undertaker, it's a bad omen.

DON AL. Ceremony of some sort going on?

GIU. (*aside*). He *is* an undertaker! (*Aloud*.) No – a little unimportant family gathering. Nothing in *your* line. 655

DON AL. Somebody's birthday, I suppose?

GIA. Yes, mine!

TESS. And mine!

MAR. And mine!

GIU. And mine! 660

DON AL. Curious coincidence! And how old may you all be?

TESS. It's a rude question – but about ten minutes.

DON AL. Remarkably fine children! But surely you are jesting?

TESS. In other words, we were married about ten minutes since.

DON AL. Married! You don't mean to say you are married? 665

MAR. Oh yes, we are married.

DON AL. What, both of you?

ALL. All four of us.

DON AL. (*aside*). Bless my heart, how extremely awkward!

GIA. You don't mind, I suppose? 670

TESS. You were not thinking of either of us for yourself, I presume? Oh, Giuseppe, look at him – he was. He's heart-broken!

DON AL. No, no, I wasn't! I wasn't!

GIU. Now, my man (*slapping him on the back*), we don't want anything in your line to-day, and if your curiosity's satisfied – you can 675 go!

DON AL. You mustn't call me your man. It's a liberty. I don't think you know who I am.

GIU. Not we, indeed! We are jolly gondoliers, the sons of Baptisto Palmieri, who led the last revolution. Republicans, heart and soul, we hold 680 all men to be equal. As we abhor oppression, we abhor kings: as we detest vain-glory, we detest rank: as we despise effeminacy, we despise wealth. We are Venetian gondoliers - your equals in everything except our calling, and in that at once your masters and your servants.

DON AL. Bless my heart, how unfortunate! One of you may be 685 Baptisto's son, for anything I know to the contrary; but the other is no less a personage than the only son of the late King of Barataria.

ALL. What!

DON AL. And I trust - I *trust* it was that one who slapped me on the shoulder and called me his man! 690

707 *the Grand Canal*: The widest and most important of Venice's 180 canals, it runs for $2\frac{1}{2}$ miles bisecting the island on which the city is built.

709 *the Rialto*: The bridge across the Grand Canal mid-way between the railway station and the *Dogana*, or customs house, on the edge of the lagoon. Until 1854 the Rialto was the sole connecting link between the east and west quarters of Venice. The present bridge is the sixth on the site and dates from 1592. Each of its ends rests on 6000 wooden piles. With its picturesque arcades of shops it was a favourite meeting place for Venetians, as Shakespeare recognized when he made Shylock ask in Act I of *The Merchant of Venice*: 'What news on the Rialto?'

718 *Oh! they've often been convicted*: This line was officially included in the libretto at the time of the 1907 revival, although it was almost certainly spoken in earlier performances as an ad-lib gag. It was probably originally coined by Rutland Barrington, who created the role of Giuseppe.

722 *Oh, he's a fine fellow*: In the version of the libretto which she apparently prepared for performance in the United States (see the note to line 246), Helen D'Oyly Carte deleted this and the next line and substituted the following:

> MAR. I feel more than half convinced already.
> GIA. *and* TESS. So do we.

733 *And we may take our friends with us*: In the same American version this passage was altered to:

> MAR. And we may take all our relatives and friends with us and give them lucrative appointments even if they know nothing of the duties they are to perform?
> DON AL. Undoubtedly. That is the usual course of procedure – in Barataria.
> MAR. I'm utterly convinced.

GIU. One of us a king!

MAR. Not brothers!

TESS. The King of Barataria!   *Together*

GIA. Well, who'd have thought it!

MAR. But which is it?   695

DON AL. What does it matter? As you are both Republicans, and hold kings in detestation, of course you'll abdicate at once. Good morning! (*Going.*)

GIA. *and* TESS. Oh, don't do that! (MARCO *and* GIUSEPPE *stop him.*)

GIU. Well, as to that, of course there are kings and kings. When I say that I detest kings, I mean I detest *bad* kings.   700

DON AL. I see. It's a delicate distinction.

GIU. Quite so. Now I can conceive a kind of king – an ideal king – the creature of my fancy, you know – who would be absolutely unobjectionable. A king, for instance, who would abolish taxes and make everything cheap, except gondolas –   705

MAR. And give a great many free entertainments to the gondoliers —

GIU. And let off fireworks on the Grand Canal, and engage all the gondolas for the occasion —

MAR. And scramble money on the Rialto among the gondoliers.

GIU. Such a king would be a blessing to his people, and if I were a king, that is the sort of king I would be.   710

MAR. And so would I!

DON AL. Come, I'm glad to find your objections are not insuperable.

MAR. *and* GIU. Oh, they're not insuperable.

GIA. *and* TESS. No, they're not insuperable.   715

GIU. Besides, we are open to conviction. •

GIA. Yes; they are open to conviction.

TESS. Oh! they've often been convicted.

GIU. Our views may have been hastily formed on insufficient grounds. They may be crude, ill-digested, erroneous. I've a very poor opinion of the politician who is not open to conviction.   720

TESS. (*to* GIA.). Oh, he's a fine fellow!

GIA. Yes, that's the sort of politician for *my* money!

DON AL. Then we'll consider it settled. Now, as the country is in a state of insurrection, it is absolutely necessary that you should assume the reins of Government at once; and, until it is ascertained which of you is to be king, I have arranged that you will reign jointly, so that no question can arise hereafter as to the validity of any of your acts.   725

MAR. As one individual?

DON AL. As one individual.   730

GIU. (*linking himself with* MARCO). Like this?

DON AL. Something like that.

MAR. And we may take our friends with us, and give them places about the Court?

735 *That's always done*: This phrase did not appear in the original libretto. Its first formal appearance was in 1914, but I suspect it had been said unofficially before that.

740–43 *Stop, stop. . .* : The exchange about the admission of ladies to Barataria has been altered several times. As performed on the opening night it ran as follows:

> DON AL. Stop, stop – that won't do at all – we can't have any ladies. (*Aside.*) What will Her Majesty say!
> ALL. What!
> DON AL. Not at present. Afterwards, perhaps. We'll see.

In 1897 Gilbert changed Don Alhambra's second remark (line 742) to 'Not admitted. We must keep the place respectable at first'. This, in turn, was later changed to 'We must keep the island respectable' and finally to its present version.

749–84 *Kind sir, you cannot have the heart*
In a letter sent to Sullivan on 9 November 1889, Gilbert wrote:

> If I remember right, you expressed some doubt as to whether Gianetta's song, 'Kind sir, you cannot have the heart,' was not too long for the situation, and said something about cutting it down to one verse. This was some time ago, and perhaps you are no longer of that opinion. I have come across a song which I wrote for the same situation, and which perhaps presents better opportunities for acting than the other. Anyhow, I enclose it for your information. If you don't like it, tear it up. Or if you want the original song shortened, could it be done by taking the second half of the first verse and the first half of the second verse? Don't trouble to answer this.

In the event, Sullivan obviously decided that the song was not too long and it was preserved intact.

765 *Ah me, you men*: At this point in D'Oyly Carte performances Gianetta laid her hand on the Don's arm. As she sang the same refrain again at the end of the second verse, he was all ready to cover her hand with his own, but this time she laid it across her own heart.

Don Al. Undoubtedly. That's always done! 735
Mar. I'm convinced!
Giu. So am I!
Tess. Then the sooner we're off the better.
Gia. We'll just run home and pack up a few things (*going*) —
Don Al. Stop, stop – that won't do at all – ladies are not admitted. 740
All. What!
Don Al. Not admitted. Not at present. Afterwards, perhaps. We'll see.

Giu. Why, you don't mean to say you are going to separate us from our wives! 745
Don Al. (*aside*). This is very awkward! (*Aloud.*) Only for a time – a few months. After all, what is a few months?
Tess. But we've only been married half an hour! (*Weeps.*)

FINALE, ACT I.

SONG – Gianetta.

Kind sir, you cannot have the heart
        Our lives to part 750
    From those to whom an hour ago
        We were united!
Before our flowing hopes you stem,
        Ah, look at them,
    And pause before you deal this blow, 755
        All uninvited!
You men can never understand
        That heart and hand
    Cannot be separated when
        We go a-yearning; 760
You see, you've only women's eyes
        To idolize
    And only women's hearts, poor men,
        To set *you* burning!
Ah me, you men will never understand 765
That woman's heart is one with woman's hand!

Some kind of charm you seem to find
        In womankind –
    Some source of unexplained delight
        (Unless you're jesting), 770
But what attracts you, I confess,
        I cannot guess,

800-849 *Then one of us will be a Queen*

This proved to be one of the most popular numbers with the audience during the initial run of *The Gondoliers*. The *Daily News* reported that after its conclusion on the first night 'the excited house encored, the pit emphatically demanding "All of it!", a request laughingly granted by Sir Arthur Sullivan.' The same paper went on to note that it was also whistled from the gallery during the inordinately long interval while the complicated scenery for Act II was being assembled on stage.

The song also greatly appealed to Queen Victoria. During a Royal Command performance of *The Gondoliers* at Windsor Castle on 6 March 1891 she was observed delightedly beating time to its catchy rhythm.

This performance was the first entertainment to be given at Windsor Castle since the death of Prince Albert in 1861. Neither Gilbert nor Sullivan was present for the occasion, and the former was somewhat annoyed to discover later that his name had been left off the posters by mistake. Victoria, however, thoroughly enjoyed the piece and made the following entry in her diary, which shows the admiration of a real 'right-down regular Royal Queen' for the work of two of her most talented subjects:

To me a woman's face is quite
Uninteresting!
If from my sister I were torn,   775
It could be borne –
I should, no doubt, be horrified,
But I could bear it; –
But Marco's quite another thing –
He is my King,   780
He has my heart and none beside
Shall ever share it!
Ah me, you men will never understand
That woman's heart is one with woman's hand!

RECITATIVE – Don Alhambra.

Do not give way to this uncalled-for grief,   785
Your separation will be very brief.
To ascertain which is the King
And which the other,
To Barataria's Court I'll bring
His foster-mother;   790
Her former nurseling to declare
She'll be delighted.
That settled, let each happy pair
Be reunited.

Mar., Giu.,   Viva! His argument is strong!   795
Gia., Tess.   Viva! We'll not be parted long!
               Viva! It will be settled soon!
               Viva! Then comes our honeymoon!

(*Exit* Don Alhambra.)

QUARTET – Marco, Giuseppe, Gianetta, Tessa.

Gia.   Then one of us will be a Queen,   800
               And sit on a golden throne,
               With a crown instead
               Of a hat on her head,
               And diamonds all her own!
With a beautiful robe of gold and green,   805
I've always understood;
I wonder whether
She'd wear a feather?
I rather think she should!

At nine we went over to the Waterloo Gallery where all the seats were filled by the Ladies and Gentlemen of the Household. All the Princes and Princesses sat with me in the front row. *The Gondoliers* the last of Sir A. Sullivan's comic operas, was performed by D'Oyly Carte's company of the Savoy Theatre, and lasted about two hours and a half. The music, which I know and am very fond of, is quite charming throughout and was well acted and sung. The opening scene with the contadini singing and binding flowers, with a lovely view of Venice and the deep blue sea and sky, was really extraordinarily pretty. The dancing which often comes in was very graceful and pretty.

The dialogue is written by Gilbert and very amusing. The Grand Inquisitor (Mr Denny) was excellent and most absurd, also Mr Rutland Barrington, who is very fat and one of the gondolieri. Miss Jessie Bond is a clever little actress and sings nicely. The dresses are very gay and smart and the whole ensemble brilliant and well put on the stage. In the last scene there were eighty people on the stage, which for an extemporized one was wonderful. I really enjoyed the performance very much. Afterwards I spoke to Mr D'Oyly Carte and complimented him. We then went to the Drawing-room, into which all the company came, but I only stayed a short while. Everybody was much pleased.

The Gondoliers found favour with the Royal Family in general. The Prince of Wales, later to become King Edward VII, saw the opera at least four times. Would it have been quite so popular in royal circles, I wonder, if Gilbert and Sullivan had kept in a 'Baratarian National Anthem' which was cut out at an early stage of their work? In it the subjects of Barataria told their monarch exactly what to do. The first line was 'As long as you are good as gold', and subsequent lines enjoined the king to:

> Knuckle down with humble mien
> And keep your crown and sceptre clean.

831 *She'll bear away the bell*: To bear away the bell is to carry off the prize. It probably derives from the old custom of presenting a little gold or silver bell as a prize to the winners of horse races.

ALL.　　　　　Oh, 'tis a glorious thing, I ween,　　　　　810
　　　　　　　To be a regular Royal Queen!
　　　　　　　No half-and-half affair, I mean,
　　　　　　　But a right-down regular Royal Queen!

MAR.　　　　　She'll drive about in a carriage and pair,
　　　　　　　　With the King on her left-hand side,　　　815
　　　　　　　　　And a milk-white horse,
　　　　　　　　　　As a matter of course,
　　　　　　　　Whenever she wants to ride!
　　　　　　　With beautiful silver shoes to wear
　　　　　　　　Upon her dainty feet;　　　　　　　820
　　　　　　　　　With endless stocks
　　　　　　　　　Of beautiful frocks
　　　　　　　And as much as she wants to eat!

ALL.　　　　　　Oh, 'tis a glorious thing, I ween, etc.

TESS.　　　　　Whenever she condescends to walk,　　　825
　　　　　　　　Be sure she'll shine at that,
　　　　　　　　　With her haughty stare
　　　　　　　　　And her nose in the air,
　　　　　　　　Like a well-born aristocrat!
　　　　　　　At elegant high society talk
　　　　　　　　She'll bear away the bell,　　　　　830
　　　　　　　　　With her 'How de do?'
　　　　　　　　　And her 'How are you?'
　　　　　　　And 'I trust I see you well!'

ALL.　　　　　　Oh, 'tis a glorious thing, I ween, etc.　　835

GIU.　　　　　And noble lords will scrape and bow,
　　　　　　　　And double themselves in two,
　　　　　　　　　And open their eyes
　　　　　　　　　In blank surprise
　　　　　　　　At whatever she likes to do.
　　　　　　　And everybody will roundly vow　　　　840
　　　　　　　　She's fair as flowers in May,
　　　　　　　　　And say, 'How clever!'
　　　　　　　　　At whatsoever
　　　　　　　　She condescends to say!　　　　　845

852 *ebullition*: A sudden outburst or state of agitation.

870 *And all shall equal be*: This line had a particular message for the members of the D'Oyly Carte Opera Company, as Jessie Bond, who created the role of Tessa, noted many years later in an article, 'Memories of an Old Savoyard', which is quoted in Leslie Baily's *The Gilbert and Sullivan Book*. In the summer of 1889, she recalled, she was in the midst of an argument with Gilbert about her salary and her *prima donna* status:

> Gilbert snapped out that he was tired to death of artists who thought that they were responsible for the success of the operas, and that he intended to put a stop to the whole thing. 'We'll have an opera,' he exclaimed, rather angrily, 'in which there will be no principal parts. No character shall stand out more prominently than another.' Surely enough, when *The Gondoliers* was written a little later, we discovered that it contained more than the usual number of big parts. In case we missed the significance of that, he gave the two gondoliers their duet which told that 'all shall equal be'.

871 *peruke*: A variation of the word periwig, meaning a wig.

875 *Coutts*: One of the most exclusive banking houses in Britain, which numbers the Queen among its customers. It had its origins in the late seventeenth century in a goldsmith's and money-lender's business in the Strand, where Coutts now has its modern headquarters. In the eighteenth century the firm was taken over and greatly developed by two Scottish brothers, Thomas and James Coutts, who gave their name to the business.

ALL.　　　　Oh, 'tis a glorious thing, I ween,
　　　　　　To be a regular Royal Queen!
　　　　　　No half-and-half affair, I mean,
　　　　　　But a right-down regular Royal Queen!

　　　　　　(*Enter Chorus of Gondoliers and Contadine.*)　　　　850

CHORUS.

Now, pray, what is the cause of this remarkable hilarity?
This sudden ebullition of unmitigated jollity?
Has anybody blessed you with a sample of his charity?
Or have you been adopted by a gentleman of quality?

MAR. *and* GIU.　　Replying, we sing　　　　　　　　　855
　　　　　　　　As one individual,
　　　　　　As I find I'm a king,
　　　　　　　　To my kingdom I bid you all.
　　　　　　I'm aware you object
　　　　　　　　To pavilions and palaces,　　　　　860
　　　　　　But you'll find I respect
　　　　　　　　Your Republican fallacies.

CHORUS.　　As they know we object
　　　　　　　　To pavilions and palaces,
　　　　　　How can they respect　　　　　　　865
　　　　　　　　Our Republican fallacies?

MARCO *and* GIUSEPPE.

MAR.　　　For every one who feels inclined,
　　　　　　Some post we undertake to find
　　　　　　Congenial with his frame of mind –
　　　　　　　　And all shall equal be.　　　　　870

GIU.　　　The Chancellor in his peruke –
　　　　　　The Earl, the Marquis, and the Dook,
　　　　　　The Groom, the Butler, and the Cook –
　　　　　　　　They all shall equal be.

MAR.　　　The Aristocrat who banks with Coutts –　　875
　　　　　　The Aristocrat who hunts and shoots –
　　　　　　The Aristocrat who cleans our boots –
　　　　　　　　They all shall equal be!

888 *Sing high, sing low*: In his *Treasury of Gilbert and Sullivan* Martyn Green says that a conundrum traditionally put to new members of the D'Oyly Carte Company was 'Who are the two Chinese characters in *The Gondoliers*?' The answer, of course, is Sing-Hi and Sing-Lo.

907 *Then hail! O King*: In early libretti, this chorus was longer. After the line 'But do not bend the knee' it continued:

> It may be thou –
>   Likewise it may be thee –
> So hail! O King,
>   Whichever you may be.

908 *Come, let's away*: In the licence copy this line is printed: 'Then let's away – our island home awaits me –'.

GIU. The Noble Lord who rules the State –
      The Noble Lord who cleans the plate –   880

MAR. The Noble Lord who scrubs the grate –
      They all shall equal be!

GIU. The Lord High Bishop orthodox –
      The Lord High Coachman on the box –

MAR. The Lord High Vagabond in the stocks –   885
      They all shall equal be!

BOTH. For every one, etc.

               Sing high, sing low,
               Wherever they go,
                    They all shall equal be!   890

CHORUS.   Sing high, sing low,
               Wherever they go,
                    They all shall equal be!

      The Earl, the Marquis, and the Dook,
      The Groom, the Butler, and the Cook,   895
      The Aristocrat who banks with Coutts,
      The Aristocrat who cleans the boots,
      The Noble Lord who rules the State,
      The Noble Lord who scrubs the grate,
      The Lord High Bishop orthodox,   900
      The Lord High Vagabond in the stocks –

      For every one, etc.

          Then hail! O King,
               Whichever you may be,
          To you we sing,   905
               But do not bend the knee.
          Then hail! O King.

          MARCO *and* GIUSEPPE (*together*).

   Come, let's away – our island crown awaits me –
      Conflicting feelings rend my soul apart!
   The thought of Royal dignity elates me,   910
      But leaving thee behind me breaks my heart!
                    (*Addressing* GIANETTA *and* TESSA.)

934 *Than forty-five*: Another example of Gilbert's obsession with women in their forties. Readers will recall that in *The Pirates of Penzance* Ruth sings that her love has been accumulating for forty-seven years, and that the same age is given to the lady who figures in the Bab Ballad 'Haunted' (see the note to line 172, page 96). The judge in *Trial by Jury* tells us that the rich attorney said of his daughter:

> She may very well pass for forty-three
> In the dusk, with a light behind her!

GIANETTA *and* TESSA (*together*).

Farewell, my love; on board you must be getting;
  But while upon the sea you gaily roam,
Remember that a heart for thee is fretting –   915
  The tender little heart you've left at home!

GIA.   Now, Marco dear,
                        My wishes hear:
                          While you're away
                      It's understood   920
                      You will be good
                          And not too gay.
                      To every trace
                      Of maiden grace
                          You will be blind,   925
                      And will not glance
                      By any chance
                        On womankind!

                      If you are wise,
                      You'll shut your eyes   930
                        Till we arrive,
                      And not address
                      A lady less
                        Than forty-five.
                      You'll please to frown   935
                      On every gown
                        That you may see;
                      And, O my pet,
                      You won't forget
                        You've married me!   940

And O my darling, O my pet,
Whatever else you may forget,
In yonder isle beyond the sea,
Do not forget you've married me.

TESS.   You'll lay your head   945
                      Upon your bed
                        At set of sun.
                      You will not sing
                      Of anything
                        To any one.   950

974 *Xebeque*: A small, three-masted ship used for carrying merchandise in the Mediterranean.

You'll sit and mope
All day, I hope,
   And shed a tear
Upon the life
Your little wife   955
   Is passing here.

And if so be
You think of me,
   Please tell the moon!
I'll read it all   960
In rays that fall
   On the lagoon:
You'll be so kind
As tell the wind
   How you may be,   965
And send me words
By little birds
   To comfort me!

And O my darling, O my pet,
Whatever else you may forget,   970
In yonder isle beyond the sea,
Do not forget you've married me.

QUARTET.   O my darling, O my pet, etc.

CHORUS (*during which a 'Xebeque' is hauled
          alongside the quay*).   975

Then away { they / we } go to an island fair
   That lies in a Southern sea:
We know not where, and we don't much care,
   Wherever that isle may be.

THE MEN (*hauling on boat*).   One, two, three,   980
                     Haul!
                One, two, three,
                     Haul!
                One, two, three,
                     Haul!   985
                With a will!

993–1000 *Away we go*
  Both the licence copy and the first American edition of the libretto give Marco another
  four lines in this song:

        And the birds all twitter
         Through the winter weather,
        Like a spinnet and a zither
         That are played together.

  The licence copy then continues:

ALL.   The pull, yeo ho! and again, yeo ho! (*hoisting sail*)
           And again yeo ho! with a will!
           When the breezes are a-blowing,
           Then our ship will be a-going,
           When they don't we shall all stand still!
           And away we go to the island fair,
           That lies in a southern sea,

           $\left.\begin{matrix} \text{We} \\ \text{They} \end{matrix}\right\}$ know not where, and $\left\{\begin{matrix} \text{we} \\ \text{they} \end{matrix}\right.$ don't much care,

           Wherever that isle may be.

          END OF ACT I

The above version of the final chorus was also used at the first night and early
performances at the Savoy Theatre, where it followed the present shortened version
of Marco's solo.

ALL.   When the breezes are blowing
          The ship will be going,
          When they don't $\left\{\begin{array}{l}\text{we shall}\\\text{they will}\end{array}\right\}$ all stand still!
          Then away $\left\{\begin{array}{l}\text{they}\\\text{we}\end{array}\right\}$ go to an island fair,   990
          We know not where, and we don't much care,
          Wherever that isle may be.

                    SOLO – MARCO.

          Away we go
            To a balmy isle,
          Where the roses blow   995
            All the winter while.

ALL (*hoisting sail*).   Then away $\left\{\begin{array}{l}\text{we}\\\text{they}\end{array}\right\}$ go to an island fair
          That lies in a Southern sea:
          Then away $\left\{\begin{array}{l}\text{we}\\\text{they}\end{array}\right\}$ go to an island fair,
          Then away, then away, then away!   1000

(*The men embark on the 'Xebeque'.* MARCO *and* GIUSEPPE *embracing* GIANETTA *and* TESSA. *The girls wave a farewell to the men as the curtain falls.*)

                    END OF ACT I

6 *cup and ball*: A game played with a ball which is attached by string to a rod which has a cup at one end of it. The object is to toss the ball and catch it in the cup.
morra: A favourite Italian game in which two people face each other and alternately raise their hands quickly. The object is to guess how many fingers are being held up. The winner is the first player to guess correctly nine times.

15–22 *Two kings, of undue pride bereft*
This duet is not included in the licence copy sent to the Lord Chamberlain. Instead it contains at this point a solo for Pietro, one of the gondoliers brought over by Marco and Giuseppe to Barataria, who has been appointed a judge by the island's new rulers. The song was adapted before the opening night into the duet now sung by Marco and Giuseppe. Here it is:

PIETRO.
Two monarchs free from all ambition,
Who do not presume on their condition,
 But do their very best to please
 And justify their bread and cheese.
A people dignified and polished,
Who class distinctions have abolished,
 And, one and all, with zeal combine
 To make their monarchs toe the line.
When joined in such harmonious tether,
Both king and people pull together.
 No wonder peace and plenty smile
 Upon this highly-favoured isle.

ALL.
When joined in such harmonious tether, etc.

ACT II

SCENE. – *Pavilion in the Court of Barataria.* MARCO *and* GIUSEPPE, *magnificently dressed, are seated on two thrones, occupied in cleaning the crown and the sceptre. The Gondoliers are discovered, dressed, some as courtiers, officers of rank, etc., and others as private soldiers and servants of various degrees. All are enjoying themselves without reference to social distinctions – some playing cards, others* 5 *throwing dice, some reading, others playing cup and ball, 'morra', etc.*

CHORUS OF MEN *with* MARCO *and* GIUSEPPE.

Of happiness the very pith
    In Barataria you may see:
A monarchy that's tempered with
    Republican Equality. 10
This form of government we find
The beau-ideal of its kind –
A despotism strict, combined
    With absolute equality!

MARCO *and* GIUSEPPE.

Two kings, of undue pride bereft, 15
    Who act in perfect unity,
Whom you can order right and left
    With absolute impunity.
Who put their subjects at their ease
By doing all they can to please! 20
And thus, to earn their bread-and-cheese,
    Seize every opportunity.

CHORUS.   Of happiness the very pith, etc.

MAR. Gentlemen, we are much obliged to you for your expressions of satisfaction and good feeling – I say, we are much obliged to you for your 25 expressions of satisfaction and good feeling.

48 *We want our tea*: This was one of several gags introduced by Rutland Barrington into early performances. Gilbert specifically approved it, and the line was included in the libretto for the 1907 revival.

There is an amusing story, recounted in Leslie Baily's *The Gilbert and Sullivan Book*, about Richard D'Oyly Carte's explanation of the gags in *The Gondoliers* to Queen Victoria after the Royal Command performance at Windsor in March 1891. It comes from the magazine *The Era*:

> Her Majesty, who followed her copy of Mr Gilbert's libretto closely, observed that certain additions were made to the text by the leading performers. Mr Carte was summoned to the elbow of Royalty and the Queen graciously inquired of him the meaning of these interpolations which she had noticed.
>
> 'These, your Majesty,' said Mr Carte, 'are what we call gags.'
>
> 'Gags?' replied the Queen, 'I thought gags were things that were put by authority into people's mouths.'
>
> 'These gags, your Majesty,' answered the manager, bowing profoundly, 'are things that people put into their own mouths without authority.'
>
> The Queen smiled benignly and seemed perfectly satisfied with the ready reply.

61–124 *Rising early in the morning*
Giuseppe's famous catalogue of the duties of a working monarch is said to have greatly amused Queen Victoria. Gilbert's original version of the song, contained in the licence edition, is worth quoting in full although on the whole I think the revised version now sung is an improvement. It will be noted that it has a slightly different metre. The first six lines are the same in both cases. The first version then proceeds:

> First we polish off some batches
> Of political despatches,
> > Give the usual assent
> > To some Acts of Parliament.
> If the business isn't heavy
> We may hold a Royal *levée*,
> > Or review the household troops –
> > Shalloo humps! and shalloo hoops!

ALL. We heard you.

MAR. We are delighted, at any time, to fall in with sentiments so charmingly expressed.

ALL. That's all right.

GIU. At the same time there is just one little grievance that we should like to ventilate.

ALL (*angrily*). What?

GIU. Don't be alarmed – it's not serious. It is arranged that, until it is decided which of us two is the actual King, we are to act as one person.

GIORGIO. Exactly.

GIU. Now, although we act as *one* person, we are, in point of fact, *two* persons.

ANNIBALE. Ah, I don't think we can go into that. It is a legal fiction, and legal fictions are solemn things. Situated as we are, we can't recognize two independent responsibilities.

GIU. No; but you can recognize two independent appetites. It's all very well to say we act as one person, but when you supply us with only one ration between us, I should describe it as a legal fiction carried a little too far.

ANNI. It's rather a nice point. I don't like to express an opinion off-hand. Suppose we reserve it for argument before the full Court?

MAR. Yes, but what are we to do in the meantime?

MAR. *and* GIU. We want our tea.

ANNI. I think we may make an interim order for double rations on their Majesties entering into the usual undertaking to indemnify in the event of an adverse decision?

GIOR. That, I think, will meet the case. But you must work hard – stick to it – nothing like work.

GIU. Oh, certainly. We quite understand that a man who holds the magnificent position of King should do something to justify it. We are called 'Your Majesty', we are allowed to buy ourselves magnificent clothes, our subjects frequently nod to us in the streets, the sentries always return our salutes, and we enjoy the inestimable privilege of heading the subscription lists to all the principal charities. In return for these advantages the least we can do is to make ourselves useful about the Palace.

SONG – GIUSEPPE *with* CHORUS.

Rising early in the morning,
    We proceed to light the fire,
Then our Majesty adorning
    In its workaday attire,
        We embark without delay
        On the duties of the day.

On returning, *inter alia*,
We plate-powder the regalia,
    (With a special rubbing down
    For the sceptre and the crown.)
Then in view of cravings inner,
We go down and order dinner,
Do some labour literary
For our private secretary,
Spend an hour in titivating
All our gentlemen-in-waiting.
Then, if nothing up is cropping,
We may do a little shopping,
Buy some fruit and vegetables,
Or be useful in·the stables.
After that we generally
Go and dress our private *valet*,
    Or have a *tête-à-tête*
    With the presentation plate,
Or we run on little errands for the Ministers of State.

After luncheon (making merry
On a bun and glass of sherry)
    If we've nothing in particular to do,
    We create a peer or two –
Make a Royal Proclamation,
Or receive a Deputation –
    Toddle off, in semi-state,
    To a function or a *fête*.
After that, we take our orders
From the keepers and the warders.
    We prepare their tea and toast,
    Take their letters to the post;
Then we go and stand as sentry
At the Palace (private entry),
While the warrior on duty
Goes in search of beer and beauty.
He relieves us if he's able
Just in time to lay the table,
Hand the beef and the potaters
(We are admirable waiters).
After dinner, in a manner,
We perform on the pianner
(All our little skill invoking),
While the gentlemen are smoking.
    If objection there is none,
    We may go to bed at one,
With the gratifying feeling that our duty has been done!

ALL.   After dinner, in a manner, etc.

103 *the Garter or the Thistle or the Bath*: Three orders of knighthood in Great Britain. The Most Noble Order of the Garter is the highest. It was instituted by Edward III in *c.* 1348. Legend has it that it originated when the Countess of Salisbury had accidentally lost her garter at a court ball. It was picked up by the king, who, noticing the looks of the spectators, rebuked them by binding the blue band around his own knee, saying as he did so '*Honi soit qui mal y pense*' ('Evil be to him who evil thinks').

First, we polish off some batches
Of political despatches,
    And foreign politicians circumvent;
Then, if business isn't heavy,   70
We may hold a Royal *levée*,
    Or ratify some Acts of Parliament.
Then we probably review the household troops –
With the usual 'Shalloo humps!' and 'Shalloo hoops!'
Or receive with ceremonial and state   75
An interesting Eastern potentate.
    After that we generally
    Go and dress our private *valet* –
(It's a rather nervous duty – he's a touchy little man) –
    Write some letters literary   80
    For our private secretary –
He is shaky in his spelling, so we help him if we can.
    Then, in view of cravings inner,
    We go down and order dinner;
Then we polish the Regalia and the Coronation Plate –   85
    Spend an hour in titivating
    All our Gentlemen-in-Waiting;
Or we run on little errands for the Ministers of State.

    Oh, philosophers may sing
    Of the troubles of a King;   90
Yet the duties are delightful, and the privileges great;
    But the privilege and pleasure
    That we treasure beyond measure
Is to run on little errands for the Ministers of State.

CHORUS. Oh, philosophers may sing, etc.   95

After luncheon (making merry
On a bun and glass of sherry),
    If we've nothing in particular to do,
We may make a Proclamation,
Or receive a deputation –   100
    Then we possibly create a Peer or two.
Then we help a fellow-creature on his path
With the Garter or the Thistle or the Bath,
Or we dress and toddle off in semi-state
To a festival, a function, or a *fête*.   105
    Then we go and stand as sentry
    At the Palace (private entry),

The Most Ancient Order of the Thistle is the highest Scottish order of knighthood and ranks second only to the order of the Garter. It was instituted by King James VII of Scotland and II of England in 1687. The Most Honourable Order of the Bath dates from 1399 and derives its name from the ceremony of bathing which was formerly practised at the inauguration of a knight as a symbol of purity.

120 *of worries there are none*: The phrase was originally 'of troubles there are none'. It was changed to 'worries' in the third edition of the libretto.

141–68 *Take a pair of sparkling eyes*
This eternal favourite of amateur tenors has always evoked a mixed response from critics. The *Sunday Times* review of the first night described it as 'one of Sir Arthur Sullivan's inspirations – a strain of the purest melody, exquisitely accompanied by divided strings *pizzicati* in imitation of a guitar'. More recently, however, writing in the foreword to the 1962 Oxford University Press edition of the Savoy Operas, Lord David Cecil complained of its 'insensitiveness of taste' and of 'a genteel vulgarity . . . which is distressing'.

Sullivan composed the tune to the song, which began in Gilbert's first version 'Take a pair of bright blue eyes', at five o'clock in the morning of 9 November 1889. He had been working solidly since 5.15 the previous afternoon after taking a three-and-a-half-hour rehearsal earlier that day. During his marathon session through the night he had also composed 'There lived a King' and had rewritten the opening of Act I and Luiz and Casilda's two duets, 'Ah, well-beloved' and 'There was a time'. It is small wonder that for the last two lines which form the coda of 'Take a pair of sparkling eyes' he borrowed and transposed a theme which he had already used in a ballad entitled 'A Life That Lives for You'.

For a long time it was customary in D'Oyly Carte productions for all other performers to leave the stage when one of the principals was singing a solo aria. This practice was started by Gilbert, who wrote in a letter to Helen D'Oyly Carte in June 1909: 'Giuseppe should leave the stage during the refrain of the first verse of "Take a pair".'

145 *Having passed the Rubicon*: The Rubicon was a small river which separated ancient Italy

Marching hither, marching thither, up and down and to and fro,
  While the warrior on duty
  Goes in search of beer and beauty   110
(And it generally happens that he hasn't far to go).
  He relieves us, if he's able,
  Just in time to lay the table,
Then we dine and serve the coffee, and at half-past twelve or one,
  With a pleasure that's emphatic,   115
  We retire to our attic
With the gratifying feeling that our duty has been done!

  Oh, philosophers may sing
  Of the troubles of a King,
But of pleasures there are many and of worries there are none; 120
  And the culminating pleasure
  That we treasure beyond measure
Is the gratifying feeling that our duty has been done!

CHORUS. Oh, philosophers may sing, etc.
       (*Exeunt all but* MARCO *and* GIUSEPPE.) 125

GIU. Yes, it really is a very pleasant existence. They're all so singularly kind and considerate. You don't find them wanting to do this, or wanting to do that, or saying 'It's my turn now'. No, they let us have all the fun to ourselves, and never seem to grudge it.

MAR. It makes one feel quite selfish. It almost seems like taking 130 advantage of their good nature.

GIU. How nice they were about the double rations.

MAR. Most considerate. Ah! there's only one thing wanting to make us thoroughly comfortable.

GIU. And that is?   135

MAR. The dear little wives we left behind us three months ago.

GIU. Yes, it *is* dull without female society. We can do without everything else, but we can't do without that.

MAR. And if we have that in perfection, we have everything. There is only one recipe for perfect happiness. 140

SONG – MARCO.

  Take a pair of sparkling eyes,
   Hidden, ever and anon,
    In a merciful eclipse –
   Do not heed their mild surprise –
    Having passed the Rubicon,   145
    Take a pair of rosy lips;

from Cisalpine Gaul. When Julius Caesar crossed it in 49 B.C. he passed beyond the limits of his territory and became an invader. The incident has given rise to the expression 'to cross the Rubicon', meaning to take an irrevocable step.

182 *And we wanted variety*: This line was originally sung 'And we long for variety'.

Take a figure trimly planned –
Such as admiration whets –
(Be particular in this);
Take a tender little hand,   150
Fringed with dainty fingerettes,
Press it – in parenthesis; –
Ah! Take all these, you lucky man –
Take and keep them, if you can!

Take a pretty little cot –   155
Quite a miniature affair –
Hung about with trellised vine,
Furnish it upon the spot
With the treasures rich and rare
I've endeavoured to define.   160
Live to love and love to live –
You will ripen at your ease,
Growing on the sunny side –
Fate has nothing more to give.
You're a dainty man to please   165
If you are not satisfied.
Ah! Take my counsel, happy man;
Act upon it, if you can!

(*Enter Chorus of Contadine, running in, led by* FIAMETTA *and* VITTORIA.
They are met by all the Ex-Gondoliers, who welcome them heartily.)   170

SCENA – CHORUS OF GIRLS, QUARTET, DUET *and* CHORUS.

Here we are, at the risk of our lives,
From ever so far, and we've brought your wives –
And to that end we've crossed the main,
And don't intend to return again!

FIA.   Though obedience is strong,   175
              Curiosity's stronger –
            We waited for long,
              Till we couldn't wait longer.

VIT.   It's imprudent, we know,
              But without your society   180
            Existence was slow,
              And we wanted variety –

BOTH.   Existence was slow, and we wanted variety.

ALL.   So here we are, at the risk of our lives,

189–92 *Tessa! Giuseppe . . .*: In the licence copy, Marco, Giuseppe, Tessa and Gianetta are given a brief quartet after their mutual greetings and before the girls embark on their long series of questions. It was struck out before the opening performance although the caption 'Quartet' remains in the vocal score to this day.

> A pleasanter kind of surprise
> We ⎱
> You ⎰ possibly couldn't devise.
> It's a genuine species of joy
> Which hasn't a grain of alloy!
> When husband is parted from wife
> A slice is cut out of his life;
> And when they're united again
> The pleasure makes up for the pain.

185

And we've brought your wives –
And to that end we've crossed the main,
And we don't intend to return again!

(*Enter* GIANETTA *and* TESSA. *They rush to the arms of* MARCO *and* GIUSEPPE.)

GIU.	Tessa!	
TESS.	Giuseppe!	*Embrace.*
GIA.	Marco!	
MAR.	Gianetta!	

190

TESSA *and* GIANETTA.

TESS.   After sailing to this island –
GIA.   Tossing in a manner frightful,
TESS.   We are all once more on dry land –   195
GIA.   And we find the change delightful,
TESS.   As at home we've been remaining –
         We've not seen you both for ages,
GIA.   Tell me, are you fond of reigning? –
         How's the food, and what's the wages?   200
TESS.   Does your new employment please ye? –
GIA.   How does Royalizing strike you?
TESS.   Is it difficult or easy? –
GIA.   Do you think your subjects like you?
TESS.   I am anxious to elicit,   205
         Is it plain and easy steering?
GIA.   Take it altogether, is it
         Better fun than gondoliering?
BOTH.   We shall both go on requesting
         Till you tell us, never doubt it;   210
Everything is interesting,
         Tell us, tell us all about it!

CHORUS.   They will both go on requesting, etc.

TESS.   Is the populace exacting?
GIA.   Do they keep you at a distance?   215
TESS.   All unaided are you acting,
GIA.   Or do they provide assistance?
TESS.   When you're busy, have you got to
         Get up early in the morning?
GIA.   If you do what you ought not to,   220
         Do they give the usual warning?
TESS.   With a horse do they equip you?
GIA.   Lots of trumpeting and drumming?

244 *I've done*: In the version originally intended by Gilbert, Tessa and Gianetta had not, in fact, quite done at this point. The licence copy contains the following additional lines:

> GIA. Your employer won't be angry, will he?
> MAR. My employer?
> GIA. The old gentleman in mourning.
> GIU. O lord, I forgot him! But he won't know – he's not here. He's in Spain, hunting after Nurse.
> GIA. Then we may stay?
> MAR. Stay? I should think you might! Why, we've been longing for this! (*kisses her*).
> TESS. That accounts for it. And now – which of you is king?
> GIU. That we shan't know, etc.

253 *Dance a cachucha, fandango, bolero*: A tall – not to say exhausting – order. These three Spanish dances all have different rhythms and speeds. The cachucha, which is what is actually played and danced in *The Gondoliers*, is the fastest. It is danced by couples and includes the completion of a circle by four quarter-turns and a backward glissade of alternate feet at the second and fourth sections of the measure.

The fandango is a slowish dance in six-eight time, usually danced by one couple and accompanied by castanets.

The bolero, which Gilbert has, of course, already used for the surname of the Grand Inquisitor, is a slow minuet-like dance which was also normally danced by only two people at a time. My information tells me that it was invented by one Zerezo in 1780, so the Baratarians must have been very well ahead of their time to be dancing to it in 1750.

254 *Xeres. . . Manzanilla, Montero*: Xeres is an old Spanish word for the fortified wine which we call sherry; the name derives from the town of Xeres (now Jerez) in Andalusia, which is famous for its wine. Manzanilla is a light dry sherry, and Montero is a wine from the Pyrenees region of Spain (the word literally means mountaineer).

TESS.	Do the Royal tradesmen tip you?
GIA.	Ain't the livery becoming!	225

TESS. Does your human being inner
          Feed on èverything that nice is?
GIA. Do they give you wine for dinner;
          Peaches, sugar-plums, and ices?
BOTH. We shall both go on requesting   230
          Till you tell us, never doubt it;
Everything is interesting,
          Tell us, tell us all about it!

CHORUS. They will both go on requesting, etc.

MAR. This is indeed a most delightful surprise!   235
TESS. Yes, we thought you'd like it. You see, it was like this. After you left we felt very dull and mopey, and the days crawled by, and you never wrote; so at last I said to Gianetta, 'I can't stand this any longer; those two poor Monarchs haven't got any one to mend their stockings or sew on their buttons or patch their clothes – at least, I hope they haven't – let us all pack   240 up a change and go and see how they're getting on.' And she said, 'Done', and they all said, 'Done'; and we asked old Giacopo to lend us his boat, and *he* said, 'Done'; and we've crossed the sea, and, thank goodness, *that's* done; and here we are, and – and – *I've* done!

GIA. And now – which of you is King?   245
TESS. And which of us is Queen?
GIU. That we shan't know until Nurse turns up. But never mind that – the question is, how shall we celebrate the commencement of our honeymoon? Gentlemen, will you allow us to offer you a magnificent banquet?
ALL. We will!   250
GIU. Thanks very much; and, ladies, what do you say to a dance?
TESS. A banquet *and* a dance! Oh, it's too much happiness!

CHORUS *and* DANCE.

Dance a cachucha, fandango, bolero,
Xeres we'll drink – Manzanilla, Montero –
Wine, when it runs in abundance, enhances   255
The reckless delight of that wildest of dances!
    To the pretty pitter-pitter-patter,
    And the clitter-clitter-clitter-clatter –
      Clitter – clitter – clatter,
      Pitter - pitter – patter,   260
    Patter, patter, patter, patter, we'll dance.
Old Xeres we'll drink – Manzanilla, Montero;
For wine, when it runs in abundance, enhances
The reckless delight of that wildest of dances!

265 *Cachucha*: This wild dance has always given the D'Oyly Carte ladies an opportunity to show their paces, and other things as well. The first-night review in the *Topical Times* commented: 'The attractions of *The Gondoliers* are numerous. To begin with, the chorus wore comparatively short skirts for the first time, and the gratifying fact is revealed to a curious world that the Savoy chorus are a very well-legged lot'.

271 *Sorry you're late*: This was one of Rutland Barrington's gags later incorporated in the libretto.

276 *the servants'-hall*: Helen D'Oyly Carte obviously thought that the classless Americans would not know the meaning of this term. In her version prepared for performance in the United States, this line was changed to 'But surely, surely the kitchen rather than the drawing room is the proper place for these gentry', to which Giuseppe's reply was 'We have appropriated the kitchen and the attic'.

279–80 *accessible only by tickets. . .* : The line about the Lord Chamberlain was almost certainly another of Barrington's gags. Gilbert's original line was simply 'It's the Royal Apartment, and we permit no intruders'. The Lord Chamberlain is the official in overall charge of the Royal Household. He was also, until 1968, the censor of all plays performed in Britain. Like all other dramatists, Gilbert was required to send copies of his new works to the Lord Chamberlain's office for licensing before they could be performed.

294–5 *A plate of macaroni and a rusk*: In Helen D'Oyly Carte's American version this becomes 'prezels or a Boston cracker?'

298 *Yes – gout*: Not gout, but the equally uncomfortable condition of rheumatism affected one of the D'Oyly Carte's distinguished line of Grand Inquisitors and nearly caused a minor revolution in the way this scene was played.

When she took over the running of the company in 1948 on the death of her father, Dame Bridget D'Oyly Carte was very surprised to find that shortly after coming on in this scene, Don Alhambra sat down on the royal throne and remained there for his conversation with Marco and Giuseppe and the singing of 'There lived a King'. Even for a monarchy remodelled on Republican principles, this seemed rather presumptuous and disrespectful behaviour on the part of one so proper. She inquired about the origins of this practice and eventually found that it had been introduced ten years or so earlier for the benefit of the then Don Alhambra, Sydney Granville, who

CACHUCHA.   265

(The dance is interrupted by the unexpected appearance of DON ALHAMBRA, *who looks on with astonishment.* MARCO *and* GIUSEPPE *appear embarrassed. The others run off, except Drummer Boy, who is driven off by* DON ALHAMBRA.)*

DON AL. Good evening. Fancy ball?   270
GIU. No, not exactly. A little friendly dance. That's all. Sorry you're late.
DON AL. But I saw a groom dancing, and a footman!
MAR. Yes. That's the Lord High Footman.
DON AL. And, dear me, a common little drummer boy!
GIU. Oh no! That's the Lord High Drummer Boy.   275
DON AL. But surely, surely the servants'-hall is the place for these gentry?
GIU. Oh dear no! *We* have appropriated the servants'-hall. It's the Royal Apartment, and accessible only by tickets obtainable at the Lord Chamberlain's office.   280
MAR. We really must have some place that we can call our own.
DON AL. (*puzzled*). I'm afraid I'm not quite equal to the intellectual pressure of the conversation.
GIU. You see, the Monarchy has been re-modelled on Republican principles.   285
DON AL. What!
GIU. All departments rank equally, and everybody is at the head of his department.
DON AL. I see.
MAR. I'm afraid you're annoyed.   290
DON AL. No. I won't say that. It's not quite what I expected.
GIU. I'm awfully sorry.
MAR. So am I.
GIU. By the by, can I offer you anything after your voyage? A plate of macaroni and a rusk?   295
DON AL. (*preoccupied*). No, no – nothing – nothing.
GIU. Obliged to be careful?
DON AL. Yes – gout. You see, in every Court there are distinctions that must be observed.
GIU. (*puzzled*). There are, are there?   300
DON AL. Why, of course. For instance, you wouldn't have a Lord High Chancellor play leapfrog with his own cook.
MAR. Why not?
DON AL. Why not! Because a Lord High Chancellor is a personage of great dignity, who should never, under any circumstances, place himself in   305
the position of being told to tuck in his tuppenny, except by noblemen of his

was in his mid-sixties and suffered badly from rheumatism. When Granville finally left in 1942 after thirty-five years with the company, his successor, Richard Walker, continued the business of sitting down on the throne, and so what had been intended as a temporary expedient became established as a regular practice. Dame Bridget, however, put a stop to it and ever since, gout or no gout, the Don has respectfully remained standing in the presence of their Majesties the Kings of Barataria. In fact, it seems that earlier Dons than Sydney Granville may also have sat down for the singing of 'There lived a King'. George Low has drawn my attention to the souvenir brochure published by the *Sphere* for the D'Oyly Carte London season of 1924 in which there is a photograph of Leo Sheffield as the Don, sitting on the throne and singing to Giuseppe. He also points to a drawing of an even earlier production reproduced in Raymond Mander and Joe Mitcheson's *Picture History of Gilbert and Sullivan* which shows the Don sitting cross-legged on the floor while singing to the gondoliers.

308 *tuck in his tuppenny*: tuck in his head. The Grand Inquisitor was very advanced to be using this particular colloquialism in 1750. According to the *Oxford English Dictionary* its first recorded use in England was not until 1859.

322 *Rhenish wine*: Wine produced in the Rhine region. It figures prominently in one of Gilbert's *Bab Ballads*, 'The Baron Klopfzetterheim'.

324 *at junket or at jink*: A junket is a feast or banquet, particularly one at public expense. The word jink is more usually found in its plural form, and most commonly in the phrase 'high jinks' meaning pranks, frolics or generally lively and boisterous occasions.

325 *toddy*: A drink made with hot water, whisky, sugar and sometimes also lemon juice, which is said to be particularly efficacious in easing colds and influenza. Making great play with its Scottish associations, Sullivan scored an accompaniment to Marco and Giuseppe's line 'With toddy, must be content with toddy' which suggests the droning of bagpipes at the start of a reel.

336 *shovel hats*: A stiff broad-brimmed hat, turned up at the sides and with a shovel-like curve at the front and the back, which was formerly worn by many ecclesiastics.

own rank. A Lord High Archbishop, for instance, might tell a Lord High
Chancellor to tuck in his tuppenny, but certainly not a cook, gentlemen,
certainly not a cook.

    Giu. Not even a Lord High Cook? 310

    Don Al. My good friend, that is a rank that is not recognized at the
Lord Chamberlain's office. No, no, it won't do. I'll give you an instance in
which the experiment was tried.

      SONG – Don Alhambra, *with* Marco *and* Giuseppe.

Don Al.   There lived a King, as I've been told,
               In the wonder-working days of old, 315
               When hearts were twice as good as gold,
                   And twenty times as mellow.
               Good-temper triumphed in his face,
               And in his heart he found a place
               For all the erring human race 320
                   And every wretched fellow.
               When he had Rhenish wine to drink
               It made him very sad to think
               That some, at junket or at jink,
                   Must be content with toddy. 325

Mar. *and* Giu. With toddy, must be content with
                   toddy.

Don Al.   He wished all men as rich as he
               (And he was rich as rich could be),
               So to the top of every tree
               Promoted everybody. 330

Mar. *and* Giu. Now, that's the kind of King for me.
                   He wished all men as rich as he,
                   So to the top of every tree
                   Promoted everybody!

Don Al.   Lord Chancellors were cheap as sprats, 335
               And Bishops in their shovel hats
               Were plentiful as tabby cats –
                   In point of fact, too many.
               Ambassadors cropped up like hay,
               Prime Ministers and such as they 340

344 *Lords-Lieutenant*: The office of Lord-Lieutenant was created in 1549 to take over the military duties of the sheriff. Later the duties became more administrative and involved the recommendation of local magistrates and justices of the peace to the Lord Chancellor. Lords-Lieutenant are still the Queen's representatives in each county, although their functions now are largely ceremonial.

347 *With Admirals all round his wide dominions*: This provides Sullivan with the opportunity for another musical joke. This time he accompanies Marco and Giuseppe's line with a snatch of hornpipe.

367 *shoddy*: Woollen yarn obtained by shredding refuse woollen rags, which, with the addition of some new wool, is made into a kind of cloth. The word has more generally come to mean any worthless material made to look like something of superior quality. Sullivan's original accompaniment to Marco and Giuseppe's refrain 'Of shoddy, up goes the price of shoddy' included a few bars of 'Yankee Doodle Dandy' to show what he thought of the American pirate versions of his operas.

                Grew like asparagus in May,
                   And Dukes were three a penny.
                On every side Field-Marshals gleamed,
                Small beer were Lords-Lieutenant deemed,
                With Admirals the ocean teemed   345
                   All round his wide dominions.

MAR. *and* GIU. With Admirals all round his wide dominions.

DON AL.   And Party Leaders you might meet
                In twos and threes in every street
                Maintaining, with no little heat,   350
                   Their various opinions.

MAR. *and* GIU. Now that's a sight you couldn't beat –
                Two Party Leaders in each street
                Maintaining, with no little heat,
                   Their various opinions.   355

DON AL.   That King, although no one denies
                His heart was of abnormal size,
                Yet he'd have acted otherwise
                   If he had been acuter.
                The end is easily foretold,   360
                When every blessed thing you hold
                Is made of silver, or of gold,
                   You long for simple pewter.
                When you have nothing else to wear
                But cloth of gold and satins rare,   365
                For cloth of gold you cease to care –
                   Up goes the price of shoddy.

MAR. *and* GIU. Of shoddy, up goes the price of shoddy.

DON AL.   In short, whoever you may be,
                 To this conclusion you'll agree,   370
                When every one is somebodee,
                   Then no one's anybody!

MAR. *and* GIU. Now that's as plain as plain can be,
                To this conclusion we agree –

ALL.   When every one is somebodee,   375
                   Then no one's anybody!

386 *lucky dog*: This was originally 'lucky fellow'.

401 *what will Her Majesty say*: This line was originally 'What will the Duke say', which was a popular Victorian catch-phrase. It occurs several times in Don Alhambra's dialogue in the first edition of the libretto. I cannot discover when this particular line was changed to its present form, but it would be nice to think that it was for the Command performance before Queen Victoria in 1891.

416 *There's something in that*: A handwritten addition to Helen D'Oyly Carte's corrected copy of the 1907 libretto has Giuseppe saying to Tessa at this point 'Go in the corner'. This was no doubt originally another Barrington gag. It does not appear in the next master copy of the libretto prepared by J. M. Gordon in 1914.

(GIANETTA *and* TESSA *enter unobserved. The two girls, impelled by curiosity, remain listening at the back of the stage.*)

DON AL. And now I have some important news to communicate. His Grace the Duke of Plaza-Toro, Her Grace the Duchess, and their beautiful daughter Casilda – I say their beautiful daughter Casilda —   380

GIU. We heard you.

DON AL. Have arrived at Barataria, and may be here at any moment.

MAR. The Duke and Duchess are nothing to us.

DON AL. But the daughter – the beautiful daughter! Aha! Oh, you're a   385
lucky dog, one of you!

GIU. I think you're a very incomprehensible old gentleman.

DON AL. Not a bit – I'll explain. Many years ago when you (whichever you are) were a baby, you (whichever you are) were married to a little girl who has grown up to be the most beautiful young lady in Spain. That   390
beautiful young lady will be here to claim you (whichever you are) in half an hour, and I congratulate that one (whichever it is) with all my heart.

MAR. Married when a baby!

GIU. But we were married three months ago!

DON AL. One of you – only one. The other (whichever it is) is an   395
unintentional bigamist.

GIA. *and* TESS. (*coming forward*). Well, upon my word!

DON AL. Eh? Who are these young people?

TESS. Who are we? Why, their wives, of course. We've just arrived.

DON AL. Their wives! Oh dear, this is very unfortunate! Oh dear, this   400
complicates matters! Dear, dear, what will Her Majesty say?

GIA. And do you mean to say that one of these Monarchs was already married?

TESS. And that neither of us will be a Queen?

DON AL. That is the idea I intended to convey. (TESSA *and*   405
GIANETTA *begin to cry.*)

GIU. (*to* TESSA). Tessa, my dear, dear child —

TESS. Get away! perhaps it's you!

MAR. (*to* GIA.). My poor, poor little woman!

GIA. Don't! Who knows whose husband you are?   410

TESS. And pray, why didn't you tell us all about it before they left Venice?

DON AL. Because, if I had, no earthly temptation would have induced these gentlemen to leave two such extremely fascinating and utterly irresistible little ladies!   415

TESS. There's something in that.

DON AL. I may mention that you will not be kept long in suspense, as the old lady who nursed the Royal child is at present in the torture chamber, waiting for me to interview her.

437 *O Mount Vesuvius*: Is it too fanciful to speculate whether the fact that Tessa chooses for her apostrophe the famous volcano on the edge of the Bay of Naples suggests that it might be visible from Barataria? In that case, the southern sea in which the island stands is that part of the Mediterranean known as the Tyrrhenian, which is certainly southern to the Venetians, and Barataria lies somewhere between Sardinia and Sicily.

438 *a vulgar fraction*: A common-or-garden fraction in which the numerator and denominator are represented by numbers placed the one above and the other below a horizontal line. For complex, compound, continued, decimal, proper and improper fractions, consult the modern Major-General in *The Pirates of Penzance*. He is, after all, very well acquainted with matters mathematical. I'm not.

442–87 *In a contemplative fashion*
This quartet, so splendidly muddled and yet at the same time so tightly controlled, is perhaps the supreme example of Sullivan's trick of setting several different vocal themes one against another. He himself wrote in a letter to a friend, quoted in Leslie Baily's *The Gilbert and Sullivan Book*:

> You get the germ of it in *The Sorcerer* and it is afterwards worked in a greater degree in *The Pirates* (the policemen's chorus with the counter theme for the sopranos). In *The Mikado* there is amongst others the Trio for the three men in the first act, with all three different themes going at the same time. The most ingenious bit of work (certainly the most difficult) is the quartet in *The Gondoliers*, 'In a contemplative fashion'.

Certainly both composer and librettist seem to have laboured over this more than any other number in the opera. Sullivan first asked Gilbert to rewrite his original draft at the end of August 1889, and on 12 September he received an amended version and the following letter:

> Will this do? It is dactylic, but it is difficult to get the contrast you want without dactyls. Probably it will be impracticable to set the accompanying lines, 'In a contemplative fashion,' so as to be a running accompaniment to the verses as they now stand. If so, I suppose they could be omitted during the verses and introduced at the end to finish with. If the verses won't do, send them back and I'll try again.

GIU. Poor old girl. Hadn't you better go and put her out of her suspense?   420
DON AL. Oh no – there's no hurry – she's all right. She has all the illustrated papers. However, I'll go and interrogate her, and, in the meantime, may I suggest the absolute propriety of your regarding yourselves as single young ladies. Good evening!

(*Exit* DON ALHAMBRA.)   425

GIA. Well, here's a pleasant state of things!
MAR. Delightful. One of us is married to two young ladies, and nobody knows which; and the other is married to one young lady whom nobody can identify!
GIA. And one of us is married to one of you, and the other is married   430
to nobody.
TESS. But which of you is married to which of us, and what's to become of the other? (*About to cry.*)
GIU. It's quite simple. Observe. Two husbands have managed to acquire three wives. Three wives – two husbands. (*Reckoning up.*) That's two-   435
thirds of a husband to each wife.
TESS. O Mount Vesuvius, here we are in arithmetic! My good sir, one can't marry a vulgar fraction!
GIU. You've no right to call me a vulgar fraction.
MAR. We are getting rather mixed. The situation is entangled. Let's try   440
and comb it out.

QUARTET – MARCO, GIUSEPPE, GIANETTA, TESSA.

In a contemplative fashion,
    And a tranquil frame of mind,
Free from every kind of passion,
    Some solution let us find.   445
Let us grasp the situation,
    Solve the complicated plot –
Quiet, calm deliberation
    Disentangles every knot.

TESS. I, no doubt, Giuseppe wedded –
    That's, of course, a slice of luck.
 He is rather dunder-headed,
    Still distinctly, he's a duck.
	THE OTHERS. In a con- 450
	    templative fashion, etc.

GIA. I, a victim, too, of Cupid,
    Marco married – that is clear.
 He's particularly stupid,
    Still distinctly, he's a dear.
	THE OTHERS. Let us
	    grasp the situation, etc. 455

MAR. To Gianetta I was mated;
    I can prove it in a trice:
 Though her charms are overrated,
    Still I own she's rather nice.
	THE OTHERS. In a con-
	    templative fashion, etc.
	
	    460

Sullivan clearly found that the new version was not satisfactory and sent it back to be altered once again, as on 22 September we find Gilbert writing to him:

> I have altered 'In a contemplative fashion' as suggested. The only question is whether the two last verses which the two girls sing at each other, and with which the two men have nothing to do, wouldn't be better in the original flowing metre, as lending itself to the volubility of two angry girls. I don't care a pin myself which it is, but I thought you might find the original dactylic metre better for the purpose.

In the event, the dactylic metre (i.e. one long syllable followed by two short ones) was used for the girls' angry utterances at the end and it produces a splendid crescendo of confusion before the controlled calmness of the final ensemble lines, 'Quiet, calm deliberation/Disentangles every knot!'

481 *Messer*: From the old Italian word *Messere*, meaning sir or master.

Giu. I to Tessa, willy-nilly,
    All at once a victim fell.
  She is what is called a silly,
    Still she answers pretty well.

THE OTHERS.   Let us
  grasp the situation, etc.

465

MAR.   Now when we were pretty babies
          Some one married us, that's clear –

GIA.   And if I can catch her
             I'll pinch her and scratch her
         And send her away with a flea in her ear.

470

GIU.   He whom that young lady married,
          To receive her can't refuse.

TESS.   If I overtake her
          I'll warrant I'll make her
        To shake in her aristocratical shoes!

475

GIA. (*to* TESS.).   If she married your Giuseppe
          You and he will have to part –

TESS. (*to* GIA.).   If I have to do it
          I'll warrant she'll rue it –
        I'll teach her to marry the man of my heart!

480

TESS. (*to* GIA.).   If she married Messer Marco
          You're a spinster, that is plain –

GIA. (*to* TESS.).   No matter – no matter.
          If I can get at her
        I doubt if her mother will know her again!

485

ALL.   Quiet, calm deliberation
          Disentangles every knot!

                 (*Exeunt, pondering.*)

(MARCH. *Enter procession of Retainers, heralding approach of* DUKE, DUCHESS, *and* CASILDA. *All three are now dressed with the utmost magnificence.*)

490

CHORUS OF MEN, *with* DUKE *and* DUCHESS.

    With ducal pomp and ducal pride
    (Announce these comers,

509 *She's excelled by none*: In the version originally intended for performance and printed in the licence copy, the solo 'On the day when I was wedded', now sung by the Duchess of Plaza-Toro slightly later in Act II, did not appear. Instead, she and the Duke were given the following song immediately after their duet 'This polite attention touches':

DUCH.	Oh, a mother is a mother,
	Though of ducal state,
	And her love she cannot smother
	Like the low-born mate
	Of a butcher, or a baker –
DUKE.	Or a baker's man –
DUCH.	Or a parish undertaker –
DUKE.	Or a publican –
DUCH.	Or a cowman, or a ploughman –
DUKE.	Or an artisan –
DUCH.	Or a pieman, or a flyman –
DUKE.	With his shandrydan.
DUCH.	Or a soldier, or a sailor,
	Or a tinker, or a tailor,
	Or a jockey, or a jailor –
DUKE.	With his big black van.

527 *Oh! couldn't he, though*: This line was not in the original first-night libretto and was almost certainly an ad-lib which was later authorized.

O ye kettle-drummers!)
Comes Barataria's high-born bride.   495
(Ye sounding cymbals clang!)
She comes to claim the Royal hand –
(Proclaim their Graces,
O ye double basses!)
Of the King who rules this goodly land.   500
(Ye brazen brasses bang!)

DUKE *and* This polite attention touches
DUCH.   Heart of Duke and heart of Duchess
Who resign their pet
With profound regret.   505
She of beauty was a model
When a tiny tiddle-toddle,
And at twenty-one
She's excelled by none!

CHORUS.   With ducal pomp and ducal pride, etc.   510

DUKE (*to his attendants*). Be good enough to inform His Majesty that His Grace the Duke of Plaza-Toro, Limited, has arrived, and begs —
CAS. Desires —
DUCH. Demands —
DUKE. And demands an audience. (*Exeunt attendants.*) And now, my   515
child, prepare to receive the husband to whom you were united under such interesting and romantic circumstances.
CAS. But which is it? There are two of them!
DUKE. It is true that at present His Majesty is a double gentleman; but as soon as the circumstances of his marriage are ascertained, he will, *ipso*   520
facto, boil down to a single gentleman – thus presenting a unique example of an individual who becomes a single man and a married man by the same operation.
DUCH. (*severely*). I have known instances in which the characteristics of both conditions existed concurrently in the same individual.   525
DUKE. Ah, he couldn't have been a Plaza-Toro.
DUCH. Oh! couldn't he, though!
CAS. Well, whatever happens, I shall, of course, be a dutiful wife, but I can never love my husband.
DUKE. I don't know. It's extraordinary what unprepossessing people   530
one can love if one gives one's mind to it.
DUCH. I loved your father.
DUKE. My love – that remark is a little hard, I think? Rather cruel, perhaps? Somewhat uncalled-for, I venture to believe?
DUCH. It was very difficult, my dear; but I said to myself, 'That man is   535

538–89 *On the day when I was wedded*
As already pointed out in the note to line 509, this song, although written, was missing from the licence copy and was not originally destined for performance. Gilbert was unhappy that, placed where it now is, it held up the action. He first proposed to Sullivan that it be moved to Act I, since, as he pointed out, the Duchess 'will have plenty to say in Act II and as present arranged she has practically nothing in Act I'. Later he suggested that it be dropped completely. However, it was saved, but whether by the entreaties of Sullivan or of Rosina Brandram, who played the Duchess, I have not been able to establish.

551 *this Tartar*: Originally a native inhabitant of the region of Central Asia extending eastward from the Caspian Sea, 'Tartar' has come to mean one who is savage, irritable and violent.

a Duke, and I *will* love him.' Several of my relations bet me I couldn't, but
I did – desperately!

SONG – DUCHESS.

On the day when I was wedded
  To your admirable sire,
I acknowledge that I dreaded   540
  An explosion of his ire.
I was overcome with panic –
For his temper was volcanic,
  And I didn't dare revolt,
  For I feared a thunderbolt!   545
I was always very wary,
  For his fury was ecstatic –
His refined vocabulary
  Most unpleasantly emphatic.
  To the thunder   550
    Of this Tartar
  I knocked under
    Like a martyr;
  When intently
    He was fuming,   555
  I was gently
    Unassuming –
  When reviling
    Me completely,
  I was smiling   560
    Very sweetly:
Giving him the very best, and getting back the very worst –
That is how I tried to tame your great progenitor – at first!

But I found that a reliance
  On my threatening appearance,   565
And a resolute defiance
  Of marital interference,
And a gentle intimation
Of my firm determination
  To see what I could do   570
  To be wife and husband too
Was the only thing required
  For to make his temper supple,
And you couldn't have desired
  A more reciprocating couple.   575

592–6 *Shady*: In the American version prepared by Helen D'Oyly Carte, this passage is
altered to:

> DUKE. Shady? A nobleman shady who is listed upon the Stock Exchange, and is
> upon the point of declaring an extra dividend? A nobleman shady who has never
> commanded a premium of less than ten per cent since he was first floated? A nobleman
> shady who is regularly sought for by Savings Banks, Trust Companies, executors, widows
> and – and –
> DUCH. Sheriffs.
> DUKE. And so forth, as an investment which combines unsurpassed profit with
> unequalled security! Oh fie!

596 *floated at a premium*: The expression used when the initial sale of shares in a company
commands a price in excess of their nominal value.

598 *he was applied for over and over again*: When a public company is formed it issues a
prospectus designed to attract investors. Those who want to invest then apply for
shares.

601 *the Limited Liability Act*: Limited liability is a condition under which the loss that an
owner, or shareholder, of a business may incur is limited to the amount of capital
invested by him and does not extend to his personal assets. In Britain the Duke of
Plaza-Toro could not legally have formed himself into a limited liability company until
the mid-nineteenth century. However, in Spain, and indeed in Barataria, company
legislation may well have been more advanced!

   The idea of individuals forming themselves into limited companies is picked up
again in *Utopia Limited*, where Mr Goldbury, the company promoter, has 'applied the
Limited Liability principle to individuals, and every man, woman and child is now a
Company Limited with liability restricted to the amount of his declared Capital! There
is not a christened baby in Utopia who has not already issued his little Prospectus!'

607 *Recorders*: A magistrate or judge appointed by the Crown to exercise certain criminal
and civil jurisdictions. Recorders were originally people with legal knowledge
appointed by mayors to record the proceedings of their courts and the customs of their
cities.

610 *baronetted*: Baronets are members of the lowest hereditary titled order, which was
instituted by James I in the early seventeenth century. They are styled 'Sir', and the
title is normally shortened to 'Bart.' after their names.

Ever willing
  To be wooing,
We were billing –
  We were cooing;
When I merely   580
  From him parted,
We were nearly
  Broken-hearted –
When in sequel
  Reunited,   585
We were equal-
  Ly delighted.
So with double-shotted guns and colours nailed unto the mast,
I tamed your insignificant progenitor – at last!

CAS. My only hope is that when my husband sees what a shady family   590
he has married into he will repudiate the contract altogether.
DUKE. Shady? A nobleman shady, who is blazing in the lustre of
unaccustomed pocket-money? A nobleman shady, who can look back upon
ninety-five quarterings? It is not every nobleman who is ninety-five quarters
in arrear – I mean, who can look back upon ninety-five of them! And this,   595
just as I have been floated at a premium! Oh fie!
DUCH. Your Majesty is surely unaware that directly Your Majesty's
father came before the public he was applied for over and over again.
DUKE. My dear, Her Majesty's father was in the habit of being applied
for over and over again – and very urgently applied for, too – long before he   600
was registered under the Limited Liability Act.

RECITATIVE – DUKE.

To help unhappy commoners, and add to their enjoyment,
Affords a man of noble rank congenial employment;
Of our attempts we offer you examples illustrative:
The work is light, and, I may add, it's most remunerative.   605

DUET – DUKE *and* DUCHESS.

DUKE.   Small titles and orders
               For Mayors and Recorders
                  I get – and they're highly delighted –

DUCH.   They're highly delighted!

DUKE.   M.P.s baronetted,   610

611 *gazetted*: Promotions in the armed forces are published along with many other official appointments in *The London Gazette*, a Government publication which appears every Tuesday and Friday.

612 *Aldermen knighted*: Aldermen were important co-opted members of certain local authorities. With the reorganization of local government they have now largely disappeared.

The first section of the Duke and Duchess's song recalls the second verse of 'Henceforth all the crimes that I find in *The Times*', a song from Act II of *Ruddigore*, now seldom performed, in which Sir Ruthven Murgatroyd pours scorn on:

> Ye well-to-do squires, who live in the shires,
> Where petty distinctions are vital,
> Who found Athenaeums and local museums,
> With views to a baronet's title –
> Ye butchers and bakers and candlestick-makers
> Who sneer at all things that are tradey –
> Whose middle-class lives are embarrassed by wives
> Who long to parade as 'My Lady',
> Oh! allow me to offer a word of advice,
> The title's uncommonly dear at the price!

For all Gilbert's jeering at the honours system, he had no hesitation in accepting the knighthood which was conferred on him in 1907. Indeed, it was for long a matter of some irritation to him that Sullivan, who was knighted in 1883, had been honoured while he had not. Perhaps small titles and orders were not to be sneered at too much after all.

Sham Colonels gazetted,
And second-rate Aldermen knighted –

Duch.   Yes, Aldermen knighted.

Duke.   Foundation-stone laying
I find very paying: 615
It adds a large sum to my makings –

Duch.   Large sums to his makings.

Duke.   At charity dinners
The best of speech-spinners,
I get ten per cent on the takings –   620

Duch.   One-tenth of the takings.

Duch.   I present any lady
Whose conduct is shady
Or smacking of doubtful propriety –

Duke.   Doubtful propriety.   625

Duch.   When Virtue would quash her,
I take and whitewash her,
And launch her in first-rate society –

Duke.   First-rate society!

Duch.   I recommend acres   630
Of clumsy dressmakers –
Their fit and their finishing touches –

Duke.   Their finishing touches.

Duch.   A sum in addition
They pay for permission   635
To say that they make for the Duchess –

Duke.   They make for the Duchess!

Duke.   Those pressing prevailers,
The ready-made tailors,
Quote me as their great double-barrel –   640

648 *Companies bubble*: A bubble is a worthless, unstable, unsound project, usually in the financial or commercial sphere. The most famous was the South Sea Bubble of 1720, when the price of shares in the South Sea Company rose out of all proportion to its earnings as a result of massive over-speculation, with the inevitable aftermath of a disastrous crash and the ruin of thousands. The bursting of the South Sea Bubble led to tight restrictions on the formation of joint-stock companies in Britain, which were not eased until 1855, when limited liability companies – the kind formed by the Duke of Plaza-Toro – were permitted.

655 *écarté*: A French card game which involves discarding cards. The word *écarté* means discarded.

DUCH.   Their great double-barrel –

DUKE.   I allow them to do so,
               Though Robinson Crusoe
                    Would jib at their wearing apparel –

DUCH.   Such wearing apparel!   645

DUKE.   I sit, by selection,
               Upon the direction
                    Of several Companies bubble –

DUCH.   All Companies bubble!

DUKE.   As soon as they're floated   650
               I'm freely bank-noted –
                    I'm pretty well paid for my trouble –

DUCH.   He's paid for his trouble!

DUCH.   At middle-class party
               I play at *écarté* –   655
                    And I'm by no means a beginner –

DUKE (*significantly*). She's not a beginner.

DUCH.   To one of my station
               The remuneration –
                    Five guineas a night and my dinner –   660

DUKE.   And wine with her dinner.

DUCH.   I write letters blatant
               On medicines patent –
                    And use any other you mustn't –

DUKE.   Believe me, you mustn't –   665

DUCH.   And vow my complexion
               Derives its perfection
                    From somebody's soap – which it doesn't –

690–91 *Allow me to present*: The original libretto printed in the licence copy has some extra lines and some extra business at this point, as follows:

> GIU. (*indicating* DUCHESS). The young lady one of us married? Marco, I begin to hope it was you.
> DUCH. (*pleased at the mistake*). Pardon me – her mother. This is our daughter (*presenting* CARLOTTA) – the Queen, and wife of one of you.
> GIU. Delighted, I'm sure – if it's me.
> MAR. Some time since we met – if it's me.
> GIU. (*aside to* MARCO). Neat little body!
> MAR. But not a patch on Gianetta.
> CAR. (*curtseying*). Gentlemen, I am the most obedient servant, etc.

DUKE (*significantly*). It certainly doesn't!

DUKE.	We're ready as witness	670
	To any one's fitness	
	To fill any place or preferment –	

DUCH.   A place or preferment.

DUCH.	We're often in waiting	
	At junket or *fêting*,	675
	And sometimes attend an interment –	

DUKE.   We enjoy an interment.

BOTH.	In short, if you'd kindle	
	The spark of a swindle,	
	Lure simpletons into your clutches –	680
	Yes; into your clutches.	
	Or hoodwink a debtor,	
	You cannot do better	

DUCH.   Than trot out a Duke or a Duchess –

DUKE.   A Duke or a Duchess!   685

(*Enter* MARCO *and* GIUSEPPE.)

DUKE. Ah! Their Majesties. Your Majesty! (*Bows with great ceremony.*)
MAR. The Duke of Plaza-Toro, I believe?
DUKE. The same. (MARCO *and* GIUSEPPE *offer to shake hands with him.
The* DUKE *bows ceremoniously. They endeavour to imitate him.*) Allow me to   690
present —
GIU. The young lady one of us married?

(MARCO *and* GIUSEPPE *offer to shake hands with her.* CASILDA *curtsies
formally. They endeavour to imitate her.*)

CAS. Gentlemen, I am the most obedient servant of one of you. (*Aside.*)   695
Oh, Luiz!
DUKE. I am now about to address myself to the gentleman whom my
daughter married; the other may allow his attention to wander if he likes, for
what I am about to say does not concern him. Sir, you will find in this young
lady a combination of excellences which you would search for in vain in any   700

709 *what do I find*: The cue for another of Barrington's gags. After the Duke's 'what do I find?', Giuseppe came in with 'What have I lost?' This was added to the libretto prepared for the 1907 revival but was cut by 1914.

728 *I'll take off anything else in reason*: There was some more ad-libbing at this point. Marco said 'You've done it now', to which Giuseppe replied 'I don't mean what they mean'. Once again, this was included in the libretto prepared for the 1907 revival but was cut again in 1914.

735 *They are very off-hand with us*: Barrington extended this line to 'No, they're a mean lot. They wouldn't stand for anything, besides they are very off-hand with us – very off-hand indeed.'

739 *We've got a carriage*: Another Barrington gag, this time approved by Gilbert and allowed to be permanently enshrined in the libretto.

742 *a soupçon of this sort of thing*: Barrington generally interpolated at this point 'What song?' *Soupçon* is, of course, a perfectly respectable French word meaning a suggestion, very small quantity or slight trace. For the 'business' at the end of this phrase, the following words, also devised by Barrington, were introduced for the Duke to show the kind of thing he had in mind: 'Saw you in the Park this morning: Little Heartkiller: anytime you're passing – pass'. Gilbert emphatically did not approve of this last gag. He wrote to Helen D'Oyly Carte in June 1909: 'I never sanctioned "any time you are passing, pass". I don't know what it means: it seems arrant nonsense.'

young lady who had not the good fortune to be my daughter. There is some
little doubt as to which of you is the gentleman I am addressing, and which
is the gentleman who is allowing his attention to wander; but when that
doubt is solved, I shall say (still addressing the attentive gentleman), 'Take
her, and may she make you happier than her mother has made me.'   705

DUCH. Sir!

DUKE. If possible. And now there is a little matter to which I think I am
entitled to take exception. I come here in state with Her Grace the Duchess
and Her Majesty my daughter, and what do I find? Do I find, for instance,
a guard of honour to receive me? No!   710

MAR. *and* GIU. No.

DUKE. The town illuminated? No!

MAR. *and* GIU. No.

DUKE. Refreshment provided? No!

MAR. *and* GIU. No.   715

DUKE. A Royal salute fired? No!

MAR. *and* GIU. No.

DUKE. Triumphal arches erected? No!

MAR. *and* GIU. No.

DUKE. The bells set ringing?   720

MAR. *and* GIU. No.

DUKE. Yes – one – the Visitors', and I rang it myself. It is not enough!
It is not enough!

GIU. Upon my honour, I'm very sorry; but you see, I was brought up
in a gondola, and my ideas of politeness are confined to taking off my cap to   725
my passengers when they tip me.

DUCH. That's all very well in its way, but it is not enough.

GIU. I'll take off anything else in reason.

DUKE. But a Royal Salute to my daughter – it costs so little.

CAS. Papa, I don't want a salute.   730

GIU. My dear sir, as soon as we know which of us is entitled to take
that liberty she shall have as many salutes as she likes.

MAR. As for guards of honour and triumphal arches, you don't know
our people – they wouldn't stand it.

GIU. They are very off-hand with us – very off-hand indeed.   735

DUKE. Oh, but you mustn't allow that – you must keep them in proper
discipline, you must impress your Court with your importance. You want
deportment – carriage —

GIU. We've got a carriage.

DUKE. Manner – dignity. There must be a good deal of this sort of   740
thing – (*business*) – and a little of this sort of thing – (*business*) – and possibly
just a *soupçon* of this sort of thing! – (*business*) – and so on. Oh, it's very
useful, and most effective. Just attend to me. You are a King – I am a subject.
Very good —

745–80 *I am a courtier grave and serious*
This celebrated song in which Marco and Giuseppe are taught courtly manners and graces was originally written for Don Alhambra. It was then transferred to the Duke of Plaza-Toro. It was also changed from a trio to a quintet by bringing in Casilda and the Duchess.

The version of the song printed in the licence edition, part of which is quoted in Leslie Baily's *The Gilbert and Sullivan Book*, is substantially different from that actually performed on the first night and subsequently. Here it is:

SONG – DUKE.

Now I'm about to kiss your hand –
   Look haughty, proud and somewhat freezy;
Yet gracious, affable and bland –
   It's not particularly easy.
   (*They endeavour to carry out his instructions.*)
Humph! Pretty well; it's not supreme –
   If anything, it's *too* unbending.
   (*They endeavour to modify their demeanour.*)
Now that's the opposite extreme –
   Don't be so deuced condescending!

MAR. *and* GIU. (*depressed*).
   Oh hard to please some people seem!
     At first our pose was too unbending;
   Then came the opposite extreme –
     We were too deuced condescending!

DUKE.
   Now try a cold, Imperial air –
     Half-close your eyes and stick your nose out;
   Assume a blank and vacant stare –
     Shut up your mouth and turn your toes out.
     (*They carry out his instructions.*)
   That's very good, that's very fair;
     That's dignified, yet blandly winning!
   Upon my honour, I declare
     That's very good for a beginning.

MAR. *and* GIU. (*cheerfully*).
   That comes of taking proper care –
     We're dignified and blandly winning!
   Upon my honour, I declare
     That's very good for a beginning.

DUKE.
   Now walk about with stately stride,
     Your army ready to review it,
   Put on a quantity of side –
     (*They endeavour to carry out his instruction.*)
   No – not too much – don't overdo it!
     (*They modify their manner.*)
   That's capital! That's excellent!
     You've caught the style of thing precisely!
   Both gentlemen I compliment,
     I think you do it very nicely!

MAR. *and* GIU. (*joyfully*).
   We've got it now! That's what he meant!
     We've caught the style of thing precisely!

GAVOTTE.

DUKE, DUCHESS, CASILDA, MARCO, GIUSEPPE.

DUKE.	I am a courtier grave and serious Who is about to kiss your hand: Try to combine a pose imperious With a demeanour nobly bland.	745
MAR. *and* GIU.	Let us combine a pose imperious With a demeanour nobly bland.	750

(MARCO *and* GIUSEPPE *endeavour to carry out his instructions.*)

DUKE.	That's, if anything, *too* unbending – Too aggressively stiff and grand;	

(*They suddenly modify their attitudes.*)

	Now to the other extreme you're tending – Don't be so deucedly condescending!	755
DUCH. *and* CAS.	Now to the other extreme you're tending – Don't be so dreadfully condescending!	
MAR. *and* GIU.	Oh, hard to please some noblemen seem! At first, if anything, *too* unbending; Off we go to the other extreme – Too confoundedly condescending!	760
DUKE.	Now a gavotte perform sedately – Offer your hand with conscious pride; Take an attitude not too stately, Still sufficiently dignified.	765
MAR. *and* GIU.	Now for an attitude not too stately, Still sufficiently dignified.	

(*They endeavour to carry out his instructions.*)

DUKE (*beating time*).

	Oncely, twicely – oncely, twicely – Bow impressively ere you glide.	770

(*They do so.*)

MAR. (*to* GIU.).	That's capital!
GIU. (*to* MAR.).	That's excellent!
ALL.	I think $\left\{ \begin{matrix} \text{we} \\ \text{you} \end{matrix} \right\}$ do it very nicely!

781 *Gavotte*: A stately dance, originating from France, which resembles the minuet but is more lively. The gavotte at the end of 'I am a courtier' was originally designed to be danced by Giuseppe and the Duke, with Marco accompanying them on his mandolin. This was because both Rutland Barrington and Frank Wyatt were excellent dancers. When the song became a quintet, the dance was revised to involve all five principals on stage.

788 *I'd rather not – you*: Another Barrington gag, as is the phrase in the next line, 'I – we, that is, several of us'.

797 *Then you are married*: At this point Barrington interpolated 'Yes, here's some of them'.

802–3 *we shall get hopelessly complicated*: The first American edition of the libretto, which was printed in Cincinnati in 1889, has a different quintet at this point followed by a lengthy passage of dialogue missing from the English edition. It is cued in as follows:

> MAR. It's a difficult position. It's nobody's fault – let us treat it good-humoredly and make the best of it.
> CAS. Oh yes; let's make the best of it by all means.
> TESS. *and* GIU. Certainly, let's make the best of it.
> MAR. Very well. It seems that we two have married you three. Now I have a proposition to make which I think will meet the difficulty.

QUINTET.

MARCO, GIUSEPPE, CASILDA, TESSA, GIANETTA.

MAR.	Till time shall choose
	    To solve the hitch
	Which wife is whose –
	    Whose wife is which,
	Our three young brides must please agree
	To act as one and not as three.

CAS., TESS., GIA.	Your three young brides hereby agree To act as one, and not as three. Then you must be, till that is done, Two gentlemen rolled into one.
MAR. *and* GIU.	Then we will be, till that is done, Two gentlemen rolled into one.

ALL.	Till time shall choose
	    To solve the hitch
	Which wife is whose –
	    Whose wife is which,
	The three young brides hereby agree
	To act as one and not as three;
	And both their lords, till that is done,
	Two gentlemen rolled into one!

Capital both, capital both – you've caught it nicely!
That is the style of thing precisely!

DUCH. *and* Capital both, capital both – they've caught it nicely! 775
CAS.   That is the style of thing precisely!

MAR. *and* Oh, sweet to earn a nobleman's praise!
GIU.   Capital both, capital both – we've caught it nicely!
    Supposing he's right in what he says,
    This is the style of thing precisely! 780

(GAVOTTE. *At the end exeunt* DUKE *and* DUCHESS, *leaving* CASILDA *with*
MARCO *and* GIUSEPPE.)

GIU. (*to* MARCO). The old birds have gone away and left the young
chickens together. That's called tact.

MAR. It's very awkward. We really ought to tell her how we are 785
situated. It's not fair to the girl.

GIU. Then why don't you do it?

MAR. I'd rather not – you.

GIU. I don't know how to begin. (*To* CASILDA.) A – Madam – I – we,
that is, several of us — 790

CAS. Gentlemen, I am bound to listen to you; but it is right to tell you
that, not knowing I was married in infancy, I am over head and ears in love
with somebody else.

GIU. Our case exactly! *We* are over head and ears in love with
somebody else! (*Enter* GIANETTA *and* TESSA.) In point of fact, with our 795
wives!

CAS. Your wives! Then you are married?

TESS. It's not our fault.

GIA. We knew nothing about it.

BOTH. We are sisters in misfortune. 800

CAS. My good girls, I don't blame you. Only before we go any further
we must really arrive at some satisfactory arrangement, or we shall get
hopelessly complicated.

QUINTET AND FINALE.

MARCO, GIUSEPPE, CASILDA, GIANETTA, TESSA.

ALL. Here is a case unprecedented!
   Here are a King and Queen ill-starred! 805
  Ever since marriage was first invented
   Never was known a case so hard!

GIA., TESS. *and* CAS. (*speaking together*). I think that is a very satisfactory arrangement.

MAR. *and* GIU. (*speaking together*). Ingenious, isn't it, Jenny?

GIA., TESS. *and* CAS. (*surprised*). Jenny?

MAR. *and* GIU. I must call you something, you know.

GIA., TESS. *and* CAS. Well, if you call me Jenny, I shall call you Thomas.

MAR. *and* GIU. Oh hang it all – Tommaso!

GIA., TESS. *and* CAS. No – Thomas.

MAR. *and* GIU. But it's so British!

GIA., TESS. *and* CAS. Never mind that. The question is, will you always be true to me?

MAR. *and* GIU. My dear Jenny, can you doubt it?

GIA., TESS. *and* CAS. Certainly. How can I trust a husband who married one-third of me when I was a baby and waited twenty years before he married the remainder?

MAR. *and* GIU. It does sound dilatory. Regard it as an instalment on account.

GIA., TESS. *and* CAS. And now I come to think of it, you've only married two-thirds of me, after all.

MAR. *and* GIU. I've married as much as I might.

GIA., TESS. *and* CAS. But I've married the whole of you!

MAR. *and* GIU. Pardon me – one-third of you is still single.

GIA., TESS. *and* CAS. My dear Thomas, what is the use of one-third of me being single when I don't know which third it is?

The above dialogue led straight into the singing of the quintet 'Here is a case unprecedented' (originally 'Here is a fix unprecedented'). Presumably both this dialogue and the song 'Till time shall choose' were performed in the first American production. They were also clearly originally intended to be used in the opening performance in London, as they occur in broadly the same form in the licence copy sent to the Lord Chamberlain. The licence copy has a slightly different version of the dialogue, and particularly of the last speech for Marco and Giuseppe: 'Besides, I'm married all over, whereas one-third of you is single, and can do what it likes'.

A note in Sullivan's diary for 2 December 1889, just five days before the opening night, apparently explains the dropping of this entire passage: 'Gilbert came down after rehearsal at Savoy . . . settled to cut dangerous dialogues at end of the piece'.

The licence copy also contains a second verse for 'Here is a fix unprecedented':

MAR. *and* GIU.	Here is a King – an extremely rich one –
	Somebody's married him – deuce knows who!
GIA., TESS. *and* CAS.	A third of myself – but I don't know which one –
	Is married to half of ye or you!
	O moralists all,
	How can you call
	Marriage a state of union true,
	When half of myself $\Big\}$ but I don't know which one
	One third of myself
	Has married two thirds $\Big\}$ of ye or you!
	Is married to half

The lines now sung from 'O moralists all' to 'ye or you?' (817–21) were not sung in early performances. They first appear in the third edition of the libretto (*c.* 1912).

826 *She will declare*: At this point the licence copy has the following ensemble to be sung by all:

> O time of eager expectation!
> Moment of uneasy doubt!
> O period of perturbation!
> Truth, at last, is coming out!

MAR. *and*	I may be said to have been bisected,
GIU.	By a profound catastrophe!

CAS., GIA.,	Through a calamity unexpected	810
TESS.	I am divisible into three!	

ALL.
    O moralists all,
     How can you call
    Marriage a state of unitee,
  When excellent husbands are bisected,   815
    And wives divisible into three?
     O moralists all,
     How can you call
    Marriage a state of union true?

CAS., GIA.,	One-third of myself is married to half of ye	
TESS.	or you.	820
MAR. *and*	When half of myself has married one-third	
GIU.	of ye or you?	

(*Enter* DON ALHAMBRA, *followed by* DUKE, DUCHESS,
and all the CHORUS.)

FINALE.

RECITATIVE – DON ALHAMBRA.

Now let the loyal lieges gather round –
The Prince's foster-mother has been found!   825
She will declare, to silver clarion's sound,
The rightful King – let him forthwith be crowned!

CHORUS. She will declare, etc.

(DON ALHAMBRA *brings forward* INEZ, *the Prince's*
foster-mother.)   830

TESS.	Speak, woman, speak –	
DUKE.	We're all attention!	
GIA.	The news we seek –	
DUCH.	This moment mention.	
CAS.	To us they bring –	835
DON AL.	His foster-mother.	
MAR.	Is he the King?	

840–47 *The Royal Prince was by the King entrusted*

Gilbert had originally written a song for Inez. However, he later changed it to eight lines of recitative for reasons which he explained in a letter to Sullivan: 'firstly, because I thought the audience wouldn't care for a set ballad from a stranger at the end of the piece; and secondly, because the situation became too like the situation at the end of *Pinafore*, where little Buttercup explains she has changed the children at birth'.

Inez, described by Gilbert in an earlier letter to Sullivan as 'a Spanish bandit's wife – a picturesque, fierce, melodramatic, old woman', has, I think, the doubtful distinction of being on stage for a shorter time and having less to sing than any other principal in the Savoy Operas, not counting those with minor walk-on, non-speaking roles like Mr Bunthorne's solicitor in *Patience*. The notary in *The Sorcerer* has the same number of solo lines, but he also has a part in an ensemble and appears on stage on three separate occasions.

GIU.   Or this my brother?

ALL.   Speak, woman, speak, etc.

RECITATIVE – INEZ.

The Royal Prince was by the King entrusted   840
To my fond care, ere I grew old and crusted;
When traitors came to steal his son reputed,
My own small boy I deftly substituted!
The villains fell into the trap completely –
I hid the Prince away – still sleeping sweetly: 845
I called him 'son' with pardonable slyness –
His name, Luiz! Behold his Royal Highness!

(*Sensation.* LUIZ *ascends the throne, crowned
and robed as King.*)

CAS. (*rushing to his arms*). Luiz.   850
LUIZ. Casilda! (*Embrace.*)

ALL.   Is this indeed the King?
                    Oh, wondrous revelation!
            Oh, unexpected thing!
                    Unlooked-for situation!   855

MAR., GIA.,   This statement we receive
GIU., TESS.   With sentiments conflicting;
            Our hearts rejoice and grieve,
                Each other contradicting;
            To those whom we adore   860
                We can be reunited –
            On one point rather sore,
                But, on the whole, delighted!

LUIZ.   When others claimed thy dainty hand,
                    I waited – waited – waited,   865

DUKE.   As prudence (so I understand)
                    Dictated – tated – tated.

CAS.   By virtue of our early vow
                    Recorded – corded – corded,

875 *A royal crown and a golden throne*: In the licence copy this is the last line of the opera. According to Leslie Baily, Gilbert postponed writing the finale until Sullivan had decided on a rhythm which would bring the opera to an exhilarating climax. The composer eventually decided on a reprise of the cachucha used earlier in Act II. Gilbert at first intended to preface it with a gallop, but this was later deleted. It went:

> With the cymbals clanging,
> > And the trumpets tooting,
> And the tabors banging,
> > And the fluters fluting,
> And the drummers drumming,
> > And the harpers twiddling,
> And the hautboys humming,
> > And the fiddlers fiddling –
> Let us sing, let us shout, let us ring, let us rout,
> Let us drink, let us dance, let us prank, let us prance.

The full version of this gallop is in Gilbert's papers in the British Library. It includes the following delightful lines:

> From the country of the thistle
> > Bring the bagpipe's drone,
> And the little penny whistle
> > And the loud trombone!

876 *Once more gondolieri*: In early performances the reprise of this song was given to Marco and Giuseppe only, and not, as now, to all.
884 *premé, stalì*: Two genuine gondoliers' cries. *Premé* means push down on your pole, *stalì* means stop.

DUCH.   Your pure and patient love is now   870
             Rewarded – warded – warded.

ALL.   Then hail, O King of a Golden Land,
             And the high-born bride who claims his hand!
             The past is dead, and you gain your own,
             A royal crown and a golden throne!   875

             (*All kneel:* LUIZ *crowns* CASILDA.)

ALL.   Once more *gondolieri*,
                  Both skilful and wary,
                  Free from this quandary
                       Contented are we. Ah!   880
                  From Royalty flying,
                  Our gondolas plying,
                  And merrily crying
                       Our '*premé*,' '*stalì!*' Ah!

             So good-bye, cachucha, fandango, bolero –   885
                  We'll dance a farewell to that measure –
             Old Xeres, adieu – Manzanilla – Montero –
                  We leave you with feelings of pleasure!

                         CURTAIN